AF653359

What the Experts say .

"It is a well written book. It gives a good and precise overview of marketing rather than the encyclopedia type of books written by both Indian and foreign authors."

Prof. (Dr.) M. J. Xavier,
Executive Director, VIT Business School;
Former Director, Indian Institute of Management Ranchi

"Vijay Prakash Anand's book provides a hands-on view of marketing. of particular mention here, are his Indian examples that help one connect with the industry, the customer and the marketing concepts. This book can serve as a guide to an MBA student."

Prof. (Dr.) Rajani Gupte,
Vice Chancellor, Symbiosis International University, Pune

"This book on Marketing Management reflects the author's depth of knowledge and his vast experience of the subjects covered."

Kwang Ro Kim, Vice Chairman,
Onicra Credit Rating Agency of India Limited,
Former Vice Chairman & CEO, Videocon Industries Ltd.,
Former President, MD and Head of LG Electronics India

"This is one of the best books in Marketing that I have come across anywhere. The text is simple and eloquently written and covers almost all aspects of marketing in a systematic and intuitive way. Vijay has done a commendable job."

Prof. (Dr.) Ved Prakash Sharan,
Pro Vice Chancellor, Ranchi University

"This book, written by Prof. Vijay highlights the most recent trends in marketing worldwide, while maintaining an India specific focus......sure to become the Bible of Marketing in the near future."

Prafull Dwivedi, CEO,
VLCC International LLC, Dubai – UAE

"This book is a useful slot for course content in marketing in Indian management schools. As a textbook it has right blend of theory and examples drawn from a range of industries. It is easy to read, effective and connects well using simple and evocative Indian examples and case studies."

Jasjit Singh Bawa,
Senior Manager - Brand, Renault India

"I think relevance of content, practicality, comprehensiveness, ease of understanding are a few words that define the book 'Marketing Management - An Indian Perspective' written by Mr. Vijay Prakash Anand. The book is very well structured, language is very simple and examples used are very relevant."

Vikas Mehra, Ex Sales Head – Inside, *Microsoft*,
CEO and Founder, Zinc Consulting

"An excellent book, written in simple language....highly recommended for both students of marketing as well as marketing professionals."

Shashi Shalini Kujur, I.P.S.
India Post, West Bengal Circle, Kolkata

"The examples and case studies given in the book are excellent. This is the first marketing book that I truly enjoyed while reading and has the potential to become a best seller."

Anglia Ruskin University

Sarat C Das, Editor, U Asia, UK,
Visiting Faculty, Anglia Ruskin University Outcentre, London

"This is one of the best marketing book, I have come across in the Indian context by an Indian author."

SPJ S P Jain School of Global Management
DUBAI • MUMBAI • SINGAPORE • SYDNEY

Prof. K. H. Iyer
Former Dy. Chairperson,
S. P. Jain, Mumbai, Trainer and Consultant

"I had earlier enjoyed the lectures by Prof. Vijay Prakash Anand. Now this book makes the learning of marketing even more fun with hundreds of Indian examples."

KARVY
Bringing industry, finance and people together

Mr. Rajat Khare
Cluster Head, Karvy, Gurgaon

"Marketing has always been Greek and Latin to me, until I read Marketing KISS.....this book is an eye opener and provides fascinating peek into the world of marketing .....thoroughly recommended."

goibibo.com

Mr. Sachin Verma
Tech Lead, www.goibibo.com

Readers Speak...

"Marketing Management – An Indian Perspective, is the concise Gita of Marketing. It helped me understand marketing in the simplest manner."

Ms. Gauri, Student
MMS, IES Management College, Mumbai University, Mumbai

"This book is quite good and strictly according to the need of Marketing Students of Indian Region. The language of this book is very simple and examples from Indian economy make it more sophisticated for the MBA students. This book is bound to be an asset for the students as well as faculty along with working professionals."

Atul Goyal, Assistant Professor, Department of Business Administration,
Jind Institute of Engineering & Technology, Jind

"Marketing has always been Greek and Latin to me, until I read the Marketing Management by Prof. Vijay Prakash Anand."

Mr. Sachin Verma, Web Administrater, ibibo.com, Gurgaon

"The book written by Prof. Vijay Prakash Anand is really an epitomic book for management students. This book has been written with the help of a lot of paragon examples, which enhances the concept of a particular topic in whiz-bang way.!!! Any body would be infatuated with the content; which is written in a very simple way. Simply an "all wool and a yard wide" book.

Kunal Kishor, Student,
Shri Ram Murtii Smarak International Business School, Lucknow

---

"This book is extremely useful for every mgmt. students & people who is related to corporate world. Indians will love it after reading it's most recent interesting examples & anecdotes concerning more of Indian brands along with International brands."

Anurag Shukla, Janalakshmi Financial Services, Kanpur

"The best thing about Vijay Sir is the clarity and simplicity ....."

Durgesh Rawat, Student,
Shaheed Shukhdev college of business studies, Delhi University

---

"With more than 275 photos, tables and illustrations, Marketing Management has not only helped me to understand Marketing, but it also has helped me to master the subject."

Mr. Abhinav Anand, Student, Bharti Vidyapeeth, Pune

"Vijay Sir is excellent in making the students understand the complex principles of marketing in the most interesting manner with examples in the Indian context."

Mr. Manimoy Paul, (PGDM – EMPI),
Head – Post Production, Mahuaa Bangla Channel, Kolkata

Marketing Management

An Indian Perspective

Vijay Prakash Anand
Jaipuria Institute of Management, Lucknow
Visiting Professor, IIM Ranchi

Published by:
biztantra
Ideas for Tomorrow!
An Imprint of dreamtech PRESS

© Copyright 2016 by the Author

The book may not be duplicated in any way without the express written consent of the publisher, except in the form of brief excerpts or quotations for the purpose of the review. The information contained herein is for the personal use of the reader and must not be incorporated in any commercial programmes, other books, databases, or any kind of software without written consent of the publisher. Making copies of this book or any portion thereof for any purpose other than your own is a violation of copyright laws.

Limits of Liability/ Disclaimer of Warranty

The author and publishers have used their best efforts in preparing this book. The author makes no representation or warranties with respect to the accuracy or completeness of the content of this book, and specifically disclaims any implied warranties of merchantability or fitness for any particular purpose. There are no warranties which extend beyond the description contained in this paragraph. No warranty may be created or extended by sales representatives or written sales materials. The accuracy and completeness of the information provided herein and the opinion stated herein are not guaranteed and warranted to provide any particular results, and the advice and strategies contained herein may not be suitable for every individual. Neither Biztantra (Dreamtech Press) nor the author shall be liable for any loss of profit or any commercial damages, including but not limited to special, incidental, consequential, or other damages.

Trademarks

All brand names and product names used in this book are trademarks, registered trademarks, or trade names of their respective holders. Dreamtech Press is not associated with any product or vendor mentioned in this book.

ISBN: 978-93-5119-825-3

Reprint: 2025

Printed at: Nisha Enterprises

Dedicated to
My dear wife Poonam
&
My lovely kids Arjun
and Aryan

Dedicated to

My dear wife Poonam

&

My lovely kids Arjun

and Aryan

PREFACE

Preface to Second Edition

It gives me immense pleasure in forwarding you the second edition of 'Marketing Management, An Indian Perspective'. It has almost been four years, since the first edition of this book was presented to you. Since then, the world of marketing has changed and so is your book. Based on the feedback received from the readers, academia and industry over the past four years, this book has been revised and updated. I am thankful to all the readers and well wishers, who gave their inputs to improve the book. I am also thankful to Prof. M. J. Xavier, Executive Director, VIT Business School and Former Director, IIM Ranchi for his encouragement and support.

I am very happy to share that this book has been recommended as Text Book of Marketing in many B-Schools in India including IIM Ranchi. Within two months of the publication of the first edition, this book was recommended as the Text Book for Marketing at IIM Ranchi for PG Executive Programme.

As far as second edition is concerned, the second edition is thoroughly revised and updated in accordance with today's marketing needs and challenges. Besides updating the internal content of the book, there are two major additions in the book. Three new chapters have been introduced namely Rural Marketing, International Marketing and Green Marketing; while in every chapter there are several marketing insights in boxes to make the content more relevant and current.

I am also grateful to my publisher Rahul Gupta, Biztantra for the help and support throughout in updating the book. I would also like to thank M. V. Shastri, Ishwar Singh and Rishi Ballabh at Biztantra for editing and designing the book.

Lastly I thank my family: my parents, my wife Poonam and my little kids – Arjun and Aryan for their unconditional support and encouragement in completing the second edition of the book.

Vijay Prakash Anand

Preface to First Edition

'Marketing Management – An Indian Perspective' is a concise yet comprehensive guide on the fundamentals on marketing and its relevance in today's marketplace. This book not only provides a foundation for developing the skills required for an MBA/ PGDM student; but it also serves as a must have resource for marketing professionals and entrepreneurs to become efficient and effective marketer. The book, divided into 15 chapters covers all aspects of the marketing domain and has been written in a way so as to be thoroughly engaging as well as thought provoking.

This book is based on my knowledge and understanding of Marketing in the last 14 years in the diverse areas of Advertising, Marketing, Academics and Research. Besides the hands on experience in the marketing field, teaching students in top B-Schools has helped me to shape up this book, as it is required by the management students in India. With the right mixture of marketing theory with the practices across India and the world, this book takes a lot of examples from the Indian companies to understand the concepts better. With more than 275 photos, illustrations, tables and graphs, this book helps you understand marketing in the current business scenario in the most lucid manner.

I express my gratitude to all my colleagues and students from B-schools for extending their support and encouragement. I am also thankful to my wife Poonam and my son Arjun for being a source of incessant motivation and support to me in writing the book.

I am grateful to Mr. Rahul Gupta at Biztantra for relentlessly pursuing this project with me for a long time. I would like to thank Mr. Yoginder Singh and his editorial team for giving their timely inputs. I am thankful to Mr. Arun Kumar and Mr. Ishwar Saini for their valuable inputs in shaping the book.

Vijay Prakash Anand

About the Book

This book 'Marketing Management – An Indian Perspective' covers the fundamental concepts in marketing with the contemporary issues in marketing from an Indian perspective. This hands-on guide with real life Indian examples shall help you understand and utilize various marketing concepts and tools to identify and fulfill the customers' needs. Right from the basics and overview of Marketing, it covers market oriented strategic planning, marketing research, segmentation, targeting and positioning, competition, consumer and business markets, branding, new product development, pricing, distribution strategies and integrated marketing communications in fifteen chapters. It also foretells what the future of marketing is and how a company can benefit from it in the hypercompetitive arena. In the fifteenth chapter, we have given an overview on topics like Services Marketing, Rural Marketing, International Marketing, Retail Marketing, E-Commerce, Customer Relationship Management and Green Marketing.

This book provides the foundation for developing the skills required for an MBA student with lots of Indian examples and more than 275 photos, tables and diagrams to understand the Marketing better. It also serves as a must have resource for marketing professionals and entrepreneurs to become efficient and effective marketer.

Excerpts...

Today, marketing is not just the domain for the marketing department in a company. It's a philosophy now; it's a business orientation, which needs to be imbibed in the corporate vision and mission to be successful in the market. All the successful marketers in India like Tata, Reliance, Mahindra, Birla, Bharti Airtel, Marico, HUL, Dabur etc are thriving by understanding and delivering value to the Indian consumers to serve them in a better way than their competition.....

About the Book

This book [illegible] concepts in marketing with the [illegible] Indian perspective. The [illegible] help you understand [illegible] [illegible] communications to other stakeholders. It also speaks about the [illegible] Management, Services Marketing, International Marketing, Retail [illegible] Customer Relationship Management [illegible] Marketing by Vijay [illegible]

About the Author

Prof. Vijay Prakash Anand is a management post graduate in Marketing from Symbiosis, Pune and an economics honours graduate from St. Xavier's College, Ranchi. He has more than 18 years of experience in the field of Marketing, Advertising, Corporate Communications, Academics and Research. He has taught at leading B-Schools in India like IIM Ranchi, Symbiosis, Pune, Bharti Vidyapeeth, Pune, Pune University MBA Department as a visiting faculty member and in EMPI Business School, New Delhi, NIILM Centre for Management Studies, New Delhi and IES Management College, Mumbai University, Mumbai as a full time faculty member. His book 'Marketing Management, An Indian Perspective' is recommended as a text book for Marketing at IIM Ranchi. He also writes a blog on marketing at www.marketingbyvijay.wordpress.com and has a YouTube Channel named 'Marketing by Vijay'. His areas of research include Digital marketing and Green Marketing. He is currently working as a faculty member in the area of Marketing at Jaipuria Institute of Management, Lucknow and is a Visiting Professor at IIM Ranchi.

BRIEF CONTENTS

Detailed Contents

Chapter 17: Green Marketing

Chapter 1

Overview of Marketing

Chapter Structure

- Introduction to Marketing
- Importance of Marketing: Marketing is Everything
- *Marketing Insight 1.1: What Made Maruti Celerio a Grand Success in India*
- *Marketing Insight 1.2: The Monk Who wants a Billion-dollar Company*
- Scope of Marketing
- *Marketing Insight 1.3: Prof. Shelby D. Hunt on the Definition of Marketing*
- Elements of Marketing
- *Marketing Insight 1.4: Deodorant Market Getting Hotter in India*
- Marketing Vs Selling: Two Commonly held, Mistaken views of Marketing
- History of Marketing
- Philosophies of Marketing Management
- Fortune at the Bottom of the Pyramid
- Marketing Mix
- *Marketing Insight 1.5: Fortune at the Bottom of the Pyramid*
- Summary
- Discussion Questions
- References

"A customer is the most important visitor on our premises. He is not dependent on us. We are dependent on him. He is not an interruption in our work. He is the purpose of it. He is not an outsider in our business. He is part of it. We are not doing him a favour by serving him. He is doing us a favour by giving us an opportunity to do so."

-Mahatma Gandhi

Introduction to Marketing

Marketing as a term is widely used in the management of a business and in our day-to-day life. In the era of customer and competition driven business world, marketing is not just the domain for the marketing department in a company. It's a philosophy; it's a business orientation now. It is imbibed in the corporate vision and mission of the successful companies. All the successful companies in India like Tata, Reliance, Mahindra, Bharti Airtel, Maruti, Birla, Bajaj, Dabur, Patanjali etc are thriving by understanding and delivering value to the Indian consumers to serve them in a better way than their competitors.

Importance of Marketing: Marketing is Everything

Marketing is just not selling. Marketing is neither just a business function. Marketing is a lot more complex than selling and just being a business function. In a path breaking article **'Marketing is everything'**, **Regis McKenna** has stated,

'Marketing today is not a function; it is a way of doing business. Marketing is not a new ad campaign or this month's promotion......Its job is not to fool the customers, nor to falsify the company's image. It is to integrate the customer into the design of the product and to design a systematic process for interaction that will create substance in the relationship.'[1]

Marketing spans across all the aspects of your business and across all customer contact points including your company's web site, how do you answer the phones, your marketing and PR campaigns, your sales process, how your sales representatives present themselves (in person and on the phone), how you implement your products and/or services, how you manage your customers (customer service), and how you solicit customer feedback.

In fact, your business starts and ends with marketing. You need to be marketing oriented all the time to succeed and sustain in the business for a long time.

'The aim of marketing is to make selling superfluous. The aim of marketing is to know and understand the customer so well that the product or service fits him and sells itself. Ideally, marketing should result in a customer who is ready to buy. All that should be needed then is to make the product or service available.'[2]

There have been innumerable examples of products and services, where the customers have flocked to buy the products or use the services; like Apple's iPods, iPhones and now iPads, Sony's Walkman, Nintendo Video Game, Toyota Lexus, Microsoft Windows etc. In the Indian context also, many products and services have made their mark among the customers. Ford Ecosport, Maruti Suzuki Baleno and Celerio, Patanjali products are excellent examples to understand how a business can be driven by identifying and fulfilling needs of the customers.

Marketing Insight 1.1

What Made Maruti Celerio a Grand Success in India

Maruti Celerio

India's largest car maker, Maruti Suzuki India states that Celerio was a gamble which went on to carve a great success story for the company. The company didn't even considered going for a market research before launching their Celerio product. Moreover, the company introduced the vehicle in the market's most roughest phase. Commenting on this, Mayank Pareek, COO (Marketing & Sales) said, " At times you have to go with just that gut feeling." And he did go by his intuitions. " I was tense as we launched in the midst of a full-blown slowdown," he added.

The gamble certainly paid off, as Celerio has bagged bookings over 35,000 units; significant considering the current sluggish market conditions. More interestingly, the AMT version contributes 49 per cent to this massive response from Indian buyers. Compared to last year's March records, this year Maruti posted a 5.5 per cent decline in total sales. And even the small segment cars could not help carmakers overcome the downfall, as it too registered a decline of 11 per cent in comparison to last year's data. Talking about the gearless vehicle, Mayank Pareek said, "This is the right time to go gearless and the response to Celerio has proved us right. For more than 50 per cent of buyers, this variant is their second car."

The major reason behind Celerio's success is taken to be the changing socio-economic conditions, and also the altering demographic profile helped a lot with this. The ease and comfort associated with gearless cars made them so popular amongst the Indian buyers. For a long time, the Indian car market has been skeptical about automatics; also their pricier tag made them not-so-popular in India. Automatic transmission driven cars were viewed as problematic from every dimension, be it with high price tag or with their high maintenance costs. And then there's a general Indian perception- higher fuel efficiency, higher are the chances behind car's success, and certainly automatic cars could not stand upto the expectations of Indians.

So, how Maruti played its cards considering all these mentioned conditions and came up with such an amazing product. Well, it just got its 3 Ps hit at the right target- Product, Pricing and Positioning. Celerio automatic is one such product which has been designed with fuel economy that matches that of manuals, thus catering the needs of Indian buyers. At the positioning front, the car has been designed to serve the convenience of the driver- just start and go. Also, now the car with automatics is busy dictating, which was earlier done by drivers with manually operated transmissions.

Besides Maruti Celerio, several other Indian companies have also given the products or services, which were really needed by the customers; but the product or service was just not available to them like Nirma, Good Knight, PVR Multiplex or Mahindra Scorpio. The successful companies all across the world are those, who constantly try to innovate and deliver the products or services, which the customers want.

Nirma

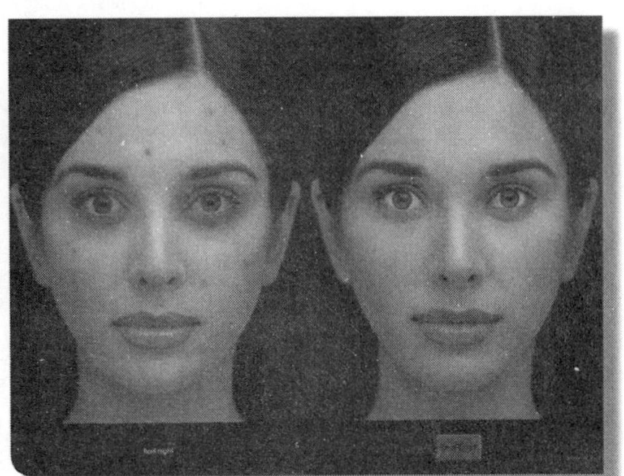

Good Knight

PVR

Mahindra Scorpio

In the recent times, Patanjali Ayurved has become a huge success in the masses in the FMCG (Fast moving Consumer Goods) category in India. It has grown by more than 150% in 2014-15 and achieved a turnover of more than Rs. 2000 crore. The success of Patanjali is all about understanding the needs of the customers well and providing high quality healthy products at cheaper prices than competition.

Marketing Insight 1.2

The Monk Who wants a Billion-dollar Company

Baba Ramdev aims to make Patanjali India's largest FMCG company. Will his missionary zeal work?

Patanjali's ₹ 2,000-crore FMCG journey began ten years ago, quite accidentally, with gooseberries. Acharya Balkrishna, the 43-year-old architect of Patanjali's growth from a cottage industry to the one that is giving MNCs sleepless nights, recounts how it all started in 2005, when a delegation of farmers met Ramdev. They were going to destroy their gooseberry plantations as there was no demand for the fruit. To stop them, Ramdev started manufacturing *amla* juice.

"At first, we had no clue how to go about it and outsourced the fruit to a food processing unit in Hoshiarpur in Punjab," says Balkrishna. The juice became a runaway hit, and Patanjali started sourcing gooseberries from all over the country to meet the demand. Today, 25 truck loads of gooseberry arrive at the Patanjali unit, where 6,000 litres of juice is processed per hour. "Now there are so many other *amla* juice manufacturers in the country. We literally created the category," says Balkrishna.

From niche to mainstream

Creating new product categories partly explains Patanjali's early success. After *amla* juice, it started making the sort of esoteric local food and personal care products (aloe vera juice, *hing* (asafoetida) digestive *golis*, *shikakai* (acacia concinna) sherbets and spices that Indians otherwise shopped for at*khadi* or *gramudyog* outlets.

"We suddenly saw a market gap that could be filled," says Balkrishna. "Whatever people demanded, we kept making," adds Ramdev, before taking a jibe at MNCs, "We don't bother with expensive market research." As the enterprise flourished, Patanjali became ambitious and started getting into established FMCG categories. The change also seems to have coincided with Ramdev's growing political clout.

Today, Patanjali, Divya Pharmacy - the Ayurvedic medicine manufacturing company, and Patanjali Gram Udyoga Unit, produce nearly 600 products. Patanjali has now muscled into noodles, cornflakes and cookies. The group employs about 15,000 people in its units.

Ramdev says the business has grown 150 per cent this year, and may close this fiscal with a turnover of ₹5,000 crore. Though Ramdev claims that he and Balkrishna don't set targets, in the next breath, he throws a ₹10,000-crore-turnover-in-three-years goal.

The growth, he adds, will come through expansions into everything from baby care to garments. "From bio-fertilisers to healthy food, to organic cotton clothes, we will produce anything that can make India and Indians beautiful," declares his acolyte Balkrishna.

But how is noodles making Indians beautiful? Both Ramdev and Balkrishna insist it's not an incongruous product for them, but are weaning Indians away from '*videshi*' junk food by offering healthier local alternatives. "*Swadeshi* is our goal" says Ramdev, and declares, "noodles – which resembles our*sevaiyan* (vermicelli) - is quite Indian."

But why are they so antagonistic to MNCs? After all the FMCG market in India is currently a ₹2 lakh-crore market and there is enough room for everyone. Anurag Mathur, partner, PwC India, says: "Macroeconomic trends show that there is enough opportunity in the secular packaged food industry for both, the MNCs and Indian companies." Mathur says the market will double in five years.

Yet Ramdev seems to be obsessed to best Nestle's Maggi. He personally tasted the Patanjali noodles and sent it back to the R&D lab 13 times, before he was satisfied. The yoga guru says his only motive is to see that the 'money of this land should not go overseas.' He declares: "Collective prosperity and charity are our goals. The profits from the FMCG business will be used to build 500 Acharya Kulams across the country." These are K12 schools that will impart *vedic* education. The first of these is already up in Roorkee. Also being launched are Ayurvedic colleges and research institutes. "Next year, we will be starting animal-based trials for medicines for blood pressure, cancer and hepatitis," says Ramdev.

Ramping up distribution

Soon after sewing up a deal with Patanjali, Kishore Biyani of Future Group forecast that it would be among the top three FMCG manufacturer in a few years. "I would say Patanjali can become No.1 ahead of HUL. This is not based on optimistic high expectations but based on fact," says Aditya Pittie, CEO of Pittie group who is the pan-India distributor for Patanjali's modern trade and Mumbai distributor for its general trade (kirana shops) business. "In Mumbai, we are seeing 30 per cent growth month-on-month," says Pittie.

Initially, Patanjali's consumers came from its massive yoga and Ayurveda network. Patanjali Yog Samiti has 1 lakh branches, and 5 lakh teachers. Across India, there are 10,000 Patanjali Chikitsalaya and Aarogya Kendras. Ramdev claims he has interacted with at least 20 crore people who have attended his camps. Now, the group is trying to expand its consumer base through professional channels. There are 80 super distributors and 700 distributors and 5,000 franchisee stores. After the much hyped deal with Biyani's Future Group, Patanjali is now going after almost every other modern trade brand – from Spencer's to More, to place its products.

"Our aim is that 15 per cent to 20 per cent of Patanjali's turnover should come from modern trade," says Pittie. The Group is setting up giant Patanjali Mega Marts too.

The bumps ahead

The push for high growth comes with challenges. Sourcing of raw material, for instance, will be critical to cope with the volumes. Patanjali has already faced that with gooseberries. To reach online consumers faster (Grofers and Big Basket now stock Patanjali products), it must have manufacturing units and warehouses across the country.

Patanjali's product portfolio is unwieldy. That's a challenge that Mudra and McKann Erickson, who have been roped in to handle advertising for Patanjali, will have to overcome. From a zero-advertising strategy , Patanjali has done a U-turn, emerging as the third biggest television advertiser in the country.

Also, as Naresh Gupta, Managing Partner, Bang in the Middle, an advertising agency, points out, for the brand to move into the big league, it has to appeal to those who don't buy into Baba's personal belief system. He says, "Today Ramdev is also a political figure and to merge commerce with politics has not been easy or successful for anyone."

Peter Drucker has also stated that **'The purpose of business is to create a customer, the business enterprise has two – and only two –basic functions: marketing and innovation. Marketing and innovation produce results; all the rest are costs. Marketing is the distinguishing, unique function of the business.'**[3]

Whether you take the example of Yahoo or Google or Apple or Tata or Reliance; all the successful companies rely heavily on constant innovation and marketing of their products or services.

Scope of Marketing

What is Marketing? – Definitions of Marketing

The Chartered Institute of Marketing defines marketing as **'The management process responsible for identifying, anticipating and satisfying customer requirements profitably'**

Oxford Dictioneries define Marketing **'as the process of performing market research, selling products and /or services to customers and promoting them via advertising to further enhance sales.'**

Kotler Philip, Gary Armstrong, Veronica Wong, and John Saunders is of the view that **'Marketing as an integrated process through which companies build strong customer relationships and create value for their customers and for themselves.'** It generates the strategy that underlies sales techniques, business communication, and business developments.

Paliwoda, Stanley J and John K. Ryans believe in a different concept called the **value-based marketing**, which states the role of marketing to contribute to increasing shareholder value.

American Marketing Association's (AMA) has defined as following:

'Marketing is an organizational function and a set of processes for creating, communicating, and delivering value to customers and for managing customer relationships in ways that benefit the organization and its stakeholders.'

Above definition was applicable till Sept., 2007. Now with the ever changing business environment, the definition of Marketing also underwent a lot of change from Oct., 2007. Now, AMA defines Marketing as:

'Marketing is the activity, set of institutions, and processes for creating, communicating, delivering, and exchanging offerings that have value for customers, clients, partners, and society at large.'[4]

Marketing Insight 1.3

Marketing Insight 1.3

Prof. Shelby D. Hunt on the definition of Marketing

AMA defines Marketing as:

'Marketing is the activity, set of institutions, and processes for creating, communicating, delivering, and exchanging offerings that have value for customers, clients, partners, and society at large.'[4]

While commenting on the definition given By AMA, Prof. Shelby D. Hunt in his book – "Marketing Theory" said that '2007 definition is a positive step toward viewing marketing as a profession... First, consider the phrase, 'Marketing is the activity'. This phrase, which substitutes for 'marketing is the organizational function', recognizes that marketing is an action word. Specifically, 'marketing' is a gerund, a verbal form that ends in –ing that is used as a noun, but conveys the meaning of a verb, 'to market'. That is marketing is something that organizations as well as individuals (e.g., entrepreneurs and consumers) engage in or do. Because the definition is put forth by AMA, a professional association, it should be stressed that the definition implies that the activity of marketing is to be conducted ethically and responsibly. It is also important to stress that with the deletion of, 'marketing is the organizational function', marketing is not something that is done just by those in organizations formal marketing departments. Rather, modern marketing practice and theory views marketing, among other things, as an orientation that is recommended as a guiding philosophy for the entire organization and its employees.

Second, consider the phrase 'Set of institutions and processes'. This phrase uses 'institutions in two ways: 1) 'institutions' refers to type of organizations that engage in marketing, for example, manufacturers, wholesalers, retailers, advertising agencies, distributors and marketing research firms; 2) 'institutions' refers to the formal and informal norms that guide, inform and regulate ethical, responsible ethical, responsible and legal marketing....The phrase 'institutions and processes' also implies that the marketing systems in a society (e.g. channels of distribution, networks and supply chains) are central to the practice and study of marketing.

Third, consider the phrase ' for creating ....offerings'. This phrase stresses that it is market offerings that are being exchanged, not just tangible goods (Vargo and Lusch, 2004). Drawing on resource-advantage theory, 'a market offering is a distinct entity that 1) is composed of a bundle of attributes, which 2) may be tangible or intangible, objective or subjective and which 3) may be viewed by some buyer(s) as a want satisfier'. Therefore, the phrase 'for creating, communicating, delivering and exchanging offerings' delineates four central components of marketing activity: 1) 'Creating' means developing new (both radically new and incrementally new) market offerings, often as a result of marketing research that explores consumers needs, wants, tastes and preferences. 2) 'Communicating' implies the use of advertising, personal selling, sales promotion and other vehicles to inform potential customers and clients about the availability and the attributes of market offerings. 3) Delivering means the process of moving market offerings and their ownership from production to consumption, a process that often involves using intermediaries. 4) 'Exchanging' market offerings captures the historical focus of the purpose of marketing and includes discrete, individual or 'transactional exchanges and long-term, multiple or relational exchanges. It is important to stress that exchanging implies that the parties find mutually agreed upon terms of exchange, including the prices of each of the components of the market offerings (e.g. the prices of tangible goods, warranties and delivery).

Fourth, the phrase 'offerings that have value for customers, clients, partners' identifies three key constituencies or stakeholders of marketing. 1) In the case of fro-profit organizations, the constituencies of 'customers' is paramount. Indeed, it is customers' perceptions of rivals' market offerings that determine their relative value...2) In the case of nonprofit institutions though these organizations engage in marketing, they do not see themselves as having 'customers'. Rather they normally see themselves as having clients (or members and donors) for whom services are provided (and from whom donations are solicited). Again, it is nonprofit organizations' clients, whose perception determines the relative value of the organisations' market offerings. 3) The inclusion of 'partners' recognizes that the importance of collaborative networks and alliances in modern marketing practice. All partners in such arrangements must perceive the value to be obtained from participating in the partnerships.

Fifth, the phrase 'offerings that have value for....society at large' acknowledges that, ...society is always the ultimate client for a truly professional discipline. Recall that the framework maintains that marketing must be responsive to society's need for high quality products and services that are reasonably priced, reasonably promoted and conveniently available. The definition, therefore, acknowledges that the ethical and responsible practice of marketing benefits society – and the normal, everyday practice of marketing, I argue, is ethical and responsible. That is creating market offerings that have value to customers and clients benefits society. Exchanging market offerings benefit society. Therefore, marketing benefits society.

Marketing is not just an organizational function, but it is an activity and a set of institutions are involved. Now the customers, organisation and its stakeholders have also been rephrased as Customers, Clients, Partners and Society at large. Now Customer Relationship Management (CRM) is as important as Partner Relationship Management (PRM). Societal welfare is as important as the company's welfare. Panasonic's 'Eco Ideas', Nokia's 'Take Back Campaign', HP's 'Power to Change' and Toyota's initiative for Hybrid Green Vehicles are few examples of corporate initiative for the society at large.

Philip Kotler, a well known authority on marketing has termed marketing as a **'societal process by which individual and groups obtain what they need and want through**

creating, offering and freely exchanging products and services of value with others.' Marketing can also be said as the process of **'satisfying needs and wants through an exchange process'.**

In a simpler way, Kotler has defined Marketing in terms of **CCDVTP**, which means **creating, communicating and delivering value to the target market at a profit.**

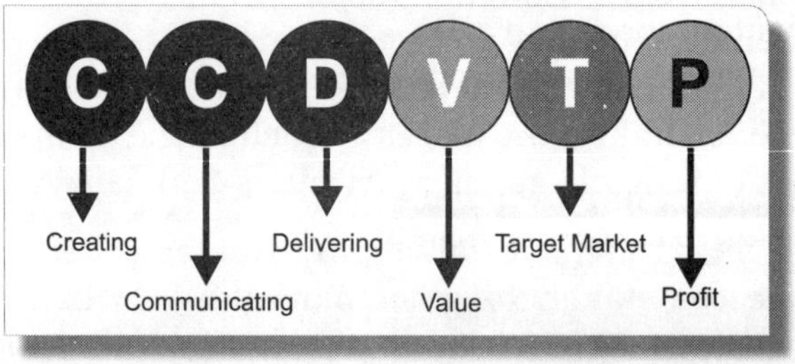

Thus, **Marketing is all about identifying and meeting human and social needs and that too in a profitable way.** Ultimately, the objective of any business activity is to make profits.

On the whole, we can say that CCCCC STP PPPP encompasses all the aspects in marketing. Sounds confusing, let me clarify, Marketing is all about 5Cs, STP and 4Ps. 5Cs stands for Customers, Company, Competitors, Collaborators and Context. While STP stands for Segmentation, Targeting and Positioning; whereas 4Ps represent the Marketing Mix i.e. Product, Price, Place and Promotion.

Figure 1.1

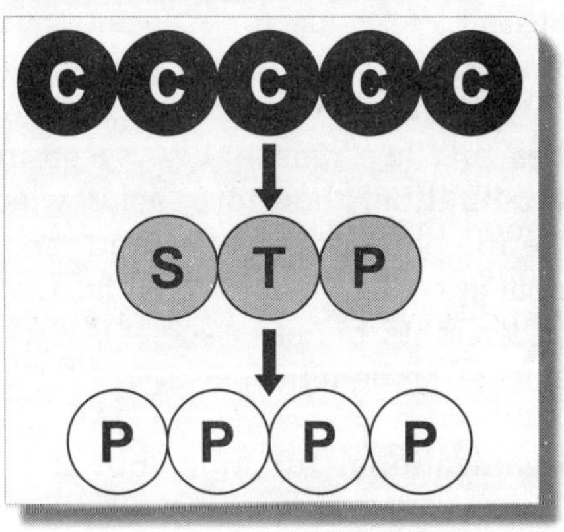

Marketing Structure

What is Marketed?

A marketer does not only market goods and services, but he or she also markets eight other entities like Events, Experiences, Persons, Places, Properties, Organisations, Information and Ideas.7 The ten entities, which can be marketed are as follows:

1. **Goods**: Goods are physical, tangible articles, which can satisfy a need. All across the world, most of the country is engaged in manufacturing and producing goods like Toothpaste, Washing Powder, Cosmetics, Cars, Petrol etc.

   Now, goods are not only marketed by companies, but also by individuals. In the era of Internet Marketing, individuals can also sell goods through the Internet. In India, you have got websites like www.ebay.in, www.olx.in to sell your products online. Besides these websites, goods can also be sold and bought through shopping sites like www.flipkart.com, www.snapdeal.com, www.amazon.in, www.infibeam.com, www.homeshop18.com etc.

Pepsodent Toothpaste

Surf Excel Detergent Powder

2. **Services**: Services are non physical and intangible in nature and can satisfy a need. Banking, Courier, Hotel, Airline, Multiplex, Train, Doctors, Lawyers, Management Consultants are all examples of services. With the advancement in the economy, a country moves from a good producing country to a service oriented country. For example, USA, which is one of the most developed countries in the world, is having a 70% - 30% mix of goods and services.

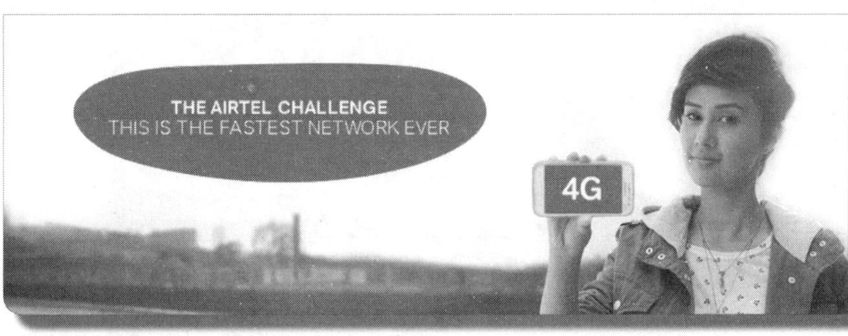

Airtel

State Bank of India

But some services are inclusive of product, like the restaurant, where a customer gets a tangible good in the form of say a masala dosa and gets it served at his table. In the other case, a service like mobile is backed by huge investments in equipments.

In the study of marketing all the ten entities, which can be marketed, are generally clubbed together as goods and services.

3. **Experiences**: Experiences can be also marketed with the usage of goods, services and with a dose of technology. India's first amusement park in Delhi - Appu Ghar, Essel World in Mumbai, Disney Land in USA and Sentosa Island in Singapore are examples of experiences, which needs to be marketed.

Essel World, Mumbai

4. **Events**: Events like ICC Cricket World Cup 2015, FIFA World Cup Brazil 2014, Shahrukh Khan's Temptation World Tour in 2009, Commonwealth Games in Delhi in 2010, Olympics, Asian Games, T20 World Cup, Wimbledon, Shakira's Concerts etc. needs marketing to get the audience and spectators.

ICC Cricket World Cup 2015

5. **Persons**: Peter Montoya's book 'The Brand called You' and Tom Peters' advise to each person to become a brand, says a lot about the marketing of a person. For example, Mahendra Singh Dhoni, the captain of Indian Cricket Team, earned $10 million (Rs 48 Crore) in 2008 and became the world's richest cricketer; followed by Sachin Tendulkar with $8 million (Rs 38.5 Crore). In 2007, the highest earning celebrity in the world was Oprah Winfrey with an earning of $260 million. Other celebrities are also not far behind with Filmmaker Steven Spielberg earning $110 million, Sportsman Tiger Woods earning $100 million and Actor Johnny Depp earning $92 million.

   All these celebrities are marketed by an agent or a personal manager or by a talent management company like Percept Talent Management; which manages Celebrities like Amitabh Bachchan, Shah Rukh Khan, Katerina Kaif, Aamir Khan, Priyanka Chopra, Yuvraj Singh, A. R. Rahman, Shekhar Suman besides others.

Lux

Tag Heuer

Pepsi

6. **Places**: Incredible India, Kerala: The God's Own Country, and Malaysia: Truly Asia, are different advertising campaigns to attract tourist to these places. Places are marketed to bring more tourists, residents, factories and offices. Tourism boards, real estate companies, advertising and promotional agencies and public relations organizations generally market the places.

Kerala – God's Own Country

7. **Properties**: Properties including real estate properties and financial properties, both need to be marketed. Every Saturday, The Times of India comes out with a supplement called Times Property for the real estate properties to be marketed; while Hindustan Times comes out with HT Estates on the same day. Companies like DLF, HDIL, Omaxe, Rahejas, Unitech etc. are real estate companies, who regularly market their real estate

properties. Financial properties like shares, bonds, debentures, mutual funds etc. also need to be marketed to the individual as well as institutional investors.

Amrapali

Birla Sun Life Mutual Fund

8. **Organisations**: Life is Good (LG), Let us make things better (Philips), Experience Change (Videocon), Count on us (Maruti Suzuki) etc are examples of fortifying the image of the company in the mind of its target publics. Even social organisations like CRY (Child Relief and You) also market themselves to gain visibility and attract funds.

Videocon

General Motors

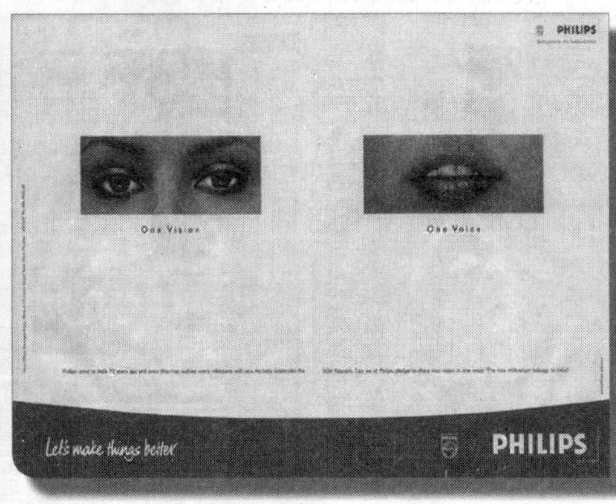

Philips

9. **Information**: Encyclopedia Britannica, Manorama Year Book, Penguin CNBC TV18 Business Year Book, Magazines like Overdrive, Smart Photography, Digit, Business World, Screen, Filmfare, Femina; and DVDs / CDs like Budget Demystified, Being Business Leaders are examples of how information is marketed. Schools, Colleges, Institutes and Universities also produce and market information to the students and their guardians.

CNBC TV18 CDs and Books

> **'The production, packaging and distribution of information is one of our society's major industries.'[8] – Carl Shapiro and Hal Varian**

10. **Ideas**: 'An idea can change your life' – the famous baseline of Idea Cellular fits correctly as far as marketing of ideas is concerned. Ideas like Condom 'Bindaas Bol' campaign, Oral Contraceptives 'Goli Ke Jamjoli' campaign, 'Pulse Polio' campaign, NACO campaign to spread awareness against AIDS etc. effectively market the social concerns by their respective bodies like USAID, Child and Reproductive health, Health ministry, Govt. of India and National AIDS Control Organisation (NACO).

End Polio

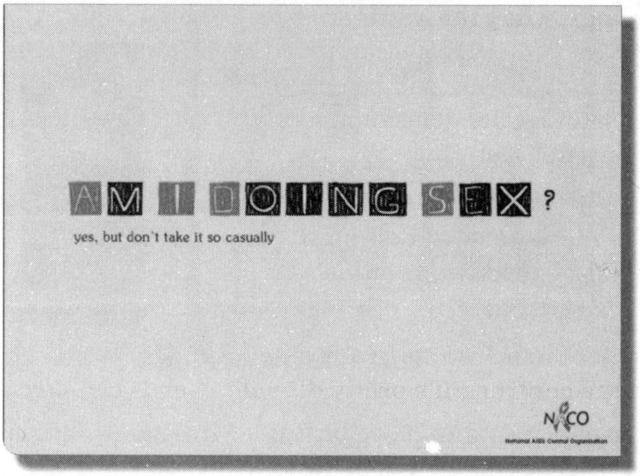

NACO

Elements of Marketing

Needs, Wants, Demands,

As you know, Marketing is all about identifying and meeting human and social needs and that too in a profitable way. Needs are basic human requirements. You need air, water, food, shelter and clothing to survive. You also need education as well as entertainment. Once these needs are specified by you, it become wants. For example, you are hungry and want to eat samosa or vada pao. Similarly a south Indian guy would like to have a dosa or idli. Our society and culture leads to our wants.

Mercedes Benz

Wants become demands, when the wants are backed by the ability to pay. Everybody would like to drive a Mercedes, but everyone cannot afford it. That's why, only those wants, which are backed by purchasing power, will be calculated as demands. For a marketer, demand plays a great role in managerial decision making. This help to forecast the demand, while doing the strategic market planning.

Here it's very important to understand that **'Marketers don't create needs; needs preexist marketers'.** But the marketer can definitely create the desire for its product through a television commercial or through an ad in the magazine or in the newspaper or on the internet.

Understanding the needs and wants of the customer lies at the core of marketing. But it is not that easy. On the contrary, it's pretty difficult. Needs can be classified in five types:

a) **Stated Needs**: Those needs, which are stated by the customer like a cheap motorbike.
b) **Real Needs**: Now the real need is not restricted to cheap price of the bike only. But it should also have good mileage for lower operating cost.
c) **Unstated Needs**: Here the customer may expect cheap spare parts and good after sales service.
d) **Delight Needs**: The customer may want free accessories or extended warranty.
e) **Secret Needs**: The customer may also like to be seen by his friends and acquaintances as a smart consumer.

Thus the marketer needs to be market savvy to not just understand the stated needs. But he should also try to help customers learn, what they want.

Customer and Consumer

The consumer is the one who consumes or uses the goods and services produced. While the customer buys goods or services for his own use or for others use. The basic difference lies in its purchase and its uses. It may also be inferred that the customer is not always the primary consumer. Generally in business to consumer (B2C) marketing, the term consumer is used, while in business to business (B2B) marketing, the term customer is used.

Thus, the line of difference between customer and consumer is very thin. Both these words can be used concurrently in marketing. The famous quote 'Customer is King' refers to both consumers as well as customers.

Markets

In economics, the concept of market means any structure that allows buyers and sellers to exchange any type of goods, services and information. Traditionally, the market is meant to be a physical place, where buyers and sellers meet to buy and sell goods. Now in the internet era, the world has become a market. Earlier the barter system was used for the transacting business. Now, the transaction is done on the monetary basis. Market is also meant as a grouping of customers.

According to **Jeffrey Rayport and John Sviokla**

> **'With the advent of Internet, now market can be divided into two parts – marketplace and marketspace. As you know, the physical place for buying and selling is a marketplace; while marketspace is digital in nature, as buying and selling can be done on the internet.'[5]**

Mohan Sawhney has given another concept **Metamarket**, which consists of a cluster of complementary products and services, which are closely related in the minds of the consumers. These products and services may be from different industries.

> **The automobile Metamarket consists of automobile manufacturers, new car and used car dealers, financing companies, insurance companies, mechanics, spare parts dealers, auto magazines, classified auto ads in newspapers and auto websites.[6]**

Thus, right from Maruti Suzuki to MRF Tyres to Munjal Showa to State Bank of India to ICICI Lombard to Mahindra First Choice to Overdrive magazine to Zigwheels.com; all are part of the automobile Metamarket.

> Taking a cue from the concept, **Mr. Jagdish Khattar,** former MD of Maruti Suzuki has launched a venture called **Carnation Auto,** which deals in Car services, accessories, preowned cars, new cars and DC design Kits.

Consumer Markets and Business / Industrial Markets.

Markets can be classified on the basis of the **product** itself, or on the basis of the **end-consumer**, or both. The market is most commonly classified as following:

Consumer Markets and

Business Markets or **Industrial Markets** or **Organizational Markets**

International Markets

Nonprofit and Governmental Markets

- **Consumer Markets:** Consumer markets are the markets for products and services like Car, LCD TV, Refrigerators, Toothpaste, Ice Cream, Apparels and Air travel bought by individuals for their own or family use. In the consumer market, companies try to identify and meet the needs of the consumer through their product and service offering. Additionally, they try to position the products into the consumers mind for better awareness and purchases. In the last few years, products like deodorants, handwash, dishwash etc. have emerged as a new category under **Fast Moving Consumer Goods** (FMCG).

Consumer markets can be classified in five ways:

1. **Fast Moving Consumer Goods (FMCG)**
2. **Consumer Durables**
3. **Soft Goods**
4. **Yellow Goods**
5. **Services**

Marketing Insight 1.4

Deodorant market getting hotter in India

Let me ask you two multiple choice questions.

Q1. Name the market leader in deodorant category in India?

a) Park Avenue b) Axe c) Fogg d) Old Spice

Q2. Identify the market size of deodorant in India?

a) Rs. 1122 crore b) Rs. 295 crore c) Rs. 2100 crore d) Rs. 3900 crore

I hope, you got it right. The answer for both the questions is the 'c' option; i.e. Fogg is the market leader in deodorant category and the market size is worth Rs. 2100 crore.

Let us get into the deodorant market deeper. In the last few years, Deodorant has come up very fast in the Fast Moving Consumer Goods (FMCG) category. From a minuscule market size of Rs. 283 Crore in 2007, it has grown to more than Rs. 2100 crore in 2014. (Kindly check out the table 1 below). Besides the market size, it is also the fastest growing product in the FMCG category. Against the growth rate of 9 percent in FMCG, it is growing at 16 percent in India. This kind of growth also makes India, as the fastest growing deodorant markets in the world. These facts and figures make every FMCG company drool over this category. That's why; you find the presence of all the big as well as regional companies vying for the consumer's attention. Let us check out the brands in this category. I have listed down 22 brands; while in reality there may be a larger number, due to presence of many regional players (Kindly check out the table 2 below).

Table 1 : Deodorant Market Size in India

Sl. No.	Year	Deodorant Market Size(In Rs. Crore)
1	2007	283
2	2008	393

Sl. No.	Year	Deodorant Market Size(In Rs. Crore)
3	2009	**567**
4	2010	**793**
5	2011	**1129**
6	2012	**1521**
7	2014	**2100 (Approx.)**

(Source : Euromonior International)

Table 2 : Deodorant Brands in India

Sr. No.	Brand	Company	Brand Ambassador	Market Share
1	Fogg	Vini Cosmetics	-	17%
2	Park Avenue	Helene Curtis India (Part of Raymond)	-	8%
3	Axe	Hindustan Unilever Limited (HUL)	Ranbir Kapoor	Over 6%
4	Wild Stone	McNroe	Dia Mirza	Around 6%
5	Old Spice	Proctor & Gamble (P&G)	Arjun Rampal	
6	He	Emami	Hrithik Roshan	
7	Layer'r Shot	Adjavis Venture	Imran Khan	
8	Envy	Vanessa Care	Irrfan Khan	
9	Provogue	Provogue	Fardeen Khan	
10	Addiction	Mankind Pharma	Sunny Leone	
11	Garnier	Garnier	John Abraham	
12	Dove	HUL		
13	Rexona	HUL		
14	Set Wet	Marico		
15	Cinthol	Godrej		
16	Nivea	Nivea India		
17	Engage	ITC		
18	Spinz	Cavincare		
19	Fa	Jyothy		
20	Yardley	Wipro		
21	KS Deo (Kama Sutra)	J. K. Ansell (Part of Raymond)		
22	Rover	VEMB Retail		

Deodorant market is also unique in India, with market being dominated by companies of Indian origin, rather than MNCs. According to the recent Economic Times report – based on the March 2014 quarter Nielsen data, Fogg leads the market with 17% market share and is followed by Park Avenue with 8%. While Axe has slipped to third place with only 6% market share and its market share is now almost identical to Wild Stone. Although Axe has been in the market for long, it just took four years for Fogg to become the leader in the market.

Fogg

Axe Blast

Now let us check out what makes Fogg the leader in the market. For the same, we need to understand the marketing strategy of Fogg. Fogg is owned and marketed by a company called Vini Cosmetics, which was founded by Darshan Patel. Darshan Patel was the former promoter of Paras Pharma, which was later sold to Reckitt Benckiser. Earlier with Paras Pharma, Patel had successfilly marketed Moov, Krack Cream, Livon, Itchgard and Dermicool. He applied a strategy to break the clutter in this highly fragmented category, by giving more value to the customer.

If we think in terms of marketing from the theoretical perspective per se; a company can differentiate its product from the competition, on the basis of the marketing mix i.e. 4Ps – Product, price, place and promotion. In this case, being a FMCG product; Fogg played the first P i.e. Product card quite well. They found out that the deodorant can be differentiated by having less gas and more perfume. In turn, it will also provide more value to the customers. Now the customers were guaranteed to have 800 sprays from a bottle of Fogg Royal priced at Rs. 170/-. Thus the functionality of having more number of sprays in a bottle worked wonders for Fogg and it became the leader in the market. The functionality was also adopted well in the promoting the product with the tagline 'No Gas, Only Deo'. This kind of positioning was also different from the competition – including Axe, which emphasized only on the seduction aspect to sell their deodorants.

Wild Stone

He

Now let us analyse the positioning of various companies in the segment. Before 2013, Axe Ad was featuring a promotional campaign showing 'Angels falling on the earth'.

But it was not received well in India. To arrest the sales graph, HUL roped in Ranbir Kapoor as the brand ambassador. But this strategy has also not shown results. In comparison to Axe, Park Avenue deodorant has hold its ground well and have managed to keep their market share intact by product differentiation through innovation in pack sizes and by launching new fragrances. Other competitors are busy playing the card of seduction like Wild Stone, KS, Provogue etc., while others are relying on copying Fogg's strategy. Now few companies are trying to combine the seduction card with the functionality part like Addiction. New players like 'He' deo by Emami is banking on Hrithik Roshan, while 'Envy' deo by Vanessa is relying heavily on Irrfan Khan to do the trick. Besides these brands, few other brands like Set Wet, Spinz, Fa, Nivea, Yardley, Cinthol etc. are lost in the market game, without having a mark on the marketing horizon. Thus, it will be very interesting to see as to how these companies fight out in the cluttered deodorant market in the coming years and emerge a winner.

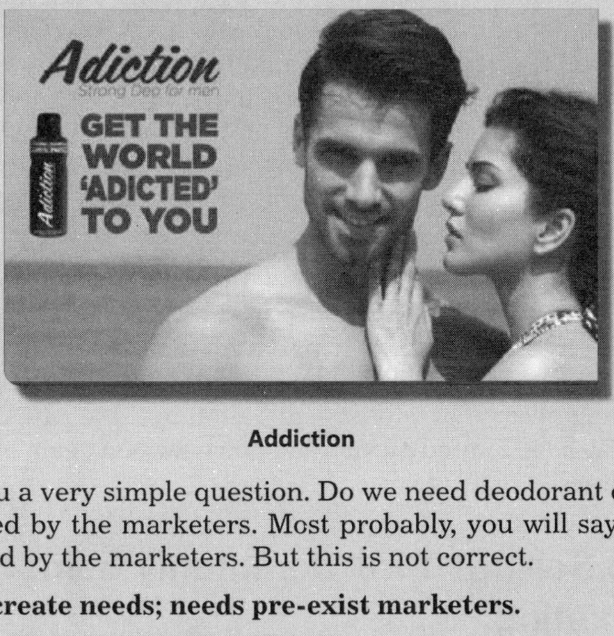

Addiction

Now let me ask you a very simple question. Do we need deodorant or the need for the deodorant is created by the marketers. Most probably, you will say that the need for deodorant is created by the marketers. But this is not correct.

Marketers do not create needs; needs pre-exist marketers.

Marketers just influence demand by communicating the benefits of the products to the customers, making the product available and by pricing it attractively. Customers are influenced by the society and this in turn creates demand for the product. In case of deodorant, a customer can very well live without it; but the societal influences keep him asking for the product. Thus, marketers do not create needs.

- **Business Markets:** In Business market, the buying and selling takes place among businesses. It includes profit as well as not for profit businesses, government agencies (Local, State and National) and institutions (Schools, Hospitals). The business buying is quite different from consumer buying, as the buyers are well informed and a professional approach is taken up, while taking purchase decisions. Business markets include the finished goods like PCs, office furniture, raw materials and components like steel, paint, timber, plastics, steering and services like security, courier, accounting and legal services. With respect to the consumer market, the buyers and sellers in the business market are relatively small in number.

Most of the times, the products and services are similar in the consumer markets and business markets like a fan or a TV or a courier service. The classification of the market depends upon the usage by the consumer or the business entity. A fan or a TV bought by a customer for his home use is a part of the consumer market, while the same brand of Fan or TV becomes a part of the business market, if it is bought by a hotel or by an educational institution.

- **International Markets:** Markets are not restricted within the borders. Now it is difficult to find a leading company not having international market. Maruti Suzuki sells more cars in India than its own domestic marketing Japan. Tata Group has the largest number of employees in the manufacturing sector in England than any English Company. Opportunities in these markets bring more challenges also. A company needs to take decisions not only on the front of country selection, but also needs to adapt products and services to the respective country. The difference in currency, culture, language, legal and political conditions bring far more challenges than the domestic market.
- **Nonprofit and Governmental Markets:** Nonprofit and Governmental markets pose a pricing challenge to the company. Most of the time pricing plays a crucial role in purchase decisions. Generally government purchasing is done through tenders, where bids are invited from different companies. The lowest bidder gets the order. That's why pricing needs a careful consideration in these cases. Similarly, nonprofit organisations also have limited purchasing power, which again calls for better pricing from the companies.

Marketing Vs Selling: Two Commonly held, Mistaken views of Marketing

In the marketing parlance, the term marketing is mostly mistaken for selling. You think that Marketing is selling. Secondly you also feel that marketing is just a department in the company. But marketing is a lot more than selling. Let me delve deeper into it.

Marketing is Selling

The most common type of confusion is that Marketing is selling. Although Selling is a part of Marketing; on the whole, it is much more than selling. Marketing starts much before the selling exercise. Marketing at first, identifies the unfulfilled needs and desire of the customer and then it measures the extent by which a profitable opportunity for the company exists. For example – Anand Mahindra saw the opportunity for launching a low cost SUV in the form of Scorpio in the market and then he and his marketing team at Mahindra assessed the situation of selling this kind of SUV in the market. Once they were convinced about the market opportunity, they got into production of the SUV. Here in this case, marketing started right after finding the unfulfilled needs of the masses; but selling started only after the production of Mahindra Scorpio. Marketing does not stop at the point of sales; but goes much beyond than that. That's why it helps the marketers to look at the marketing expenditures as an investment, not as a cost. They should look out for long term goals rather than short term results.

Marketing is Mainly a Department

This is the second most common type of confusion among the people. Generally in an organization, marketing functions as a department. This department consists of trained and experienced people in marketing to implement the company's marketing strategy. But marketing is not just a department, but it is a philosophy; a culture the organization imbibes to fulfill the customer needs.

History of Marketing

The history of marketing dates back to the beginning of civilisation. It started with the barter system and when the volume of business grew up; traders came into existence. With the industrial revolution happening in the late 18th and early 19th century, the business expanded manifold. Again with the subsequent progress in transportation and communication system, the business grew across the borders of a country.

In the Indian context, the Kautilya's famous book 'Arthashastra' talked about the relationship between the sellers and buyers. It also dealt with the earnings of the traders Marketing as a topic first appeared in the first half of the 20th century, with reference to distribution. The process of distribution and the determination of price through the demand and supply paved the way for studies in marketing. That's why economics is known as the mother of marketing. In the early stage, marketing was also known for selling and advertising only. But subsequently with the development of marketing as a management study, it got the right place it deserved through the various principles and theories.

Philosophies of Marketing Management

As far as the company orientation towards the marketplace is concerned, it has gone through various stages with the development. On the whole, it can be divided into five concepts:

The Production Concept

In the beginning, after the industrial revolution took place; the manufacturers were selling, whatever they could produce; as there was shortage of different products. It led to the stage where businesses adopted the **Production Concept**. Production concept is the oldest concept in the business and is based on the philosophy that consumers prefer products, which are widely available and inexpensive. For the business to be successful, maintaining high production efficiency, mass distribution and low costs was essential. The companies in China like Haier, TCL etc follow the same philosophy, based on the huge and inexpensive labour availability.

The Product Concept

The emphasis on production concept led to the difficulty in selling the products, which eventually forced the businesses to go for product differentiation. It was also found out that customers prefer those products that offer the most quality, performance or innovative features. This kind of business orientation led to the **Product Concept**. But a new and better product may not be always successful, unless it is marketed properly.

The Selling Concept

Product concept further led to **Selling Concept**; when selling became difficult even after having a good product at a cheaper price. Empahsising upon the selling concept, **Sergio Zymen**, Coca-Cola's former VP of Marketing has said,

> **'The purpose of Marketing is to sell more stuff to more people more often for more money in order to make more profits.'**

Selling concept holds that every product needs aggressive marketing to be sold. It happens mostly with the unsought goods like Insurance, Mediclaim policies, Demat accounts, Encyclopedias etc. and when there is overcapacity.

The Marketing Concept

With the increasing competition, the businesses started to discover that it is useful to produce what the customers want; rather than what can be produced by the company. This philosophy is known as **Marketing Concept**. It emerged in the 1950s with an objective of providing right products for the customers. Famous direct marketer **Lester Wunderman** has said,

> 'The chant of the **Industrial Revolution** was that of the manufacturer who said, **'This is what I make, won't you please buy it.'**

> The call of the **Information Age** is the consumer asking, **'This is what I want, won't you please make it.'**

Theodre Levitt has said

> **'Selling focuses on the needs of the seller; marketing on the needs of the buyer. Selling is preoccupied with the seller's need to convert his product into cash; marketing with the idea of satisfying the needs of the customers by means of the product and the whole cluster of things associated with creating, delivering and finally consuming it.'**

It has also been found through research that companies have achieved better performance by imbibing this philosophy. For example, Dell Computers has achieved success through mass customization of the computers, notebooks and netbooks, based on the individual customers' requirements.

The Holistic Marketing Concept

In the 21st century, the marketing concept is further strengthened with the term called **Holistic Marketing Concept.** Holistic marketing concept takes into account a broad, integrated perspective. It is based on integrated marketing, internal marketing, relationship marketing and performance marketing. It includes the development and implementation of marketing programs within the organisation as well as outside the organisation.

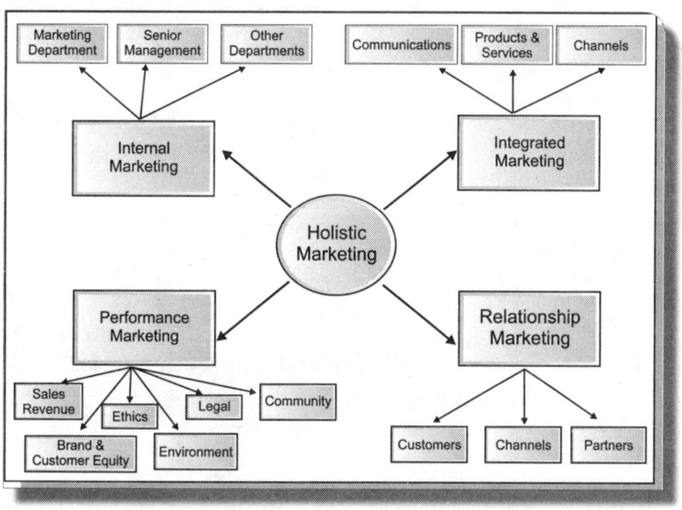

The Holistic Marketing Concept

Integrated marketing tries to build synergy among the product and services, channels of distribution and communications. It tries to integrate the marketing mix i.e. McCarthy's 4P's – Product, Price, Place and Promotion Whereas internal marketing deals with the relationship and the coordination among the marketing department with the senior management and other departments like finance, accounts, human resources, information technology etc. Relationship marketing deals with effective implementation of CRM (Customer Relationship Management) and PRM (Partner Relationship Management); while performance marketing calls for marketing activities as well as broader concerns of the society. It contains financial accountability, brand and customer equity on the one hand and ethics, environmental, legal and community concerns on the other in the form of social responsible marketing.

Socially responsible marketing calls for marketing beyond the objective of just making profits. It talks about fulfilling the need of a customer in such a way that will help to preserve the ecology and enhance the customers and society welfare. With the growing concern, the concept 'Green Marketing' is gaining popularity day by day.

Nokia 'Take Back'

Panasonic 'Eco Ideas'

HP 'Power to Change'

Nokia's 'Take Back' campaign for recyling old mobile phones, **HP's 'Power to Change'** campaign to save electricity and **Panasonic's 'Eco Ideas'** to produce energy efficient products, to reduce CO2 emissions across all their manufacturing sites and to spread awareness about the environmental activities through celebrity endorsers in India and all across the world, are examples of being a environment friendly, socially responsible company.

Marketing Mix

'Plan your work and work your plan'.

The philosophy of planning is as important in the business as it is in life. In the same way, marketing also needs a plan to reach its objectives and that is called marketing Plan. Marketing plan includes an executive summary with the SWOT analysis of the company, company's marketing strategy, market assessment in terms of segmentation, targeting and positioning, its marketing and financial goals, sales revenue and marketing budget forecast on yearly, quarterly and monthly basis and monitoring, evaluating and controlling the action plan.

The marketing plan leads to segmenting and targeting the market. Once the segments are identified, marketing mix helps the company to achieve its objectives.

The origin of marketing mix dates back to 1948, when **James Culliton** talked about a recipe for the marketing. Taking this recipe forward, **Neil H. Borden** coined the term 'marketing mix' in the American Marketing Association Presidential Address and said

'The marketing mix is the set of marketing tools the firm uses to pursue its marketing objectives in the target market.'[7] - Neil H. Borden

Neil Borden talked about twelve marketing tools – product planning, pricing, branding, channels of distribution, personal selling, advertising, promotions, packaging, display, servicing, physical handling and fact finding and analysis; under marketing mix. Then Professor **Richard Clewett** used a framework where he talked about four tools – product, price, distribution and promotion. **E. Jerome McCarthy** changed 'distribution' to 'place' and gave the famous **4Ps of Marketing.**[8]

1. **Product,**
2. **Price,**
3. **Place and**
4. **Promotion**

These four P's represent the set of marketing tools into four broad groups from the seller's point of view. Out of these four P's, a company can change its price and advertising and promotions in the short term. But it can change the product or can develop a new product or can modify the place i.e. distribution channel, only in the long run. For example, Chevrolet reduced the price of its hatchback car Spark by over fifty thousand rupees and it did so by announcing it through advertisements.

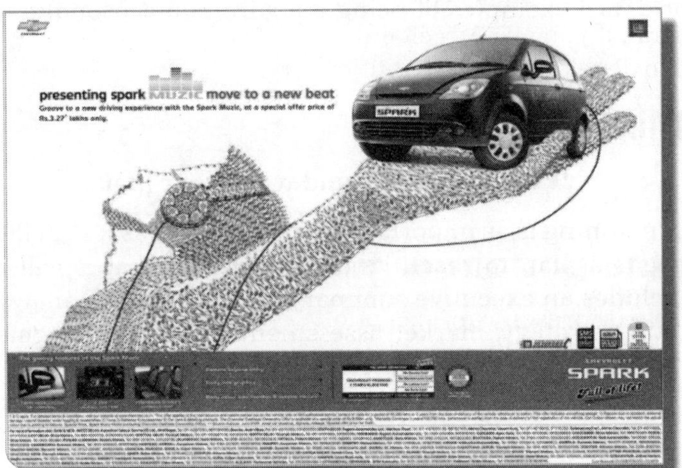

Chevrolet Spark

Again, after the Tata DoCoMo's offer of 1 paisa per second tariff scheme, Reliance announced its scheme of 50 paise per minute through a half page advertisement in almost all the newspapers.

Tata DoCoMo

Reliance Mobile

On the contrary, launching a new SUV like Mahindra Scorpio can take up to five years in the making. Again, if you are Aircel and launching your telecom services in the Indian market, you need to develop your distribution channel and it can take up months together.

Marketing Insight 1.5

Marketing Insight 1.5

Fortune at the Bottom of the Pyramid

Low-income markets present an exceptional opportunity for the world's wealthiest companies – to seek their fortunes and bring prosperity to the aspiring poor.

Nirma Vs.Wheel

The concept of the "Fortune at the Bottom of the Pyramid" was coined by C. K. Prahalad, Professor of Corporate Strategy and International Business at the University of Michigan, USA. The economic pyramid shown below illustrates the concept really well. According to this pyramid, more than 4 billion consumers constitute the BOP (Bottom of the Pyramid). This is indeed a massive, untapped opportunity.

The traditional assumption is that the poor have no purchasing power and therefore do not present a viable market. Is this true? Not really, if you know how to convert the poor into consumers! The real source of market promise is not the wealthy few in the developing world, or even the emerging middle – income consumers: It is the billions of aspiring poor who are joining the market economy for the first time. In short, the poorest populations raise a prodigious new managerial challenge for the world's wealthiest companies: selling to the poor and helping them improve their lives by producing and distributing products and services in culturally sensitive, environmentally sustainable, and economically profitable ways.

Four Consumer Tiers

EXHIBIT 1: THE WORLD ECONOMIC PYRAMID

Annual Per Capital Income*	Tiers	Population in Millions
More Than $20,000	1	75-100
$1,500- $20,000	2 & 3	1,500-1,750
Less Than $1,500	4	4,000

Based on purchasing power parity in U.S. $
Source: Adapted from (Prahalad and Hart 2002)

Four Consumer Tiers

At the very top of the world economic pyramid are 75 to 100 million affluent Tier 1 consumers from around the world. This is a cosmopolitan group composed of middle and upper-income people in developed countries and the few rich elites from the developing world. In the middle of the pyramid, in Tiers 2 and 3, are poor customers in developed nations and the rising middle classes in developing countries, the targets of MNCs' past emerging-market strategies.

Now consider the 4 billion people in Tier 4, at the bottom of the pyramid. Their annual per capita income — based on purchasing power parity in U.S. dollars — is less than $1,500, the minimum considered necessary to sustain a decent life. For well over a billion people — roughly one-sixth of humanity — per capita income is less than $1 per day.

In fact, given its vast size, Tier 4 represents a multitrillion-dollar market. According to World Bank projections, the population at the bottom of the pyramid could swell to more than 6 billion people over the next 40 years, because the bulk of the world's population growth occurs there. The quality and quantity of products and services available in Tier 4 is generally low. Therefore, much like an iceberg with only its tip inplain view, this massive segment of the global population – along with its massive market opportunities – has remained largely invisible to the corporate sector.

Wheel vs. Nirma

Hindustan Unilever Ltd. (HUL), a subsidiary of Great Britain's Unilever PLC and widely considered the best managed company in India, has been a pioneer among MNCs exploring markets at the bottom of the pyramid. For more than 50 years, HUL has served India's small elite who could afford to buy MNC products. In 1969, Dr. Karsanbhai Patel started selling Nirma in Gujrat and went on to sell it nationally by 1985. Patel was offering detergent products for poor consumers, mostly in rural areas. In fact, Nirma created a new business system that included a new product formulation, low-cost manufacturing process, wide distribution network, special packaging for daily purchasing, and value pricing.

HUL, in typical MNC fashion, initially dismissed Nirma's strategy. However, as Nirma grew rapidly, HUL could see its local competitor was winning in a market it had disregarded. Ultimately, HUL saw its vulnerability and its opportunity: In 1995, the company responded with its own offering for this market, drastically altering its traditional business model. HUL decentralized the production, marketing, and distribution of the product to leverage the abundant labor pool in rural India, quickly creating sales channels through the thousands of small outlets where people at the bottom of the pyramid shop. HUL also changed the cost structure of its detergent business so it could introduce Wheel at a low price point. Unilever's own analysis of Nirma and HUL's competition in the detergent business reveals even more about the profit potential of the marketplace at the bottom of the pyramid.

Contrary to popular assumptions, the poor can be a very profitable market — especially if MNCs change their business models. Specifically, Tier 4 is not a market that allows for the traditional pursuit of high margins; instead, profits are driven by volume and capital efficiency. Margins are likely to be low (by current norms), but unit sales can be extremely high. Managers who focus on gross margins will miss the opportunity at the bottom of the pyramid; managers who innovate and focus on economic profit will be rewarded. Nirma has become one of the leading branded detergent makers in the world. Meanwhile, HUL, stimulated by its emergent rival and its changed business model, registered a 20 percent growth in revenues per year and a 25 percent growth in profits per year between 1995 and 2000. Over the same period, HUL's market capitalization grew to $12 billion — a growth rate of 40 percent per year. HUL's parent company, Unilever, also has benefited from its subsidiary's experience in India.

Answer the following:

1. **Do you agree with the statement: 'Low-income markets present an exceptional opportunity for the world's wealthiest companies'?**
2. **Discuss the reasons for the success of Wheel in the Indian market.**
3. **Unilever has adopted the bottom of the pyramid as a corporate strategic priority. Is it right for the Unilever to do so?**

Let us start by answering the questions posed above one by one.

1. Do you agree with the statement: 'Low-income markets present an exceptional opportunity for the world's wealthiest companies'?

Now you all know that 'Low-income markets present an exceptional opportunity for the world's wealthiest companies' and thus the answer to the first question is yes. With more than 4 billion people in this category, low income markets make it very lucrative for the multinational corporations (MNCs). As you know that every company needs to sustain itself and grow in the market to fulfill their ultimate objective of making more and more profits. But, high income markets are limited and these markets have already been catered by different MNCs since long. So, there is lesser possibility to expand these markets. In that way, low income markets are totally untapped market and provide a huge opportunity for the marketers; as it did also in the case of Wheel for Hindustan Unilever Limited (HUL).

Let us come to the second question:

2. Discuss the reasons for the success of Wheel in the Indian market.

Before getting into answering it now, let us go back in 1969; where the story originates. In 1969, Dr. Karsanbhai Patel launched Nirma detergent powder to cater to the unmet needs of the customers for a low cost detergent powder. At that point of time, HUL's Surf was priced at Rs. 15/- a kg and that was too costly for the bottom of the pyramid customers. Dr. Patel launched Nirma at Rs. 3.50/- a kg and the same became a huge success.

Let us get into marketing theory a bit, to understand this scenario better. As you know, Marketing is all about identifying and fulfilling the needs of the customers. These customer needs can be classified into two categories -

1) Unmet needs and

2) Met Needs

Good companies try to meet the needs of the customers, which are already met; while Great Companies try to fulfill both unmet needs as well as met needs.

Nirma

Nirma is a very good example of fulfilling the unmet needs of the customers. Once you fulfill the unmet needs, you also get the **first mover advantage**; as there is no competition and you can have a free run in the market. It happened with Nirma also and it had almost a free run till late 1980s. But at last, in 1988, HUL woke up and launched Wheel to counter Nirma. At almost same point of time, Ghari detergent powder also entered the market and the market became highly competitive. In the next phase, around 2010, HUL started thinking of giving Wheel brand a mega push by undertaking two distinct strategies to counter both the players – Nirma and Ghari in one go.

Ghari

As you know, a brand can only sustain and grow itself in the market, when it can differentiate itself with the similar / me-too products. The answer to differentiation lies into the marketing mix of any product i.e. 4Ps and 7Ps, if it is a service. You need to tweak one of the Ps or more than one P to differentiate yourself and win over the market. In the case of Wheel, the product was similar to Nirma and Ghari and differentiation with respect to price and place was not possible. Nirma and Ghari were already there in the market for many years and were also very frugal in their expenses; which made them quite competitive in the market. Thus, the possibility of breaking the price barrier and selling Wheel at a lesser price than Nirma and Ghari was ruled out.

Now the only thing left was the promotion. The most obvious choice in this P was to get a Brand Ambassador / Celebrity Endorser and that's what HUL did. HUL roped in Salman Khan and Prachi Desai to endorse Wheel. Although the choice of Prachi Desai was simple, due to her massive fan following among housewives due to Saas Bahu serials. But choosing the male brand ambassador was pretty difficult.

Although it may seem easy to you; but think again. Is that so easy? For a company like HUL; the possibilities in selecting the brand ambassador was wide open; right from Amitabh Bachchan to Sachin Tendulkar to M S Dhoni to all the khans in the industry – Salman Khan, Shahrukh Khan, Aamir Khan, plus Akshay Kumar, Hrithik Roshan and so on. Next comes the question – how do you select a brand ambassador? Brand ambassador is decided on the basis of the target market, you cater to. Now, who is the target market for a product like Wheel detergent powder, which sells for Rs. 40/- a kg. Yes, You are right, the target customer for Wheel is the bottom of the pyramid customer, who earns $1500 a year. In monthly terms, he earns $125 a month i.e. Rs. 7500/- per month. Now, a person who earns on an average Rs. 7500/- and even less is hooked to what? Cricket, Cinema or something else. Most probably it will be cinema and for the Hindi belt in India; it will be specifically Bollywood cinema.

Wheel

Now comes the next question, Which Bollywood film star can he associate himself with? He can only associate with the film star; whom he can identify himself with. If it would have been 1980s, the choice was fairly simple – Amitabh Bachchan. Then Govinda and now yes, you are right, it is Salman Khan. Salman Khan was the only film star, who was popular with the masses, since his film Wanted in 2009. At that point of time, Shahrukh Khan was always acting as an NRI in USA in most of his films, while Aamir khan was seen as a Class actor, not an actor of the masses.

With the massive success of Wanted in 2009 that too in single screen theatres in tier II and tier III cities, semi urban and rural locations, made the choice for Salman Khan very obvious for HUL. The success story still continues with hits after hits like Dabbang, Ek tha Tiger, Bodyguard, Ready, Dabbang 2, Jai Ho and now Kick; which is ruling at the box office.

Besides promotion, HUL also created another differentiation, that too in the product. Now let me ask you one question, how do you understand that the clothes which you are going to wear is fresh? Yes, you smell it. And HUL smelt that too and incorporated artificial fragrance into Wheel, with photographs of Lemon, Jasmine, Sandal etc. to make consumers believe that it contains real ones.

Now let us come to the third question:

3. Unilever has adopted the bottom of the pyramid as a corporate strategic priority. Is it right for the Unilever to do so?

Yes, it is perfectly right for Unilever to replicate the same strategy across other similar markets. That's why they launched Ala in Brazil. Now catering to the needs of the bottom of the pyramid customers has become a trend for all the companies. These companies try to innovate and introduce products to suit their needs. HUL'S Pure It and Tata Swach is a good example in the water purifier segment. Many companies have introduced small sachets / packages in the FMCG category to target more and more customers from the price point ranging from a meager 50 paise to Rs. 10. You name any brand and it's there with the likes of Colgate, Parachute, Sunsilk, Parle G, Pepsodent, Fair & Lovely.

1. **Product**: The product is the starting point for marketing. A Product is anything that can be offered to a customer to satisfy his or her need or want. Whether it's a television or insurance policy, the product offers a total bundle of benefits to the customers. Typically in marketing, the term product is used for any good or service or any other entities, which can be marketed. According to Philip Kotler, ten entities can be marketed: Goods, Services, Experiences, Events, Person, Places, Properties, Organisations, Information and Ideas.

   Under product, factors like form, (size, shape, physical structure), performance quality, conformance quality, durability, reliability, reparability, style, design, product variety, quality, design, features, brand name, packaging, size, service, warranty, return, company reputation, pre sale information, post sale technical support, repair service, service distinction, ordering ease, delivery, installation, customer training, customer consulting, maintenance and repair are also taken into account to offer the value to the customers.

   A company needs to have some product to sell. If the company is new; then it should develop a product to sell in the market. In case of products, which are already there in the market, the company needs to differentiate its market offering. In case of new products, how should the company develop its product? Once it has launched a new product in the market and competitors are coming up with 'me-too' products, then how should a company react? When the company should expand the product line with brand and line extensions, without diluting the brand? When is the time to cut down the product line? All these questions are answered in a separate chapter under the Product.

2. **Price**: Price, the second P in the marketing mix, has a great relevance in business. Price is the only element in marketing, which produces revenue for the business organization. It is also the easiest element in the marketing mix, which can be adjusted in the short term. Price is also important as it communicates the value proposition. Price is the money; you pay for any product or service. The name may be different like airfare, tuition fee, college fee, hotel tariff, insurance premium, interest charges, rent, lease rental, retainer fee, consultancy fee, salary, commission, wage, toll or honorarium; but it means the same.[9]

   When a company wants to modify its marketing mix, price is the only factor in the marketing mix, which can be adjusted in the short run. All the other factors like product, place and promotion; may take a longer time to change. GM cut the price of its Spark cars on 12th Oct., 2007 by a whopping Rs. 53000/- by just announcing in a press conference. Similarly, Reliance cut its mobile tariffs to 50 paise per minute, reacting to the offer given by Tata DoCoMo's 1 paisa per second. In the era of hyper competition, pricing is the easiest way to react in the market. After Tata DoCoMo's offer of 1 paisa per second tariff rate in mobile services, almost every company in the mobile service segment like Airtel, BSNL, MTNL, Vodafone, Idea, Aircel, Reliance and Tata Indicom, has reduced their tariff rates.

   Pricing does not only take into account the Maximum retail price (MRP), but it also takes into account discounts, allowances, payment terms, credit terms and zero percent financing. The price for any product or service is decided on the basis of the company's price objective, the demand for the product, the estimation of costs and your competitors' costs, price and offers. Pricing is discussed in detail in a separate chapter.

3. **Place**: Place is very critical for the success of any business. Place means a marketing channel or trade channel or a distribution channel to reach out to the customers. Marketing channels are sets of interdependent organisations involved in the process of making a product or service available for use or consumption.[10] It is a set of mechanism or the network via which a firm goes to the market. It serves mainly four functions. The marketing channel helps to generate the demand for the company. The company then, fulfills the demand and also provides after sales service through them. It also helps in giving the information and feedback to the company from the customers.[11] For example, the leading car manufacturer in India, Maruti Suzuki has 933 dealers in 666 cities across India to sell its 14 brands of cars with more than 150 variants. It has also got 3060 service points across more than 1454 cities in India with more than 315 Maruti True Value outlets.

Maruti Suzuki Baleno

Place takes into account distribution channels, lot size, product assortment (breadth, length and width of product lines), locations, inventory, transport, logistics, coverage, 24/7 availability etc. Place is also dealt in detail in a separate chapter.

4. **Promotion:** Promotion, the fourth P of marketing, includes Advertising, Sales promotions, Public Relations, Direct Marketing, Personal Selling, Internet marketing and Interactive marketing. Now it is known as integrated marketing communications, where a company tries to integrate all its communication efforts to get maximum returns on their promotional expenditure.

   Once the product is developed in accordance with the needs of the customers, it needs to be priced attractively and then it needs to be available at the point of purchase. But, the customer will ask about your product in the market, only when he or she is aware about it. Again awareness or communication to the customer should be in such a way that the customers choose your product over competitors' product.

   Today customers are communicated through various communication channels like Print Advertisement, TV Commercials, Posters, Leaflets, Point of purchase (POP) Materials, Hoardings, Video Films, Directories, Sales Meeting, Fairs and Trade Shows, Online Shopping, Telemarketing, Catalogue Marketing, Contests, Seminars etc. Promotion is discussed further in the chapter Integrated Marketing Communications.

4 Cs and 4 As of Marketing

All these four Ps represent the set of marketing tools from the seller's point of view. But, there is something from the buyer's point of view also and this concept is given by **Robert Lauterborn**. He suggested four Cs corresponding to four Ps; which talks about the Customer benefits.[12]

Four Ps	Four Cs
Product	Customer Solution
Price	Customer Cost
Place	Convenience
Promotion	Communication

In addition to 4Ps and 4Cs, Prof. **Jagdish Sheth** came out with **4As**. He said that consumers will buy the products, only if there is

1. **Awareness,**
2. **Acceptability,**
3. **Affordability and**
4. **Accessibility**

Others have suggested few other Ps to be added in the four Ps of marketing. In 1970s, **Nickels and Jolson** proposed Packaging to be added.[13] **Philip Kotler** proposed to add politics and public opinion, as marketing depends upon a receptive government and receptive public. On the whole, four Ps cover almost everything in marketing and that's why it is still the most formidable base for understanding marketing.

7 Ps of Marketing

As far as products are concerned, four Ps still rule the marketing arena. But in the case of services and for knowledge based economy, **Booms and Bitner** has suggested another three Ps, besides 4 Ps like product, price, place and promotion; totaling it to 7Ps of Marketing.[14] These additional Ps are required for services marketing, as services have the characteristics of inseparability, intangibility, heterogeneity and perishability. Services range from an airline services to banking to courier to hotels. These additional P's are:

5. **People,**
6. **Process and**
7. **Physical Evidence**

5. **People**: All people, who directly or indirectly influence the perceived value of the product or service, including knowledge workers, employees, management and consumers comes under the 5th P of Marketing. In any service, the use of appropriate staff and people are of utmost importance for its success.

6. **Process**: In the case of process; procedures, mechanisms and flow of activities helps the marketer to satisfy the consumer in a better way. For example – Dominos Pizza serves its customers not only through its restaurants, but also with its 30 minutes guaranteed

home delivery in India. Mc Donald's serves its customers with freshly made burgers and French fries within two minutes of the order due to its streamlined process. Through physical evidence, a service marketer gives a tangible character by using certificates, tickets, logos etc.

Domino's Pizza

Mc Donald's

7. **Physical Evidence**: Physical evidence deals with the direct sensory experience of a product or service that allows a customer to measure whether he or she has received value. For example, if you travel first class on an aircraft, you expect enough room to be able to lie down. Again, once you walk into a restaurant, you expect a clean and friendly environment. All these factors are very important in giving the right value to the consumers.

Air India

All the above 3Ps helps a marketer to effectively implement the marketing plan for services.

Summary

- Marketing as a term is widely used in the management of a business and in our day-to-day life. In the era of customer and competition driven business world, marketing is not just the domain for the marketing department in a company. It's a philosophy; it's a business orientation now. It is imbibed in the corporate vision and mission of the successful companies.
- AMA defines marketing as 'the activity, set of institutions, and processes for creating, communicating, delivering, and exchanging offerings that have value for customers, clients, partners, and society at large.'
- A marketer does not only market goods and services, but he or she also markets eight other entities like Events, Experiences, Persons, Places, Properties, Organisations, Information and Ideas.
- Needs are basic human requirements. You need air, water, food, shelter and clothing to survive. Once these needs are specified by you, it become wants. Wants become demands, when the wants are backed by the ability to pay. Marketers don't create needs; needs preexist marketers.
- Markets can be classified on the basis of the **product** itself, or on the basis of the **end-consumer**, or both. The market is most commonly classified as following: **Consumer** Markets and **Business M**arkets (Industrial Markets or Organizational Markets), International Markets and Nonprofit and Governmental Markets.

- As far as the company orientation towards the marketplace is concerned, it has gone through various stages with the development. On the whole, it can be divided into five concepts: production concept, product concept, selling concept, marketing concept and holistic marketing concept.
- Jerome McCarthy classified different marketing activities as marketing mix tools, which include four P's i.e. product, price, place and promotion applicable for products. Whereas, for services, Booms and Bitner has suggested another three Ps, besides 4 Ps like product, price, place and promotion; totaling it to 7Ps of Marketing. These additional Ps are people, process and physical evidence. It is required for services marketing, as services have the characteristics of inseparability, intangibility, heterogeneity and perishability.

Discussion Questions

1. Define Marketing? Discuss the five stages of company orientations towards the marketplace.
2. What do you mean by Marketing Mix? Why do you require additional P's for marketing services?
3. Discuss the statement 'Selling focuses on the needs of the seller; marketing on the needs of the buyer. Selling is preoccupied with the seller's need to convert his product into cash; marketing with the idea of satisfying the needs of the customers by means of the product and the whole cluster of things associated with creating, delivering and finally consuming it.' How marketing concept is different from Holistic marketing concept.
4. What is the difference between Selling and Marketing? Do you agree with the statement 'Marketing is everything'?
5. Write an essay on five marketing success stories in India in the last ten years.
6. How different is product marketing from service marketing? Discuss in light of seven P's of marketing.
7. Short Notes:
   a. Needs, Wants, Demands
   b. Customer and Consumer
   c. Business Markets and Consumer Markets
   d. Governmental Market
   e. Events

References

1. Regis McKenna, '**Marketing Is Everything**', Harvard Business Review, 1991
2. Peter F. Drucker, Management : Tasks, Responsibilities, Practices, New York : Harper and Row, 1973, pp64-65
3. Peter F. Drucker, 'Innovation and Entrepreneurship', Harper Paperbacks, 2006
4. American Marketing Association definition of Marketing approved by American Marketing Association Board Of Directors, Oct., 2007
5. Jeffrey Rayport and John Sviokla, 'Managing in the marketspace', Harvard Business Review, Nov.-Dec. 1994, p. 141-50 and 'Exploring the Virtual Value Chain', Harvard Business Review, Nov.-Dec. 1995, p. 75-85
6. Mohan Sawhney, 'Seven Steps to Nirvana', McGraw Hill, 2001
7. Neil H. Borden, 'The concept of the Marketing Mix', Journal of Advertising Research, June, Vol. 4, pp. 2–7, 1964
8. E. Jerome McCarthy, 'Basic Marketing : A Managerial Approach', 1960 1st ed. / 13th ed., Irwin, Homewood Il, 2001
9. Referred from David J. Schwartz, 'Marketing Today: A Basic Approach', 3rd Edition, Harcourt Brace Jovanovich, 1981, p.271
10. Louis W. Stern and Adel I. El-Ansary, 'Marketing Channels', Prentice Hall, 1996
11. Robert J. Dolan, 'Going to Market', Harvard Business School Publishing, 1999
12. Lauterborn, R (1990) "New Marketing Litany: 4 Ps Passe; C words take over", Advertising Age, October 1, 1990, pg 26
13. Nickels, William G. & Jolson, Marvin A. (1976) 'Packaging - The Fifth 'P' In The Marketing Mix', Advanced Management Journal, Winter, Vol. 41, Iss. 1, p. 13
14. Bitner, J. and Booms, B. (1981) Marketing strategies and organizational structures for service firms, in Donnelly, J. and George, W. Marketing, American Marketing Association, Chicago, 1981

CHAPTER 2

Market Oriented Strategic Planning

Chapter Structure

- Value in Marketing
- The 5 Cs of Marketing Analysis
- Customer Value, Satisfaction and Retention
- Value Delivery Process
- Market Oriented Strategic Planning
- Igor Ansoff's 'Product Market Expansion Grid'
- *Marketing Insight 2.1: Maruti Readies Plan for LCV Foray*
- *Marketing Insight 2.2: Asian Paints Enters the Kitchen with Sleek Deal*
- *Marketing Insight 2.3: Wipro: from a Vegetable Oil Maker to an IT Major*
- *Marketing Insight 2.4: ITC Takes a Big Bite of FMCG Pie*
- Summary
- Discussion Questions
- References

"The primary function of the marketing plan is to ensure that you have the resources and the wherewithal to do what it takes to make your product work."

- Jay Levinson

Value in Marketing

'The central role of marketing in the enterprise stems from the fact that marketing is the process by which a firm creates value for its chosen customers.'[1]

Marketing revolves around value. It is all about creating communicating, delivering, and exchanging offerings that have value for customers, clients, partners, and society at large.

'Value is created by meeting customer needs. Thus a firm must define itself not by the product it sells, but by the customer benefit provided.'[1]

The value creation done by the company is an ongoing process. The company needs to sustain this process of value creation over a period of time to sustain itself in the market. The company's marketing strategy helps to create the value on a sustainable and continuous basis. In Indian market, business groups like Tatas, Birlas, Ambanis etc. have been quite successful at creating value over a period of time through a bouquet of products and services under their belt.

Whatever the big names you hear in the business world like Ford, General Motors, Sony, Disney, Coke, McDonald's, HP; all had been in the business for more than 50 years. But, it does not mean that only older companies are successful in the business. In fact, a lot of new companies have been tremendously successful in Indian as well as global markets like Infosys, Wipro, HCL, Airtel, Apple, Microsoft, Google, Yahoo etc.

HP

Stressing upon the importance of Marketing in any business organisation, **David Packard**, Co-Creator, Hewlett Packard (now known as HP) once said that

'Marketing is far too important to leave to the marketing department.'

Actually, the whole company should strive to deliver the promised value. Otherwise the marketing will fail. Regis McKenna also argued that

Marketing management encompasses all factors that influence a company's ability to deliver value to customers; it must be 'all-pervasive, part of everyone's job description, from the receptionists to the Board of Directors.'

Thus, Marketing is both a business function and a business orientation. We mostly think in terms of marketing as a business function, in terms of what it does through Sales,

Market Research, Advertising, Promotion, Public Relations, Distribution and so on. But it's the marketing orientation towards the business, which makes a company successful.

The 5 Cs of Marketing Analysis

Marketing is the process via which a firm creates value for its chosen customers. Value is created by meeting customers' needs. The plan by which value is created on a sustainable basis is the firm's Marketing Strategy. The success of any business depends upon its marketing strategy.

Going further, Marketing Strategy is guided by 5 Cs, which leads the firm to go forward in fulfilling the needs of the customer. Traditionally only three Cs - Customers analysis, Company analysis, and Competitors analysis; were considered for doing the marketing analysis, which is known as Marketing Triangle (See figure 2.1).

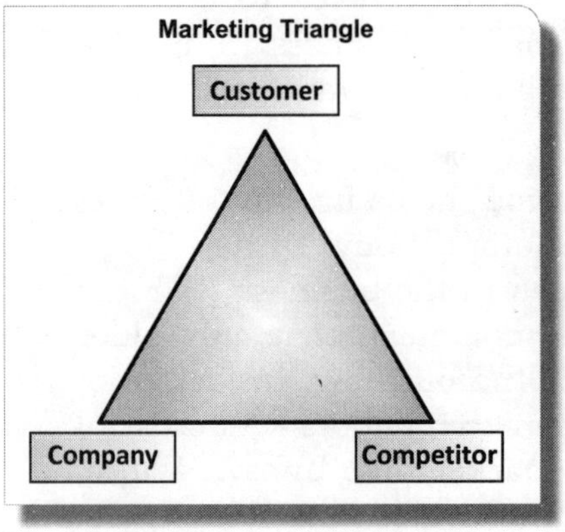

Figure 2.1: Marketing Triangle

But now, it has been broadened to include another 2 Cs i.e. Collaborators and Context. In the figure 1.3, the five major areas of marketing decision making is shown below. To understand it further, we will take the example of Tata Nano again.

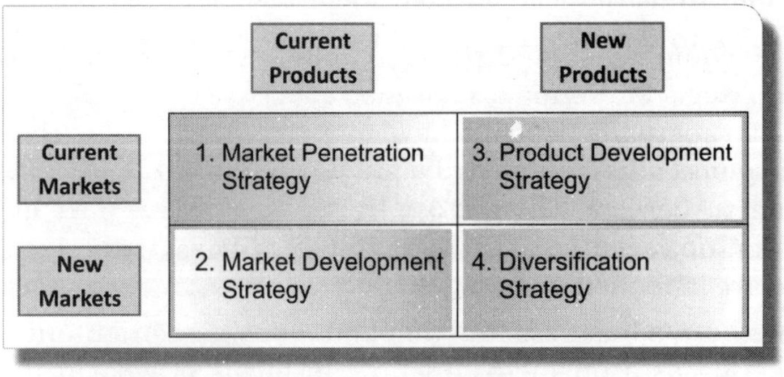

Figure 2.2: The 5 Cs of Marketing Analysis

1. **Customer Needs**: A company seeks to satisfy certain needs. Now, what are these needs? Who are involved in the process and what role does each one of them play? How does the customer seek information? What criteria does he use to evaluate various alternatives? How important is price for the customer? Where does the customer buy from? etc. Once you are better off answering questions, you will be close to your customer and the customers will be close to your company.

   For doing the same, the marketing department of the firm tries to divide a potential market into distinct subsets of consumers with a common need or characteristic. The same can be found out through Marketing Research. Then, it selects one or more segments to target with right kind of positioning and specially designed marketing mix.

   In the case of Tata Nano, Tata Motors wanted to satisfy the need of a car for common people, at the price which they can afford. Captain Gopinath dreamt of common man flying through an airlines and came up with Air Deccan. (Currently Air Deccan has been taken over by Kingfisher Airlines and is renamed as Kingfisher Red). Karsanbhai Patel found the need of a cheap washing powder for common people and launched the hugely successful Nirma. In the same way, Ajay Bijli motivated cinegoers through PVR Multiplex and made watching movie a pleasurable experience. Anand Mahindra understood the need of the customer of having a Sports Utility Vehicle (SUV) just for Rs. 7 Lacs.

2. **Company**: Company analysis is as important as customer analysis. As it will help to understand what a company can do or what it can't. There are several ways and measures like SWOT (Strength, Weakness, opportunity, Threat) Analysis, Core Competency Analysis and BCG (Boston Consultancy Group) Matrix besides other methods to analyse the company externally and internally. It also requires an understanding of the company's finances, its research and development (R&D) capabilities, its supply and distribution channel management capability, the strength of its brands and other assets.

   In the case of Tata Nano, Tata Motors was already having the expertise of manufacturing and distributing vehicles. In the same way, Mahindra had been selling its tractors and jeeps for a long time. But Karsanbhai Patel started afresh, while Captain Gopinath had the experience in the Aviation industry. Ajay Bijli was also informed about the film exhibition business due to its Priya Movie Theatre in Delhi.

   It is not that a company needs to have experience to succeed in the marketplace. But you can also succeed, if you have the pulse of the market. You understand the needs of the customers. Microsoft, Google, Apple, Nirma are all the examples for understanding what you can do, what you can offer to fulfill the needs of the customers. All these companies are launched by first generation entrepreneurs and they made it big in the market.

3. **Competition**: Once you understand the customers and your core competency, you need to understand the market players i.e. Competitors. Competition is all about current and potential offerings that a customer may consider. You need to assess the strengths and weaknesses of the competitors; as it will help out to differentiate your product and services from others. For Tata Nano, although there is no competition at the price point of Rupees One Lac, but a customer may think about buying Maruti 800 instead of Tata Nano LX model, which costs almost Rs. 1.8 Lacs on road. In the case of Mahindra Scorpio, the competition was limited due to rival offerings in the market available for more than Rs. 14 lacs. In the case of Nirma, the competition was from Wheel and with the movie multiplex experience, the single screen cinema halls were the competition.

   Once you are already there in the market with your product or service offering, a company needs to be careful all the time as the competition can take the fizz away. As it happened in the case of Bajaj Auto, which was the largest two wheeler manufacturer twenty years back. But in the 1990s, with the onslaught of Hero Honda, it slipped into oblivion. Again identifying the customer needs, it's back in the business at no. 2 position with clear leadership in above 100cc segment of motorbikes with Pulsar, Discover and XCD bikes.

Bajaj Pulsar 150 DTS-i

You might also be familiar with Onida being one of the leading TV Brands in India few years back, with its one of the most successful Devil Ad campaign. Now Samsung and Sony is leading the market. So, beware of competition; as it cannot make your business, but it may certainly break your business.

Onida Television

Sony Bravia LED Television

4. **Collaborators**: For the success of any business organisation or firm, its' very essential to maintain a relationship with the customers. But, it is also very important to maintain the relations with the collaborators, who are the partners in the progress of the firm. That's why you need to take care of **Customer Relationship Management (CRM)** and **Partner Relationship Management (PRM)** as well. Collaborators mainly include your distribution channel partners and suppliers besides others.

   The Success of Tata Nano to deliver the car at Rs. One Lac price point is the example of how collaborators can help you deliver your dream. The bouncing back of Bajaj has also been partly due to its collaborators, which helped them to sell their bike Bajaj Boxer at almost four thousand cheaper than the largest selling bike Hero Honda Splendor.

   Collaborators help you to manufacture and deliver your goods and services to the customer in a better way than your competitors and that's why they also need to be motivated.

5. **Context**: Context whether it is cultural, technological, regulatory and legal factors, can play a greater part in influencing your business decisions, your strategic marketing decisions. It's also important, because it is ever changing. Now the business is not done as it was done earlier. The advent of Internet, Web and Mobile Technologies has led the distribution and communication system to be totally revamped. Few years back, E-Commerce (Electronic Commerce – Doing business electronically mainly through internet) started the online business revolution and now it is extended to M-Commerce (Mobile Commerce). Now with Mobile Banking, your bank is now in your pocket.

Tata Indigo CS : The Most Compact Sedan in the World

Similarly, regulatory and cultural factors can also influence your marketing exercise. For example in India, if you manufacture a car which is lesser than four meters in length, you get excise benefits. Now all the sedans are above four meters and so these cars don't get the excise benefits. Taking the legal context to the market scenario, Tata Motors launched a new version of its Tata Indigo called Tata Indigo CS (Compact Sedan). This model is the cheapest sedan in the world with a price tag of less than Rupees four lacs for petrol variant.

In the same way, India is becoming a small car manufacturing hub of the world, due to the strong and growing inherent demand and the excise benefits provided to small cars. This excise benefit is applicable to only those cars, which are having less than four meters length and not more than 1200 cc petrol engines and 1400 cc diesel engines. That's why; most of the small cars in India are having either up to 1200 cc petrol engines or up to 1500 cc diesel engines.

Mont Blanc Watch

Similarly Mall Culture in India, high disposable income and living for today culture has led to the growth of branded products. The launch of world famous brands like Harley Davidson, Tag Heuer, Bentley, Gucci, Mont Blanc are all examples of changes in the mindset of the customers, changes in the cultural context of the customers.

Customer Value, Satisfaction and Retention

There are three drivers of successful relationship between customers and marketers. These are as following:

1. Customer Value,
2. Customer Satisfaction and
3. Customer Retention.

Customer value is the ratio between customers' perceived benefits (economic, functional and psychological) and the resources (monetary time, effort, psychological) used to obtain these benefits. The perceived value is relative and subjective. That's why it is often argued that the firm should look out for value proposition rather than Unique Selling Proposition (USP). Philip Kotler has also defined Marketing

> **'as the art and science of choosing target markets and getting, keeping and growing customers through creating, delivering and communicating superior customer value.'[2]**

Once the creation of value takes place, it leads to the customer satisfaction i.e. the individual's perception of the performance of the product or service in relation to his or her expectation. Then customer satisfaction leads to customer retention.

Nescafe

The overall objective of providing value to customers continuously and more effectively than the competition is to have and to retain highly satisfied customers. Because there is **customer lifetime value (CLV)** attached to every customer. For example, you go to your college canteen every day and have samosa or sandwich with tea or coffee say Nescafe every day. Although you are spending just forty five rupees a day, you will be spending approximately Rs. Twenty seven thousand in two years during your MBA/PGDM program.

To understand it better, for example you have passed out from the college; you get a good placement and start working in an MNC. You want to buy your first car and then you decide to buy a car from Maruti Suzuki, Tata Motors or Hyundai. In this case, when you buy the car, you have a long term association as you will be requiring spare parts and regular servicing. It is all part of the customer lifetime value. Now, you want to upgrade your car from a hatchback to a sedan due to increase in your income or social status or the needs for a bigger car for your family. If you had been satisfied with your first car say Maruti Alto, there is a good probability that you will continue with the brand by buying a Swift Dzire. In this way, you become brand loyal. But if you are not satisfied, then you won't upgrade the car from the same company. Not only that, you will also advise your family, friends, relatives and acquaintances not to buy any car from that car manufacturer.

Maruti Suzuki Swift 2011

The moral of the story is that if your company is selling a FMCG (Fast Moving Consumer Goods) product, which is bought frequently and of low value or selling a high value product like Car, LCD TV, notebook or an air conditioner, you should take care of every customer, as there is CLV attached to the customers.

Marketing is all about creating value, capturing value and sustaining value through the analysis of 5 Cs, correct know how of STP and the implementation of its marketing mix via 4 Ps. This will help the firm to be competitive and profitable in the market by customer acquisition (adding new customers) and Customer Retention (retaining old customers).

Value Delivery Process

In this dynamic world, the rules of business have changed. Earlier a company used to make the product and then the marketing started as shown in the following figure in the traditional physical process sequence.

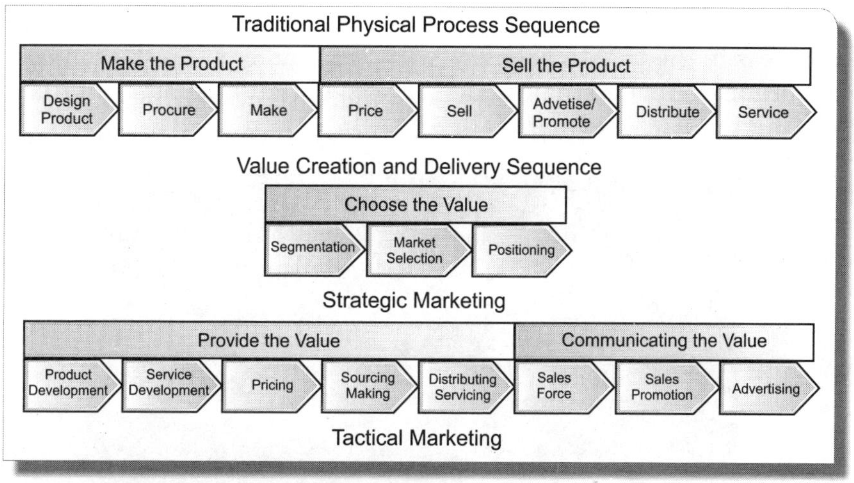

(Source : Michael J. Lanning and Edward G. Michaels, "A Business is a value delivery system", McKinsey staff paper no. 41, June, 1988)

Now the value creation and delivery takes place in three phases as shown above. It starts with Segmentation, Targeting and Positioning (STP) and then it moves on to providing the value through first 3P's in the stages of product development, pricing, sourcing and distributing. Then it moves on to communicating value through sales force, promotions and advertising. This process has got cost implications. That's why generally the pricing of a product goes up to three to four times of the manufacturing cost.

Market Oriented Strategic Planning

Tata, Birla, Coke, Mc Donald's, Ford, General Motors Disney have one thing common. These companies are in the business for more than 75 years. All this has been possible due to their long term vision and strategic planning. Market oriented strategic planning has helped these companies to stay ahead in the market than their competition, by looking at a long term outlook of growth rather than short term focus on profits. That's why, **Philip Kotler** has rightly said

'It is more important to do what is strategically right than what is immediately profitable.'[3]

In the changing business scenario, market oriented strategic planning is must for any company. It does not only take into account the company's objectives, capabilities and resources; but it also takes into account the changing market opportunities. The objective of the strategic planning is to ensure that the company hits both the targets of profits as well as growth. For example : To keep the growth momentum with more and more profits, Tata launched their GSM service in the market in the name of Tata DoCoMo; besides its successful business in the CDMA segment with Tata Indicom. In the same way, Reliance (Anil Ambani Group) launched their GSM services in the same name of Reliance Mobile, as it is present in the CDMA segment.

Mahindra Xylo

In the same way, to keep the growth momentum, Mahindra launched their successful SUV Scorpio and then they launched Xylo. With Xylo, Mahindra is racing ahead in the market now, competing against the market leader Toyota Innova. Tata Motors not only acquired Land Rover and Jaguar, but also launched Nano, Indica Vista and Indigo Manza to cater to different segments of customers.

Strategic Intent

Generally most of the large companies work on the four organizational levels:

1. Corporate Level
2. Division Level
3. Business Unit Level and
4. Product Level.

Corporate headquarters devises and guides the organisation on all the levels. Strategic intent helps the management team to understand where they want to go and how to arrange their priorities, so as to achieve the organizational goals. According to Hamel and Prahlad,

'Strategic Intent envisions a desired leadership position, which is more than an unfettered ambition, involving an active management process.'

It also consists of a mission statement and a vision statement.

On the whole, strategic intent process concludes the following:

1. Current environment of the business
2. Core competencies of the current business
3. Future position of the business
4. A set of strategic intent statements including mission and vision statements

Taking into account the current environment of business, its core competencies and its future position; a set of mission and vision statements are developed to show the right path. A mission statement defines company's business, its objectives and its approach to attain the objectives. A vision statement describes the desired future position of the organisation.

A company needs to do SWOT Analysis for doing the same. SWOT Analysis is the overall evaluation of its internal environment i.e. Strengths and Weaknesses and its external environment i.e. opportunities and threats. Based on the assessment of its internal as well as external environment, a company may progress on the path of its vision and mission.

Once a company looks forward to expand its businesses, it can do so in any of the three ways:

1. **Intensive Growth Opportunities**: By identifying opportunities to achieve further growth within current businesses
2. **Integrative Growth Opportunities**: By identifying opportunities to acquire or build businesses that are related to current businesses
3. **Diversification Growth Opportunities**: By identifying opportunities in the unrelated attractive businesses

Igor Ansoff's 'Product Market Expansion Grid'

In case of Intensive Growth Opportunities, Igor Ansoff has suggested a 'Product Market Expansion Grid'.[4]

	Current Products	New Products
Current Markets	1. Market Penetration Strategy	3. Product Development Strategy
New Markets	2. Market Development Strategy	4. Diversification Strategy

Product Market Expansion Grid

Product market expansion grid can help the company to identify the market opportunities in respective markets and products. The first thing a company can consider is to gain more market share in the existing or current products in the current markets. This is called Market penetration strategy. Or, the company can look forward to expand its markets for current products through Market Development Strategy. The next thing a company can consider as to whether it can develop new products to its current markets and it is called Product Development Strategy. Lastly the company can take up the diversification strategy i.e to develop new products for new markets.

Cadbury Dairy Milk

As far as market penetration strategies are concerned, the company can encourage its current customers to buy more or it can try to attract competitor's customers or it can induce non users to start using the product. This type of strategy is quite prevalent. If you remember the Cadbury's campaign, 'Kuchh Khaas hai Zindagi Mein' and then 'Kuchh Meetha Ho jaye', it is a very good example of how a company can achieve growth as well as profits through market penetration strategies. Cadbury has not only increased its sales of chocolates, but also tried to expand the market by promoting it as a substitute of our age old sweets.

In Diwali, there is the tradition of gifting sweets and dry fruits. To cater to this business opportunity, Cadbury comes out with special gift packages of chocolates for the customers. Even Kurkure, Bikaji, Lays now comes out with gift hampers in Diwali as a part of market penetration strategy.

Moser Baer

Besides intensive growth opportunities, the company can also look forward to integrative growth through backward, forward and horizontal integration. Moser Baer, the second largest manufacturer of optical media i.e. CDs, DVDs and Blu Ray Discs; in the world have gone further and forwardly integrated its business by not only selling home videos on CDS, DVDs and Super DVDs, but also getting into media content creation including film production.

Maruti Suzuki is also entering into the India's fast growing small commercial vehicle space, besides its passenger vehicle business. Earlier Maruti was only offering Omni Cargo Van in the commercial vehicle space. Recently Asian Paints has also acquired 51% stake in Sleek Group, a leading organised player in the modern kitchen space; to move up the value chain. Now Asian Paints will be able to sell a new home-buyer paint, water proofing and a modular kitchen under one roof

Marketing Insight 2.1

Marketing Insight 2.1

Maruti Readies Plan for LCV Foray

Co's new 2-cylinder, 800 cc diesel engine may be key to the successful development of a pick-up truck by 2017

Tata Ace

Maruti Suzuki, India's largest car manufacturer is exploring a foray into India's fast growing small commercial vehicle space. The segment is currently dominated by Tata Motors Ace with over 50% market share. Though the Japanese carmaker had the Omni Van, used as a cargo vehicle, it did not have a competitive offering in the load-carrier segment, due to the absence of a small diesel engine.

But with the development of company's two-cylinder, 800 cc, diesel engine for the passenger car shifting to India, it is actively exploring options to use the potential workhorse to enter the small pick up truck market, ET learns.

The project is codenamed 'AP' and if the exercise fructifies into an actual investment, the possible entry into light commercial vehicle (LCV) space could happen "between 2015 and 2017", according to informed sources. ET has learnt that the company is likely to develop an all-new platform or may use the Suzuki carry pick up truck platform which is sold in South East Asia and may tweak it to handle the overloading abuse in the country. When contacted, a Maruti Suzuki spokesperson replied that the company does not comment on future product plans.

According to Frost & Sullivan, the Indian small and light commercial vehicle segment is likely to grow by a compounded annual growth rate of 18% over the next five years to 8,30,000 units by 2016. With the development of infrastructure, the country is expected to shift to hub-and-spoke model of transporting goods. In the hub-and spoke model heavy trucks ply on big highways, or hubs, and small commercial vehicles act as spokes in cities where the movement of heavy vehicles is restricted.

According to Frost & Sullivan, the Indian small and light commercial vehicle segment is likely to grow by a compounded annual growth rate of 18% over the next five years to 8,30,000 units by 2016. With the development of infrastructure, the country is expected to shift to hub-and-spoke model of transporting goods. In the hub-and spoke model heavy trucks ply on big highways, or hubs, and small commercial vehicles act as spokes in cities where the movement of heavy vehicles is restricted.

In the April-November period, the mini truck and the pick-up truck segment combined (i.e. weight not exceeding 3.5 tonnes) posted a growth of 24% with sales of 2,75,900 units. In the same period, market leader Tata Motors posted a growth of 22.9% selling 1,57,183 units. Despite the entry of major players like M&M, Piaggio and Ashok Leyland, Tata Motors continues to lead with a market share of 57% this fiscal. Experts believe Maruti Suzuki may prove a major threat to Tata Motors as it has a wider reach in the country.

Deepesh Rathore, MD of IHS Automotive, says the technological entry barrier are limited in the mini truck space and the segment is one of the fastest growing segments in the Indian automotive industry with further potential to grow large volumes. “Despite the entry of many players in small truck space, Tata Motors continue to enjoy over 50% of the market share and the others too are growing, that clearly shows that there is a room for more players.

Maruti Suzuki can certainly be a strong challenger to Tata Motors with the widest possible reach, but having a suitable diesel engine is the key,” said Rathore.

Just like the passenger car space, even in the mini-truck category, the demand is getting upgraded from 0.5-1 tonne segment of Ace Zip to 2-tonne segment of Tata Motors Super Ace, Mahindra Genio and Ashok Leyland Dost category. While M&M and Piaggio fared well in the last fiscal with their Maxximo and Ape mini trucks, the two automobile companies have seen sales dipping over 20% and 70% respectively, in the current fiscal.

Experts say it will be interesting to watch, which space Maruti Suzuki would prefer to enter. “There is a clear upgrading happening from sub-one-tonne trucks to higher payload trucks of 2 tonnes and above and it is clearly seen in the numbers of Ashok Leyland Dost which has been a run away success and Tata Motors and M&M’s pick-up trucks, too, continue to register double-digit growth. Since Maruti Suzuki’s project is at an early stage, they will be watching this evolution very closely,” said an analyst with a leading broking firm.

Marketing Insight 2.2

Asian Paints Enters the Kitchen with Sleek Deal

Company buys 51% stake in modular kitchen space player to move up the value chain

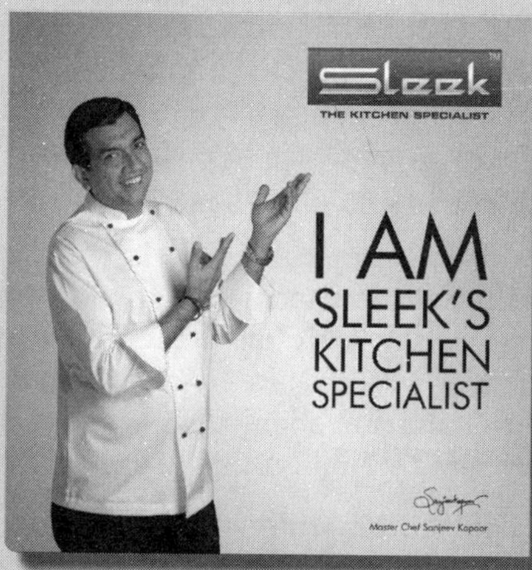

Sleek

It's always been more about homes than paint – so for Asian Paints, moving into providing kitchen solutions is a logical step up the value chain. It has acquired a 51% stake in Sleek Group, a leading organised player in the modern kitchen space. It's the first such step for the decorative paints company following its decision taken in July 2012 to explore opportunities in areas of home improvement and décor.

"It may be an un-related business for a paints company, in terms of distribution and manufacturing, but we find it to be a brilliant strategy for Asian Paints as it will now be able to sell a new home-buyer paint, water proofing and a modular kitchen," says Abneesh Roy, associate director, Edelweiss Capital.

"To take our brand to the next level in a fairly nascent and unorganised market, we needed a strategic partner to develop our back-end and dealer network", says Rajesh Ahuja, managing director of Sleek International. "We found such partner in Asian Paints, the Indian multinational with a 30,000-dealer network", he adds.

Volumes in the paints business typically grow at nearly twice the rate of GDP. With GDP growth having weakened to 4.5%, paints volume growth has slowed to 9%. This has prompted Asian Paints to scout for fast-growing opportunities outside its core business. While Asian Paints has not disclosed the size of the acquisition, it is going to be funded through internal accruals by the company.

Analysts estimate Sleek's revenues at Rs. 200-250 crore, making it a small acquisition for Rs. 10,000- crore Asian Paints with current assets of over Rs. 3,000 crore. "It may be a small acquisition at this point in time, but it is in line with the company's articulated strategy of entering into home solutions — which is a big market," says Shirish Pardeshi, executive director, Anand Rathi Securities.

Similarly, Tata group always looks out for integrating its businesses. If we talk about say Tata Motors then Steel, Battery and other raw material and components are supplied from its own sister concerns. Again Reliance will make the picture complete by taking out crude oil from KG Basin to refining and then to selling its petroleum products in its own outlets.

But attractive opportunities do not only lie in the current businesses, it can lie in different businesses too. For many industrial or business conglomerates all across the world, the diversification is the driver of their growth, be it Reliance, Tata, Wipro or ITC. You name the business and the company is there into. For example, the well known Cigarettes manufacturer ITC, earlier known as Imperial Tobacco Company of India Limited, has diversified into FMCG products like packaged foods, confectionery, toiletries, incense sticks, safety matches, hotels, paperboards, information technology and agricultural products.

Marketing Insight 2.3

Marketing Insight 2.3

Wipro: From a vegetable oil maker to an IT major

Wipro

Wipro was established by Mohamed Hasham Premji in 1945 as a vegetable oil manufacturer in Amalner, Maharashtra. It was then known as Western India Products Ltd. Its main area of business was production of sunflower vanaspati oil. Later on, it moved to soaps and other consumer care products. The company filed for IPO in February 1946. In 1966, after Hasham Premji's death, the business was taken over by his son Azim Premji, who was then 21.

In 1977, the company changed its name to Wipro Products Ltd. In 1982, the company was renamed Wipro Ltd. Wipro ventured into the IT business in 1981. Today, it has over 130,000 employees and clients across 54 countries. It was listed on the New York Stock Exchange in October 2000.

In February 2001, Wipro became the first Indian IT company to get ISO 14001 certification. Wipro has been ranked 1st in the 2010 Asian Sustainability Rating of Indian companies and is a member of the NASDAQ Global Sustainability Index as well as the Dow Jones Sustainability Index.

In November 2012, the company de-merged its non-IT businesses. The demerger means Wipro will hive off three units — Wipro Consumer Care & Lighting, Wipro Infrastructure Engineering and Medical Diagnostic Product & Services business — into a separate unlisted company called Wipro Enterprises.

Marketing Insight 2.4

ITC Takes a Big Bite of FMCG Pie

Gains in biscuits, snacks & noodles and headway in soaps and shampoos help co forge ahead

Aashirvaad

In August when ITC cornered a share of more than 28% in cream biscuits in urban India as per Nielsen data, it was a wake-up call for the largest cream biscuits maker Britannia. Although Britannia did not share data with ET, numbers obtained from an industry official suggests that ITC may have nosed ahead of Britannia in this segment by roughly 1 percentage point, at least for the month of August. However, both ITC and Britannia declined to confirm this (Britannia did not respond to an email with questions on the threat from ITC).

Sr. No.	Brand	Category	Revenue 2011-12 (In Rs. Crore)
1	Sunfeast	Biscuits	2000
2	Aashirvaad	Staples	1500
3	Classmate	Stationery	800
4	Bingo!	Salty Snacks	700
5	Vivel	Personal Care	500

Biscuits is just one fast-moving consumer goods (FMCG) category in which the cigarette, hotel, paper and packaging giant has garnered scale and share. Within foods, salty snacks and noodles are two categories in which ITC is making rapid gains; and, in personal care, the Kolkata-headquartered marketer is making headway with its shampoos, skin care, and soaps. This combined assault within the consumer space – along with contributions from fragmented categories like stationery – helped ITC's non-cigarette FMCG business clock a top line of Rs 5,545 crore in fiscal year 2012, with foods bringing in 60% of those revenues. More importantly, the company has hit near breakeven levels, according to a recent Credit Suisse report.

"Despite being relatively new in all these segments, we have been witnessing rapid growth and have established significant market standing across most categories," says ITC Ltd executive director Kurush Grant, who heads the FMCG business that includes cigarettes, packaged foods, personal care products and stationery products.

If, in cream biscuits, ITC is taking the fight to Britannia's labels like Bourbon, Treat and Pure Magic with its own battery of brands like Dark Fantasy, Choco Fills and Dual Dream Cream, in noodles it has thrown down the gauntlet at Nestle's Maggi. As per the recent Credit Suisse report, ITC's instant noodles brand Sunfeast Yippee! has gained double-digit market share within two years of launch, and is the second largest brand after Maggi.

Nestle has now started to offer aggressive discounts and incentives to retailers on Maggi to protect its market share. Although a Nestle India spokesperson termed the initiative as a dealer engagement programme, a recent report by Kotak Institutional Equities said Nestle's discount scheme for Maggi is possibly the first in 10-15 years.

Credit Suisse also points out that in salty snacks, ITC had gained a 15% market share in June with Bingo! potato chips, a business that has broken even in five years. PepsiCo is the leader in this business, and its spokesman said the company has strengthened its market position over the past year with the help of 25 new product and variant launches, including Baked Lay's, Aliva Multigrain Waves, Kurkure Puffcorn and Kurkure Monster Paws.

In personal care, the Credit Suisse report says ITC has gained a 6% share in the highly competitive soaps market within four years of launch and 2% in shampoos. Manish Jain, a financial analyst with Nomura Equities Research, says the gain in market share in soaps is impressive, considering the presence of established players like Hindustan Unilever and Godrej Consumer Products. "The shampoo performance has been somewhat underwhelming, although the anti-dandruff segment is growing faster. To correct this, ITC has re-launched various varieties," adds Jain.

Devendra Chawla, president, Food Bazaar category at India's largest retailer Future Group, says the success rate of ITC' FMCG brands is better than the norm in the FMCG industry in which 70% of the launches don't make the cut after the first two years. "ITC has shown the courage to launch multiple products in a year unlike most other FMCG companies that might launch at best 2-3 products annually," says Chawla.

ITC's decision to begin bottom-up in FMCG may have worked in its favour. As Credit Suisse analyst Arnab Mitra says: "Unlike P&G, which starts with premium products and slowly moves down the pyramid, ITC has started at the bottom of the pyramid to build volumes in trade, leveraging its strong distribution, and then focused on premium products backed by very strong advertising support."

ITC recently revamped the entire FMCG portfolio by launching a richer and premium variant at each level. As Mitra points out, ITC has managed to reduce the share of mass market glucose biscuits from over half of biscuit sales five years back to less than a fourth now with premium launches like Sunfeast Dark Fantasy. And, in staples, ITC has consolidated its leadership position aided by the strong performance of Aashivaad Multi Grain atta. In personal care, ITC has launched premium products across its three main brands: Fiama Di Wills, Vivel and Superia. ITC's divisional chief executive (personal care) Sandeep Kaul says the Vivel brand is now used by one-fifth of Indian households.

ITC Brands

The two key drivers for any business are Profits and Growth. To attain this, the company should plan strategically. This strategic plan can be implemented at four levels: corporate, division, business unit and product. Corporate plan guides the whole enterprise on a macro level and then it moves to its divisions and business units. Then the products plan tries to achieve its objectives in the product markets on a micro level.

Summary

- Marketing revolves around value. The value creation done by the company is an ongoing process. The company needs to sustain this process of value creation over a period of time to sustain itself in the market.
- The plan by which value is created on a sustainable basis is the firm's Marketing Strategy. The success of any business depends upon its marketing strategy.
- Marketing Strategy is guided by 5 Cs, which leads the firm to go forward in fulfilling the needs of the customer – Customers, Company, Competitors, Collaborators and Context.

- Successful relationship between customers and marketers depends on the three drivers - Customer Value, Customer Satisfaction and Customer Retention.
- In the changing business scenario, market oriented strategic planning is must for any company. It does not only take into account the company's objectives, capabilities and resources; but it also takes into account the changing market opportunities. The objective of the strategic planning is to ensure that the company hits both the targets of profits as well as growth.
- Strategic intent helps the management team to understand where they want to go and how to arrange their priorities, so as to achieve the organizational goals.
- In case of Intensive Growth Opportunities, Igor Ansoff has suggested a 'Product Market Expansion Grid'. Product market expansion grid includes Market penetration strategy, Market Development Strategy, Product Development Strategy and diversification strategy.

Discussion Questions

1. Define value in marketing? Discuss value delivery process in detail.
2. What do you mean by market oriented strategic planning? Discuss the various strategies under the product market expansion grid.
3. Discuss the 5C's of marketing analysis with an example in Indian context.
4. Discuss the various growth opportunities available to a company with an example in Indian context.
5. Short Notes

   a. Customer Value b. Customer Satisfaction

   c. Customer Retention d. SWOT Analysis

   e. Customer Lifetime Value f. Intensive Growth Opportunities

References

1. Robert J. Dolan, 'Note on Marketing Strategy', Harvard Business School Publishing, 1997
2. Philip Kotler, Marketing Management, 11th Edition, Indian Reprint, 2004
3. Philip Kotler, Marketing Management, 11th Edition, Indian Reprint, 2004
4. Igor Ansoff, Strategies for Diversification, Harvard Business Review, Sept. – Oct. 1957

CHAPTER 3

Marketing Environment

Chapter Structure

Information is Power

Marketing Information System

How do you identify a market opportunity? How best can you serve your target markets? Should you opt for intensive or integrative growth opportunity or should you go for diversification? All these questions can only be answered, if you have the information. As you know,

Information is power.

Today's business is driven by the information. The same applies to marketing also. The company needs to be informed about its customers, competitors and its context. The company needs to be aware about the changing business scenario and changing customer needs. That's why a marketing information system (MIS) should be in place to become effective and efficient in the market.

Marketing information system consists of people, procedures and systems to collect, analyse and distribute the information needed to marketing decision makers.

Big Bazaar

Marketing information system is based on internal company records like Sales information system, order to payment cycle, databases, marketing intelligence activities, marketing research and marketing decision support system. In the case of internal company records, order to payment cycle is very important. Big Bazaar has got more than 160,000 products on their shelf. With the usages of internet, intranet and extranet, companies like Big Bazaar and others are managing their sales cycles, their suppliers and their customers efficiently.

Internal Records

Internal records provide an input to the marketer for their marketing decision making. Right from order to payment cycle to the sales data to prices to costs to inventory levels to receivables and payables, all these information play a key role in decision making process.

a. **Order to Payment Cycle**: Order to payment cycle is the heart of the internal record system. Distributors, dealers, retailers send the orders to the company. On the basis of these orders, production and inventory calculations are made to produce and supply at the desired level. In the era of internet, intranet and extranet; the process has become much faster, accurate and efficient.

b. **Sales Information System:** Similarly, timely and accurate reporting on current sales is helping the companies to be at the right time, with the right product and with the right quantity. All the dealerships of Maruti Suzuki are connected through extranet and minute by minute information is updated, so that you get your white Swift or red A-Star or your blue Wagon-R in time.

c. **Databases, Data Warehousing and Data Mining:** In this information age, when there are a lot of databases like customer database, product database, sales persons database etc.; it is important that databases are managed and warehoused properly. Once databases are stored, it can be mined on the basis of marketing information required.

ICICI Bank

In India, ICICI Bank is using the techniques of data mining to acquire new customers. These customers may be totally new to ICICI or in most of the cases; ICICI Bank taps their customer base and offers them various other services. For example: If you are having an ICICI Bank Account, you have special privilege offers from the bank for new services like Home Loans, Car Loans, Credit Cards, Personal Loans and others. ICICI Bank has also got Loan on Phone Scheme and Pre Approved Offers into each of their services; so that the relationship with the customer can not only be maintained, but can also be expanded with new service offerings. Ultimately in the long run, the business of ICICI Bank will grow manifold by using the data mining techniques.[1]

d. **Marketing Intelligence System:** In the era of cut throat competition and information overload, the company needs to put in place an effective and efficient marketing intelligent system. It helps the company in understanding today's and tomorrow's customer needs better.

> **'A marketing intelligence system is a set of procedures and sources, managers use to obtain everyday information about developments in the marketing environments. Marketing Managers collect marketing intelligence by reading books, newspapers and trade publications; talking to customers, suppliers and distributors; monitoring social media on the internet via online discussion groups; e-mailing lists and blogs; and meeting with other company managers.'**
> **– Philip Kotler**

The success of marketing intelligence system lies on the following:

i. **Distributor, Dealers, Retailers**: Distributors, dealers and retailers are the backbone of the marketing information system. They can provide data on day to day happening of the market, as they are aware about the company as well as the competitors. Most of the times, retailers keep multiple products at their shop. These retailers can give the information needed by the marketing intelligence system.

Many companies are also hiring mystery shoppers to gauge the customer experience and service quality, all across the world. But who is a mystery shopper?

> **A Mystery Shopper is like an undercover agent. Your job is to evaluate a business – either through onsite visits or telephone calls – as if you were an actual shopper or potential customer looking for a particular service. You need to evaluate and provide feedback about the greeting and attitude of store employees and the location's appearance.**

Bare International

Bare International is one of the companies, who are helping the companies to understand the market better in India and 100 other countries in the world. Companies like Bare International assign shopping research assignment to its affiliated shoppers. Each mystery shopping research assignment is different because each of their clients are different, right from restaurants to gyms to department stores to multiplexes to telecom services provider to car dealerships to something else. Mystery Shoppers learn specific information about individual businesses prior to each assignment, so that evaluations are performed correctly. So, if you want to enjoy movie at a multiplex free of cost or you want to go shopping without paying anything, then you can also become a mystery shopper by joining an organisation like Bare International (www.bareinternational.com).

ii. **Sales force**: Sales force is the link between the company and the distributors, dealers and retailers. The effectiveness of these distributors, dealers and retailers in providing information, is also dependent on the company's sales force. As the sales force is the first hand contact in the company, it can be very useful in providing the correct information.

iii. **An Eye on Competition**: In today's era of cut throat competition, a company needs to be careful all the time as the competition can take the fizz away from you. That's why

'Successful companies design and operate systems for gathering continuous intelligence about competitors.'[2]

A company needs to network itself not only with the distributors, dealers, retailers and sales force. But it should also look out for information through social networking sites and industry specific websites. It can also gather information through road shows and trade fairs.

iv. **Customer Advisory Panel**: Customer advisory panel can do wonders for the company. In top B-schools, there is an advisory panel to provide valuable insight into the course curriculum. In Indian Railways also, there is a system of customer advisory panel. In almost all the retail operation, a process of customer feedback is maintained for better insight into the business.

v. **Governmental Data**: Governmental data forms the basis of marketing calculations including market forecast. The census of India provides the biggest source, besides the National Sample Survey Organisation (NSSO) data, Economic Surveys, Industry specific surveys and others.

vi. **Private Data Sources**: Market research firms provide a lot of data to the companies. In India, ORG-MARG, A C Nielsen, IMRB, TAM Media Research etc provide syndicated research data.

Mouthshut.com

vii. **Online Customer Feedback System**: Online customer review forums like mouthshut.com and industry specific sites like motoroids.com, team-bhp.com, autocarindia.com, Vicky.in, zigwheels.com etc. for automobile industry, techtree.com, tech2.com, technoholik.com, thinkdigit.com etc. for technology can provide a lot of input for marketing. Blogs are also turning out to be a major source of customer feedback now.

A company needs to be proactive in using these resources. The management needs to be involved in getting the market updates. These updates can shape the marketing strategy and its implementation in a better way.

Marketing Environment

A company needs to understand its marketing environment to successfully operate in the market. As we have seen earlier that marketing strategy is guided by 5 Cs, which leads the firm to go forward in fulfilling the needs of the customer. These five C's are – Customers, Company, Competitors, Collaborators and Context. It's better to be aware about yourself and your competitors. But it is also important to know your context. Context whether it is cultural, technological, regulatory and legal factors can play a greater part in influencing your business decisions, your strategic marketing decisions. It's also important, because it is ever changing.

The basis of the context is the macro environment. Macro environment presents an uncontrolled environment for the company. In this environment, the company needs to operate and make profits. Everybody right from the company to the customers to the competitors operate in this environment. You, as a company need to be smart enough to create and benefit from the opportunities for your own good self. For example in India, if you manufacture a car which is lesser than four meters in length and have engines not exceeding 1200 cc for petrol and 1500 cc for diesel; you get excise benefits. You need to pay only 10% excise duty instead of 22%. Now all the sedans are above four meters and so these cars don't get the excise benefits. Taking the legal environment to the market scenario, Tata Motors launched a new version of its Tata Indigo called Tata Indigo CS (Compact Sedan). This model is the cheapest sedan in the world with a price tag of less than Rupees four lacs for petrol variant. This has been possible just due to the excise benefits of around Rs. 30,000 – Rs. 40,000/- ; which has been passed on to the customers. Now Tata motors has launched an upgraded version of Indigo CS called Indigo eCS.

Ford Ecosport

Taking a cue from Tata Motors, Maruti Suzuki has launched a sub 4 meter Dzire to avail the excise benefits and has also cut the price to make it more competitive in the market. Honda has also followed the same strategy and launched a car Amaze, based on its hatchback Brio. Now even Ford has come out with the compact SUV to get the excise benefits.

Macro environment include the following:

1. Demographic Environment,
2. Economic Environment,
3. Socio Cultural Environment,
4. Green Environment,
5. Technological Environment and
6. Legal and Political Environment

Demographic Environment

Demographic environment gives an overview of the opportunities available for a company. Marketers are interested in population, because it serves their customer base. They are also interested in knowing the size and growth rate of population, age, sex, education, income, occupation, marital status, family size, family life cycle, religion, nationality and social class of population. It helps the marketer to segment and target the market.

In India, the Indian Census provides the most credible source of information on Demography (Population characteristics), Economic Activity, Literacy and Education, Housing & Household Amenities, Urbanisation, Fertility and Mortality, Scheduled Castes and Scheduled Tribes, Language, Religion, Migration, Disability and many other socio-cultural and demographic data since 1872. The 15th National Census of the country was done in 2011. This is the only source of primary data in the village, town and ward level, it provides valuable information for planning and formulation policies for Central and the State Governments and is widely used by National and International Agencies, Scholars, business people, industrialists, and many more.

Demographic environment provides a broader picture of the market with population, population age mix and literacy data.

a. **Population:** Currently the world population is estimated to be 6.91 billion by the United States Census Bureau. Asia accounts for over 60% of the world population with more than 4 billion people. China and India together have about 37 percent of the world's population. Africa follows with 1 billion people, 15% of the world's population. Europe's 733 million people make up 11% of the world's population. Latin America and the Caribbean region to 589 million (9%), North America is home to 352 million (5%) and Oceania/Australasia to 35 million (less than 1%).[3]

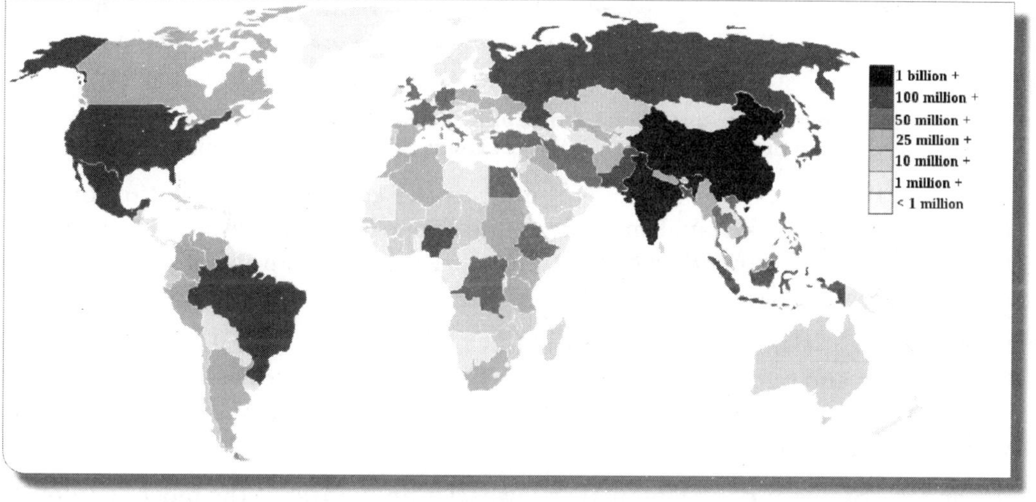

(Source: Wikipedia - http://en.wikipedia.org/wiki/Image:World_population.PNG)

Currently India accounts for 17.3% of the world population, estimated at 1.21 billion. India is the second most populous country in the world after China and followed by USA. By 2050, it is estimated that India will be the most populous country in the world.

Census of India 2011

India's population has jumped to 1.21 billion, an increase of more than 181 million during 2001-11, based on the provisional data of Census 2011.[4]

POPULATION [1]	Persons	1,21,01,93,422	
	Males	62,37,24,248	
	Females	58,64,69,174	
DECADAL POPULATION GROWTH 2001-2011		Absolute	Percentage
	Persons	18,14,55,986	17.64
	Males	9,15,01,158	17.19
	Females	8,99,54,828	18.12
DENSITY OF POPULATION [2] (per sq. km.)		382	
SEX RATIO (females per 1000 males)		940	
POPULATION IN THE AGE GROUP 0-6 [1]		Absolute	Percentage to total population
	Persons	15,87,89,287	13.12
	Males	8,29,52,135	13.30
	Females	7,58,37,152	12.93
LITERATES [1]		Absolute	Literacy rate
	Persons	77,84,54,120	74.04
	Males	44,42,03,762	82.14
	Females	33,42,50,358	65.46

General Notes

1. The figures for India and Manipur, include by sex, the estimated population, 0-6 population and literates of Paomata, Mao Maram and Purul sub-divisions of senapati district of Manipur for Census 2001 and 2011.
2. For working out density of India and the State of Jammu & Kashmir, the entire area and population of those portions of Jammu & Kashmir which are under illegal occupation of Pakistan and China have not been taken into account.

(Source: Census of India, Office of Registrar General and Census Commissioner, India, Ministry of Home Affairs, Govt. of India)

Although the population is almost equal to the combined population of the U.S., Indonesia, Brazil, Pakistan, Bangladesh and Japan (1,214.3 million), the silver lining is that after 1911-21 the past decade (2001-11) witnessed the addition of smaller population than the previous decade's growth.

Of the total provisional population of 1,210.2 million, the number of males stood at 623.7 million and females at 586.5 million. The percentage growth in 2001-11 was 17.64 — males 17.19 and females 18.12. India's population accounts for 17.5 per cent of the world's population.

Among the States and the Union Territories, Uttar Pradesh is the most populous State with 199 million people, followed by Maharashtra with 112 million people. Lakshadweep is the least populated at 64,429 people.

The percentage decadal growth rates of the six most populous States have declined during 2001-11 compared with 1991-2001. The population growth in Uttar Pradesh has declined from 25.85 per cent to 20.09 per cent, in Maharashtra from 22.73 per cent to 15.99 per cent, Bihar from 28.62 per cent to 25.07 per cent, West Bengal from 17.77 per cent to 13.93 per cent, Andhra Pradesh from 14.59 per cent to 11.10 per cent and Madhya Pradesh from 24.26 per cent to 20.30 per cent.

The overall sex ratio nationwide has increased by seven percentage points to 940 against 933 in Census 2001. Sex ratio is defined as the number of females per 1,000 males. An increase in sex ratio was observed in 29 States/Union Territories. Kerala with 1,084 has the highest sex ratio followed by Puducherry with 1,038. With 618, Daman and Diu has the lowest ratio.

This is the highest sex ratio at the national level since Census 1971 and a shade lower than 1961. Three major States - Jammu and Kashmir, Bihar and Gujarat - have shown a decline in sex ratio as compared to Census 2001. India's skewed sex ratio due to female foeticide and selective sex determination has been a cause for concern.

However, the area of grave concern remained the lowest ever child sex ratio of 914. The provisional data showed that the child sex ratio [0 to 6 years] came down to 914 females per 1,000 males against 927 in Census 2001. It showed a continuing preference for male children in the last decade.

An increasing trend in the child sex ratio was seen in Punjab, Haryana, Himachal Pradesh, Gujarat, Tamil Nadu, Mizoram and the Andaman and Nicobar Islands, but in the remaining States/UTs, the ratio showed a decline. While the overall sex ratio has improved since 1991, the decline in child sex ratio has been unabated since the 1961Census. The total number of children in the age group of 0-6 is now 158.8 million, less by five million since 2001.

The literacy rate has gone up from 64.83 per cent in 2001 to 74.04 per cent, an increase of 9.21 percentage points.[5]

Table 1: Distribution of population, sex ratio, density and decadal growth rate of population : 2011

State/ UT Code	India/State/Union Territory #	Total population			Sex ratio (females per 1000 males)	Density (Per sq. km)	Decadal growth rate
		Persons	Males	Females			
1	2	3	4	5	6	7	8
	INDIA	**1,210,193,422**	**623,724,248**	**586,469,174**	**940**	**382**	**17.64**
01	Jammu & Kashmir	12,548,926	6,665,561	5,883,365	883	124	23.71
02	Himachal Pradesh	6,856,509	3,473,892	3,382,617	974	123	12.81
03	Punjab	27,704,236	14,634,819	13,069,417	893	550	13.73
04	Chandigarh #	1,054,686	580,282	474,404	818	9,252	17.10
05	Uttarakhand	10,116,752	5,154,178	4,962,574	963	189	19.17
06	Haryana	25,353,081	13,505,130	11,847,951	877	573	19.90
07	NCT of Delhi #	16,753,235	8,976,410	7,776,825	866	11,297	20.96
08	Rajasthan	68,621,012	35,620,086	33,000,926	926	201	21.44
09	Uttar Pradesh	199,581,477	104,596,415	94,985,062	908	828	20.09
10	Bihar	103,804,637	54,185,347	49,619,290	916	1,102	25.07
11	Sikkim	607,688	321,661	286,027	889	86	12.36
12	Arunachal Pradesh	1,382,611	720,232	662,379	920	17	25.92

State/ UT Code	India/State/Union Territory #	Total population			Sex ratio (females per 1000 males)	Density (Per sq. km)	Decadal growth rate
		Persons	Males	Females			
1	2	3	4	5	6	7	8
13	Nagaland	1,980,602	1,025,707	954,895	931	119	-0.47
14	Manipur	2,721,756	1,369,764	1,351,992	987	122	18.65
15	Mizoram	1,091,014	552,339	538,675	975	52	22.78
16	Tripura	3,671,032	1,871,867	1,799,165	961	350	14.75
17	Meghalaya	2,964,007	1,492,668	1,471,339	986	132	27.82
18	Assam	31,169,272	15,954,927	15,214,345	954	397	16.93
19	West Bengal	91,347,736	46,927,389	44,420,347	947	1,029	13.93
20	Jharkhand	32,966,238	16,931,688	16,034,550	947	414	22.34
21	Orissa	41,947,358	21,201,678	20,745,680	978	269	13.97
22	Chhattisgarh	25,540,196	12,827,915	12,712,281	991	189	22.59
23	Madhya Pradesh	72,597,565	37,612,920	34,984,645	930	236	20.30
24	Gujarat	60,383,628	31,482,282	28,901,346	918	308	19.17
25	Daman & Diu#	242,911	150,100	92,811	618	2,169	53.54
26	Dadra & Nagar Haveli#	342,853	193,178	149,675	775	698	55.50
27	Maharashtra	112,372,972	58,361,397	54,011,575	925	365	15.99
28	Andhra Pradesh	84,665,533	42,509,881	42,155,652	992	308	11.10
29	Karnataka	61,130,704	31,057,742	30,072,962	968	319	15.67
30	Goa	1,457,723	740,711	717,012	968	394	8.17
31	Lakshadweep#	64,429	33,106	31,323	946	2,013	6.23
32	Kerala	33,387,677	16,021,290	17,366,387	1,084	859	4.86
33	Tamil Nadu	72,138,958	36,158,871	35,980,087	995	555	15.60
34	Puducherry#	1,244,464	610,485	633,979	1,038	2,598	27.72
35	Andaman & Nicobar Islands#	379,944	202,330	177,614	878	46	6.68

(Source : Census of India, Office of Registrar General and Census Commissioner, India, Ministry of Home Affairs, Govt. of India)

State/ UT Code	India/State/Union Territory #	Literacy rate (%)		
		Persons	Males	Females
1	2	12	13	14
	INDIA	**74.04**	**82.14**	**65.46**
01	Jammu & Kashmir	68.74	78.26	58.01
02	Himachal Pradesh	83.78	90.83	76.60

State/ UT Code	India/State/Union Territory #	Literacy rate (%)		
		Persons	Males	Females
1	2	12	13	14
03	Punjab	76.68	81.48	71.34
04	Chandigarh #	86.43	90.54	81.38
05	Uttarakhand	79.63	88.33	70.70
06	Haryana	76.64	85.38	66.77
07	NCT of Delhi #	86.34	91.03	80.93
08	Rajasthan	67.06	80.51	52.66
09	Uttar Pradesh	69.72	79.24	59.26
10	Bihar	63.82	73.39	53.33
11	Sikkim	82.20	87.29	76.43
12	Arunachal Pradesh	66.95	73.69	59.57
13	Nagaland	80.11	83.29	76.69
14	Manipur	79.85	86.49	73.17
15	Mizoram	91.58	93.72	89.40
16	Tripura	87.75	92.18	83.15
17	Meghalaya	75.48	77.17	73.78
18	Assam	73.18	78.81	67.27
19	West Bengal	77.08	82.67	71.16
20	Jharkhand	67.63	78.45	56.21
21	Orissa	73.45	82.40	64.36
22	Chhattisgarh	71.04	81.45	60.59
23	Madhya Pradesh	70.63	80.53	60.02
24	Gujarat	79.31	87.23	70.73
25	Daman & Diu #	87.07	91.48	79.59
26	Dadra & Nagar Haveli #	77.65	86.46	65.93
27	Maharashtra	82.91	89.82	75.48
28	Andhra Pradesh	67.66	75.56	59.74
29	Karnataka	75.60	82.85	68.13
30	Goa	87.40	92.81	81.84
31	Lakshadweep #	92.28	96.11	88.25
32	Kerala	93.91	96.02	91.98
33	Tamil Nadu	80.33	86.81	73.86
34	Puducherry #	86.55	92.12	81.22
35	Andaman & Nicobar Islands #	86.27	90.11	81.84

The Goldman Sachs BRIC countries i.e. Brazil, Russia, India and China, has projected that *India* would become the *third largest* economy by 2050. That's why all the large multinational corporations (MNCs) are lining up in India to do business.

b. **Populaion Age Mix**: Besides the size and growth rate, population age mix is also very important. Population age mix helps to understand the demand size of various products and services. For example –India's young population require mobiles, laptops, electronic gadgets, home appliances, mutual funds, homes, milk, diapers, toys etc; whereas Japan's older population require more of healthcare, insurance and other products and services.

c. **Literacy:** As per the provisional data of 2011 census, the literacy rate in India is 74.04%. Males literacy rate stands for 82.14%, while only 65.46% females are literate. Higher level of literacy leads to demand for education and related products like newspapers, magazines, books etc. Now Internet literacy is also important for a marketer

Economic Environment

Economic environment of any economy defines the market for products and services. The size of an economy is defined in terms of gross domestic product (GDP). Indian economy is eleventh largest in the world by nominal GDP and fourth largest on the basis of purchasing power parity (PPP). Since 1991, with liberalization and globalisation, Indian economy has been growing at a higher pace. This size of the economy presents huge opportunities for companies.

Besides GDP, income distribution is another important factor for a marketer. Currently the income distribution in India is as follows:

	2007 Household Income	2009 Household Income
< 75 K	13.6 %	11.0 %
75 – 150 K	21.6 %	19.1 %
150 – 300 K	28.9 %	27.9 %
300 – 500 K	12.6 %	15.9 %
500 – 1000 K	11.2 %	11.4 %
> 1000 K	12.0 %	14.7 %

Household incomes have reached the level of Rs 3.61 million crores in 2009. There is dramatic different shifts in the higher and the lower income categories. Whereas the proportion of households earning less than Rs 75,000 pa has reduced by 2.6% and the proportion earning between Rs 75,000 and Rs 150,000 pa has reduced by 2.5%, the proportion earning over Rs 10 lac pa has increased by 2.7% and the proportion earning between Rs 3 lac pa has increased by 3%. The three higher income categories have all seen an increase in proportion while all the three lower income categories have seen a decrease in proportion. This clearly indicates the propensity of consumption to shift from basic goods to higher value goods and services, which is clearly borne out by the consumption figures.

The consumption shift means a lot for the marketer, as it can guide the current and future path of the company. The major changes in the consumption pattern are:

1. People are spending proportionately less on food items. Fast Moving Consumer Goods (FMCG) demand is expected to increase.
2. We are spending more on transportation, which is a combination of running our own vehicles as well as making use of transport services. This calls for more demand for automobile industry on the whole.
3. We are spending more on health and well-being. The cost of medical care has gone up. Increase in life expectancy also means people live longer with greater need for medical care. More demand for health care also means more opportunities for private health sector.
4. We are spending more on communications. Telecom companies are expected to grow.

All the above factors mean a lot to the marketer; as it entails rise in the consumption of FMCG products, rise in the demand for automobile, demand for healthcare and demand for mobile services and mobile handsets. The increase in consumption means increased opportunities for a marketer.

Besides the GDP and per capita income, the economic environment concerning inflation, interest rate and stage of the business cycle also means a lot to the marketer. Currently India is facing a high inflation rate situation, which has also led to the rise of interest rate in the economy. The situation of high inflation rate combined with high interest rate is slowing down the Indian economy. It is not only affecting the core areas, but also has a great impact on the other sectors. Right from the Housing to the Automobile to Cement to Sanitary ware to Steel to Clothing, it is affecting the whole economy.

The stage of the business cycle also means a lot to the marketer. It either helps the companies to grow or it makes them shrink. Recently USA was gripped with recession between end of 2007 to June, 2009. It not only eroded the demand in US, but it also led to hundred thousands of employees losing their jobs. The recession also spread into European countries and affected the demand as well as livelihood of many people. These recessionary trends also had a great impact on Indian as well as other Asian economies, with the international business linkages.

Socio-Cultural Environment

Language, culture, norms, religious beliefs, values etc. form the socio cultural environment. The socio cultural environment plays a major role in defining the needs and wants of the consumers, as their lifestyle patterns and consumption behavior depends upon these factors. In India, these factors become too prominent than the other developed economies like USA and UK, as India is a land of cultural diversity and regional differences. With more than 33 major languages and six major religions, India presents a dramatic picture to the marketer with a wide diversity in the consumption habits and needs and wants of the consumers. For example, the preferred drink in northern part of India is tea, while it is lassi (sweet curd) in Punjab and coffee in southern states. The breakfast habits are also very different, right from rajma-chawal and curry–rice in the Delhi, Punjab and adjoining states to Puri, Bhaji, Jalebi in norther states to Idli, Dosa in southern states. Fesivals are also very different in different regions. If Ganesh Puja is the major festival in Maharashtra, the same place is occupied by Durga Puja in West Bengal, Orissa, Jharkhand and Northern States. While Holi and Chhath takes the centrestage in Bihar; Onam in Kerala, Pongal in Tamilnadu and Ugadi in Karnataka and Andhra Pradesh is celebrated widely. Diwali has the distinction of only festival, which is celebrated all across India.

On the language front also, official language Hindi is widely spoken in India, while English is recognized as an additional language for office work. There are 22 scheduled languages under eighth schedule of Indian Constitution including Assamese, Bengali, Bodo, Dogri, Gujrati, Kannada, Kashmiri, Konkani, Maithili, Malayalam, Manipuri, Marathi, Nepali, Oriya, Punjabi, Sanskrit, Santhali, Sindhi, Tamil, Telugu and Urdu. Besides these official languages, several other languages and dialects are also spoken and used widely like Bhojpuri in northern parts of India.

Multiplicity and diversity in the socio cultural environment creates a lot of complexities for the marketer. That's why an advertisement for a product or service may not need only to be dubbed for different regions or states, but it may also require different celebrity endorser to

Parle Monaco

do the same. On the similar lines, Bhojpuri star Ravi Kishan has been signed for promoting Parle Monaco in the Hindi belts of Uttar Pradesh and Bihar, while Bengali actress Rituparna Sengupta will do the same in Eastern part of India. Again in 2010, Dabur signed Ravi Kishan to endorse its Chyawanprash brand exclusively for localised below-the-line activities such as interactions with consumers, dealers and stockists in UP and Bihar. Telecom services provider Bharti Airtel released ads for rural audiences featuring Rajpal Yadav, a popular star in the North, with the tagline - 'Airtel bajega toh tarraki bolegi'. Similarly, despite Coca Cola

Thums Ad featuring Salman Khan

Thums Ad featuring Mahesh Babu

having national star Salman Khan as brand ambassador for its Thums Up brand, it uses Telugu actor Mahesh Babu for endorsing the same brand in the South.

Regional diversity does not only require a marketer to plan their promotional exercises, but it also requires making necessary changes in the product and service offerings on a global scale. McDonalds, the world's largest chain of burgers, operate in 119 countries. Based on the local taste and preferences, it modifies its product line. In India, it sells Aloo Tikki more, while it does not serve any beef products as in USA, due to religious sentiments here. In some countries, it offers rice burgers as well as shrimp burgers.

Green Environment

With growing environmental concerns, the word 'Green' has received a lot of attention in the recent times. For a marketer, it has become very important to be in synch with the natural environment, as it provides a lot of opportunities and also creates challenges to adapt to the changing business environment. The importance can also be understood with the modifications in AMA's definition of marketing with the addition of three words 'Society at large'. Earlier marketing was only meant for benefitting the organisation and its stakeholders. Now it also means that the product and services should benefit the society on the whole. It is for that reason only that a company like Pepsi India has only one out of four major links to talk about its products, that too by saying 'Nourishing and Delighting India'. The other three links deals with 'Innovation to Transform Lives', 'Tomorrow Better than Today: Environment' and 'Empowering Growth with Fun at Work'. Here the environmental concerns are shown more than the junk nature of their aerated drinks and food products. Now, societal welfare is as important as the company's welfare.

For a marketer, going green has become the new success mantra in marketing to differentiate the products and services from their competition. It has also become a platform for innovation. Now, more and more organisations are trying to follow the green path either directly or indirectly. Whether it is the case of Panasonic with the 'Eco-Ideas' implemented in their production facilities or the case of ICICI Bank with the 'E-statements' saving hundreds of trees every month; marketers all across the world are trying to relate their products and services to the 'Green' to be more marketing savvy and innovative.[6]

Nissan Leaf

Green also means new opportunities for a company like Toyota with Toyota Prius, the hybrid car or Nissan with Nissan Leaf. There might be changes in the packaging as well as in the advertising.

Technological Environment

'Change is the only constant' – This proverb applies beautifully to the technological environment. While technological developments have done good to the society in the area of healthcare, communications etc, it has also done bad with the development of weapons of mass destruction like nuclear bombs, missiles, machine guns etc.

The technological environment has a great impact on the markets and businesses. Many times, it creates a business opportunity or it ruins a business. Mobile technology created business for companies like Airtel, Vodafone, Idea etc, but it also ruined the business for Pagelink, Mobilink and other players in the paging services. Similarly, the business of

BSNL and MTNL got divided and shrunk also with other players in the market. In the MP3 player category, it created an opportunity and Apple took the lead through its iPods. But it also ruined the business for Sony Discman and Walkman. Sony is still struggling to make a mark in that space.

You not only need to be careful about the competitors only, you also need to be careful about changing business space. Canon, Nokia, Pentax etc are competing against one another for the market share in the camera market, whereas a non camera company Nokia is selling the largest number of cameras in the world today through its mobile phones. Now you need to be in the printer business like HP to be successful in photo printing space. Again technology is also paving the way for mass customization as it is made possible by Dell for its Laptops and Desktops and Asian Paints for its more than thousand of shades of paints.

Now a company cannot sit on its past laurels to be successful in market. It needs to be proactive in understanding the changing needs of the consumers and moves by its competitors. It needs to innovate.

Legal and Political Environment

Legal and political environment also influences a marketer. Through various legislations, a government tries to moderate and regulate the role of the business in the society. With a stable political system in a country, businesses benefit a lot as there is coherence in the legal and business policies. It is all due to the excise policy of Govt. of India that India is becoming global hub for the small car market. Various laws like Monopolies Restrictive Trade Practices (MRTP), Foreign Exchange Management Act (FEMA), Value Added Tax (VAT) etc are governing the businesses in India. Soon, Goods and Services Tax (GST) will have a significant impact on almost all aspects of businesses operating in the country, including the supply chain, sourcing and distribution decisions, inventory costs and cash flows, pricing policy, accounting and IT systems and transactions management.

Jago Grahak Jago

On the consumer side, Consumer Protection Act (COPRA) protects the interests of consumers. The provisions of the Act came into force with effect from 15th April, 1987. Consumer Protection Act imposes strict liability on a manufacturer, in case of supply of defective goods by him, and a service provider, in case of deficiency in rendering of its services. The term "defect" and "deficiency", as held in a catena of cases, are to be couched in the widest horizon of there being any kind of fault, imperfection or shortcoming. Furthermore, the standard, which is required to be maintained, in services or goods is not restricted to the statutory mandate. But it is applicable to that claimed by the trader, expressly or impliedly, in any manner whatsoever.[7] The Ministry of Consumer Affairs, Food and Public Distribution also runs an awareness campaign called 'Jago Grahak Jago'.

Environmental Scanning

LG Curved 3D OLED TV

Environmental scanning is of utmost importance for a marketer as it does not only create opportunities, but it also creates challenges to the company. It helps the marketer in taking the right decisions for present as well as future. HP saw the opportunity coming in the form for digital printing; that too in the home; leaving the film processing and development shops in red. Tata saw it through Tata Nano; while Apple is keeping the market on its toe with their innovative offerings like iPods, iPhones and iPads. Now Samsung has launched Galaxy Round with a curved display, while LG has launched World's first curved OLED TV with 4.3 mm slim screen. Again, taking a leaf from the success of Toyota Prius, Nissan has launched Leaf, its electric car. Constant scanning of the marketing environment is going to be the key of success. Being aware and being innovative is the only formula, which can make a company survive and grow in the market.

Marketing Insight 3.1

Cadbury Steps Up the Game as Sales Slip

Brand owner Mondelez is investing heavily in sales and route-to-market expansion in India

Cadbury brand owner Mondelez International is investing heavily in sales and route-to-market expansion in India, a priority market for the American food giant where sales have slumped to their lowest since 2005. "We increased our sales infrastructure with one lakh visicoolers in the market and the company took big strides by expanding into rural India and reaching seven states in 2013," a spokeswoman for Cadbury India said.

According to data provided by Mondelez, its India business grew in the "low-teens" in 2013. It was 21% in 2012 and over 30% in the preceding years. Cadbury India attributed it to economic slowdown, increase in commodity prices and the depreciation in the rupee. Although India is one of the fastest growing markets for chocolates, domestic sales of the commodity have fallen with consumers spending less due to the economic slowdown. In 2013, growth in overall food segment slowed to 11.6%, from over 17% in the previous year, data showed.

At the annual performance presentation last week, Mondelez's chief financial officer, David Brearton, said, "While economic conditions are likely to remain difficult, especially in emerging markets, we intend to leverage market share gains to offset potential volatility." Despite the cloudy outlook, Mondelez's. 4,000-crore plus Indian unit last year announced plans to invest $190 million to build the country's largest chocolate manufacturing plant near Hyderabad. "Given our advantaged portfolio and footprint, strong fundamentals and ongoing investments, we're confident that we're well positioned to take on the opportunity, as this market turns around," said the spokeswoman for Cadbury India, which is in the process of transitioning its legal name to Mondelez India Foods.

Cadbury Shots

In the Rs. 6,000-crore domestic chocolate segment, Cadbury has over 67% marketshare, followed by Nestle at 21% and Ferrero at 6%. Increasing market share, however, may not be easy for Cadbury, which has been pushing its pricier brand 'Silk' and lowestpriced 'Cadbury Shots'. Rival Nestle, which grew 7% in 2013, too is focusing on its new brand, Alpino, and Munch. In the health beverage section, Cadbury's Bournvita faces competition from Heinz India's Complan.

Summary

- Marketing information system consists of people, procedures and systems to collect, analyse and distribute the information needed to marketing decision makers. It is based on internal company records like Sales information system, order to payment cycle, databases, marketing intelligence activities, marketing research and marketing decision support system.
- A marketing intelligence system is a set of procedures and sources, managers use to obtain everyday information about developments in the marketing environments. It works on the feedback provided by distributors, dealers, retailers, its sales force and its advisory panel. It also relies on governmental and non governmental data and online feedback system.
- A company needs to understand its marketing environment i.e. macro environment to successfully operate in the market. It presents an uncontrolled environment for the company. Macro environment include the following: demographic environment, economic environment, socio cultural environment, green environment, technological environment and political legal environment.

- Environmental scanning is of utmost importance for a marketer as it does not only create opportunities, but it also creates challenges to the company. It helps the marketer in taking the right decisions for present as well as future.

Discussion Questions

1. Define Marketing Information System? How does it help the marketer?
2. What do you mean by marketing environment? Discuss its major components.
3. Define Marketing Intelligence System? Discuss its components.
4. Short Notes:
    a. Mystery Shopping
    b. Demographic Environment
    c. Economic Environment
    d. Technological Environment
    e. Environmental Scanning
    f. Order to Payment Cycle
    g. Data Warehousing and Data Mining

References

1. Vijay Prakash Anand and Praveen Kumar, 'Data mining as a tool for building and managing better Customer relationships', 2008
2. Leonard M. Fuld, 'The New Competitor Intelligence: The complete resource for finding, analysing and using information about your competitors', John Wiley, 1995
3. "World Population Prospects: The 2008 Revision Population Database". Esa.un.org. 2009-03-11. Retrieved 2010-12-29
4. Census of India, Office of Registrar General and Census Commissioner, India, Ministry of Home Affairs, Govt. of India
5. Vinay Kumar, Census 2011 puts India's population at 1.21 billion, The Hindu, 1st April, 2011
6. Vijay Prakash Anand, 'Go Green : The New Success Mantra in Marketing', 2011
7. Consumer Protection Act (COPRA), India

Self Assessment Questions

   a. [illegible] Environment   b. Demographic Environment

4. Census of India, Government of India, [illegible]

6. Vijay Prakash Anand, [illegible]

CHAPTER 4

Marketing Research

Chapter Structure

"Some people use research like a drunkard uses a lamppost: for support, not illumination."

-David Ogilvy

Marketing Research

The success of the marketing strategy depends a lot on the marketing research. It deals with specific issues relating to marketing product and services.

According to American Marketing Association,

'Marketing Research is the function that links the consumer, customer, and public to the marketer through information used to identify and define marketing opportunities and problems; generate, refine, and evaluate marketing actions; monitor marketing performance; and improve understanding of marketing as a process.

Marketing research specifies the information required to address these issues, designs the method for collecting information, manages and implements the data collection process, analyzes the results, and communicates the findings and their implications.'

The term marketing research is commonly interchanged with market research.

Market research is concerned specifically with markets, while marketing research is concerned specifically about marketing processes.[1]

Whether you are developing a new product like Tata Nano or Maruti Suzuki Swift or developing an idea to be propagated or launching a new service; you need to understand the market and its customers. Most of the time companies are engaged in meeting the existing demand of a product. These companies try to fulfill the same need in a better, cheaper and user friendly way.

But Business is not only about marketing. It's also about innovation. Many companies who are pioneer in innovation are also the companies which are respected a lot; are also the companies who are leaders in their respective business segment. Intel, Microsoft, Sony, Apple, Mahindra, Tata, PVR, Maruti Suzuki etc are the companies; which try to sense the customers and deliver whatever they want. The foundation of these innovations and their marketing successes is none other than marketing research.

Marketing Research in Real Life

Case 1: Condom Bindaas Bol

The government of India launched a campaign for increasing public awareness to expand the usage of Condoms. But it failed. Because the campaign was based on a false assumption that people are not aware about condoms and once they will be informed, the usage will increase. But it never happened. Based on a marketing research, it was found out that people were too shy to ask for condoms in a shop.

Condom Bindaas Bol

Then, in September 2006, a new campaign "Condom Bindaas Bol" was launched to decrease the embarrassment associated with purchasing condoms. With a series of humorous television advertisements, the campaign developed by Lowe India became very successful. The campaign encouraged people to talk openly about condoms and to use the word freely at the point of purchase. It was possible only due to marketing research.

Case 2: Titan Raga

Like many other companies, Titan, the topmost brand in watch category in India, used marketing research to its advantage. Till 1991, there was a women's watch segment. But it was poorly catered segment, as in the market all the companies including Titan sold downsized versions of male watches to women. Then on the basis of an in depth marketing research, Titan understood the needs of women and launched a collection of watches exclusively designed and crafted for women called Titan Raga.

Titan Raga

The product became hugely successful. Now Titan has Zoop – exclusively for Kids, Nebula, Octane, Orion and Edge catering to different market segments besides Raga Diva and Raga Flora.

Case 3: Honda Amaze

In the compact sedan segment, Honda launched Amaze in 2013 on the basis of a marketing research and customer feedback. The research and feedback from the customers showed that a large no of customers wanted a diesel car with good fuel efficiency, with a combination of space inside the car. Honda not only met both the requirements, but exceeded the customer expectation by launching the car with its Earth Dreams technology, which gave not only the class leading mileage of 25.8 Kms to a litre, but was also class leading as far as power was concerned by delivering 100 bhp.

Honda Amaze

For developing Amaze, Honda India's Senior Vice President and Director Shigeru Yamazaki along with the top executives home visits of Brio buyers to understand their needs and learn from them, to develop a sedan. Their efforts paid in a big way, with an order book of more than 30,000 within few days of its launch.

Marketing Insight 4.1

Marketing Insight 4.1

Honda goes all out to woo customers with Amaze

Honda Amaze

Late as it may be in entering the diesel segment in the Indian auto market, Honda is, however, leaving no stone unturned to ensure that its entry level sedan 'Amaze', slated for launch next month, becomes a success. Apart from readying maintenance package, extended warranty schemes and exchange offers with the Amaze, top executives of the company's Indian arm Honda Cars India Ltd (HCIL) are even doing home visits of first time buyers, who bought its Brio hatchback earlier, to learn from their needs.

"The Amaze is a critically important car for us. Not only are we entering a new segment of an entry-level sedan, we are also introducing our first diesel engine here. It is a growing segment and this should help us grow," HCIL Senior Vice President (Sales and Marketing) Jnaneswar Sen told PTI. Stressing on the importance to meet customer requirements, he said: "With Amaze, we are expecting a lot of first time buyers. Our senior management people, even including our Senior Vice President and Director Shigeru Yamazaki, are doing home visits of Brio buyers to understand their needs and learn from them."

Sen further said the company expects a lot of self driven customers for Amaze as compared to its other sedans which are mostly chauffeur driven. "Therefore, we are preparing for quick service, road-side assistance, maintenance package of two years or 40,000 km, extended warranty. We are ensuring that cost of maintenance is low," he said, adding HCIL would also have exchange offers for Amaze with old cars of any brand.

The entry level sedan Amaze qualifies for the excise duty benefit, enjoyed by small cars in India and will directly take on Maruti Suzuki's Swift DZiRE, the current undisputed segment leader. At present, any car with a petrol engine capacity under 1,200 cc or diesel engine under 1,500 cc, but length shorter than four metres, attract an excise duty of 12%.

HCIL will introduce the Amaze in both petrol and diesel options. It has already been launched in Thailand with a petrol engine only. The car is based on the platform of its existing small car Brio, which was developed exclusively for the Asian markets. The company had said it would locally produce the 1.5 litre diesel engines for Amaze at its Tapukara plant in Rajasthan while, the car will be rolled out from its Greater Noida plant.

Case 4: Colors Channel

In the fiercely competitive general entertainment satellite channels business segment, Colors was launched on 21st July, 2008. Within a span of one and half year, the channel has grabbed the number one position, leaving behind Star Plus. Based on a marketing research, Colors has well managed to keep its promise of 'cohesive viewing', with its differentiated content, coupled with disruptive scheduling and peppered with some of the biggest blockbuster Hindi movies. Programs like Balika Vadhu and Uttaran has ended the saas bahu era with a fresh approach towards programming and content like Khatron Ke Khiladi and Big Boss have only fortified its position further.

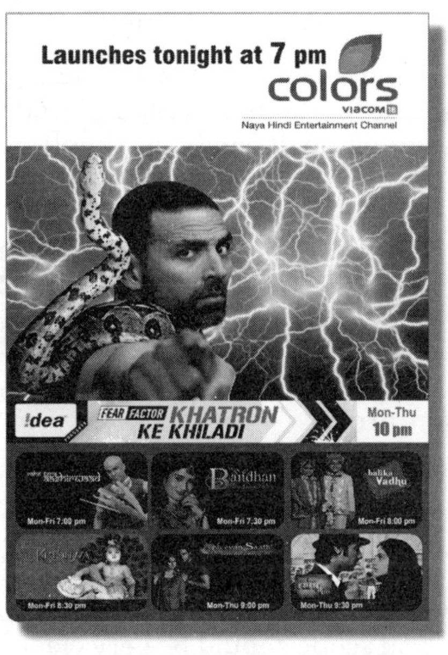

Colors Entertainment Channel

Thus the success of Titan, LG, Colors and so many other companies and even government organisations are based on a solid foundation of marketing research. It helps the companies to provide the relevant, accurate and reliable information to take the right business and marketing decision.

Formal and Informal Marketing Research

Marketing is all about identifying and satisfying customer needs. In this process, a marketer has to take many strategic and tactical decisions. These decisions help to understand the marketing opportunity and tap the right kind of market segment. It does not end here, but it becomes more complex with decisions ranging right from the product to the pricing to the distribution channel and the promotions. It is everyone's responsibility in the company to understand the market and the customers. Both markets and the customers can be understood by the help of the following.

1. **Formal market research and**
2. **Informal market research**

Formal market research is a $16.5 billion dollars industry worldwide. Generally large companies spend 1 to 2% of company's sales on marketing research. In India, there are three types of research firms - syndicated service research firms like NCAER, AC Nielsen, ORG-MARG, IMRB etc., custom marketing research firms, which carries out research work in accordance with the client's requirement and specialty line marketing research firms. Besides the formal marketing research, there are creative and affordable ways of finding out information through hiring students from an MBA College for a summer or winter assignment and through regular monitoring of published information and actions.

Marketing Research refers to the formal collection, analysis and reporting of external data, that is relevant to a specific marketing situation faced by the company. Based on the complexity of the marketing situation, it can be as simple as a customer feedback form to a nationwide survey.

'The process of listening to the voice of the market and conveying information about it to appropriate management' is all about marketing research. - Vincent Barabba and Gerald Zaltman

Steps to Marketing Research

Marketing Research starts with developing a research brief, collecting field data and preparing Data Analysis and Reports. On the whole, there are six steps to marketing research:

Define the problem and research objectives

In the first step, the content and scope should be very clear as to what is to be researched. It is also important to know that what kinds of decisions are required on the basis of the research.

Develop the Research Plan

Once the marketing problem is defined with the research objectives, the second step is to find the necessary information. The information gathering requires decisions to be taken for data sources, research approaches, research instruments, sampling plan and contact methods.

The data sources can be classified into two categories:

- **Primary Data:** Primary data is data collected directly from the market place – customers, retailers, distributors, suppliers, sales persons etc. for a specific purpose. While, secondary data is collected for another purpose and already exist in the market. That's why it saves time as well as money in the research process.
- **Secondary Data:** Secondary source of data includes published reports, industry or trade statistics, news coverage etc. Selected sources of secondary data are Census of India, National readership survey (NRS), National Council of Applied Economic Research (NCEAR), Thompson Urban and Rural Indices, Economic Times, Business Today, Business World coverage, Capital Market Database, CRISIL Reports, Bombay Stock Exchange (BSE) Directory etc.

Many companies also keep their databases retrieved from past sales records. These internal databases help companies like Shoppers Stop, Citibank, Jet Airways, Airtel and Kingfisher Airlines a lot for maintaining a long relationship with the customers. Although secondary data offers the advantage of time and money, yet most of the time it suffers from inadequacy, inaccuracy, unavailability and irrelevancy.

Marketing Insight 4.2

Marketing Mavens Making Data Work

Shoppers Stop

A month ago Shoppers Stop, India's oldest big box retailer, was an indirect beneficiary of a surge in the stockmarket indices. As the markets rose some 8% in early-to-mid September, the retailer took a punt that Gujaratis, whose purchases are closely linked to upswings on the bourses, would go on a spree. And, true to form, they did, adding 25% in incremental growth on sales to Gujarati customers in mid-to-late September when the stock markets rose around 8%. It isn't Gujaratis alone that the retailer has targeted. In the past, Shoppers Stop has used analytics to target promotions at Muslim shoppers during Id, the holy month, and tailor promotions specifically at them. Like with its Gujarati promotion, it used the 2.6 million members of its First Citizen customer loyalty program and name searches to yield additional revenues of Rs. 1 crore in August this year.

Shoppers Stop has found other ways to mine its data. For instance, it has even devised special programs for working women — who shop most often in the middle of the day — to keep them coming into its stores. Shoppers Stop's marketing chief Vinay Bhatia is the man responsible for juicing out every drop of data from the retailer's loyalty program. "Vinay is able to string together data strategy and analytics and use them to devise winning campaigns," says S. Swaminathan, co-founder and CEO of Hansa Cequity, a marketing solutions firm.

By doing this, the lifestyle retailer can throw up surprising bits of data on consumers (example: women are most likely to buy salwar tops and men's undergarments together) that allows Shoppers to tweak its promotions and push them to buy more of the 15 broad categories it vends. "Analytics allows me to tailor programs for individual consumers and track their spending to the last naya paisa," says Bhatia.

This intense focus on analytics is already paying dividends; in fiscal year 2012 Shoppers Stop earned additional revenues of some Rs. 35 crore; and it has already beaten this figure in the first six months of this fiscal year. It expects to earn up to Rs. 70 crore this year.

An adventure sports junkie, who recently made a trip to Thailand to explore its underwater caves, Bhatia is bringing some of this adrenalin to work. He has been pushing Shoppers Stop to try new technologies whenever they surface (like QR or quick response codes and augmented reality), build targeted programs for individual consumers and make Brand Shoppers Stop stand out in an increasingly competitive market. "From putting the brand at the centre of our business, we want to make the customer our focus," says Bhatia.

The challenge for Bhatia is to not just unearth more and more shopping patterns, but to find innovative ways to communicate them to consumers. While an earlier generation of customers took their cues from linear advertising and promotions, Bhatia thinks Gen Y is breaking the mould. "Our target consumer is urbane and constantly networked," he says. "Digital and social media today play a critical role in reaching them."

Shoppers Stop has been quick off the blocks on this front, with some 3.6 million fans for its Facebook page, nearly 4,000 followers on Twitter and a growing presence on Pinterest, the latest rage in the social media space. "We need to be setting the trend and not be a follower on this front," he adds. Bhatia then wants to move from a linear approach to advertising (via the regulation TV and print ads) to using Shoppers Stop's interconnected ecosystem – which includes its content-rich website and mobile application – to attract the consumer. The online initiatives are dovetailed with promotions that are aimed at converting more and more consumers into shoppers.

As a marketer, Bhatia has in the past hawked everything from paints to suitcases and firmly believes that the consumer and not the company is king. So, the first thing he did when he started at Shoppers Stop nearly four years was to spend a week on the floor, actually playing shopping assistant. It's there he discovered that it is easy to knot your own tie, but harder to put one on a potential customer; and that a disproportionate number of people bought shirts, but didn't bother with trousers to match. That was nearly five ago when Shoppers Stop had some 24 stores; today the retailer has 54 and expects to add some eight more a year for at least the next three years.

As far as primary source of data is concerned, it offers the advantage of accuracy, adequacy and being relevant. But at the same time, it's a time consuming process and needs a lot of money. You can collect primary data from the whole of it or a part of it. Taking the data from the entire population is known as Census; while taking a part of the population is called Sample.

In most of the research cases, census cannot be taken, that's why a sample size is chosen from the census, which represents the census. Sampling procedure can be random or it can be purposive and judgmental. In the case of random sampling, the samples are collected randomly. For example, you take the sample as every fifth person entering in a shopping mall for a survey. Although this method is free from researcher bias, yet it may not have the right sample in the process. On the contrary, in the case of purposive and judgmental sampling, the researcher can select its respondent in the sample and may also ask one question to the respondent and based on the reply may either continue or leave the investigation.

There are five ways to collect the primary data:

Kishore Biyani

1. **Observational Research**: Observational research happens in the real life surroundings. This technique is based on the behaviour shown in the actual shopping environment as to how does a consumer buy, what he buys. On the basis of the observation, the findings are generated. These findings are found to be useful in tracking brand preference and brand movement. Besides the researchers, this technique has been used regularly by Mr. Kishore

Biyani, Managing Director of Pantaloon Retail (India) Limited and Group Chief Executive Officer (CEO) of Future Group,. In his book 'It Happened in India', he talked about the observational research for understanding the psyche of Indian buyers.

2. **Focus Group Research**: A Focus Group is a small group of six to twelve people, who are guided by a moderator to discuss a product or service or the image of a company or a political party. The moderator throws a question to the participants and in turn a discussion happens. Based on the findings of the discussion, the outcome is noted. Focus Group research is useful in exploratory research; but the findings cannot be generalized. With the advent of Internet, now many companies are using the online focus group research.

3. **Survey Research**: Survey research is a widely used tool to collect data for descriptive research. It is used to find out knowledge of products and services, preferences, satisfaction, price resistance and so forth from the population. As most of the time, it is not possible to go through the whole population; a sample survey is used to find out the required information. Survey can be conducted anywhere: in your office, on the road or in the mall or elsewhere.

4. **Behavioural Data**: In the era of Internet and Bar Codes, the tracking of consumer purchasing behaviour is possible. This helps in understanding the consumer's buying pattern and preferences. Unlike the survey, the respondent can not tell lie, as it is based on the actual purchases. With the usage of Data Warehousing, Data Mining and Web Mining, the behavioural data leads to know a lot about the customers.

Shoppers Stop's First Citizen Club

Many companies are utilizing the power of Behavioural data through their loyalty programmes like Shoppers Stop's First Citizen Club, Pantaloon's Green Card, Lifestyle Inner Circle Cards, Kingfisher Airlines' King Club Programme, Taj Group's Taj Inner Circle, Leela Hotels' Connoisseur Club. Online shopping websites also offers different reward programmes and offers for its loyal customers on websites like amazon.com, futurebazaar.com, rediff.com, ebay.in, indiatimes.com etc.

Marketing Insight 4.3

Marketing Insight 4.3

India a global analytics hub as companies dig for data

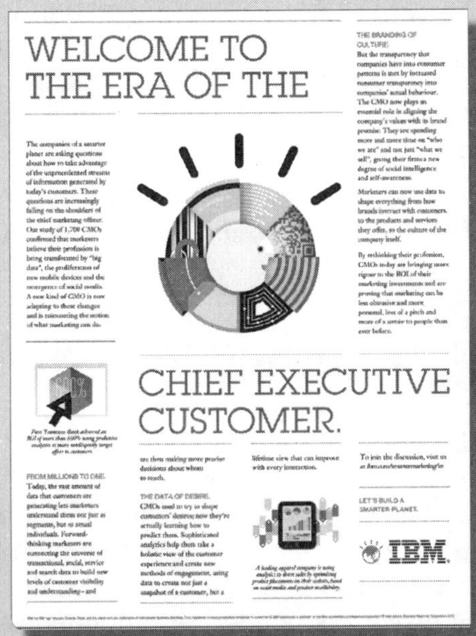

IBM

Most Indian parents push their children to do well in mathematics. That push is now paying an unexpected dividend. India is becoming one of the big global hubs of analytics, a field that has math and statistics at its core. And everybody from MNCs to Indian startups is tapping into this capability.

Analytics is becoming important globally thanks to the explosion of data. Corporates have their internal data, but increasingly, they now have to deal with related external data, coming from social media, blogs, image and video sites, sensors and more. Companies have to find all that is being said about them in these spaces, organize this data deluge, generate insights, make predictions, and finally produce recommendations for action.

"Corporate leaders today need to know more than how to run a data warehouse or build a dashboard. There is demand for people who have that uncanny knack of knowing which metrics are valuable for the organization they serve," says C K Guruprasad, search consultant for the technology practice at global executive search firm Heidrick & Struggles India.

Pradeep Nair, director in IBM India's software group, uses the delightful example of Pele to explain the new analytics phenomenon. Dribble skills in football, he says, is something that many players have. "Pele had in addition this uncanny ability to know where the ball would be before it got there. Now companies want that kind of capability," he says.

Analytics solutions involve technology, as also human intervention to further refine the results that technology provides. IBM, which has a major analytics centre of excellence in India that services the globe, recently announced that its analytics is enabling Jet Airways to accurately calculate, track and report aircraft emissions, and optimize its fuel usage by detailed analysis of each flight. HCL Technologies is creating a digital lobby for an MNC bank that can track what account holders aretalking about it on Facebook and LinkedIn. This will help bank staff to serve their customers better.

IBM, Accenture, Genpact and the big Indian IT companies all have fairly broad analytics practices today. Numerous startups too have emerged, with proprietary analytics technologies and methodologies. Startups tend to be more focused.

Mu Sigma focuses on marketing, supply chain and risk analytics. AbsolutData, founded by Indians in California but which has its delivery centre in Delhi, helps optimize marketing spends and fine tune marketing strategies by analyzing customer behaviour. Fractal Analytics, also founded by Indians in California and with its delivery centre largely in India, focuses on building customer loyalty and reducing waste in corporate operations. Among its many successes is one where it helped a customer to establish the right level of unit price discounts needed to influence shoppers to purchase more expensive large product packages and thus increase total sales for these product categories.

iCreate is today a wellknown name in banking analytics. So is Manthan Systems in retail. Manthan develops analytics solutions for global retailers like McDonald's and Lowe's to understand things like where to locate stores, how to lay out stores, which items to keep in each store and which items are best kept together. Capillary Technologies, also in retail analytics, focuses on capturing a customer's profile and purchases to make appropriate offers at appropriate times.

Nabler analyses digital trails left behind by people through their activities on websites to help companies understand their customers better and improve their product offerings. Activecubes provides analytics services in areas such as sales, marketing, supply chain, operations, and risk management. Redwood Associates has an online analytical job product called Look Beyond Resumes that allows job seekers to understand what they are best suited for, and corporates to understand which candidate is the best fit for a vacancy.

In 2010, India is estimated by Avendus Capital to have delivered $375 million of the total data analytics outsourcing of $500-550 million. Avendus estimates a talent shortage of

140,000-190,000 professionals with analytical capabilities in the US by 2018, representing about 40% of the total demand. "This talent supply gap will create a $20 billion offshore opportunity," says Amit Singh, executive director in the financial services provider.

Venkat Viswanathan, CEO of Chennai-based analytics company LatentView Analytics, says the growth in analytics in India is thanks to the IT sector. "Though Eastern Europe and China are attractive locations for analytics talent, companies are familiar with India's IT prowess, and hence look up to us to deliver analytics solutions," he says.

5. **Experimental Research**: Experimental research is often done by many companies before introducing the product in the market or to understand the impact of changes in price. As it is based on cause and effect relationship, this is the most scientific valid research. For example, Bisleri wants to implement a different bottle design for its mineral water. To understand the customer response, it can put both the designs on an interval in a shop. After a certain period of time, the results will be tabulated to understand the customer response.

Many companies go for test marketing their product or service in one place, before taking it to the national level. In India, two cities – Pune and Hyderabad is well known for test marketing exercises due to its cosmopolitan population and relatively cheaper real estate prices. Reliance started their retail operations from Hyderabad. For Kishore Biyani, the test market was Kolkata, where he opened his first Big Bazaar store.

Research Instruments

There are four research instruments to collect primary data. These are:

1. **Questionnaires**: Questionnaire is the most widely used tool for collecting primary data. It consists of a set of questions given to the respondent by the researcher. The success of this technique lies in preparing right kind of questions with suitable alternatives or no alternative. The question can be of two types:

   a. **Closed End Questionnaire**: Closed End questions are easier to interpret, answer and tabulate, as it provides all the possible answers. For example, if you ask the respondent that whether he uses Colgate Tooth Paste, and if the options are yes and no; then it's very easy to interpret, answer and tabulate.

   b. **Open End Questionnaire**: In the open end questions, the respondent can answer in his / her own words. The answer often reveals more about what people think about. If you ask the respondent that what does he feel about Colgate, then the answer may reveal a lot many things to the researcher than just the answer to the question. A good questionnaire should be specific, simple to understand and without any bias. It should not contain any technical jargon and should avoid questions with a negative in them.

Closed End Questions	
Dichotomous Question with two possible answers	Yes No
Multiple Choice Question with three or more answers	a) b) c) d)
Rating Scale Scale that rates the attributes on a 1 to 5 Scale from Excellent to Poor	1 Excellent 2 Very Good 3 Good 4 Fair 5 Poor
Likert Scale Scale that rates some attribute from agreement to disagreement	1 Strongly Agree 2 Agree 3 Neither agree nor disagree 4 Disagree 5 Strongly Disagree
Importance Scale Scale that rates some attribute from Important to Not at all important	1 Extremely Important 2 Very Important 3 Important 4 Somewhat Important 5 Not at all important
Intention to Buy Scale Scale that rates the intentions to buy	1 Definitely Buy 2 Probably Buy 3 Not Sure 4 Probably Not Buy 5 Definitely Not Buy
Semantic Differential Scale that connects two bipolar words. Respondent selects a point to voice his or her opinion	Big......................Small Heavy ....Light Modern ....Traditional

Open End Questions	
Completely Unstructured The question can be answered in innumerable ways	What do you feel about Colgate Toothpaste?
Word Association One word is presented to respondent at one time and the respondent mentions the word which comes first to his mind	Chocolate .... Airline .... Jeans ....
Sentence Completion Respondents are supposed to complete the sentence	I like Swift because ....
Story Completion	
Picture	
Thematic Apperception Test (TAT)	

2. **Psychological Tools (Behaviour Mapping, Consumer Journeys, Storytelling)**: Ernest Dichter, the master of depth interviewing, is of the opinion that Qualitative research ('Head Shrinking') gave far more insight than questionnaire based, quantitative

research ('Nose Counting'). The consumers' feelings and beliefs can only be understood by qualitative techniques using psychological tools like Depth interviews, Laddering technique and Rorshach tests.

In depth interviews, the researcher tries to gain a deeper insight into the consumers' feelings and belief about the product. It has led to many surprise findings, which have been quite useful for many companies. Laddering technique also helps to find out the inner desire and feelings about the product. For example, if you ask a person who owns a Tata Safari that 'Why have you bought Tata Safari'; then the answer might be 'he likes the looks of the vehicle'. If you probe him further 'why does he like' then he may answer because 'it adds to his macho personality'. Again if you probe further and ask 'why does he want to project a macho image' and he may answer, 'Because gals like macho guys.' The process continues till the researcher gets to the deeper reason for buying a Tata Safari.

Tata Safari

By using metaphors to non verbal images, Zaltman introduced a technique called Zaltman Metaphoric Elicitation Technique (ZMET). In this technique, respondents are asked to use his / her imagination and let the product be described with a picture or non verbal image. This helps the researcher to understand the feelings about the product.

3. **Mechanical Devices**: Sometimes mechanical devices are also used in marketing research. As far as Satellite channels are concerned, the viewership for any channel is decided by Television audience measurement (TAM). This helps to gauge the time spent on television viewing and the time spent on any particular channel by the viewer. The data compiled through the device is calculated cumulatively and called Television Rating Points (TRP) in terms of Gross Rating Points and Target Rating Points.

In India, television ratings are collected by two main organizations - TAM India and Audience Measurement Analytics Limited (aMap). aMap polls the meters (6000 households) using GSM network and provides ratings overnight. While TAM India collects data manually (physical visits) and releases data weekly. aMap also has a stand-alone digital panel (aMapDigital) to measure TV viewing in DTH homes.

Just like the readership survey for the newspapers i.e. Indian Readership Survey (IRS), it gives a framework for the advertisers to place their products in the right programmes, satellite channels to rethink about the programming strategy and content creation houses like Balaji Telefilms to add some spice from their different serials.

Galvanometer is another device to gauge the interest or emotions or feelings aroused by exposure to a particular picture or Ad. Another device tachistoscope flashes an ad to a subject with an exposure interval that may range from less than one hundredth of a second to several seconds. After each exposure, the respondent describes everything he or she recalls.[2]

4. **Qualitative Measures**: Qualitative research has also gained importance in the course of time. The Depth Review, The Group Depth Interview, Retail Store Audit, Product Testing and Corporate Image Study are some of the ways, which helps the marketer to understand the consumers. Semi structured questionnaire are used in the depth interview. Similarly, more consumers are interviewed in the case of Group Depth Interview.

   In retail store audit, the database gathered from the retail store helps in understanding the retail sales trends, movement of products from shelves to the consumer and inventory level required. Through the retail store audit only, it was found that the average shelf time in a normal grocery store was almost two to three months. But with the advent of organized retail like Big Bazaar, Spencer's, Reliance Fresh etc the average shelf time has been reduced to nine days to two weeks.

Once the research approach and instruments are finalized, the next question of sampling plan needs to be answered. Sampling plan consists of sampling unit, sampling size and sampling procedure. In the case of sampling unit, the target population should be clearly defined by the researcher. Then the number of samples is also taken into consideration. A large sample size will always give a better and reliable result, but many times it will not be possible for the researcher. Sample size of approximate one percent of the population, generally gives reliable results. The third question is sampling procedure as to how does the samples are chosen. In the case of probability sampling, every member of the population has got equal chance of selection. On the contrary, in non-probability sampling, the respondents are selected on the basis of accessibility.

Once the samples are selected, the researcher can contact them on mail, telephone, or through online interview or through personal interview. Now the mail questionnaire is losing their sheen due to internet and online questionnaire or interview has taken the lead. The best way is the personal interview, but it is also the most time consuming and a costly process. Personal interviews can either be arranged or can happen through intercept.

Marketing Insight 4.4

India Inc Suddenly Rises to Sleep Disorder

ITC Hotel

Wake-up calls often signify a sudden end to slumber. But for India's stationery-tohospitality major ITC, the wake-up call came in the form of a study that argued for more and more sleep — deep, peaceful, and recurring. ITC, which owns the country's second-largest hotel chain, undertook a study last year which found that 70% of business travellers found it difficult to sleep in the unfamiliar surroundings of a hotel room. Worse, around 82% respondents were worried that this would affect their business performance the next day.

For Nakul Anand, ITC's business chief and executive director, it indeed was a wake-up call. Anand, who firmly believes that he is in the business of selling sleep, says a hotel can offer the finest services, great restaurants and stunning architecture, but if the guest hasn't slept well, all that effort comes to nothing. Sure enough, he's got on to the act of selling sleep, and so are a slew of companies across the electronics, healthcare and technology sectors. ITC now boasts of 'sleep menu' across all its hotels, which includes a choice of pillow sizes and density, a range of calming aromatherapy essential oil sprays, in-room foot massages and even a 'dream kerchief' — a handkerchief doused in aromatherapy oils. Companies such as Philips and GE are expanding their in-home sleeping aid devices business, while demand for anti-snoring devices and sleep products too is growing.

The likes of GSK Consumer Healthcare and The Himalaya Drug Company have recently ventured into the segment. Even mobile phone applications related to sleep are seeing a huge market in India. "India is one of the most sleep-deprived nations," says Philips India Senior Director (home healthcare) Bidur Dhaul.

Philips recently undertook a survey with The Nielsen Company with 5,600 respondents across 25 cities in India. It threw up some shocking figures: 93% of the respondents were sleep-deprived, 58% felt their work suffered due to lack of sleep, and 11% actually fell asleep at work. Worse, only 2% discussed their problems with a doctor, a fact that points towards the market potential. Globally, the market for sleep aids is estimated to be more than $33 billion by 2014, according to a study by BCC Research. While industry estimates put the market for sleep products in India at around Rs 16,000 crore, GE estimates that nearly 70 million Indians are affected by sleep disorders and need some technology or interventional support.

Philips has set up 200 sleep labs in hospitals and clinics across the country that would help doctors accurately diagnose sleep disorders. The company says its in-home sleeping aid devices are growing at a double-digit rate. While the Philips range of in-home sleeping aids is sold in the Rs 25,000-60,000 range, GE India has rolled out products priced between Rs 30,000 and Rs 4 lakh. "Even though the market is in its infancy in India, it has grown four-fold in the past three years and has tremendous potential," says GE Healthcare India General Manager (life care solutions) Ashutosh Banerjee. ITC has started a sleep index for its hotels whereby it tracks reasons why a guest has not slept well. The company is also working on a chocolate made with natural ingredients that has a soothing effect and would induce sleep, says Anand.

The Himalaya Drug Company has rolled out a sleep tea, which acts as a relaxant and mild sedative. The company's two other sleep-support products — Ashvagandha and Tagara — too are growing year-on-year at 42% and 15%, respectively, says business head Mukesh Patney. The sales of over-the-counter anti-snoring products by GSK and Umesh Modi Group's Modi Omega India too are growing at a fast pace. "We get at least 15 calls per day for information about the product from customers, which we believe is a great initial response," says Himani Modi, ED at Modi Omega Pharma India. "Even a few years ago, snoring was not considered a problem in India. The scenario is changing, now it is considered an embarrassment as well as a problem," says Modi. Standing testimony to the findings of the sleep surveys is the turnaround trends in popular apps — technology is often blamed for many losing their daily sleep.

Analysing Buyer Preferences

One of the core areas of marketing research is to analyse the buyer preferences. The preference of the buyer is as important in the product development stage as in the marketing communication. There are two approaches:

1. **Concept Testing**: Concept Testing is meant to test an idea, based on a response scale. If you want to find out that in a particular locality say Connaught Place in New Delhi, whether an upmarket Chinese restaurant will work or not; then it can be found out through concept testing. Importance Scale and Intention to buy scale can be used to understand the buyer preferences on the factors like food quality, menu variety, ambience, service quality and ample parking from the respondents.
2. **Conjoint Analysis**: Conjoint analysis has become important to understand buyer preferences in the recent times. As many products and services offer a bundle of benefits; it becomes difficult from the buyer's point of view to make the right judgment. For example, a mobile phone is not just a communication device, it's a radio, it's a camera, it's your personal digital assistant, it's your mp3 player, it's an internet surfing device, it's your mailing device and it's your video player also.

Conjoint analysis is a statistical technique to predict the tradeoffs between different attributes. It helps the company to understand that which combination of different attributes of a product or service will make it more buyers friendly. Although the data is collected individually, the analysis is done cumulatively to understand, which attributes are more important to the buyer and which others are not so important. It helps the company in product or service development as it has helped LG in making their touch screen mobile phone 'Pop' GD510 known as LG Cookie Pep in Indian market.

Based on the conjoint analysis, LG has developed this product by putting more emphasis on the functionality of a full touch screen phone without the extra bulk and unnecessary features that resulted in higher prices. According to the research, many users were put off by the complexity of feature-laden phones, but still desired the easier navigation and larger screens of full touch screen phones. The LG Cookie Pep is designed to include the key features these users craved, without the overhead of features they didn't use.

Customer Price Sensitivity

Customer price sensitivity is another area which is important for marketers. India is a very price sensitive market and the companies who understand the Indian consumers are the companies, which are hugely successful. It can happen in India only where Maruti Suzuki produces more cars as well as revenue and profit than its parent company in Japan. It is all due to understanding the Indian customers well, pricing the product properly and giving a service support, which none can match. Going further, Maruti Suzuki is concentrating more on fuel efficiency to make it cheaper for its customers to run the cars. It has recently launched their KB series of engines, as fuel efficiency is the second most concern besides the price of the vehicle or sometimes top concern for the Indian customers. That's why, Maruti Suzuki focuses on the fuel efficiency in their popular television commercials (TVC) with the tagline 'Kitna Deti Hai' - How much it gives (i.e. mileage). On the contrary, Apple's iconic iPhone, which is successful all across the world, have not been quite successful officially in India due to its high pricing. That's why Aircel has launched iPhone 4 with an offer of 100% money back plans on its 24 months postpaid offer.

Collect the Information

The third step of the marketing research is as important as the second stage, as the reliability of data depends upon the data collection phase. This stage is the most expensive and time consuming and is also prone to error. The respondent or the interviewer can be biased and can give dishonest answers. Sometimes, it becomes difficult to meet the respondent and sometimes the respondent does not cooperate with the researcher.

To make this process simpler and better, now a lot of technologies like mobile, web and bar codes are used to gather data. Now, online questionnaire, interactive kiosks, data mining and web mining is helping out the researcher to find out the correct picture.

Analyse the Information

Once the data is collected, it needs to be analysed. Through various statistical techniques, the marketing researcher tabulates the data and frequency distribution. It then uses averages and measures of dispersion to generate the findings.

Marketing Insight 4.5

Marketing Insight 4.5

From big databases to the big screen

Amazing Spider-Man 2

One of the most overused terms of the current decade has to be ‘big data’. Newspapers and business magazines write about it. Consultancy firms publish learned -sounding white papers on how it will transform business. Computer service providers boast about their capabilities in the area. It is not all hype, though – the use and analysis of big data has percolated into almost every business. Now, big data takes the next step – to the big screen.

Vinny Bruzzese is a former statistics professor who has been called “the reigning mad scientist of Hollywood.” He is the CEO of The Worldwide Motion Picture Group (WMP), a film research company. “Over the past ten years Vincent has worked on over 1,000 films, impacting the development, execution, marketing or release of each one,” says the WMP website.

Bruzzese offers a service called script evaluation. "For as much as $20,000 per script, Mr Bruzzese and a team of analysts compare the story structure and genre of a draft script with those of released movies, looking for clues to box-office success. His company, Worldwide Motion Picture Group, also digs into an extensive database of focus group results for similar films and surveys 1,500 potential moviegoers," writes Brookes Barnes at The New York Times. Bruzzese's advice is along the lines of "a cursed superhero never sells as well as a guardian superhero" or "films with bowling scenes don't do well".

'Script doctors' have always been a staple of Hollywood. These were uncredited writers who were called in to tighten up scripts; Ben Hecht, one of the most famous writers from Hollywood's golden age, was a script doctor for Alfred Hitchcock films. The actress Carrie Fisher was another. Fisher worked uncredited on Spielberg's Hook, Lethal Weapon 3 and other movies. Even current wunderkind Joss Whedon was a script doctor for a long long time – working on movies like Speed, Twister, Waterworld and X-Men.

But Bruzzese's brand of script doctoring has others up in arms. Esther Zuckerman writes at The Atlantic: "Bruzzese just seems so ridiculous. His suggestions seem to ignore beloved films in favor of box office glory. For instance, he suggests that bowling scenes doom a movie, clearly ignoring the legions of fans who fancy themselves The Dude or Daniel Day-Lewis's Oscar-winning performance set in a bowling alley."

Present the Findings

In the fifth stage, the marketing researcher presents the findings. On the basis of the findings, the marketing decisions can be taken by the management.

Make the Decision

Based on the findings by the researcher, the management can make the decision in favour of the research findings, if they find it suitable. They can also go against the research findings, if they don't believe the findings or if they think otherwise.

The marketing research is supposed to help in the decision making process through the insight, it provides in the marketing situation. But, it can only be a guiding force. The ultimate responsibility lies with the management only, as they are the only responsible people to own up the decisions.

On the whole, a good marketing research should be based on a scientific method, should apply creativity, should be cost effective, should be based on healthy skepticism and should be ethical in nature.

Marketing Decision Support System

In the marketing decision making, marketing decision support system (MDSS) helps the marketing people to make better decisions. The concept of MDSS is given by John Little.

'Marketing Decision Support System is a coordinated collection of data, systems, tools and techniques with supporting software and hardware by which an organization gathers and interprets relevant information from business and environment and turns it into a basis for marketing action.'[3] – John Little

There are several decision models used by marketing managers like **John Little's** marketing mix model **BRANDAID**, **Little and Leonard Lodish's MEDIAC** for media planning, **Silk and Zaragoza's DETAILER** for sales people, **Abraham and Lodish's PROMOTER** for sales promotion, **Lodish's CALLPLAN** for sales people, **Montgomery, Hess and Samuels' GEOLINE** for sales and service territories etc.

Demand Forecasting

Marketing information system including marketing research, gives an insight into available market opportunities. It is very essential for a company to understand the quantum of demand in the market. The assessment of demand leads to plan the finances, manufacturing, purchases and human resources.

Demand forecasting is a quantitative estimation of the demand of a product or service by customers during some defined future period. The demand forecasting can be done either for the industry or for a company or its individual products. For example – Demand forecasting can be done for Soaps on the whole and then it can be done for say, Hindustan Unilever Limited (HUL) and then it can be done for an individual brand say, Lux.

Jaguar

Demand forecasting for a multinational corporation like Tata Group companies say Tata Motors can also be done at global, country, region, state and district level. Again the forecasting will be different for various products / services and its different brands and its variants. Right from Jaguar, Land Rover (JLR) to Tata Motors' commercial vehicles to passenger vehicles will all form the complete picture. Thus, right from Tata Nanos to Tata Arias to Tata Trucks and Buses to Jaguars and Land Rovers will complete the picture of Tata Motors.

Demand forecasting can be done either for short term say a quarter or three to six months or it can be done for medium term between one to three years or it can be done for a long period say five to ten years. The duration also varies depending upon the nature of the business. Generally core infrastructural sector's time frame will be much longer than say a FMCG company.

Although the long term demand forecasting is very important from the business planning, financial planning and manpower planning purposes, yet with the dynamic business environment today, a company needs to keenly watch and plan for short term as well as medium term requirements. With volatility in the business environment today, coupled with technological and other changes; a company needs to look out for short as well as medium term forecasting. In the short term, a company may gain form planning for the right manufacturing schedule, right purchasing schedule, right financial schedule and realistic sales targets.

The size of a market can be divided into four broad categories.

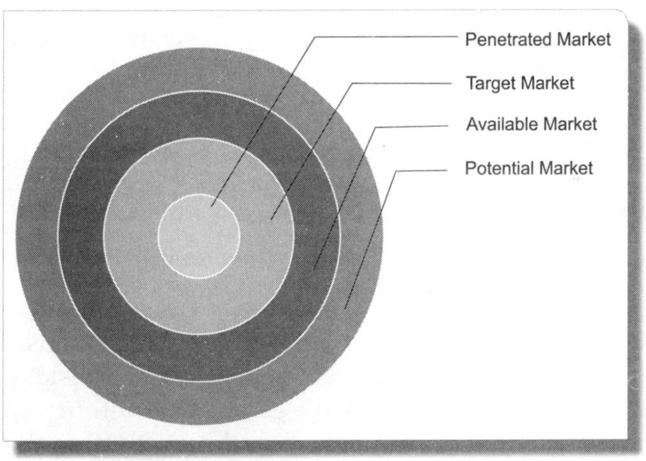

1. Potential Market: The market potential for a product or service includes all the consumers, who are interested in the product. The interest may not be backed by the income.

2. Available Market: A marketer is more interested in finding out the available market of a product or service, as these consumers are not only interested in the product, but they also have the income and accessibility to buy the product.

3. Target Market: The target market is the market targeted by the company to market its products. For example – A company may decide to market its product say, only

in northern part of India as Ghari Detergent has done in first stage. Then the target market is only restricted to the northern part of India.

4. Penetrated Market: The actual market and its set of consumers form the penetrated market.

Methods of Demand Forecasting

Although there are several methods of forecasting the demand for a product or a service, yet no forecasting method is useful for all the products. A company should use more than one forecasting method for correct decision making. The choice of the forecasting method also differs from product to product to the objective of the company to data availability besides others. Although forecasting may act as a light to guide the path, but it may not be accurate all the time in this dynamic business environment. For example, the forecasting done for two cars i.e. Maruti Suzuki Swift and Mahindra Logan, met with different fate in reality. Maruti Suzuki Swift was launched in 2005 with the sales target of 4000 units a month. But it became a runaway hit among the car buyers and sold more than 40000 cars in the first six months, which is almost 65% higher than the forecast. The success story does not end here. It went on to sell as many as 12000 units a month on an average. To continue the success story, Maruti also introduced the sedan version of swift in the name of Swift Dzire. Now Dzire is also selling 10000 units a month on an average. On the other hand, Mahindra and Ranault's partnership came to an end with the debacle of their joint venture product Logan. With a sales forecast of 50000 units a year, Logan could not achieve even its 15% of its target.

Following are the forecasting methods, which are generally used. All these methods are divided into two categories i.e. Survey methods and Statistical Methods.

- **Survey Methods**

  Survey methods help a marketer to forecast the demand based on the buyer intentions, expert opinions and the feedback from the market

  - Survey of Buyer Intentions: In survey of buyer intentions, a sample size of current and / or potential customers is selected and is asked about the purchase intentions of a particular product at a given price within a specified period. Then the data is extrapolated to the whole population, to have the right forecast.

    But the sample may not be the representative of the population. This may result in inaccurate demand forecast. It may also be possible that the intentions may not translate into the actual purchases by the consumers.

  - Sales Force Composite: Sales force composite is based on the collective data provided by the sales people all across the region or state or territory or country. In terms of reliability, it scores better than the other methods, as it is based on the real data collected by right people. Although there are still chances of being over estimation or under estimation.

- Reasoned opinion: Reasoned opinion is also known as Delphi method, which is a variant of poll and survey method. This method was developed by Rand Corporation, USA for technical changes in the late 1940s. Just like sales force composite, this method uses the opinions of the experts and a group of knowledgeable individuals anonymously to estimate the future demand. But, this method can also be subjective, as it is based on somebody's estimation.
- Test Marketing: Under test marketing, a company test markets its products in a limited geographical area, which may be representative of the whole population to measure the demand. Test marketing also facilitates feedback on the packaging, pricing, design, likability etc. besides gauging the demand. In India, Pune and Hyderabad has been a major testing ground for FMCG companies. Now Lucknow is also added to the list, with Hindustan Unilever Ltd. (HUL) test marketing its mobile tea/coffee vendors. Now the test marketing has expanded to Hyderabad, Mumbai and Patna.

Statistical Methods

Demand forecasting based on statistical methods is used a lot by companies, due to its nature of being logical and unbiased. As it depends upon the historical data and its extrapolation, it is reliable and useful for a company. But, it lacks the dynamism associated to the business, where past may not give correct picture of the present. Secondly, it cannot be used for new products, as there will be no historical data.

Demand forecasting can either be done by time series analysis or regression analysis.

- Time Series Analysis: Time series is a statistical arrangement of data in a chronological order. Its' analysis helps a company to analyse the trend in the future. The arrangement of data can be done in the form a graphical representation or it can be in the form of a table. Time series analysis helps to give us a trend, long term tendency of the data. It can also show us the seasonal variations due to festivals, holidays, weather, fashions etc. Similarly, cyclical variations like boom, recession, depression and recovery can also help us in analysis. Sometimes unforeseen events like flood, war, epidemic, fire etc leads us to residual variations, which can also help in demand forecasting. Following methods can be used under time series analysis.
  - ✓ Graphical Method
  - ✓ Semi Averages Method
  - ✓ Moving Averages Method
  - ✓ Least Squares Method
- Regression Analysis: Regression analysis is one of the most popular methods of demand forecasting. It analyses the average relation between two or more variables mathematically. Under simple regression, analysis is done for two variables

only. While under multiple regression, it is done for multiple factors simultaneously.

This method is not only descriptive, but also prescriptive and objective in nature. It analyses time series and cross section data for more accuracy. But, when explanatory variables are not chosen realistically, it may be misleading. In the case of autocorrelation, the analysis results may be biased.

Demand Forecasting for New Products

Demand forecasting for new products is more complex than the old and existing products. It requires a good understanding of the consumer per se, besides the points of differentiation from the competition. Generally it has been found that demand forecasting for new products in the year one has been off the target. It becomes more difficult, if the product or service is totally new to the market like Tata Nano, Ginger Hotels, Mahindra Scorpio, Tata Ace or say Mahindra Quanto.

Mahindra Quanto

The demand for new products can be estimated on the basis of old products and its data in the similar category or product segment. Another tried and tested method is the test marketing for the product to understand the interest and willingness to buy the product at a given price point. For FMCG products, another method, which works for calculating the year one data, is the retail simulation. In retail simulation, the consumer is asked to choose the top 5 or 10 brands in a product category. Then the new product is added to the list and the feedback in the form of choice is counted. Thus survey of buyers' intention is understood in the above way, besides the survey approach. When the product is just an improvement on existing product, then the demand can be estimated with an evolutionary approach and be projected as an outgrowth.

Summary

- The success of the marketing strategy depends a lot on the marketing research. According to American Marketing Association, 'Marketing Research is the function that links the consumer, customer, and public to the marketer through information - information used to identify and define marketing opportunities and problems; generate, refine, and evaluate marketing actions; monitor marketing performance; and improve understanding of marketing as a process.'
- The term marketing research is commonly interchanged with market research. Market research is concerned specifically with markets, while marketing research is concerned specifically about marketing processes.
- Marketing Research refers to the formal collection, analysis and reporting of external data, that is relevant to a specific marketing situation faced by the company. Based on the complexity of the marketing situation, it can be as simple as a customer feedback form to a nationwide survey.
- Marketing Research starts with developing a research brief, collecting field data and preparing Data Analysis and Reports. On the whole, there are six steps to marketing research: define the problem and research objectives, develop the research plan, collect the information, analyse the information, present the findings and make the decision.
- The data sources can be classified into two categories: primary data and secondary data. Primary data is data collected directly from the market place – customers, retailers, distributors, suppliers, sales persons etc. for a specific purpose. While, secondary data is collected for another purpose and already exist in the market. That's why it saves time as well as money in the research process.
- There are five ways to collect the primary data: observational research, focus group, surveys, behavioural data and experiments
- There are four research instruments to collect primary data. These are: questionnaires, psychological tools (qualitative measures) like behavior mapping, consumer journeys, storytelling; mechanical devices like galvanometer, tachistocope etc. and qualitative measures like the depth review, the group depth interview, retail store audit, product testing and corporate image study.
- Buyer preferences can be analysed with the help of concept testing and conjoint analysis.
- Marketing Decision Support System is a coordinated collection of data, systems, tools and techniques with supporting software and hardware by which an organization gathers and interprets relevant information from business and environment and turns it into a basis for marketing action.

- Demand forecasting is a quantitative estimation of the demand of a product or service by customers during some defined future period. The demand forecasting can be done either for the industry or for a company or its individual products.
- Demand forecasting methods are divided into two categories i.e. survey methods and statistical methods. Survey methods include survey of buyer intentions, sales force composite, reasoned opinion and test marketing. Statistical methods include time series analysis and regression analysis.

Discussion Questions

1. Define Marketing Research. Discuss the importance of Marketing Research for a company with examples.
2. Explain the six steps in marketing research process.
3. Differentiate between primary data and secondary data. Discuss the five ways to collect the primary data in detail.
4. What do you mean by Demand Forecasting? Discuss the various methods for forecasting demand.
5. Short Notes:

   a. Marketing Decision Support System
   b. Concept Testing
   c. Conjoint Analysis
   d. Time Series Analysis
   e. Secondary Data
   f. Target Market

References

1. McDonald, Malcolm, Marketing Plans, 6th ed., Oxford, England: Butterworth-Heinemann, 2007
2. Roger D. Blackwell, James S. Hensel, Michael B. Phillipes and Brian Sternthal (Dubuque IA: Kendall / Hunt 1970), Laboratory Equipment for Marketing Research; Wally Wood, 'The race to replace memory', Marketing and Media Decisions, July 1986; Gerald Zaltman 'Rethinking Marketing Research : Putting People Back In" Journal of Marketing Research 34, No4 (Nov., 1997, 424-37
3. John D. C. Little, "Decision Support System for Marketing Managers", Journal of Marketing, Summer 1979

CHAPTER 5

Consumer Markets

Chapter Structure

"With the advent of Internet, now market can be divided into two parts - marketplace and marketspace. As you know, the physical place for buying and selling is a marketplace; while marketspace is digital in nature, as buying and selling can be done on the internet."

- Jeffrey Rayport and John Sviokla

"What a man can be, he must be"

- Abraham Maslow

"In the factory, we make cosmetics; in the store, we sell hope"

- Charles Revson, Founder, Revlon

Consumer and Business Markets

In economics, the concept of market means any structure that allows buyers and sellers to exchange any type of goods, services and information. Traditionally, the market is meant to be a physical place, where buyers and sellers meet to buy and sell goods. Now in the internet era, the world has become a market. Earlier the barter system was used for business transactions. Now, the transaction is done on the monetary basis. Sometimes market is also meant as a grouping of customers.

According to **Jeffrey Rayport and John Sviokla**

> **'With the advent of Internet, now market can be divided into two parts – marketplace and marketspace. As you know, the physical place for buying and selling is a marketplace; while marketspace is digital in nature, as buying and selling can be done on the internet.'[1]**

Mohan Sawhney has given another concept **Metamarket**, which consists of a cluster of complementary products and services, which are closely related in the minds of the consumers. These products and services may be from different industries.

> **The automobile Metamarket consists of automobile manufacturers, new car and used car dealers, financing companies, insurance companies, mechanics, spare parts dealers, auto magazines, classified auto ads in newspapers and auto websites.[2]**

Thus, right from Maruti Suzuki to MRF Tyres to Munjal Showa to State Bank of India to ICICI Lombard to Mahindra First Choice to Overdrive magazine to Zigwheels.com; all are part of the automobile Metamarket.

Taking a cue from the concept, **Mr. Jagdish Khattar**, former MD of Maruti Suzuki has launched a venture called **Carnation Auto,** which deals in Car services, accessories, preowned cars, new cars and DC design Kits.

Markets can be classified on the basis of the **product** itself, or on the basis of the **end-consumer**, or both. The market is most commonly classified as following:

- **Consumer Market** and
- **Business Market** or **Industrial Market** or **Organizational Market**

In this chapter, we are going to discuss consumer markets, while business markets will be discussed in next chapter.

Consumer Market

Consumer markets are the markets for products and services like Car, LED TV, Refrigerators, Toothpaste, Ice Cream, Apparels, Air travel etc., bought by individuals for their own or family use. In the consumer market, companies try to identify and meet the needs of the consumer through their product and service offering. Additionally, they try to position the products into the consumers mind for better awareness and purchases. Consumer markets can be classified in the following way:

1. **Fast Moving Consumer Goods (FMCG):** Fast Moving Consumer Goods widely known as FMCG, generally include a wide variety of frequently purchased products such as toothpaste, shampoo, soap, cosmetics, hair oil and detergents, as well as other non-durables such as plastic goods, CFL bulbs, paper & stationery and glassware. FMCG may also include chocolates, pharmaceuticals, packaged food products and soft drinks.

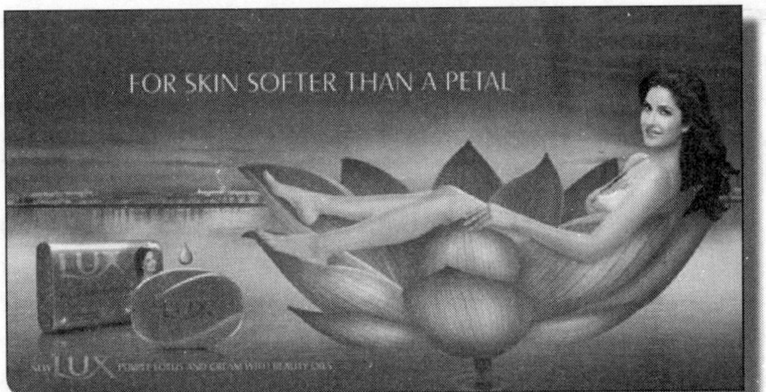

Lux

Marketing Insight 5.1

A Perfect 10! HUL's 1,000cr Club Swells

Brand Stand Dove, Pond's & Clinic Plus Join The Elite Club In FY13

Dove

Hindustan Unilever now owns ten 1,000-crore plus brands after Dove, Pond's and Clinic Plus crossed the mark in annual sales last fiscal, making it perhaps the first instance of three brands a firm joining the elite club in the same year. The trio have joined Rin, Surf Excel, Wheel, Brooke Bond, Lux, Lifebuoy and Fair & Lovely in the 1,000-crore club that accounted for more than 60% of Hindustan Unilever's annual sales of 25,810 crore last year. The country's largest FMCG company has three-dozen brands in its portfolio.

While its largest brand, Wheel, took almost three decades to hit the 1,000-crore sales mark first in 2005, Dove has now become the fastest brand to match this feat, reaching the landmark in two decades after its launch in 1993. In fact, with sales of 100 crore in 2007, the personal care brand has grown ten times in just over five years as it transformed from a bathing bar launched in 1993 to virtually all new age categories such as conditioners, deodorants, hair-oil, body and face wash. "Dove is leading the agenda of driving premiumisation," an HUL spokesperson said. This focus on premium offerings helped Hindustan Unilever post its highest operating margin in a decade at 20% for the year ended March 2013. No wonder, two premium brands — Pond's and Dove —crossed the 1,000-crore mark in the same year. "The categories of the future are what we are talking about, all of them are more aspirational and more premium. If you accept the fact that the general trend is going to be uptrading and premiumisation in the market, every category will see the trend," Hindustan Unilever CEO Nitin Paranjpe said while declaring the annual results last month. "Our job is to identify those and take steps well before it becomes obvious and imperative for everyone to act. We will benefit when the tipping point comes in any of these categories," he said.

Under Paranjpe, HUL has made a broader push upmarket in new and pricier categories that have helped the company's share price and net profit rise to record levels five years after he took the top position.

The company has been stretching most brands in premium categories. Dove was part of many these forays, helping the two decade-old premium brand to pick up sudden pace in recent years.

Piyul Mukherjee, co-founder and director at qualitative research firm Quipper Research, says, "When Dove was launched in early 90's, most companies including HUL (then Hindustan Lever) thought that liberalisation would translate into consumers buying more premium brands. However, it didn't happen as customers saved money for big-ticket items such as durables."

Emerging categories contribute almost 14%, or more than 1,000 crore, in HUL's personal care segment. Now, personal care accounts for nearly half of the firm's profits but less than a third in its total sales.

"This is the 1,000 crore that could become the 10,000-15,000 crore ten, fifteen years down the road and it's the business responsibility and strategy to really seed some of the categories," Hindustan Unilever Chairman and Unilever COO Harish Manwani said at the time of the firm's annual results.

HUL's upscale drive is not restricted to personal products, which has seen faster rollouts of new brands or categories.

Its largest segment, laundry, which has historically seen several instances of price wars in the mass and mid-priced segments, is being upgraded as well. The firm launched its most expensive laundry product, Surf Excel liquid detergent, earlier this month. It also launched Comfort One Rinse watersaving fabric conditioner and entered fabric blues segment with Rin Perfect Shine in the last six quarters.

In the foods category — which accounts for more than half of the Anglo-Dutch multinational's sales but less than a fifth of its Indian arm — Hindustan Unilever's push for premium products included launch of Magnum ice cream and Lipton iced tea. In personal care, it brought in TRESemme hair care range and extended Lux into deodorant and Dove into hair oil.

However, Hindustan Unilever with operating margin of 20.2% still trails some of its global rivals such as Colgate and Nestle that boast of higher margins as their portfolios are skewed towards premium offerings. Colgate, the market leader in oral care, reported an operating margin of 22.3% while Nestle had 22%. HUL's margin is, however, still higher than those of homegrown companies such as Godrej Consumers, Britannia, Dabur and Marico.

These goods are of low unit value with high volume potential and require frequent repurchase. In 2013, the market size was Rs. 2.2 lakh-crore in India. The top 10 companies in the FMCG sector are Hindustan Unilever Limited (HUL), ITC, Nestle India, Amul, Dabur, Asian Paints, Cadbury India, Britannia Industries, Procter & Gamble and Marico Industries. Other leading companies in this segment are Reckitt Benckiser, GlaxoSmithKline, Pepsi, Coke, Himalaya, Bajaj, Godrej etc.

Apple iPOD

Now there is a new subset of FMCG called **Fast Moving Consumer Electronics (FMCE)**, which include innovative electronic products like MP3 players, mobile phones and digital cameras. These are replaced more frequently than other electronic products.

2. **Consumer Durables:** On the contrary, Consumer durables are low volume products with high per unit value. It is also known as **White Goods or Brown Goods**. White

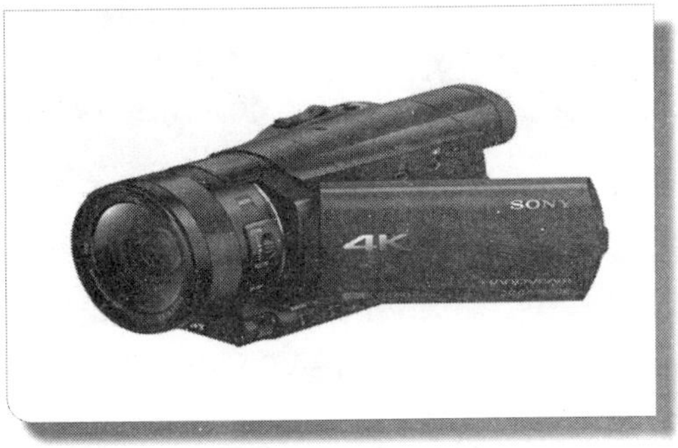

Sony Camcorder

goods include Refrigerators, Freezers, Washing Machines, Dishwashers, Microwaves etc; while Brown **goods** include TVs, DVD players, Home Theatres, Camcorders, Game consoles like Microsoft ZBox 360, Sony Playstation, Nintendo WI, personal computers etc. When the goods are not classified as White goods or brown goods, then it is called white goods on the whole, which also includes household electronics items, earlier categorised under brown goods.

3. **Soft Goods:** Soft goods are relatively priced higher than the FMCGs and lesser than the consumer durables. These goods are also low volume in nature, as it requires a shorter replacement cycle. For examples - Clothing Material, Apparels, Shoes etc.

Belmonte

4. **Yellow Goods:** Besides white and brown goods, there is another not so popular classification of Yellow Goods. Yellow Goods include material for construction and earth moving equipment, fork lift trucks and quarrying equipment. The term is also used for agricultural equipment like tractors.

JCB

Speed Post Service by India Post

Services: Beside the goods, consumer markets also require a lot of services. Goods are physical, tangible articles, while Services are non physical and intangible in nature. Services can also satisfy a need like goods. Financial services, Banking, Telecom, DTH, Courier, Hotel, Airline, Multiplex, Train, Doctors, Lawyers, Healthcare and Management Consultancy are all examples of services. Services require an additional set of marketing mix tools than the goods market like people, process and physical evidence, besides the 4Ps - product, price, place and promotion.

Consumer Behaviour

To understand the consumer market, it is very important to understand the behaviour of the consumer.

Consumer Behaviour is defined as the behaviour that consumers, whether it's an individual or, group or, a business organization, display in searching for, purchasing, using, evaluating and disposing of products and services that they expect will satisfy their needs.[3]

The principles of Consumer Behaviour lead to the development and implementation of marketing strategies. Now the consumers are also influenced by the new media like Internet, Search Engines, E-Commerce oriented websites etc.

Consumer Behaviour focuses on how individual make decisions to spend their available resources (time, money, effort) on consumption related items. That includes what they buy, why they buy it, when they buy it, where they buy it, how often they buy it, how often they use it, how they evaluate it after the purchase, the impact of such evaluations on future purchases and how they dispose of it.[4]

As an individual, everybody is unique. But everybody use or consume products or services on a regular basis. Marketers need to understand the personal and group influences that affect consumer decisions and they also need to understand, how these decisions are made. In fact, Consumer Behaviour and the decision making process is Interdisciplinary. It's a relatively new field of study started in the mid to late 1960s. There is no history or body of research of its own. It depends heavily on the concepts developed in other scientific disciplines such as Psychology (the study of the individual), Sociology (the study of groups), social psychology (the study of how an individual operates in groups), anthropology (the influence of the society on the individual) and economics.

Consumers don't always buy to maximise their benefits. Sometimes, they are also likely to purchase impulsively. They are influenced not only by family and friends, by advertisers and role models, but also by mood, situation and emotion. All these factors combine to form a comprehensive model of consumer behaviour that reflects both the cognitive and emotional aspects of consumer decision making.

Factors influencing Consumer Behaviour

A consumer's buying behaviour is influenced by culture, social and personal and Psychological factors.

Cultural Factors

A consumer's behaviour is largely shaped by his culture, subculture and social class. It has got the deepest influence on a consumer. Culture is a society's personality including language, knowledge, laws, religions, food customs, music, art, technology, work patterns, products; that give a society its distinct flavour. It is the sum total of learned beliefs, values and customs that serve to direct the consumer behaviour of members of a particular society. Beliefs and values are guides for consumer behaviour. Beliefs consist of the very large number of mental or verbal statements – I believe…, that reflect a person's particular knowledge and assessment of something (another person, a store, a product, a brand).[5]

Consumers both view themselves in the context of their culture and react to their environment based upon the cultural framework that they bring to the experience. Each individual perceives the world through his own cultural lens. For example, In the northern part of India, people generally prefer tea, while in USA, Americans prefer coffee. Similarly in Punjab, people eat more rotis than rice; while in southern India, people prefer more rice preparations. In the case of USA, it becomes bread for them.

Each culture consists of smaller sub cultures. Distinct cultural group that exists as an identifiable segment within a larger, more complex society / culture is called subculture. Subculture can be categorized on the basis of nationality (Birthplace of Ancestors), religion, geographical region, race, age, gender, occupation and social class.

A marketer needs to be aware of different needs for products, different patterns of usage and preference for certain brands. In different subcultures, advertising-media habits may be different. In turn, it requires different media to reach different sub cultural groups. Although geographical concentration of many ethnic subcultures makes the job easier for the marketers; yet it needs to be done carefully. In some cases, it has also been found that certain groups prefer to shop in certain stores.

Social Class also influences the buying behaviour of the consumer, as they tend to associate themselves in the other members of the class. In social class, the society is divided into a hierarchy of distinct status classes, so that members of each class have relatively the same status and members of all other classes have either more or less status

Generally social class structure can contain two class systems to nine class systems. If we classify it in six classes, then it can be upper-upper, lower-upper, upper-middle, lower-middle, upper-lower and lower-lower. Socio economic differences among the classes are reflected in differences in attitudes, in leisure activities and in consumption habits. This helps the marketer in understanding the customers better.

Marketing Research Society of India (MRSI) has divided India's population on the basis of urban area and rural area. MRSI has divided urban Area into eight socio economic groups based on education and occupation. These classifications are:

Urban Area Social Economic Classification	
SEC	**Description**
A1, A2	Graduates, White Coller Workers, Professionals
B1, B2	SSC Qualified, SSC, 40% Graduates, Clerical and Shopkeepers
C, D	Skilled Workers, Clerks, Salespersons
E1, E2	Unskilled Labour

Similarly, MRSI has divided rural area into four social economic classifications on the basis of education and type of house.

Rural Area Social Economic Classification	
SEC	**Description**
R1	Graduates, Pucca House
R2	Graduates, Semi Pucca House
R3	Graduates, Kuccha House
R4	SSC / Iliiterate, Kuccha House

Now, in a bid to keep pace with the fast-evolving economic outlook, consumer attitudes and preferences in the country, this system has been revamped on 3rd May, 2011 by the Media Research Users' Council (MRUC) and the Market Research Society of India (MRSI) have unveiled a new Socio-Economic Classification (SEC) system.

The new Socio-Economic Classification (SEC) system is used to classify households in India. It's based on two variables:

- Education of chief wage earner and
- Number of "consumer durables" (from a predefined list)-owned by the family. The list has 11 items, ranging from 'electricity connection' and 'agricultural land'-to cars and air conditioners. These are :

Based on the above two parameters, each household are classified in one of 12 SEC groups—A1, A2, A3, B1, B2, C1, C2, D1, D2, E1, E2 and E3. These 12 groups are applicable to both urban and rural India. The top-most new SEC class A1 comprises of 0.5% of all Indian households. Nearly 2% of urban households and less than 0.1% of rural households belong to the new SEC A1. More than half of all SEC A1 households reside in the top six Indian cities—Delhi, Mumbai, Kolkata, Chennai, Bengaluru and Hyderabad. At the other end of the spectrum, the bottom-most new SEC class E3 comprises of 10% of all Indian households. Only 2% of urban households and 13% of rural households belong to new SEC E3. Nearly 93% of all SEC E3 households are in rural India.

Social Factors

Consumer buying behaviour is also affected by reference groups and family.

- **Reference Group:** Any person or group that serves as a point of comparison (or reference) for an individual in forming either general or specific values, attitudes or a specific guide for behaviour. These reference groups serve as frames of reference for individuals in their purchase or consumption decisions.[6]

Reference groups can be divided into three types:

a. Normative reference groups: that influence general or broadly defined values or behaviour are called: Child and Family; influences the development of a basic code of behaviour

b. Comparative reference groups: that serve as benchmarks for specific or narrowly defined attitudes or behaviour : neighbouring family; influences the expression of specific consumer attitudes and behaviour

c. Indirect reference groups: Those individuals or groups with whom a person does not have direct face to face contact, such as movie stars, sports heroes, political leaders, TV personalities

The degree of influence that a reference group exerts on an individual's behaviour usually depends on the nature of the individual and the product and on specific social factors. Selected Consumer Related Reference Groups are friendship groups, shopping groups – purchase pals, work groups – colleagues, virtual groups or communities – Brand Communities and consumer action groups.

Kellogg's Tony the Tiger

There can be five major types of reference group appeals. These are celebrities, experts like Automobile mechanic, common Man – Testimonials, executive and employee spokesperson and trade spokes chapter like Kellogg's Tony the Tiger, Vodafone's Zoozoo and McDonalds' Ronald.

- **Family:** For many consumers, their family is their primary reference group for many attitudes and behaviour. Family is the prime target for many product and product categories. Two or more persons related by blood, marriage or adoption; who resides together is called family. It may be married couples or nuclear families or extended families. Socialisation is a core function of the family, besides other functions like economic and emotional support and the pursuit of a suitable lifestyle for its members. The key consumer related roles of family members include – influencers (provides info), gatekeepers (controls info), deciders, buyers, preparers (transform the product), users, maintainers (service or repairs) and disposers (disposal or discontinuation). A family consumption decisions is often influenced by its lifestyle, roles and cultural factors.[7]

  Family consumption decision making may be husband dominated, wife dominated or it may be joint. It can also be autonomic decisions i.e. either solitary or unilateral. In India, generally the decision is husband dominated, while in USA, it can be joint or may be solitary depending on the product. Now children also influence the family consumption decisions.

Personal Factors

Consumer buying behaviour is also influenced by age and stages in family life cycle, lifestyle, personality and self concept.

- **Age and Stages in Family Life Cycle:** The Family Life Cycle is a composite variable created by systematically combining such commonly used demographic variables as marital status, size of family, age of family members and employment status of the head of household. Traditional and non traditional family cycle may throw different opportunities for a marketer.

  Secondshaadi.com

  A marketer should also consider major life events like marriage, divorce, birth, relocation, job change; which may open up space for new needs. While a marriage may require the services of a marriage planner; it may also bring lots of purchases for apparels and appliances front. Divorce has opened up vistas for sites like secondshaadi.com to the services of a lawyer. Job change and relocation has created opportunities for packers and movers company like Agarwal packers and movers.

Agrawal Packers & Movers

- **Lifestyle:** Lifestyle is another personal factor, which influences the behaviour of the consumer. Lifestyle is a person's day to day pattern of living in this world. This wholesome pattern of living is expressed in terms of activities, interests and opinions, which is also known as AIO framework. It is important for a marketer to link the lifestyle of a person to the products and brands. Generally, the marketers try to project the brand personality, which imitates the target consumer personality. Once you hear about Nike (Athlete in all of us), Reebok (Success / Cricket), Levi's (American, Real and Authentic, Rugged) and Shoppers Stop (Exclusivity, Individuality); it sounds you something. The brand personality is also endorsed by the celebrity, whose personality matches the consumer's persona. That's why Akshay Kumar advertises for Levi's, while M. S. Dhoni and Bipasha advertises for Reebok.

Reebok

Marketing Insight 5.2

PepsiCo bats for IPL, Coke votes for Polls

Pepsi

NEW DELHI: As the BCCI continues to negotiate with the home ministry to keep the forthcoming IPL at home in the first week of May, when seven out of the nine phases of the election will be over, the world's largest beverage giants PepsiCo and Coca-Cola are keenly watching the space. While it is no secret that Pepsi — the title sponsor of IPL — is unhappy with the proposal of shifting the IPL to UAE or even Bangladesh, its archrival Coca-Cola is readying an aggressive sampling and distribution plan for its soft drinks, with a special focus on the 2014 general elections beginning next month.

"For beverage companies, festivals are a great way to push sales. And, it doesn't get any bigger than the festival of democracy," says Venkatesh Kini, head of Coca-Cola India, while hinting at the upcoming Lok Sabha polls.

The Atlanta-based company is trying out new models starting with its 'Happiness on the go' innovation. It has ordered hundreds of trucks that can be quickly mobilized to offer 100-150 ml beverages in cups at Rs 5 each and 200-300 ml at Rs 8-10. Each truck has the capacity to serve up to 10,000 people at once, according to company executives. "These can be sent to political rallies, melas or any large gatherings at very short notice," says Kini.

Coca-Cola

Coca-Cola's advertising sports a distinct rural flavour too, with actors Farhan Akhtar and Deepika Padukone speaking in rural dialects. Keeping in mind its rural focus, Coca-Cola executives had deliberately roped in Anurag Kashyap of Gangs of Wasseypur fame to direct the ads.

The other innovation Kini is betting on to bolster Coca-Cola's sales is a stationary dispenser (like dispenser for water) at retail points that does not require an expensive set-up. For instance, a two-litre bottle can be placed on top of a dispenser through which beverages can be served chilled in smaller cups of 100-150 ml. "These can be placed at small retail outlets," he says.

Rural markets account for one-third of the total sales of Coca-Cola. Going by urbanization trends in India, this contribution is likely to go up to 45%. Coca-Cola is present in 2.2 million outlets in the country and nearly half of them are in rural areas. So, Kini is leaving no stones unturned to capture the rural diaspora, especially during election rallies and meetings or marriages in peak summer.

PepsiCo, on the other hand, will rely heavily on distributing their products in-stadia and outside the stadia, during the IPL matches that will be held in India. According to experts in the beverage industry, Pepsi spent nearly Rs 150 crore to fully leverage their title sponsorship of the IPL last year, including the per year title sponsorship fee paid to BCCI. It sold 2 million cups of its beverages at stadiums and gained Rs 927 crore of media value according to Repucom, a sports marketing research firm. However, despite some matches being shifted to UAE, PepsiCo officials are optimistic about repeating a similar success this year as well.

"We expect to get 10 times the derived media value for our investment this year irrespective of where the tournament is held," a PepsiCo spokesperson told TOI.

The study of lifestyle is called psychographics. Psychographic can also be understood in American context through Sri Consulting – Business Intelligence (SRIC-BI) VALS (Values and Lifestyle) Model Framework. VALS is based on 4 demographic factors (Sex, Age, Education and Income) and 35 Attitudinal Questions (I am often interested in theories / I like a lot of variety in my life / I like to learn about art, culture, and history….) to profile the consumers. The VALS framework divides the American adults into eight typologies under two categories - higher resources and lower resources. Higher resources include Innovators, Thinkers, Achievers and Experiencers and lower resources include Believers, Strivers, Makers and Survivors. Although the framework is not very useful in Indian context; but it can give an insight and can be modified to suit the Indian environment. Titan, the topmost watch brand in India, offers different watches under sub brands like Octane, Orion, Edge, Heritage, WWF Collection etc to target the different psychographic customer base.

- **Personality and Self Concept:** Personality refers to the inner psychological characteristics that both determine and reflect how a person responds to his or her environment.[8] There are three distinct personality properties:

  - Personality reflects individual differences
  - Personality is consistent and enduring
  - Personality can change by major life events

  The difference in personality traits creates opportunities for different brands. That's why, we use the term brand personality; where the brand is personified with the specific mix of human traits and even gender also. The brand personality then attracts people with the similar personality traits. If Nike is about athlete in all of us, Reebok is about success factor and cricket in India; while Levi's is truly American, real, authentic and rugged. Similarly youth channel - UTV Bindaas has created a brand personality through its campaign 'What I Am', which is cool, rebellious yet responsible. This shows in their fresh and youthful programming also, which has been hit among the youth. Programs like Emotional Atyachaar, Dadagiri, Love Lockup, Date Trap etc. have made this channel India's no. 1 youth channel.

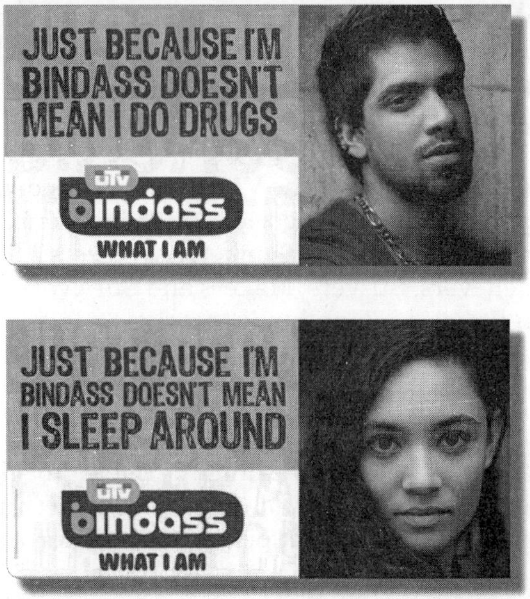

UTV Bindaas – India's no.1 youth channel

There is also a correlation between the product personality and colour. If Eveready is represented by red, generally fast food items use more of red and yellow. Every colour has a different meaning. Red represents exciting, hot and strong, while black means power, authority, mystery; white stands for goodness and purity, yellow for caution and novelty. Blue commands respect, authority, while green is secure, natural and relaxed.

Marketing Insight 5.3

Marketing Insight 5.3

Natural Selection

How CEO Philipe Haydon is turning The Himalaya Drug Company into a FMCG major

Nine years ago, The Himalaya Drug Company quietly launched a dental cream which went on to attain quite a cult following. The product wasn't advertised or widely distributed and fans had to hunt it down in select stores in cities like Mumbai, which was possibly part of the allure. The herbal formulation was developed by the company's late founder Mohammed Manal and legend has it that he left it in powder form, since he had no access to the binding technology that went into the making of tooth paste. It was his son Meraj who turned the powder into earthy brown toothpaste, the colour of Himalaya's herbal drugs.

Himalaya

This year, Himalaya finally retired the stodgy old dental cream and replaced it with a range of four new-age toothpastes — total care, whitening, gel, sensitive — which will be backed with heavy-duty advertising. That's just the beginning. The ayurvedic drug company is now planning to relaunch its full range of soaps, shampoos, lotions and creams, thereby transforming itself into a mainstream FMCG player. "That's where the growth is," says CEO Philipe Haydon. "Personal care touches many more lives. You don't have to be unwell to use toothpaste. In five years, this division will overtake our pharma operations."

Though it accounts for 40% of the company's Rs 1,200 crore annual turnover, personal care has traditionally played second fiddle to pharma at Himalaya. That changed last year, when Nielsen declared Himalaya Neem Face Wash to be number one in its category, with 18% share in a Rs 900 crore market, ahead of Fair&Lovely, Pond's and Dove from the Unilever stable. Himalaya was a first mover in face washes in 2006 and the category now constitutes half of its personal care portfolio. This success has brought home the power of brand building and the company is now ready to invest more on advertising. "We still have to be very focused on the brands we invest on. As a private company, we don't have deep pockets. I'm allocating money from pharma to build our FMCG brands. But you can be sure I'll take it all back from them soon," says Haydon.

Himalaya's rock star CEO (he plays the guitar in a band called Ministry of Blues in Bangalore) has spent nearly all his career in its pharma division, so the strategic shift can't be without heartburn. He uses a sports metaphor to compare the two business models, saying "Pharma is a contact sport, where the medical rep and doctor engage one-on-one. Personal care is like sailing, where advertising provides the wind."

One sign that big changes are afoot in any organization is the recruitment of outsiders at the top. In Himalaya, it takes the form of Rajesh Krishnamurthy, former marketing director at Colgate Palmolive, who joined nine months ago as the head of the consumer products division. With annual sales of Rs 3,000 crore, Colgate accounts for 52% of the Indian toothpaste market, so everyone's hoping Krishnamurthy might create similar magic at Himalaya. How is he handling such great expectations? "The product had already been developed before I came on board," he says, by way of deflecting some of the burden. "My mandate is to establish Himalaya in the toothpaste market, where consumers are brand loyal. We're working on a smart, stage-by-stage brand building strategy. One lesson from Colgate is that you need to have steady, consistent investment in brand building."

Krishnamurthy is not just a toothpaste man. A graduate of the Asian Institute of Management, Manila, he spent 15 years with Colgate in Malaysia, Thailand and then Venezuela, where the company has a wide product range that includes detergent, soap, shampoo and dish wash. Even as he goes about building the Himalaya toothpaste brand, Krishnamurthy is also defending the company's hard won leadership position in face wash. "We can't afford to take our eyes off this category. We intend to stay number one by introducing new variants, new packaging and expanding distribution," he says.

One weakness of Himalaya's consumer product division has been distribution, which has tended to be skewed towards organized retail and urban medical stores, where its pharma products have traditionally found shelf space. The company also has 125 exclusive Himalaya stores, mainly in tourism hot-spots where the brand has considerable traction among foreigners. But toothpaste is a category that is sold largely through grocery shops, a highly competitive mode of distribution where only in-demand brands find shelf space. "We can't survive on pharmacies, which account for just 15% of toothpaste sales in the country," says Krishnamurthy. "Himalaya Neem is now available in 4.5 lakh urban grocery outlets, thanks to the consumers pull it has generated. So we will piggy back our toothpaste on the face wash wherever we can."

Psychological Factors

Consumers are also influenced by psychological factors. These factors drive the reason for buying, that's why it is also termed as 'why' of buying. A person's buying behaviour is influenced by following major psychological processes.

- **Motivation:** Motivation is the driving force within individuals which impels them to act. This driving force is produced by a state of uncomfortable tension, which exists as the result of an unsatisfied need. Some needs are primary needs, also known as innate needs, which are physiological (biogenic) in nature. These needs include all the factors required to sustain physical life i.e. food, water, clothing, shelter, sex and physical safety. Other needs are secondary needs, which are acquired needs. These needs are developed in individuals after their birth. These are primarily psychological, which include love, acceptance, esteem and self fulfillment.[9]

Motivation is a highly dynamic construct that is constantly changing in reaction to life experiences. Rational motives can be economic sense, while emotional motives can be pride, fear, affection, status etc. According to Henry Murray, there are 28 psychogenic needs. Although everyone has the same basic set of needs, but that individual differ in their priority ranking of these needs. These needs include Achievement, recognition, exhibition, affiliation, order, and dominance.

- **Maslow's Hierarchy of Needs:** Dr. Abraham Maslow formulated a widely acceptable theory of human motivation based on the notion of a universal hierarchy of human needs. According to him, there are five basic levels of human needs from biogenic to psychogenic. The theory postulates that individuals seek to satisfy lower level needs before higher level needs emerge.[10] These needs are as follows:

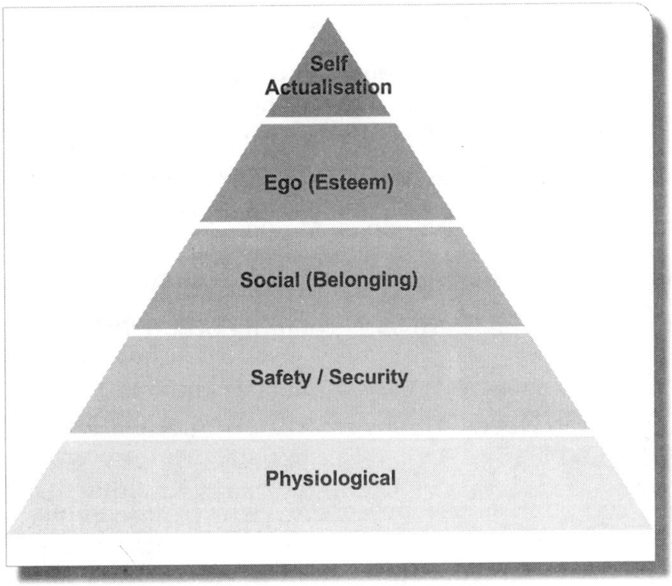

Abraham Maslow's Hierarchy of Needs

- Physiological needs: Food, Water, Air, Shelter, Sex
- Safety and Security Needs: Protection, Order, Stability (Safety, Health, Savings, Insurance, Education)
- Social Needs: Love, Affection, Friendship, Belonging
- Egoistic Needs: Inwardly directed ego (Self Esteem, success, independence, personal satisfaction) and outwardly directed ego (Prestige, Status, Recognition)
- Self Actualisation Needs: Self Fulfillment

Mercedes Benz

Men talk about women, sports and cars. Women talk about men inside sports cars.

In terms of product and services, these needs can drive demand in the following areas:

- Physiological needs: Health Foods, Medicines etc.
- Safety and Security Needs: Insurance, Mediclaim, Home Security System etc.
- Social Needs: Personal Care and grooming products, Clothes etc.
- Egoistic Needs: Big Cars, Expensive Furniture etc.
- Self Actualisation Needs: Hobby related products, adventure trips, postgraduate education etc.

- **Percception:** Perception is the process by which individuals select, organise and interpret stimuli into a meaningful and coherent picture of the world. Consumers make decisions based on what they perceive rather than on the basis of objective reality. It's all about how we see the world around us.[11] That's why product packages, brand names, ads, television commercial (TVC) etc. are used carefully in accordance with the absolute threshold, to increase the response from consumers. Generally cover page ad, use of empty space in ad, usage of yellow, ads on the floors etc. are done to cut the ad clutter and to increase the sensory input.

  On the other hand, a marketer tries to create just noticeable differences (j.n.d.), so that negative changes are not readily discernible to the public (remain below j.n.d.) and product improvements are very apparent to the customers without being wastefully extravagant (at or just above the j.n.d.). Just noticeable difference is also known as differential threshold. For example, promotional offerings like Lays 20% free in the pack or Cello Pen lasts 15% longer or Parchute Oil 100 ml free are examples of j.n.d.

Lay's Potato Chips

Parachute Oil

- **Learning:** Learning is the process by which individuals acquire the purchase and consumption knowledge and experience they apply to future related behavior. Although some learning is intentional, much learning is incidental.[12] That's why, learning is very important in consumer behavior.

  Generally a company advertises its product again and again about their brand and their benefits, to fortify its brand name in the mind of the consumers. Besides the repetition, a company also uses the ability of consumers to generalize to market their products better. Due to generalisation only, all the products look similar in a product category. To benefit from this, Big Bazaar's own private label Tasty Treat's packaging looks almost similar to its biggest competitor and market leader Kurkure.

Tasty Treat

Kurkure

Dettol

Similarly product extensions and family branding is also used in marketing to lure the consumers as Knorr or Dove or Dettol has done in the market. Now the dettol brand is not only restricted to its popular antiseptic liquid, but has also extended to soaps, liquid handwash, body wash, shaving cream and medicated plaster.

Besides repetition and stimulus generalisation, stimulus discrimination is also used in marketing through distinct positioning efforts. Positioning is an image or position that a product or service holds in the minds of the consumer.

- **Attitude:** Attitude is defined as a favourable or unfavourable predisposition that a person holds towards an object in the environement. Attitude has three components – cognitive, affective and conative i.e. behavioural. Cognitive deals with the rational and logical evaluations, while affective deals with the emotional part. Conative deals with the action tendencies. A marketer tries to find out the attitude of a consumer towards its brand through various models like Fishbein's multi attribute model and Icek Ajzen's model of behavioural intentions. Once being aware, a marketer tries to create a favourable attitude towards its products with the help of its conception and branding through its promotional messages and themes.[13]
- **Beliefs:** Beliefs are descriptive thoughts about the products and brands in the market. These brand beliefs reside in the consumer's memory, which help them to choose the brands they like. A marketer tries to create a favourable positioning to attract the consumer. In India, World Diamond Council has tried to create a belief with its positioning 'A Diamond is Forever – Heera Hai Sada Ke Liye'.

World Diamond Council

Simplified Model of Consumer Decision Making

There are three distinct but interlocking stages in the consumer decision making process:

1. **Input Stage,**
2. **Process Stage** and
3. **Output Stage.**

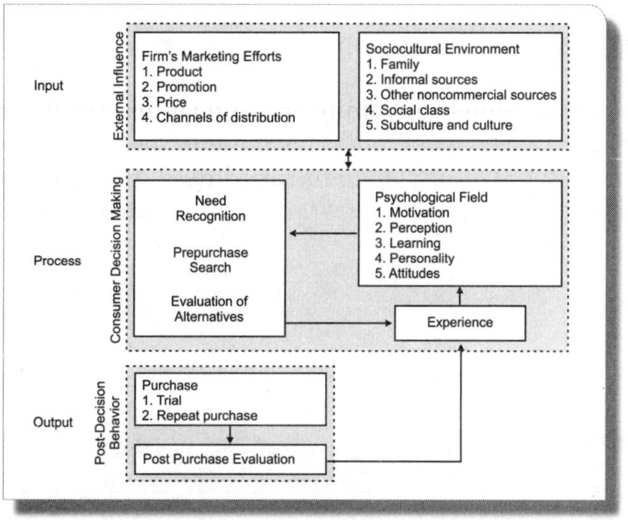

(Source: Consumer Behavior, 9/e (Paperback) By Leon G Schiffman, Leslie Lazar Kanuk)

The cumulative impact of each firm's marketing efforts, the influence of family, friends and neighbours and society's existing code of behaviour are all inputs that are likely to affect what consumers purchase and how they use what they buy.

The process stage of the model focuses on how consumers make decisions. The psychological factors inherent in each individual (motivation, perception, learning, personality and attitude) affect how the external inputs from the input stage influence the consumer's recognition of a need, pre purchase search for information and evaluation of alternatives.[14]

The experience gained through evaluation of alternatives, in turn, affects the consumer's existing psychological attributes. The output stage of the model consists of purchase behaviour and post purchase evaluation. If the consumer is satisfied, he/she will go for repeat purchase.

Consumer Buying Decision Process

The consumer buying process looks very simple from the consumers' viewpoint. But it involves a complex understanding of, who makes the buying decision to the types of buying decisions to the steps in the buying process from the marketers' viewpoint.

People generally play five roles in the buying decision. Either you can be the **'initiator'**, who put forth the idea or need for the product or service or, you can be the **'influencer'** or, you can be the '**decider**', who decides as to what is to be purchased, how is to be purchased and from where it will be purchased or, you can be the **'buyer'** making the purchase or, you can be the '**user**', who is going to consume the product or service.

Buying Behaviour

As the consumer buys a plethora of products and services right from toothpaste to a laptop to a car to an apartment, the decision for buying expensive products requires a lot of thinking and involvement.

Based on this aspect, Henry Assael has talked about four types of consumer buying based on the degree of buyer involvement and the degree of differences among brands.[15]

	High Involvement	Low Involvement
Significant Differences between Brands	**Complex Buying Behaviour**	**Variety seeking buying behaviour**
Few Differences between Brands	**Dissonance reducing Buying Behaviour**	**Habitual Buying Behaviour**

(Henry Assael, 'Consumer Behaviour and Marketing Action', Kent Publishing Co., 1987, p.87)

1. **Complex Buying Behaviour**: Complex buying behaviour happens in the case of high involvement, expensive, infrequent purchases like a car or, an apartment. Generally, there are significant differences between brands and sometimes sub brands also compete for the same consumer's attention. In the case of Rs. 3 to 4 Lacs car category, three models - Wagon R, Zen Estilo and A-Star from Maruti Suzuki compete for attention; whereas

Hyundai Grand i10

Hyundai is competing with Santro, i10 and Grand i10 in the segment. A marketer needs to differentiate its offering from the competitors' offering and position the product in such a way to influence the final decision making process of the consumer.

2. **Dissonance Reducing Buying Behaviour**: Sometimes there are little differences between the brands in the high involvement category, which leads the consumer to buy a product of his choice based on the price or his liking. After the purchase, the consumer acquires new beliefs and forms a set of attitudes. These beliefs and attitudes leads the consumer to experience the dissonance that comes from noticing that other brands would have been just as good, if not slightly better.

3. **Habitual Buying Behaviour**: Consumers have low involvement with most of the low cost, frequently purchased products sold in the market. Consumers don't spend time on deliberating over the purchase, if there are no significant differences between the brands. That's why in this category, the pricing and sales promotion schemes works in favour of the company to stimulate product trial or induce purchases.

Television advertising in this category works more than the print, because the brand beliefs are influenced by the passive learning.[16]

Marketing Insight 5.4

Marketing Insight 5.4

Growth Formula

India top revenue earner for GSK Consumer Healthcare

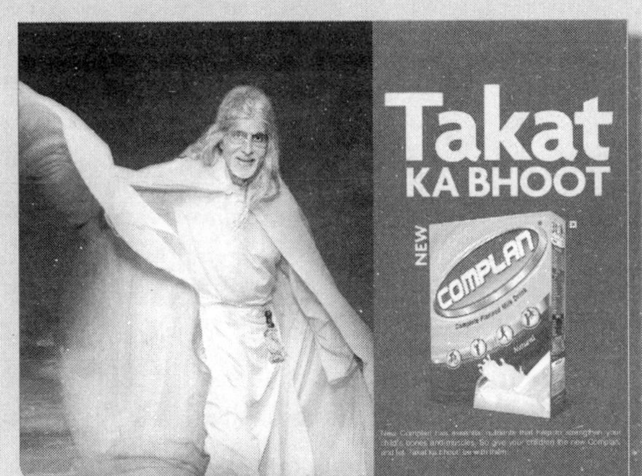

Complan

For British multinational GlaxoSmithKline Consumer Healthcare (GSKCH), India has now become the largest contributor to its global revenues, leading all emerging markets, including China, Middle East and Africa. After tasting success with its most recent venture into the oral healthcare segment in the country, the company is now pulling out all stops to boost growth by way of increasing reach and launching new products.

"The Indian unit has been growing extremely well... India contributed most to GSKCH's global growth in 2012," said Jayant Singh, executive vice-president-marketing, GSKCH.

While in India the company has largely been synonymous with its umbrella brand Horlicks, the maker of Boost, Iodex and Eno says the phenomenon is now changing. In the oral healthcare category, for instance, the company has already overtaken Colgate in the sensitive toothpaste segment with its brand Sensodyne inless than two years in modern retail outlets and pharmacies.

"Colgate has a head start in groceries. Our aim is to be present in any outlet selling toothpastes. It is just a matter of time now," Singh said. The company is evaluating launch of other products in the category from its global portfolio. With Sensodyne crossing the Rs 100 crore sales mark in India, the brand has now revised its growth target upwards of Rs 50 crore in the next three years.

In a bid to cash in on the under-penetrated sensitive oral healthcare category, the company has launched two products in less than two months in India. According to market estimates, the oral healthcare category is pegged at Rs 8,000 crore with the sensitive toothpaste segment estimated to be worth Rs 500 crore.

"The company has backed its new launches with heavy advertisements, to push its share among urban consumers. Especially in the sensitive toothpaste category, the opportunity is huge as the brand is not playing in the same segment as other companies," said Abneesh Roy, associate director, institutional equities — research, Edelweiss.

While the segment continues to be the fastest growing for GSKCH India, Singh said the company is also open to look at product extensions for brand Horlicks to capitalize on the breakfast segment. "We could expand into the ready-to-drink category for Horlicks or even snacks and muesli...but that is speculative right now. But we are already into the category and now we are only looking at how to expand," he said.

The company, which forayed into the nutritional oats category with its brand Horlicks, currently claims the third position in volume terms in the segment. Its venture into the healthy noodles category with Horlicks Foodles, however, has failed to make a mark. "Ninety percent of the noodles category is at Rs 10 price point. We do not want to play in that segment," Singh said. The company has already withdrawn the product from several markets across the country after failing to compete with Nestle's Maggi and ITC's Sunfeast Yippee.

4. **Variety Seeking Buying Behaviour:** In the case of low involvement products, when there are significant differences between the brands, consumers generally go for checking out different brands. This kind of behaviour is often found, while consumers make purchase for Biscuits and Potato Chips. The market leader tries to dominate the shelf space like Lays and Kurkure do; while the market challenger lowers the price or give more quantity like Balaji or Diamond Chips.

Stages of the Buying Decision Process

Marketing Scholars like John A. Howard, Jagdish N. Sheth, James F. engel, Roger D. Blackwell, Paul W. Miniard, Mary Frances Luce, James R. Bettman and John W. Payne, have devised a **five stage model of the buying decision process.**

The process of buying by the consumer starts long before the actual purchase and has consequences long afterward.[17]

These five stages are the following:

1. **Problem Recognition:** The buying process starts with the buyer sensing a need or a problem. The problem or need can be sensed by your internal stimuli or your external stimuli. You may be roaming in a shopping mall and may feel hungry. That leads you to the need for food. Or, you may like a Netbook at E-Zone, while roaming in the mall. In the case of food, it's the internal stimuli, while in the case of shirt; it is the influence of external stimuli, which is driving you to recognise the problem or need. Marketers try to identify and trigger your stimuli, to create an interest into their products or services, which can further be translated into purchases.

2. **Information Search**: Once you have the need or a problem, you try to search for more information regarding the product. In the case of the need for food, you may not search information, if you are familiar with the options available like McDonalds, Pizza Hut,

Apple iPad Air

KFC or a roadside dhaba etc. In case you are not familiar, then you try to search for the information. You may be longing for the recently launched Apple iPad 2. But due to non availability in Indian market, you may settle for a Netbook. Here the search for the information for a Netbook is a complicated one. Because the netbook is a costly and infrequent purchase, it gets you more involved in the purchase. You don't buy a netbook just based on the impulse. Once you identify the need, you get into the mode of heightened attention, where you become more receptive toward the information for the netbook.

Going further, you may go for active information search, where you are trying to find the information from family and friends, through mass media like Newspapers, magazines, TV or by browsing technology websites like Tech2.com or techtree.com or Thinkdigit.com or by visiting netbook showrooms or by visiting E-Zone, Croma or Jumbo stores across your city.

In any market, there are several players, who offer similar kind of products. All these brands are called **total set**. In the case of Netbook, total set consists of Asus, HP, Acer, Sony, Dell, Samsung, Lenovo, HCL, Wipro, Zenith etc. But the consumer may not be aware about all these 11 plus brands. He or she may be aware about say 7 brands - Asus, HP, Acer, Sony, Dell, HCL and Zenith. These seven brands are part of the consumer's **awareness set**. Again, the consumer may only think about HP, Acer, Sony and Dell, that becomes a part of **consideration set**. Then the consumer may strongly think about buying HP, Acer or Sony, which is a part of his or her **choice set**. Then the consumer may take the decision, which netbook to buy on the basis of the choice set.[18]

As the consumer moves from the awareness set to consideration set to choice set to the decision making, a company must leave no stones unturned to get into the consumer's awareness set first. Once they get into the awareness set, it should position the products in such a way that it makes to the final choice set and subsequently to the purchase of the product. In this respect, the fourth P of marketing – promotion is very important to communicate the right message to the right people at the right point of time.

3. **Evaluation of Alternatives:** Once the search for information is over; the consumer needs to evaluate the alternatives before he or she makes the purchase. In the case of buying salt or buying potato chips, the consumer may not think twice about a brand. But in the case of high involvement purchase like a netbook, consumer tries to evaluate all the alternatives on the basis of various benefit attributes. In buying any netbook, the varying attributes may be the processor, screen size, weight, keyboard size, battery backup, hard disk size, webcam, operating system, wireless connectivity, multimedia capability, price etc. On the basis of these attributes, the consumer will try to rank the attributes and then take the decision accordingly. For some consumers, the processor, screen size, multimedia capability, battery backup and hard disk size may be important. For others keyboard size, operating system, wireless connectivity, screen size, hard disk size and the price may be more important. Based on the individual preference, the consumer may choose the product.

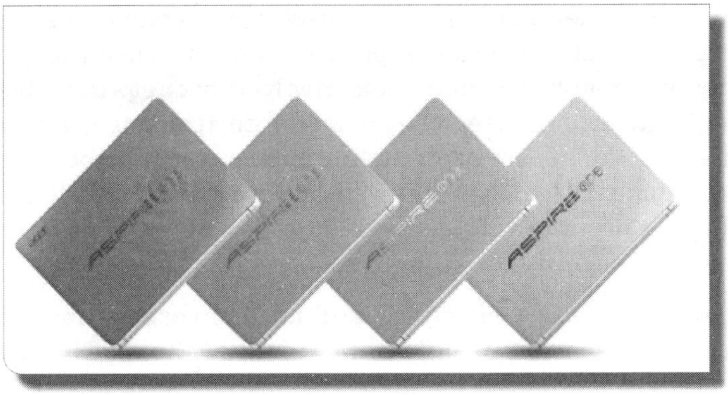

Acer Aspire One

For a company like HP or Acer, it means to provide the best combination of attributes widely applicable to the consumers. In the process, the company may emphasise more on the attributes on which they score better than their competitors. That's why Sony advertises for looks, class and quality, although the price is always higher than the competitors. Acer advertises for the best value for money netbook, while HP talks about reliability, service backup and high quality.

4. **Purchase Decision:** Based on the choice set, the consumer forms the intention to buy a certain brand. However, two factors can intervene between the purchase intention and the purchase decision.[19] These two factors are other's attitude and unanticipated situational factors. The attitude of others can be your family member, friend or acquaintance or infomediaries like Mouthshut.com, Tech2.com, Techtree.com, Amazon.com, Autocarindia.com, Zigwheels.com or some blog or a product review in newspapers and magazines. Consumers are generally influenced by these reviews. An unanticipated situational factor like losing a job or poor service by the sales person or another need becoming important, can also lead to deter you from making the purchase.

   Once a consumer has made up his mind about buying a certain product or service, he needs to decide the brand, the dealer or retailer, the quantity, purchase mode and the timing of the purchase. For buying an expensive product, besides the brand and the retailer, the consumer is more interested in knowing about the payment mode as to whether it can be made through credit card or debit card or equal monthly installment (EMI) on credit card or finance through a bank or consumer finance company like Bajaj Finance. In India, in the two-wheeler, four-wheeler and consumer electronics category, the financing mode through bank or finance company or EMI on credit card is very popular and thus important for the company.

5. **Post Purchase Behaviour:** Once you come out watching your favourite movie say Ghajini or Kites, from a multiplex, you come out telling your friend or family member that you liked the movie or you say, you disliked the movie and sometime you say it's paisa wasool. What does this mean in Marketing? This is called the post purchase

behaviour of the consumer. The behaviour results from consuming the product and the resultant satisfaction that the consumer gets. The buyer's satisfaction is a function of the closeness between the buyer's expectations and the product's perceived performance.[20] Once the buyer's satisfaction meets the perceived performance, the buyer is satisfied or the buyer is dissatisfied. In case of exceeding expectation, the buyer may be delighted. The companies should try to delight their customers. Otherwise, dissatisfied consumers will stop buying the product and take an exit option or the consumer can go for Voice option warning friends and acquaintances.[21]

Besides the post purchase use of the product, the disposal of the product is also important for the socially responsible companies like Nokia. Nokia's 'Take Back and Recycling Awareness Campaign' campaign is meant to save the environment through recycling e-waste.

Summary

- Markets can be classified on the basis of the **product** itself, or on the basis of the **end-consumer**, or both. The market is most commonly classified as following: **Consumer** Market and **Business M**arket or Industrial Market or Organizational Market.
- Consumer markets can be classified in several ways: **Fast Moving Consumer Goods** (FMCG), Consumer Durables, **Soft goods, Yellow Goods,** Services
- Consumer Behaviour is defined as the behaviour that consumers, whether it's an individual or, group or, a business organization, display in searching for, purchasing, using, evaluating and disposing of products and services that they expect will satisfy their needs.
- A consumer's buying behaviour is influenced by culture, social and personal and Psychological factors.
- Dr. Abraham Maslow formulated a widely acceptable theory of human motivation based on the notion of a universal hierarchy of human needs. According to him, there are five basic levels of human needs right from physiological, safety and security needs, social needs, egoistic needs to self actualisation needs.
- There are three distinct but interlocking stages in the consumer decision making process: Input Stage, Process Stage and Output Stage.
- The consumer buying process looks very simple from the consumers' viewpoint. But it involves a complex understanding of, who makes the buying decision to the types of buying decisions to the steps in the buying process from the marketers' viewpoint.
- Henry Assael has talked about four types of consumer buying based on the degree of buyer involvement and the degree of differences among brands. These are complex buying behaviour, dissonance reducing buying behaviour, habitual buying behaviour and variety seeking buying behavior.

- There are five stages in the buying decision process. These are: problem recognition, information search, evaluation of alternatives, purchase decision and post purchase behaviour.

Discussion Questions

1. What do you mean by consumer markets? How do you classify this market?
2. Define Consumer Behaviour. Discuss the factors influencing consumer behavior in detail.
3. Discuss the simplified model of consumer decision making.
4. Explain the consumer buying behaviour based on the degree of buyer involvement and the degree of differences among brands.
5. Discuss the five stage model of the buying decision process with examples.
6. Short Notes:
   a. Fast Moving Consumer Goods
   b. Consumer Durables
   c. Maslow's Hierarchy of Needs
   d. Information Search
   e. Dissonance Reducing Buying Behaviour
   f. Evaluation of Alternatives

References

1. Jeffrey Rayport and John Sviokla, 'Managing in the marketspace', Harvard Business Review, Nov.-Dec. 1994, p. 141-50 and 'Exploring the Virtual Value Chain', Harvard Business Review, Nov.-Dec. 1995, p. 75-85
2. Mohan Sawhney, 'Seven Steps to Nirvana', McGraw Hill, 2001
3. Leon G Schiffman, Leslie Lazar Kanuk, 'Consumer Behavior', 8/e (Paperback), Pearson, 2004
4. Leon G Schiffman, Leslie Lazar Kanuk, 'Consumer Behavior', 8/e (Paperback), Pearson, 2004
5. Leon G Schiffman, Leslie Lazar Kanuk, 'Consumer Behavior', 8/e (Paperback), Pearson, 2004
6. Leon G Schiffman, Leslie Lazar Kanuk, 'Consumer Behavior', 8/e (Paperback), Pearson, 2004

7. Leon G Schiffman, Leslie Lazar Kanuk, 'Consumer Behavior', 8/e (Paperback), Pearson, 2004
8. Leon G Schiffman, Leslie Lazar Kanuk, 'Consumer Behavior', 8/e (Paperback), Pearson, 2004
9. Leon G Schiffman, Leslie Lazar Kanuk, 'Consumer Behavior', 8/e (Paperback), Pearson, 2004
10. Leon G Schiffman, Leslie Lazar Kanuk, 'Consumer Behavior', 8/e (Paperback), Pearson, 2004
11. Leon G Schiffman, Leslie Lazar Kanuk, 'Consumer Behavior', 8/e (Paperback), Pearson, 2004
12. Leon G Schiffman, Leslie Lazar Kanuk, 'Consumer Behavior', 8/e (Paperback), Pearson, 2004
13. Leon G Schiffman, Leslie Lazar Kanuk, 'Consumer Behavior', 8/e (Paperback), Pearson, 2004
14. Leon G Schiffman, Leslie Lazar Kanuk, 'Consumer Behavior', 8/e (Paperback), Pearson, 2004
15. Henry Assael, 'Consumer Behaviour and Marketing Action', Kent Publishing Co., 1987, p.87
16. Herbert E. Krugman, 'The Impact of Television Advertising: Learning without Involvement', Public Opinion Quartely, Fall 1965, p. 349-56
17. John A. Howard and Jagdish N. Sheth, 'The Thory of Buyer Behaviour', Wiley, 1969; James F. engel, Roger D. Blackwell and Paul W. Miniard, 'Consumer Behaviour' Dryden, 1994; Mary Frances Luce, James R. Bettman and John W. Payne, 'Emotional Decisions: Trade Difficulty and Coping in Customer Choice', University of Chicago Press, 2001
18. Chem L. Narayana and Rom J. Markin, 'Consumer Behaviour and Product Performance: An alternative conceptualisation', Journal of Marketing, Oct., 1975, p.1-6; Wayne S. Desarbo and Kamel Jedidi, 'The spatial representation of Hetrogenous Consideration Sets', Marketing Science 14, No.3, pt.2, 1995, p. 326-42; Lee G. Cooper and Akihiro Inoue, 'Building Market Structures from Consumer Preferences', Journal of Marketing Research 33, No. 3, August 1996, p.293-306
19. Jagdish N. Sheth, 'An investigation of relationships among Evaluative Beliefs, Affect, Behavioural Intention and Behaviour' in John U. Farley, John A. Howard and L. Winston Rings, 'Consumer Behaviour: Theory and Application, Allyn & Bacon, 1974, pp. 89-114
20. Priscilla A. La Barbera and David Mazursky, 'A Longitudinal Assessment of Customer Satisfaction / Dissatisfaction: The Dynamic Aspect of the Cognitive Process', Journal of Marketing Research, Nov. 1983, pp.393-404
21. Albert O. Hirschman, 'Exit, Voice and Loyalty', Harvard University Press, 1970

Chapter 6

Business Markets

Chapter Structure

- Business Markets
- Defining Business Markets
- Difference between Consumer Markets and Business Market
- Business Buying Situations
- Business Buying Centre
- Business Buying Process
- *Marketing Insight 6.1: New JSW Steel Plant may Make Cars Cheaper*
- *Marketing Insight 6.2: All the Way Up*
- Summary
- Discussion Questions
- References

The decision making process by which, formal organisations establish the need for purchased products and services and identify, evaluate and choose among alternative brands and suppliers is called organisational buying."

- Webster and Wind

Business Markets

In Business market, the buying and selling takes place among businesses. It includes profit as well as not for profit businesses, government agencies (Local, State and National) and institutions (Schools, Hospitals). The business buying is quite different from consumer buying, as the buyers are well informed and a professional approach is taken up, while taking purchase decisions. Business markets include the finished goods like PCs, office furniture, raw materials and components like steel, paint, timber, plastics, steering and services like security, courier, accounting and legal services. With respect to the consumer market, the buyers and sellers in the business market are relatively small in number.

Orient Fan

Most of the times, the products and services are similar in the consumer markets and business markets like a fan or a TV or a courier service. The classification of the market depends upon the usage by the consumer or the business entity. A fan or a TV bought by a customer for his home use is a part of the consumer market, while the same brand of Fan or TV becomes a part of the business market, if it is bought by a hotel or by an educational institution.

Defining Business Markets

In Business market, the buying and selling takes place among businesses.

According to **Dwyer and Tanner, 'It include companies that consume products or services, government agencies (Local, State and National), institutions (Schools, Hospitals, Nursing Homes, Churches, Charities) and resellers.'**[1]

It is also known as **industrial marketing** or **business to business (B2B) marketing** or **Organisational Marketing**.

Webster and Wind has defined **organisational buying as the decision making process by which formal organisations establish the need for purchased products and services and identify, evaluate and choose among alternative brands and suppliers.**[2]

As far as size of the business market is concerned, 'Business marketers serve the largest market of all; the dollar volume of transactions in the industrial or business market significantly exceeds that of the ultimate consumer market.' For example, companies such as GE, DuPont and IBM spend more than **$60** million a day on purchases to support their operations.[3]

GE

Dwyer and Tanner has also stated that the purchases made by companies, government agencies and institutions **'account for more than half of the economic activity in industrialized countries such as the United States, Canada and France.'**[4]

Although the business market is bigger than the consumer market, yet only consumer market is seen and heard by you. It is because consumer market rely more on advertising and promotions to reach to its millions of consumers. While, in business markets, the number of buyers and sellers are quite small with respect to consumer market. For example - If you take into account the tyre suppliers to an automobile company like Maruti Suzuki in India. Then Maruti Suzuki will source five tyres (four for the car and one for the reserve stepney) for every car, it manufactures. The sourcing of tyres can be done from any one of the six leading manufacturers of tyres (Apollo, Bridgestone, Goodyear, JK, Ceat and MRF). On the whole, there are just 16 leading car manufacturing companies (Hindustan Motors, Maruti Suzuki, Hyundai, Chevrolet, Tata Motors, Ford, Skoda, Mahindra &

Mahindra, Renault, Fiat, Volkswagen, Nissan, Honda, Toyota, Mercedes and BMW) in India . The business market equation is 16 automobile companies sourcing tyres from 6 tyre manufacturers.

Apollo Tyres

MRF Typres

In this respect, the market becomes quite small to be targeted easily on a company to company basis. In turn, it also nullifies the need for advertising and promotions. That's why business market is not seen and heard, yet it generates more business than the consumer market. In the same tyre market, all the tyre companies need to advertise and promote their product heavily for the replacement market of the tyres, which is also called aftermarket.

Difference between Business Market and Consumer Market

Business market is very different from the consumer market with fewer large buyers. It leads to close supplier buyer relationship. The business buying requires a professional approach than the consumer buying, as the buyers are well informed. There are several buying influences right from the technical experts to sourcing people to the senior management. Several buying influences lead to multiple sales calls to close the deal. Generally the buyers are concentrated in a specific geographical area like most of the automobile companies are concentrated in and around Gurgaon, Pune, Chennai and Pantnagar region in Uttarakhand.

The demand in consumer market tends to be a direct demand, while the demand in the business market is a derived demand, which is based on the consumer demand. For example, the major demand for tyres in the business market depends upon the demand of cars by the consumers. The demand in the business market is also inelastic in nature, as the price difference in tyres will not affect the demand of tyres. It is also fluctuating in nature, as the demand is based on the consumer demand and is influenced by market sentiments.

Buying Situations

Patrick Robinson, Charles Faris and Yoram Wind are of the view that there are **three types of buying situation** in the business market: **straight rebuy, modified rebuy and new task.**[5]

1. **Straight Rebuy**: When an order is placed on a routine basis, then it's a case of straight rebuy. The product or services required are already known with the approved list of suppliers.
2. **Modified Rebuy**: If there is a modification in the regular order with respect to product specification, delivery requirement, pricing, service requirement, then it becomes a case of modified rebuy.
3. **New Task**: When there is a new requirement in the business like software, office space, security system, waste disposal system, water purification system etc., then it becomes a case of new task. Depending upon the complexity, the decision process can take days to months together.

For a marketer in the business buying process, the new task is very crucial; as it entails a great marketing opportunity for the marketer as well as a challenge for the buying organisation.

Buying Centre

Many people are involved in the process of decision making in business buying, as it is a complex as well as professional exercise.

Webster and Wind has called these decision making unit in the buying organization as **Buying Centre.** It consists of **'all those individuals and groups who participate in the purchasing decision making process, who share some common goals and the risks arising from the decisions.'**[6]

The buying centre includes the employees, who play any of the following seven roles in the purchase decision process:

1. **Initiators** demand the products, which initiates the process of buying.
2. **Users** are those people, who use the product. They may also help in defining the requirement.
3. **Infuencers** influences the decision making process. In case of technical products, the technical experts influence the decisions heavily.
4. **Deciders** decide the product requirement and supplier.
5. **Approvers** approve the decision made by the deciders.
6. **Buyers** formally authorise the purchase decision by finalising the supplier, payment terms and delivery schedule.
7. **Gatekeepers** are small people in the business organization, who can make a big difference in marketing your product. Receptionists, Telephone Operators, Personal Assistants may prevent the sales people from contacting the purchase people.

Business Buying Process

Patrick Robinson, Charles Faris and Yoram Wind have suggested **eight stages in the business buying process** and they have termed it as the **eight buyphases.**[7] As the business marketing process is complicated than the consumer marketing, it needs three more stages than the consumer marketing to complete the decision making process. Those eight stages are as follows:

1. **Problem Recognition**: The starting stage of business buying process is the same as consumer buying. In the same way, the problem can be recognized through the internal or external stimuli in the businesses. Externally the buyer can be influenced by the technological improvements in various product or service categories or processes involved in production. Internally, it may require the routine supplies.

2. **General Need Description**: Most of the time, business buyer deals with the technical products or services, which leads to defining the general need description with the required quantity.

3. **Product Specification**: Besides the general need description, the product specifications should be clearly written. It helps the company to zero in the right supplier with best matching parameters. There is a method called Product Value analysis (PVA) to reduce the cost of components by standardizing or by redesigning or by changing the methods of production in the manufacturing companies. PVA has been a great help in containing the cost of Tata Nano and Bajaj Discover, besides being a regular feature in day to day production process in every manufacturing plant.

Bajaj Discover

4. **Supplier Search**: Buying a broiler and buying a boiler are two different things and so is the search for suppliers. If you want to buy a broiler, you can go to any chicken shop; but if you want to buy a boiler, you need to do a supplier search. In the last fifteen years, the market has changed a lot due to globalization and the advancement in communication technologies like Internet and Mobile technology. Now suppliers are searched all across the world with the help of Internet.

   Various websites are helping you out in finding the right supplier for your company. These websites can be grouped under Industry centric Vertical Hubs like Plastics.com for the plastic industry, Sciquest.com for the life sciences, E-Steel.com for Steel, Imxexchange.com for Mortgages and business function centric functional hubs, MRO.com for maintenance, repair, and operating procurement, Employease.com for employee benefits administration and Celarix.com for global logistics monitoring and tracking. In India, Indiamart.com, Indianyellowpages.com, seekandsource.com and Wipro's 01markets.com are leading business to business (B2B) website.

Hong Kong based Alibaba.com is the world's largest online B2B marketplace. It has a community of more than 42 million registered users from more than 240 countries and regions.

Besides the vertical and functional hubs, a company like Dell has set up a direct extranet links to major suppliers. Coca Cola, Pepsi, Gillette, P&G, Sara Lee, Kraft and many other companies have created a buying alliance called Transora to get the lower prices for their various raw materials. Similarly, Covisint looks after the procurement of raw material and component for automotive companies like Ford, General Motors and Daimler Chrysler and Health Care Companies. These companies also have their own company buying sites like General Electric has with the Trading Process Network.

5. **Proposal Solicitation**: The proposals are sought by the business buyer for the various products and services. In the case of buying by the government market, there is the process of tender, request for prequalification and then Shortlisting of bidders happen. These bids are shortlisted on the basis of technical and commercial proposal. Directorate General of Supplies and Disposals, widely known as DGS&D is the central purchasing organisation of the government of India including Railways and Defense. Sometimes global tenders are also invited by the government.

IndianOil Technip

Refineries Division HQ., New Delhi

GLOBAL NOTICE INVITING TENDER

(International Competitive Bidding)

NIT No. / Name of Work	Sale Period/Submission Date
LSN/00785/018N/MR/1011/01/1008 Design, Engineering, Manufacturing, Testing and Supply of Heat Pump Compressor with steam turbine to IOCL's Mathura Refinery for FCCU AND PRU Revamp Project at Mathura. U.P. India. Cost of Bid documents - not applicable	23.11.2010 to 07.12.2010 (Both Days inclusive) Submission date: 21.12.2010 Upto 2.30 PM Last date of receipt of Bidder's Queries: 10.12.2010 EMD: Indian Bidder - INR 16.75 Lac Foreign Bidder-USD 37033

Contact Persons: Mr. L.S. Nagi / Mr. D.K. Dogra, Procurement Section, M/s TECHNIP KT INDIA LIMITED, A-4, Sector-1, Noida-201301, India Ph. 0120-4301445 / 4301487, Email: lsnagi@technip.com, dkdogra@technip.com

Visit : www.indianoiltenders.com for more details.

Global Tender

6. **Supplier Selection**: Just like the evaluation of alternatives, the suppliers are ranked on the basis of various attributes.

> **Anderson, Jain and Chintagunta** did a study and came out with a method called **Customer Value Assessment (CVA).** CVA uses **eight methods to assess customer value like internal engineering assessment; field value in use assessment, focus group value assessment, direct survey questions, conjoint analysis, benchmarks, compositional approach and importance ratings.**[8]

Sometimes, the companies may use a simpler approach to supplier selection, when the products or services are not of high value. But in most of the cases, the selection of suppliers is complex.

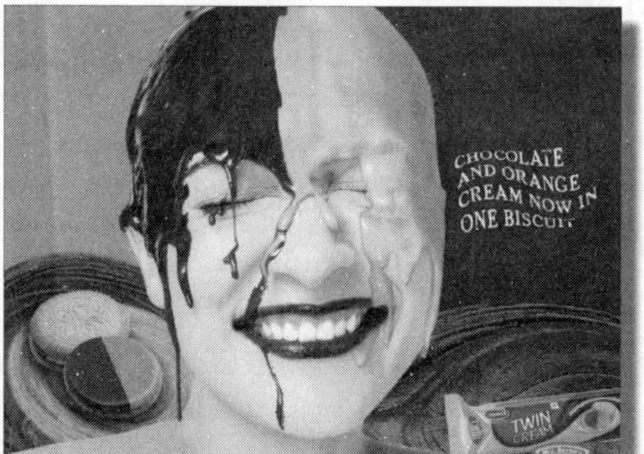

Cremica Bakery Products

McDonald's

In the case of McDonald's India also, the selection of suppliers for products like dairy and bakery products was not that easy. After a lot of quality checks and deliberations, it chose Dynamix dairy for its dairy product requirements and Cremica for its bakery and liquid products.

7. **Order-Routine Specification**: In business buying, there is a closer relationship between the buyer and the supplier. Once the supplier is finalised, a blanket contract is established with the supplier, as there will be a lot of straight rebuy or modified rebuy. These stockless purchase plans helps the company to source the products easily from the suppler, as and when it is required.
8. **Performance Review**: The success of any business also depends upon the performance of the supplier. The buyer routinely checks the performance of the supplies and decides to continue, modify or to end the business relationship with the supplier.

All the above eight stages are required in the new task situation. But in the cases of straight rebuy and modified rebuy, the stages - supplier search, proposal solicitation and supplier selection may not be required.

Marketing Insight 6.1

New JSW Steel Plant may Make Cars Cheaper

BELLARY: Your dream sedans and SUVs are expected to become lot more cheaper by next year as the imported steel used in manufacturing these cars will be made locally available by Bellary based JSW steel.

On Wednesday, the steel major formally announced the commissioning of its state-of-the-art Cold Roll Mill (CRM-2) plant to manufacture high-end products like automotive grade steel at its Vijayanagar plant in Toranagallu, about 350 km from Bangalore.

This is the first such facility in the country to manufacture outer body panels for passenger cars.

The 2.3 million tonne auto-grade steel manufacturing plant will be formally inaugurated by JSW steel chairman Sajjan Jindal on Friday and it will be attended by who is who of automotive industry.

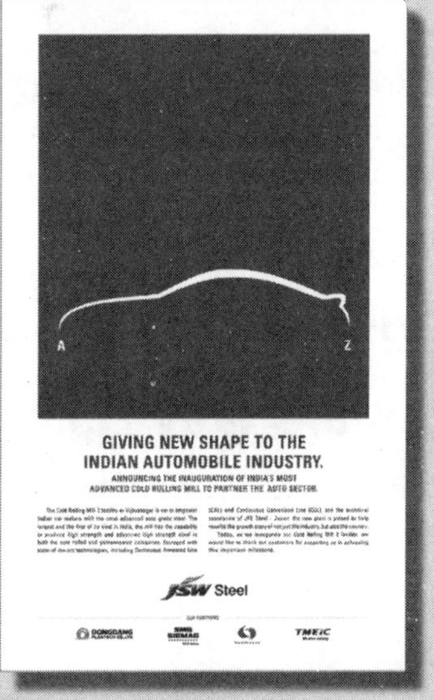

JSW Steel

"With India on road to becoming a global hub for automobiles, the demand for high end steel is likely to see an exponential growth. Keeping this in view, we have set up the new plant equipped with latest technology to produce continuously annealed cold rolled coils (up to a strength level of 980 megapascal) which was hitherto imported from other countries," said Vinod Nowal, deputy managing director, JSW steel.

He said the the new facility will benefit the car manufacturers and end buyers as the production cost of cars, SUVs, two-wheelers and home appliances will come down by about 10-15 percent by way of savings on freights, foreign exchange among other expenses. The cutting down on production cost would also provide a major relief to the automotive industry, which is reeling under negative sales growth, he said.

"Japanese car manufacturers Nissan and Honda have already shown keen interest in placing order to manufacture their SUVs in India. We expect more full-fledged orders from car makers by end of this year as more approvals are awaited," Nowal added. JSW steel has collaborated with Japanese steel major JFE for setting up CRM-2, which has a 15% stake in JSW steel with an investment of Rs 4,500 crore.

Presently, carmakers import about 20% of high quality steel from the estimated 4 million tonnes of auto-grade steel used for making outer body panels in India.

With the launch of the new facility, JSW hopes to meet at least 15% of the demand of automobile industry for high-end products including dual-phase steel and strip steel. JSW Steel already manufactures automotive steel for underbody parts and supplies to car manufacturers. The company earlier had invested Rs 1,150 crore to set up the 1 million tonne CRM plant, which is operational past few years. The new CRM-2 will manufacture exclusively outer body panels for cars and SUVs.

"For the last one year, we are working with car makers like Honda, Maruti, Toyota, Ford and Mahindra among others for their approval of our automotive steel. They were all looking forward for our new plant with superior technology," said G S Rathore, executive vice president, JSW steel.

Marketing Insight 6.2

Marketing Insight 6.2

All the Way Up

The elevator market is set to zoom up as India grows vertically. And companies are ramping up operations to bring out high-tech, high-speed lifts

Otis

In the past five years or so, as India has urbanised rapidly, the market for elevators and escalators too has grown rapidly. Sebi Joseph, managing director of Otis Elevator Company India, has overseen operations in the Philippines, Singapore and the Gulf. But Joseph believes that India is the most exciting place. "China is the world's largest elevator market with sales of 400,000 units per annum. India is the second largest market in the world today. However, the gap between the two countries is staggering," says Joseph. "India's elevator-escalator market is just about 45,000 units. That gap shows the potential the Indian market has."

It is a point that other elevator makers concur with. "Three factors are pushing the elevator market in India: rising property prices, urbanisation and an ageing population," says Neeraj Sharma, managing director, Kone India, an elevatorescalator company. "As the population gets older and more prosperous, even somebody with a two-floor bungalow is likely to install an elevator."

A 2010 McKinsey report noted that India is likely to have 68 cities with population of one million each by 2030. Europe has only 35 such cities. As cities get crowded and land gets costlier, it is likely that the buildings will get taller. What also gives elevator companies hope is the number of elevators per 1,000 people in India. For every 1,000 people, Spain has almost 20 elevators, UK 4.6, China 1.43 and India 0.16 elevators (See India is on the Ground Floor). Given this, it isn't surprising that elevator companies are excited about India.

For now, elevator manufacturers like Chennai-headquartered Johnson Lifts say the market is growing at 12-13%. However, the Indian elevator market is a unique one and not without its share of challenges.

Like Otis' Joseph points out, the Indian market, despite being the second largest, isn't the most hightech in the world: "If you look at the Gulf market, about 12,000-13,000 units are sold in a year, but most of these are for high rises. That's the case in the Philippines too. In India, the number of high rises is less, as a result of which the elevators have lower speeds and lesser number of stops."

What does it mean? In India, most lifts travel at about 0.6 m per second. At Dubai's Burj Khalifa, the world's tallest building, the lifts zip at 10 m per second. To put that in perspective, if the lift at the Burj Khalifa travelled upwards, nonstop for an hour (not that anybody would want it or that it would be feasible), it would travel about 36 km in that time.

Today, such high-tech elevators constitute less than 5% of the Indian elevator market, says V Jagannathan, executive director, Johnson. However, to travel in one of these lifts, one doesn't have to buy a ticket to Dubai. Otis is installing an elevator that travels at 6 m/second at Kohinoor, an upcoming skyscraper in Mumbai, while Kone says it will install an elevator system that will travel at 7 m/second at Palais Royale, a proposed 300-m tall building in the city.

Another significant change is the falling share of the good old collapsible-door lifts, which constitute about 30% of the market. While that is a sizable share in a 45,000-unit market, the collapsible-door segment itself has shrunk in size — from the 60% market share it had about 10 years ago.

"We expect the overall market to touch 60,000 units by 2015. The growth is driven by the residential segment, which comprises 70% of the market," says Rohit Parulekar, director, sales and marketing, Schindler India. "Another positive trend is that the manual door elevators, which form a significant part of the market, are on the decline. There is a shift towards auto-door elevators, which are safer and energy-efficient."

In value terms, factors like few high rises and low-end technology make India not as attractive a market as Dubai. Elevators can cost anywhere between 3 lakh (for the old, manual ones with rickety, collapsible doors) and 3-4 crore, depending on the technology, speed and the number of stops.

Most elevators in India, 60-70%, are sold in metros, thanks to the construction boom over the last decade. However, Tier II and Tier III cities are the next frontier, say industry watchers. Cities like Bhopal, Indore, Coimbatore and Kochi are seeing good growth, says Kone's Sharma.

However, the sales slowdown faced by the real estate industry in the last few years seems to have affected the industry's growth too. "Certainly, the slowdown in real estate has had a direct impact on the industry. Order finalisation and project completion get delayed due to this," says Jagannathan of Johnson, which sells elevators to real estate developers, government departments like CPWD, airports, hospitals and hotels.

Industry experts say the escalator segment, which mercifully is just a small fraction of the business, has been particularly hit. "Malls are the biggest buyers of escalators," says an executive. "Because the number of malls coming up isn't as high as what it was five years ago, the escalator business has been hit," he adds.

Summary

- In Business market, the buying and selling takes place among businesses. It includes profit as well as not for profit businesses, government agencies (Local, State and National) and institutions (Schools, Hospitals). The business buying is quite different from consumer buying, as the buyers are well informed and a professional approach is taken up, while taking purchase decisions.
- Although the business market is bigger than the consumer market, yet only consumer market is seen and heard by you. It is because consumer market rely more on advertising and promotions to reach to its millions of consumers. While, in business markets, the number of buyers and sellers are quite small with respect to consumer market.
- Business market is very different from the consumer market with fewer large buyers. It leads to close supplier buyer relationship. The business buying requires a professional approach than the consumer buying, as the buyers are well informed. There are several buying influences right from the technical experts to sourcing people to the senior management. Several buying influences lead to multiple sales

calls to close the deal. The demand in consumer market tends to be a direct demand, while the demand in the business market is a derived demand, which is based on the consumer demand.

- Patrick Robinson, Charles Faris and Yoram Wind are of the view that there are three types of buying situation in the business market: straight rebuy, modified rebuy and new task.
- The buying centre includes the employees, who play any of the following seven roles in the purchase decision process: initiators, users, infuencers, deciders, approvers, buyers and gatekeepers.
- Patrick Robinson, Charles Faris and Yoram Wind have suggested eight stages in the business buying process and they have termed it as the eight buyphases. These are problem recognition, general need description, product specification, supplier search, proposal solicitation, supplier selection, order-routine specification and performance review.

Discussion Questions

1. Explain the difference between consumer markets and business markets. Discuss the difference involved in marketing car tyres to consumer market and business market.
2. Define business markets? Discuss the buying situations.
3. Discuss the eight stages of the business buying process with examples.
4. Short Notes:
   a. B2B Marketing
   b. Buying Centre
   c. Modified Rebuy
   d. Supplier Search
   e. Product Specification
   f. Supplier Selection

References

1. Dwyer, F. Robert, Tanner, John F. 'Business Marketing: Connecting Strategy, Relationships, and Learning', 3rd Edition, McGraw-Hill / Irwin, 2006
2. Frederick E. Webster Jr. and Yoram Wind, 'Organisational Buying Behaviour', Prentice Hall, 1972, P.2
3. Hutt, Michael D., Speh, Thomas W. 'Business Marketing Management: A Strategic View of Industrial and Organizational Markets', 8th Edition, Thomson/South-Western, 2004
4. Dwyer, F. Robert, Tanner, John F. 'Business Marketing: Connecting Strategy, Relationships, and Learning', 3rd Edition, McGraw-Hill / Irwin, 2006
5. Patrick J. Robinson, Charles W. Faris and Yoram Wind, 'Industrial Buying and Creative marketing', Allyn & Bacon, 1967
6. Frederick E. Webster Jr. and Yoram Wind, 'Organisational Buying Behaviour', Prentice Hall, 1972, P.6
7. Patrick J. Robinson, Charles W. Faris and Yoram Wind, 'Industrial Buying and Creative marketing', Allyn & Bacon, 1967
8. James C. Anderson, Dipak C. Jain and Pradeep K. Chintagunta, 'A customer value Assessment in Business Markets: A State of Practice Study', Journal of Business to Business Marketing 1, No.1, 1993, pp.3-29

CHAPTER 7

Segmentation, Targeting and Positioning

Chapter Structure

- Segmentation, Targeting and Positioning
- *Marketing Insight 7.1: Colgate Brushes Aside Foes With an Array of Offerings*
- Market Segmentation
- How do you segment a market?
- *Marketing Insight 7.2: Culture Customisation: Wrangler, McDonald's, And Starbucks*
- *Marketing Insight 7.3:* For Luxury Watch Makers, Festive Season's Right Time to Drive Sales
- *Marketing Insight 7.4:* TIGI Products will be Sold Through Salons
- Segmenting the Market: Tata Ginger Way
- Market Targeting
- Market Positioning
- Summary
- Discussion Questions
- References

"The mass market has split into ever-multiplying, ever-changing sets of micromarkets that demand a continually expanding range of options."

- Alvin Toffler in 'Powershift'

Segmentation, Targeting and Positioning

Once the marketing analysis phase is complete, the next stage in the marketing process consists of the following:

1. **Market Segmentation,**
2. **Target Market Selection** and
3. **Product Positioning**

In the abbreviated form, it is widely known as STP - Segmentation, Targeting and Positioning, in marketing jargon. A successful marketing strategy depends a lot on these three steps.

Earlier the life was simple and so was marketing. That's why

Henry Ford with Model T

Henry Ford said that **"People can have the Model T in any colour - so long as it's black."**

That was the era of mass production, mass distribution and mass marketing. Although the era still exists, but there is a difference. In a world of more than six billion people, the needs are different and their tastes are also different. That's why Ford's model T gave way to General Motors strategy to produce different cars for different buyers, right at the top with the brand Cadillac and at the bottom with the brand Chevrolet.

In the Indian context today, if you are Colgate, you can still produce Colgate Dental Cream and sell it to millions of people in India, besides other countries. But you also need to produce Colgate Total 12, Colgate Sensitive, Colgate Max Fresh, Colgate Kids Tooth Paste,

Colgate Fresh Energy Gel, Colgate Herbal, Colgate Cibaca Family Protection, Colgate Advanced Whitening and Colgate Active Salt to complete consumers' pie. In India, Colgate Palmolive India has a market share of more than 50 percent in the oral care market.

Colgate Dental Cream

Out of that 50 percent, 35 percent market comes from a single product Colgate Dental Cream and the rest is contributed by the rest nine brands.

Marketing Insight 7.1

Marketing Insight 7.1

Colgate Brushes Aside Foes With an Array of Offerings

Co's new 2-cylinder, 800 cc diesel engine may be key to the successful development of a pick-up truck by 2017

Colgate

In a hyper-competitive consumption-driven market like India, most virtual monopolies, from Maruti Suzuki to Nokia, have had to contend with steady erosion in market share over the years. Whilst the share of India's No 1 carmaker is today well below 50%, the Finish handset manufacturer's leadership position is under constant threat from Samsung.

Against such a backdrop, one long-standing consumer brand has been not just holding on to its pole position but actually inching further head in its core category of oral care. In the first half of calendar year 2012, Colgate Palmolive India's market share in the toothpaste market stood at 54.5%, its highest since 1998, a rare instance of a market leader gaining new ground. Aggressive marketing and a huge 32% jump in advertising spend in the first quarter of fiscal year 2013 over a year ago coupled with a launch of new variants across consumer segments has helped the largely single-product company drive growth.

Analysts who met up with the company said the leadership team exuded confidence about its growth plans and medium to long-term strategy. Colgate's executive management team includes three women: along with managing director Prabha Parmeswaran, there are Sarala Menon, VP, customer service & logistics, and Rekha Rao, VP, marketing. Colgate's India top team is publicity-averse – the company was unwilling to participate in this feature – and that may not be a bad thing for the brand. "The brand is not bigger than the leadership. Its leadership is anonymous yet the brand does exceedingly well in the market," says Jagdeep Kapoor, founder Samsika Marketing Consultants.

Unlike most virtual monopolies that typically have few competitors – think Google in internet search and ESPN in sports television in the US – Colgate's rise has been in a highly competitive market. The biggest threat to Colgate in India is Hindustan Unilever Ltd (HUL), which has put its might behind two brands, Close-Up and Pepsodent. The other MNC in the game is GlaxoSmithKline Consumer Healthcare with Aquafresh and Sensodyne. Then, there are a clutch of domestic players, with Dabur leading the way with three brands on the ayurvedic platform plus the Promise label that it had acquired from Balsara in the mid-2000s. Other local brands that keep the big boys on their toes include Vicco and Anchor.

If Colgate has been able to stay convincingly ahead of the market, it's thanks to its ability to segment a category (including toothbrushes and mouthwashes) in which product differentiation is notoriously difficult to achieve. With at least 10 extensions to the flagship Colgate Dental Cream (including a kids' toothpaste and a whitening product), one mouthwash (Plax), and a wide range of toothbrush extensions (including one with a flexible head and a cheek and tongue cleaner as well as battery toothbrush), Colgate has been able to make oral care account for over 80% of its total sales. Other categories in the Colgate portfolio include the Palmolive range of personal care products (body washes and hair gels) and dishwashing paste brand Axion.

Colgate has backed its extended product range with robust distribution clout. The essentially single-brand company has one of the widest networks, touching 4.5 million retail outlets in India. "Colgate's sustained distribution strength, coupled with product innovation and creation of sub-categories such as mouthwash and sensitive oral care have helped it drive growth aggressively, explains Gautam Duggad, vice president, equity, at Motilal Oswal.

Analysts, however, warn that the HUL threat and forays like the first move by GSK in the sensitive teeth segment with Sensodyne – which forced Colgate to react with the Sensitive extension – will keep the leader on its toes. Also, if Procter & Gamble does eventually take the plunge into toothpastes by launching Crest in India, the competitive scenario could become more intense.

On the whole, a company can adopt the practice of undifferentiated marketing, where it will go for one product for all the consumers like Nirma Detergent Powder or it can offer different products for its different customer segments like HUL offers Surf Excel, Rin and Wheel or it can go after concentrated marketing by offering products for just one market segment as the specialist like Vanish Shakti Stain Remover powder by Reckitt Benckiser (India) Limited.

Surf Excel

You can be a mass marketer, but at the same time you need to be a niche marketer to sustain yourself with the changing needs of the consumer. Greater competition and unique needs of consumers has led the companies towards the market segmentation.

Market Segmentation

'Market segmentation involves dividing the market of potential customers into homogeneous subgroups. These subgroups may be distinguished in terms of their behaviour pattern, attitudes, demographic characteristics, psychographic profile and the like.' - Brian Sternthal and Alice M. Tybout

The market segments are not created by the company, but it exists in the market. The marketer needs to identify the segment and then decides as to which one he will target.

Market segmentation helps large companies to be relevant for the small groups of customers. For small companies, it helps to be the niche player in the market. It is relevant for large Fast Moving Consumer Goods (FMCG) companies like Hindustan Unilever Limited (HUL), Colgate Palmolive India, ITC and it is also relevant for a relatively small FMCG company like Ghari Detergent. At the same time, it also helps the company to differentiate their market offerings for large segment of the market. That's why you find Lux, Liril, Rexona, Lifebuoy, Hamam, Breeze, Pears and Dove coming out from the same company HUL.

Dell

Generally most of the companies are operating between the scale of mass marketing and the segment of one. On the one hand, you can think about Bentley, a fully customized car in accordance with your choice for accessories, colour, fabric, upholstery etc to the Dell Laptops and PCs. In the case of Bentley, it is meant for the lucky few, as it costs in Crores. But you can have your customized laptops and PCs at a competitive price from Dell, delivered to your home or office. Even your paint for your home or offices can be customized now. In most of the paint shops in India, you will find a computer sitting in that dusty environment of paint and hardware shop. That computer helps you to customize the paint for you and it will give your 'Merawala Green' colour paint.

Asian Paints

This is called **Mass Customisation**, which means **'production of individually customized goods and services at mass production prices'.**[1]

The concept was first used by **Stan Davis in 'Future Perfect'** in 1987. **Slywotzky and Morrison** has termed it as the **Choiceboard,** which offers

'the online customers an interactive online system that allows them to design their own products and services by choosing from a menu of attributes, components, prices and delivery options. The customer's selections send signals to the supplier's manufacturing system that set in motion the wheels of procurement, assembly and delivery.' [2]

Wind and Rangaswamy has termed it as the **Customerisation** and described it

as an operationally driven mass customisation with customised marketing in a way that helps customers to get the product of his choice.[3]

How do you segment a market?

The process of market segmentation is the process of dividing the heterogeneous market into homogeneous subgroups of similar needs and shared characteristics. The bases of market segmentation have gone a long way through different stages. It started with demographic segmentation, as the data was easily available. Then it moved on to Geographic segmentation, Geodemographic segmentation, Psychographic Segmentation and Behavioural Segmentation. Following is the five ways to segment the market:

Demographic Segmentation

Demographic segmentation is most commonly used base for segmentation. The basis of the segmentation is age, sex, education, income, occupation, marital status, family size, family life cycle, religion, nationality and social class. All these variables are either used as a single factor or in combination to segment the market.

a) **Age:** Age is most commonly used basis, as the same age group people behave in the identical manner and will have identical needs. Marketers design, produce, package and promote products differently to meet the needs of different age groups.

Kid Tricycle

For example, Colgate has different products for different age groups like Colgate Dental Cream and Colgate Kids Toothpaste. On the basis of age only, the leading toy manufacturer Fisher-Price has seven categories of toys based on the age right from Birth to 5 Months, 6 Months to 11 months, 12 months to 23 months, 2 Years, 3 Years, 4 Years to 5 Years and up. On the whole, age can be broadly categorized in the following manner :

Infant	– Newly born to 1 Year
Child	– 1 to 12 years
Adolescent	– 12 to 15
Teens	– 16 to 19
Youth	– 20 to 35
Middle Aged	– 36 to 50
Elders	– 51 to 60
Seniors	– 60 and above

Aastha Channel

Johnsons & Johnsons, JAM, Magic Pot, Aastha Channel, MTV are few of the examples on the basis of Age segmentation.

b) Income: Income has been a key driver in segmenting the market. It is based on the belief that the behaviour of the consumer changes with the changes in income. Many automobile, consumer durable, financial services, hospitality, apparels, cosmetics and travel companies segment their market on the basis of income. Broadly, on the basis of income, market can be segmented as – Low Income, Low Middle income, middle income, upper middle income and high income. It has also been found that with the increase in income, the percentage expenditure on food and other basic necessities goes down. **C. K. Prahlad** in his book **'The Fortune at the Bottom of the Pyramid'** has talked about the marketing opportunities lying at the bottom of the pyramid i.e. Lower income segment. The success of Nirma, Ghadi, and 555 are examples of successful marketing at the bottom of the pyramid.

c) **Gender:** Gender differentiation forms a fundamental segment in the marketing, as the needs of male and female are very different. Clothing and apparels, cosmetics, magazines, shoes are few of the areas, where gender differentiation creates its own market. Axe, Raymond, Pulsar are the brands targeted towards male, while Scooty, Femina, Revlon, Titan Raga are the brands targeted towards female.

Femina

Scooty

Few brands target both the genders like Reebok and Garnier, through their different products or through sub branding.

d) **Occupation**: Occupation is also an important variable in segmenting the market. The consumption behaviour of a working executive differs from a self employed person or a blue collar worker or a businessman. In the same way, there are professionals like Doctors, Lawyers, Teachers, Professors, Chartered Accountants or Traders or Students or Shopkeepers or Housewives, whose consumption habits are similar in their segment. Financial companies and banks like ICICI Bank, State Bank of India, Central Bank of India etc. regularly target these on the basis of their occupation with their different schemes. Recently State Bank of India has offered special benefits for its defense personnel customers.

e) **Education**: Education also play an important role in segmenting the market. Indian market can be classified as Illiterates, Literates, High School Passouts, University educated and professionally qualified people. The business of information like Newspapers, magazines, books etc. gets seriously affected by the education variable.

f) **Marital Status**: Being single or being married influences the behaviour patters of the customers and thus it paves the basis for market segmentation. Unmarried people generally use more of fast food and packaged food than their married counterpart. Similarly married people tend to spend a lot on consumer durables, cars, travel plans and financial products. Few businesses like Matrimonial websites, wedding management companies, wedding video and photographers are directly dependent on the status of marriage.

Shaadi.com

g) **Family Size**: Family size and structure is also an important variable in segmenting the market. With the passage of time and effective implementation of family planning measures, the average Indian family size is declining. Earlier there used to be at least 3 or 4 Children the family, which has largely gone down to two or even 1 in many families. The social fabric of life is also changing, with more and more nuclear families than the joint families. It has led to the changes in the purchasing behaviour. Earlier, if you splurge, then there was a guilt feeling of spending money. But now you feel better off after splurging. With easy credit availability and younger earning population with more nuclear families and singles living in metros and cities, a new segment has been created and the companies are cashing on it with their different product and service offerings. Most of the malls in Gurgaon are doing brisk business, thanks to the large customer base among the single males and females working in the BPOs (Business Process Outsourcing). Right from the apparels to shoes to accessories to multiplexes, all have benefited largely in the post liberalization era with the changing family size and structure.

h) **Socio Economic Status**: According to Marketing Research Society of India (MRSI), the consumption behaviour of the consumer is determined by his / her social class, which refers to the occupation of the earning members of the family. Till April, 2011, MRSI had divided Indian population in the urban area in to eight socio-economic groups of consumers on the basis of the education and occupation of the chief wage earner of the household. These groups are **SEC A1, A2, B1, B2, C, D, E1 and E2**.

A1 and A2 include graduates, white collar workers and professionals and account for 9.5% of the population. B1 and B2 include SSC qualified as well as 40 % graduates, whose occupation is clerical or are shopkeepers and account for 17% of the population. C includes skilled workers, clerks, salespersons etc and account for 19.5% of the population. D again includes skilled workers, clerks, sales persons and account for 22.4%. While, E1 and E2 include unskilled labour and account for 31.6% of the population.

Socio-Economic Classification Grid								
	Education \ Occupation	Illiterate	School upto 4 years / literate but no formal schooling	School 5-9 years	SSC/HSC	Some college but not graduate	Graduate / Post Graduate general	Graduate / Post Graduate Professional
1	Unskilled workers	E2	E2	E1	D	D	D	D
2	Skilled workers	E2	E1	D	C	C	B2	B2
3	Petty Traders	E2	D	D	C	C	B2	B2
4	Shop owners	D	D	C	B2	B1	A2	A2
5	Entrepreneurs Employees None	D	C	B2	B1	A2	A2	A1
6	Entrepreneurs Employees < 10	C	B2	B2	B1	A2	A1	A1
7	Entrepreneurs Employees > 10	B1	B1	A2	A2	A1	A1	A1
8	Self-employed professionals	D	D	D	B2	B1	A2	A1
9	Clerical/Salesmen	D	D	D	C	B2	B1	B1
A	Supervisory level	D	D	C	C	B2	B1	A2
B	Officers/Executives: Junior	C	C	C	B2	B1	A2	A2
C	Officers/Executives: Middle/Senior	B1	B1	B1	B1	A2	A1	A1

Urban Socio-Economic Classification Grid (Source : Market Research Society of India)

Till april, 2011, the Rural Indian Households are classified into **SEC R1, R2, R3 and R4.** In the rural classification, the parameters are education of the chief wage earner and the type of the house. SEC R1 includes population, who is graduate and having a pucca house, while R2 includes graduates with semi pucca house. R3 includes Grduate with Kuccha house and R4 include below SSC educated population with kuccha house.

Socio-Economic Class (SEC)- Rural			
Education	Type of House		
	Pucca	Semi Pucca	Kuchha
Illiterate	R4	R4	R4
Literate but no formal school	R3	R4	R4
Upto 4th standard	R3	R3	R4
5th to 9th standard	R3	R3	R4
S.S.C./H.S.C.	R2	R3	R3
Some College but not Graduate	R1	R2	R3
Graduate/Post Graduate (General)	R1	R2	R3
Graduate/Post Graduate (Professional)	R1	R2	R3

Note : Four Socio-Economic Classes have been labeled as R1, R2, R3, and R4.
R1 : Upper most class.
R4 : Lowest class.

Rural Socio-Economic Classification Grid (Source : Market Research Society of India)

Now, in a bid to keep pace with the fast-evolving economic outlook, consumer attitudes and preferences in the country, this system has been revamped on 3rd May, 2011 by the Media Research Users' Council (MRUC) and the Market Research Society of India (MRSI) have unveiled a new Socio-Economic Classification (SEC) system.

The new Socio-Economic Classification (SEC) system is used to classify households in India. It's based on two variables:

- ❑ Education of chief wage earner and
- ❑ Number of "consumer durables" (from a predefined list)-owned by the family. The list has 11 items, ranging from 'electricity connection' and 'agricultural land'-to cars and air conditioners. These are :

	Items owned / have access at home
	Electricity Connection
	Ceiling Fan
	LPG Stove
	Two Wheeler
	Colour TV
1a	Refrigerator
	Washing Machine
	Personal Computer/ Laptop
	Car/Jeep/Van
	Air Conditioner
1b	Agricultural Land
	NUMBER OF STANDARD 11 OWNED

(Source : New SEC System, 2011, Market Research Society of India)

Based on the above two parameters, each household are classified in one of 12 SEC groups—A1, A2, A3, B1, B2, C1, C2, D1, D2, E1, E2 and E3. These 12 groups are applicable to both urban and rural India. The top-most new SEC class A1 comprises of 0.5% of all Indian households.

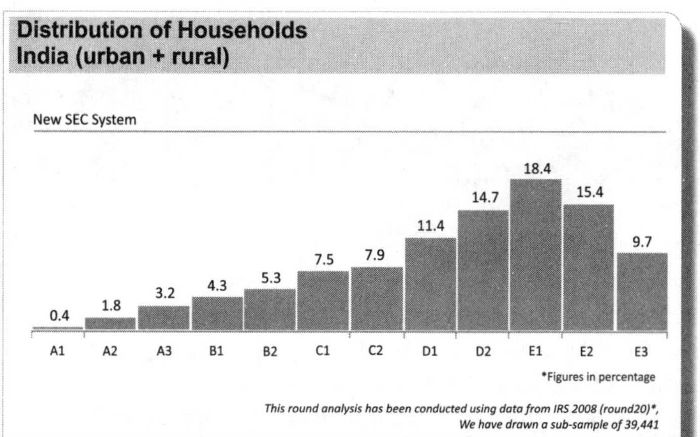

Source : New SEC System, 2011, Market Research Society of India

Nearly 2% of urban households and less than 0.1% of rural households belong to the new SEC A1. More than half of all SEC A1 households reside in the top six Indian cities—Delhi, Mumbai, Kolkata, Chennai, Bengaluru and Hyderabad. At the other end of the spectrum, the bottom-most new SEC class E3 comprises of 10% of all Indian households. Only 2% of urban households and 13% of rural households belong to new SEC E3. Nearly 93% of all SEC E3 households are in rural India.

The formulation of the new SEC system has largely been done using the Indian Readership Survey (IRS) database. The developmental work has also used IMRB's 'Household Panel' data. IRS is the largest survey of Indian households with a sample size of over 260,000—of this, roughly 175,000 are from urban India while around 85,000 hail from rural India. It was the sampling rigor and spread that led to the IRS being identified as the most appropriate database for the development of the new SEC Classification system.

Besides the above, religion, race, nationality and language are also the bases for segmenting the market.

Geographic Segmentation

Geographic segmentation is the starting point and the simplest form of segmenting the market. Here, the market is divided into countries, states, regions and cities. For a large company like LG or Samsung, it is easy to sell the products all across the country or many countries in the world; but a small player like Ghari Detergent, based in Kanpur, Uttar Pradesh needs to expand step by step in different regions of India.

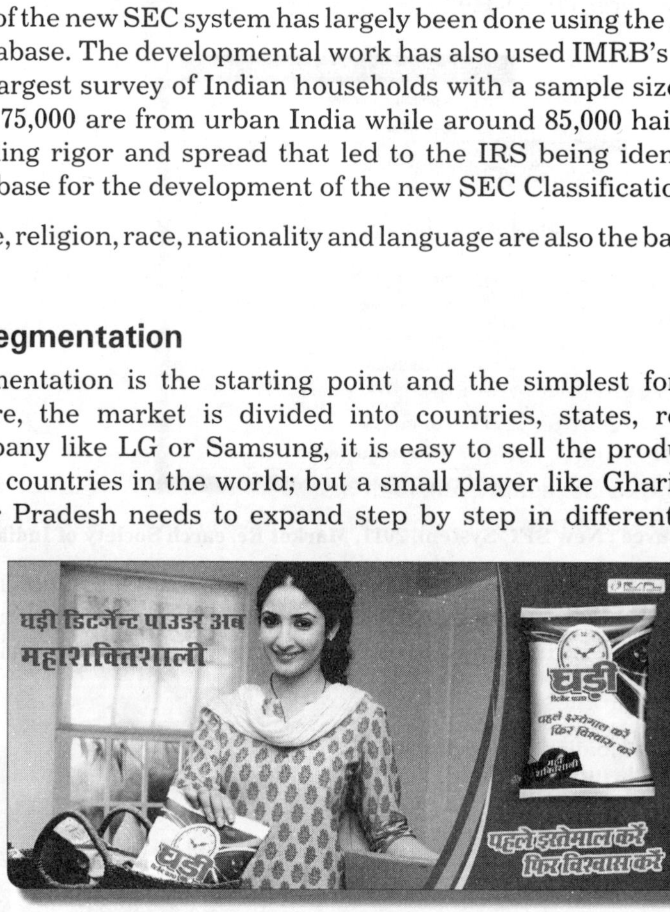

Ghari Detergent

Earlier MTR ready to eat food was sold in southern India only and then it expanded to all the other regions in India. A courier service like Vichare is only operational in Mumbai and its suburbs; but an university like Amity, is trying to expand its operations all across India besides its main campus at Noida to Jaipur, Lucknow, Gurgaon, Mumbai and so on. Nirma was also started small by Karsanbhai Patel in 1969 from a small place called Kishnapur in Gujarat and then expanded to all across India. This segmentation method helps the company to expand their markets on a logical basis.

Geodemographic Segmentation

Hindustan Unilever Pureit water purifier

Based on the philosophy of 'Birds of a feather flock together', Geodemographic segmentation combines the geographic and demographic segmentation. It is based on the philosophy that consumers staying in the same area have got similar characteristics and needs. This kind of segmentation helps the companies to market their products efficiently. For example, you won't find HUL's Pureit water purifier priced at Rs. 2000/- and now Pureit compact at Rs. 1000/- , being sold in Colaba, Mumbai, but you will find the purifier selling in the areas like Goregaon, Borivali and Mira Road in Mumbai. It is all due to the presence of the respective market segment of Pureit in these areas in Mumbai.

Psychographic Segmentation

It has often been found that people with the same demographic profile may act in a totally different manner. This happens due to the difference in their personality, lifestyle and values. Psychographics is the science of using psychology and demographics to understand the consumers better. Marketing researchers have tried to map individual lifestyle patterns to segment the market. One of the famous methods of psychographic study is AIO Framework (Activities, Interests and Opinions). AIO framework explains the individual lifestyle patterns based on the activities, interests and opinions with demographic variables.

Reebok

Levi's

Personality is also an important factor in segmenting the market. Generally, the marketers try to project the brand personality, which imitates the target consumer personality. Once you hear about Nike (Athlete in all of us), Reebok (Success / Cricket), Levi's (American, Real and Authentic, Rugged) and Shoppers Stop (Exclusivity, Individuality); it sounds you something. The brand personality is also endorsed by the celebrity, whose personality matches the consumer's persona. That's why Akshay Kumar advertises for Levi's, M. S. Dhoni, John Abraham and Nargis advertises for Reebok and Yuvraj Singh advertises for Fiat Grande Punto; while you see a young couple in Tata Indica Vista ad. Though both - Fiat Grande Punto and Tata Indica Vista are targeting the same demographic customers' profile.

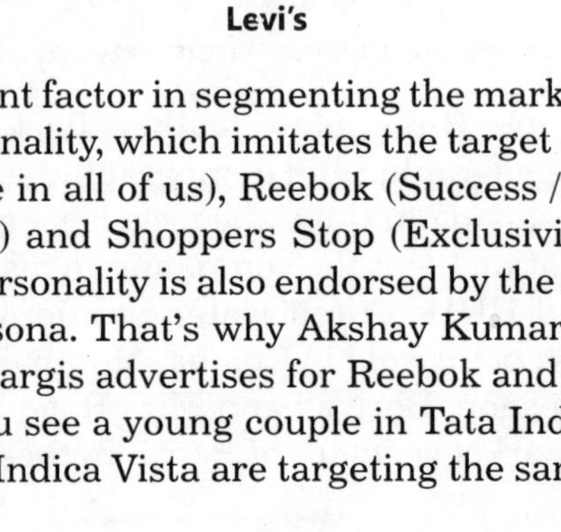

Sri Consulting – Business Intelligence (SRIC-BI) VALS (Values and Lifestyle) Model Framework.

(Source: Sri Consulting)

Psychographic Segmentation can also be understood in American context through **Sri Consulting – Business Intelligence (SRIC-BI) VALS (Values and Lifestyle) Model Framework.** VALS is based on 4 demographic factors (Sex, Age, Education and Income) and 35 Attitudinal Questions (I am often interested in theories / I like a lot of variety in my life / I like to learn about art, culture, and history....) to profile the consumers. The VALS framework divides the American adults into eight typologies

under two categories - higher resources and lower resources. Higher resources include Innovators, Thinkers, Achievers and Experiencers and lower resources include Believers, Strivers, Makers and Survivors. Although the framework is not very useful in Indian context; but it can give an insight and can be modified to suit the Indian environment. Titan, the topmost watch brand in India, offers different watches under sub brands like Octane, Orion, Edge, Heritage, WWF Collection etc to target the different psychographic customer base.

Marketing Insight 7.2

Marketing Insight 7.2

Culture Customisation: Wrangler, McDonald's, and Starbucks

Wrangler

Wrangler jeans are getting a makeover in India and going up-market in the process as parent VF Corp customises the all-American denims for the country's motorcycle-riding population and adds features to suit local needs. VF Corp hopes the strategy will add $1.1 billion in revenue to its Asia-Pacific business over the next five years.

India, with its burgeoning middle class, is a fast-growing market for international brands that want to capitalise on opportunities in Asia's third largest economy. McDonald's Corp recently announced its first vegetarian-only restaurant in the country in what many industry watchers say is a sign of how lucrative the market is and how much multinationals are tailoring to local demands. Coffee chain Starbucks Corp also customised its menu for its first Indian store to include more local flavors. "In India, they understand the western heritage that is appropriate for the brand because the Indian consumer is open to the film industry," VF Corp Chief Executive Eric Wiseman said in an interview, adding that many Indians are familiar with Westerns, unlike consumers in China.

China and India are the two hot destinations for American retailers, with the Chinese market much bigger. But many note that a large English-speaking population exposed to Hollywood and American pop culture makes the Indian shopper easier to target.

"The Wrangler position in India ... is targeted at the premium customer. The brand is aiming to tap into the potentially large segment of young consumers there whose lifestyles relate to jeans and motorcycles," Wiseman told Reuters. A study by Wrangler in India found most people travel by two-wheelers in the country, as opposed to their American counterparts who drive cars.

Taking into account traffic and climatic differences, VF Corp came up with features like water-repellant material to safeguard mobile phones and wallets, and making the fit of the jeans more motorbike-riding friendly. The new line of jeans costs about 15 per cent to 20 per cent more than the average pair of Wrangler denims, Wiseman said.

Wrangler was first sold in the US in 1947 as "cowboy" jeans and is still a popular choice for heavy-duty wear. The price for a standard pair of Wrangler regular fit jeans for men starts at about $19, according to the company's website, making them an affordable buy. Globally, the brand fetches VF Corp about $1.5 billion in revenue annually. In India, it currently brings in less than $50 million (approx Rs 260 crore), CEO Wiseman said.

"It is critical to get local, local, local," said Michael Silverstein, senior partner at The Boston Consulting Group, and co-author of the "$10 Trillion Dollar Prize," a book about the emerging Chinese and Indian middle class. Silverstein estimated there are roughly 300 million Indians who can buy a pair of jeans for the equivalent of about $20. That is almost equal to the population of the US.

Wiseman said Wrangler is developing more products along the same lines that will be introduced in India in the coming seasons. Experiments in localisation are still rare for clothing companies, mostly because they often do not have the scale or distribution capacity, said Peter Wahlstrom, an analyst with Morningstar. VF Corp is among the few companies that manufacture much of its own merchandise so it has more control over gathering raw material and distribution. Its India business is expected to grow at a rate of 22 per cent annually, while the Asia-Pacific region is expected to increase by 17 per cent.

Behavioural Segment

In the case of behavioural segmentation, the buyers are divided into different groups on the following basis.

- **Buyer's purchase decision role**
- **Product or brand usage**
- **Occasions**
- **User status and**
- **Usage rate**

On the basis of occasions, the consumers can be divided into market segments. Archies has built their business on the basis of occasional greetings. Kurkure is trying to sell more on the occasion of Diwali through its gift packs. Cadburys is trying to associate its chocolates with the happy occasion and also promoting it as a replacement of age old traditional sweets. ICICI Bank and other banks sell Gold coins on the auspicious occasions like Akshay Tritiya, Diwali etc. On Valentines Day, a company like Ferns and Petals gets the highest order to deliver flowers all across India.

Marketing Insight 7.3

For Luxury Watch Makers, Festive Season's Right Time to Drive Sales

Omega

A billboard advertisement of a luxury watch next to a busy flyover in the city is hard to miss, especially for those who associate French fashion house Hermes mainly with clothing and accessories. As Indians loosen their purse strings ahead of Dushehra and Diwali, the two big festivals that also usher in the wedding season, an increasing number of premium and luxury watchmakers are jumping on the advertising bandwagon to cash in on the air of festivity. Chanel, a French luxe brand that has been selling watches priced upwards of Rs. 2.5 lakh in India since 2005, has put up a hoarding at the swanky T3 terminal of New Delhi airport.

"The Chanel watch hoarding creates awareness, visibility and desire in an appropriate environment," Chanel India spokeswoman Marielou Phillips said, adding that it has fuelled queries about the brand's new watch collection at its boutique in the capital. India's watch market is estimated at Rs.4,500 crore, with the high-end and luxury time pieces accounting for about 20% of sales, or Rs. 850 crore.

"The idea is to establish the brand in the minds of people," said Yashovardhan Saboo, the CEO of Ethos Watch Studios, which recently started selling Hermes watches. "We will soon be displaying Hermes watches worth Rs. 80 lakh at our stores," Saboo added. Hermes watches are also available at the brand's exclusive stores in the country. Saboo says, there is untapped demand for luxury watches in India and brands have begun to realise that they need to nudge consumers to buy more.

Franck Dardenne, GM at LVMH Watch & Jewellery India, said, "Since we gain market share, we want to maintain the advertising. In the festive season, you can see TAG Heuer in newspapers every week. Dior watches and Zenith increased as well through a bigger focus." Not to be left behind, other watch brands are launching new collections and strengthening their distribution network. For instance, Swiss brand IWC Schaffhausen, from Richemont International, is appointing a representative in India and setting up a team to focus on the market.

Longines

Experts say high-end watches have witnessed steady growth over the last few years. "The cash economy is also fueling growth of luxury lifestyle in India, including sale of expensive time pieces. Because of the possibility of transactions running into lakhs and crores, a lot of Indians have started buying watches in the home turf," said Technopak India chairman Arvind Singhal. Charles Villoz, head of international sales for Swatch Group brand Longines, is of the view that despite an increase in disposable incomes, watches are still not a priority for many Indians.

"India is a huge country and the potential has not yet been exploited to the level it should have been. Even people who can afford accessible luxury, have other priorities here." Experts say that consumer taste in India is evolving and falling in line with the globaltrend. "It's not only about showing of a brand; consumers are opting for watches that are understated," said Ethos' Saboo.

According to Sunil Grover, regional GM for Corum Watches, the look and esthetics of a product still seem to rule when it comes to purchase decisions. Indian women, he adds, are now looking for bolder watches with big dials. Watchmakers, however, are not neglecting consumers looking for new technology. Seiko has rolled out 'Astron', the first solarpowered watch that can set itself using GPS technology. "The watch will tell you the local time anywhere in the world, as long as you can see the sky, just at the press of a button," said Niladri Mazumder, vicepresident sales and marketing at Seiko Watch India.

The company has decided to reach out to only 150 consumers for the new range. Even Corum and Cartier are seeing increase in demand for tourbillon watches. India, though far behind China in terms of consumption of luxury watches, has a lot in store for watchmakers. "In terms of Swiss watch exports, India ranks 24th while Hong Kong and China rank number one. But India may be the next key market. That's why we invest so much," said LVMH's Dardenne.

Kurkure

The benefits sought by the buyer vary from person to person. In the toothpaste category, somebody looks for the economy; somebody else looks out for medicinal properties to help prevent tooth decay or somebody else wants the cosmetic properties by having white, bright teeth with a fresh breath. All the benefits are answered by a single company through differentiated marketing like Colgate, which offers Colgate dental cream for economy, Colgate Total and Colgate Sensitive for medicinal properties and Colgate Maxfresh for the cosmetic properties.

Marketing Insight 7.4

TIGI Products will be Sold Through Salons

Tigi

When Hindustan Unilever's executive director Hemant Bakshi went for a 'complimentary' hair cut last week, he came out of the salon Rs. 2,500 poorer. Though his hairdo didn't cost anything at all, he splurged on almost every product used during the half an hour process — from shampoo to hair wax. And he's excited about this unusual impulse buy, because it involves his firm's foray into super premium hair-care business.

The makeshift salon was Hindustan Unilever's training ground for its professional hair products brand TIGI, popularly known as Toni & Guy after its founders, which will be sold to consumers exclusively through top salons that use these products. "TIGI actually allows us to tick many boxes in our strategy," says Bakshi, who this month completes 24 years in HUL, exactly half his life. "It allows us to complete our portfolio, have a presence in the category of the future and a presence in the channel of the future," Bakshi says.

The company will enter hair colour segment in India through the new brand, and bring in other TIGI products including gel, shampoo, wax and mousse under Bed Head and S-Factor. Unilever, the Anglo-Dutch parent of HUL, acquired TIGI's professional hair product business for $411.5 million in 2009. They carry super premium price tags, though. TIGI's shampoo, at Rs. 700-925 for 250 ml, costs almost eight times a normal one, and over four times the FMCG giant's premium brand Dove.

And TIGI products are at least 40% costlier than most products of L'Oreal, the French cosmetics giant that controls over three-fourths of the urban salon market in the country, and other competitors such as P&G's Wella and German brand Schwarzkopf. "We don't want to leave any gap in our portfolio in terms of price-points and TIGI comes and play a very important part in completing our portfolio as far as beauty is concerned in hair," Bakshi says. "We would do the same thing across all our categories."

The company will sell TIGI products through just over 40 salons in the country to start with, making its reach of 6.4 million retail outlets somewhat superfluous in this case. In comparison, L'Oreal sells its products under Professional, Matrix and Kérastase brands through more than 30,000 salons.

"Consumers go to a salon because they don't want to do colouring or other services at home. So, hairstylists can influence sales in a big way both during the service and also by advising post care products," Aseem Kaushik, director of professional products division at L'Oréal India, says. Hindustan Unilever, which has virtually covered the mass end of the market in most categories, has been focusing on premium products to improve its margins. This shift in strategy in fact helped the firm post its highest operating margin in a decade at 20% for the year ended March 2013 and also resulted in two premium brands—Pond's and Dove—crossing the Rs. 1,000-crore mark.

HUL's upscale drive is primarily reflected in personal products, which has seen faster rollouts of new brands or categories. Its recent launches include TRESemme hair care range and extending Lux into deodorant and Dove into hair oil. Emerging categories contribute almost 14%, or more than Rs. 1,000 crore, to HUL's personal care segment which, in turn, accounts for nearly half of the firm's profits but less than a third of its total sales.

User status also defines a market segment. Users can further be segmented into **first time users**, **regular users**, **ex users**, **potential users** and **non users**. In the different stages of family life cycle, a nonuser may turn into a first time user and then it can become regular user. For example, a kid may use Johnson's Baby soap for the first time and can become a regular user for few years and then the baby can leave the usage and become an ex users. On the other hand, potential user group are mother-to-be, who will buy the products relevant to their baby after a certain period of time.

Johnson's Baby Care

Usage rate also helps to segment the market. Telecom companies like Airtel, Vodafone, Reliance etc regularly segment their customers on the basis of **light, medium** or **heavy users** for their services. In the case of cigarettes, the heavy users are very loyal to the brand, but in the case of beer it has been found that either the heavy drinkers are loyal or they look out for the lowest price.

Consumers can also be segmented on the basis of varying degree of loyalty.

Loyalty is 'a deeply held commitment to re-buy or re-patronise a preferred product or service in the future despite situational influences and marketing efforts having the potential to cause switching behaviour.'[4]

George H. Brown has divided the brand loyalty status into four groups.: **Hard Core Loyals**, who buy the same brand all the time; **Split loyals**, who are loyal to two or three brands; **Shifting loyals**, who shift from one brand to another and **switchers**, who show no loyalty to any brand.5 It has been found that in beer, toothpaste, cigarettes and in newspaper category, the consumers are highly loyal to the brand.

Buyer Readiness Stage: In any market, the buyers are happened to be in different buyer readiness stage. It goes right from being unaware about the product to being aware about the product, and then progresses to interest in the product, to desire and then to the intention to buy the same.

Segmenting the Market: Tata Ginger Way

Market segmentation can only be effective, if the size of the market and purchasing power of the customers can be measured. The segment also needs to be substantial enough to justify the product or service development. The market segment also needs to be reachable and actionable. Lastly, it should be differentiable; then only the customers will be satisfied. Tata group's Ginger Hotels is a good example of market segment. There was an unfulfilled need in the market for budget hotels in the tier II cities, with the right kind of service.

Tata group's Ginger Hotels

In June, 2005, Tata Group's Indian Hotel Company Limited (IHCL), which manages Taj Hotels, Resorts and Palaces in India, launched the first-of-its-kind category of Smart Basics hotel in Bangalore under its wholly-owned subsidiary Roots Corporation Limited. The Smart Basic concept created a revolution in the world of Indian hospitality with its gennext category of hotels, which signify simplicity, convenience, informality, style, warmth, modernity and affordability. The concept was developed in association with renowned corporate strategy thinker, **Dr C. K. Prahalad**.

Ginger hotels gave the customers a unique combination of intelligently designed facilities and consistent services at extremely affordable rate ranging from Rs 1299/- to Rs 2499/- in cities like Pune, Nashik, Ahmedabad, Bhubneshwar, New Delhi, Mysore, Goa, Gawahati, Pondicherry etc. Ginger hotels provided a superior product offering and consistent experience to travellers, beyond the present offerings in the industry at a very affordable price point.

Ratan Tata

In Indian market, Tata group have been very receptive towards the customers. The customer orientation has led Tata group to come up with innovative product and service offerings. This has resulted in identifying and fulfilling the needs of different market segments through their different products and services like Ginger Hotels, Tata Nano, Tata Indigo Manza, Tata Indica, Voltas Air

Conditioners (Priced less than Rs.10000/-), Tata Salt, Tata Indicom and Tata DoCoMo. All these products and services have been very successful in the Indian market and the credit goes to a visionary like **Mr. Ratan Tata**. That's why Ratan Tata also finds a place at 12th rank in 'Thinkers 50' - the definitive listing of the world's top 50 business thinkers in 2009.[6]

Market Targeting

With an objective of maximizing profits, a company targets one or more market segments. In the target market selection process, the company evaluates the market opportunity with the understanding of the customer and analyses the competition. It also checks out its ability to reach the customers in the segment and the costs involved in reaching them. The level of customers' satisfaction with competitors' products and services are also important. If there are a lot of customers, who are dissatisfied, then the chances of success become brighter; as it happened in the case of Ginger Hotels. Then the barriers to entry, potential profitability and growth forecast should also be taken into consideration in target market selection. As it builds the foundation for the product or service or sometimes a company, extreme care is required in target market selection.

In the process of market targeting, a company can choose the following market patterns:

1. **Single Segment Concentration**: In the detergent cake and powder segment, Nirma, 555, Ghari Detergent cater to the lower segment of the customers with their cheaper products. As the company is fully dependent on that product, it involves marketing risks.
2. **Multi Segment Specialisation**: A company can also go for multiple segments. A media company like UTV produces and distributes Films under two entities – UTV

UTV

Motion Pictures and UTV Spot Boy. Under UTV Motion Pictures, it produces main stream commercial movies with big budgets like Jodha Akbar, Delhi 6, Main Aur Mrs Khanna, Kaminey under UTV Motion Pictures and small budget movies like Aamir, Dev D and Welcome to Sajjanpur under UTV Spot Boy.

ZEISS

3. **Product Specialisation**: In product specialization, the company becomes product specific. For example - Carl Zeiss, the world's leading lens manufacturer with its tagline 'We make it visible'; produces lenses for cameras, binoculars, spectacles, microscopes, mobile video and industrial metrology.
4. **Market Specialisation**: When a company specialises in serving the same market with different needs, then the company is following market specialization. In the university laboratory market, a company can sell all the products required in a lab.

Hindustan Unilever Limited

Hindustan Unilever Limited

5. **Full Market Coverage**: Large companies generally go for full market coverage with all the products and services, the customers might need. LG, Samsung, HUL, ITC, Pepsi, Colgate, Maruti Suzuki, General Motors, Hero Honda, Bajaj Auto etc are the companies, who look after the complete spectrum of customer needs through their different product offerings. That's why Maruti Suzuki sells 13 different Cars – Maruti 800, Omni, Alto, Zen Estilo, A-Star, Ritz, Swift, Wagon R, Versa, Swift DZire, Gypsy, SX4 and Grand Vitara; between the price range of Rs. 2 Lacs to Rs. 16 Lacs. Similarly, Hero Honda sells 15 different bikes – CD Dawn, CD Deluxe, Splendor+, Splendor

NXG, Passion Pro, Passion Plus, Super Splendor, Glamour, Glamour PG Fi, Achiever, CBZ X-Treme, Hunk, Karizma, Karizma ZMR and Pleasure scooters between the price range of Rs. 32000/- to Rs. 91000/-. It's not that only automobile companies are having many choices for the customers.

Even in FMCG products, a company like HUL offers 8 types of personal soaps – Breeze, Lux, Lifebuoy, Liril, Hamam, Dove, Pears, Rexona and Dove; 4 types of detergent powders – Surf Excel, Rin, Wheel and Sunlight; 4 types of skin care – Fair & Lovely, Pond's, Vaseline and Aviance; and 2 types of toothpastes – Pepsodent and Close Up.

Market Positioning

Once the market segment is identified by the company to be targeted, it needs to be positioned in the mind of the prospective customer. Positioning is creating an identity in the minds of the target market. Positioning as a concept, in marketing was popularised by advertising professionals **Al Ries and Jack Trout** through their bestseller book **"Positioning - a battle for your mind"**. This concept was first published in **1969** by Jack Trout in the paper **'Positioning is a game people play in today's me-too market place'** in Industrial Marketing. **Al Ries and Jack Trout** said that

> **'Positioning starts with a product. A piece of merchandise, a service, a company, an institution or even a person..............But positioning is not what you do to a product. Positioning is what you do the mind of the prospect. That is, you position the product in the mind of the prospect.'**[7]

Tata Bolt

Positioning is all about how does the customer perceive your product? For example, when Tata launched their first car - Indica, their tagline was 'More car, per car' and Tata Motors tried to give more value to the consumers through lower price, more space, more features and more comfort. Following this tradition they launched Tata Indigo and then through a modifications, Tata Indigo CS, the cheapest sedan in the world. Going further, they launched Tata Nano, the cheapest car in the world. Again they came up with Tata Indigo Manza with all the creature comforts in C segment at a price, which is too competitive to be true. Now they have launched Bolt and Zest to compete with the cars in the hatchback segment like Swift, Grand i10, Sail, Brio to sedans like Swift Dzire, Mahindra Logan, Ford Fiesta, Fiat Linea and Honda Amaze, which costs between Rs. 4.6 Lacs to Rs. 8 Lacs. Similarly Maruti Suzuki says 'Count on Us'. And millions of customers are counting on Maruti Suzuki by buying different cars from the Maruti stable.

The success of the positioning strategy lies in making one or two characteristics of the product or service stand out in the minds of the consumers. Positioning also takes the form of taglines or slogans that gets attached in the minds of the consumers. Amul's 'Utterly, Butterly Delicious', Nokia's 'Connecting People', Nike's 'Just do it', LG's 'Life is good', Aaj Tak's 'Sabse Tej', ICICI Prudential's 'Jeetey Raho' are few of the popular taglines that is engraved in the consumers mind.

Fevicol has been very successful in positioning the brand through its engaging television commercials (TVC); whereas the character zoozoo has become a rage in India through its Vodafone TVCs. Thus, Positioning helps in differentiating the products from the competition and also leads to top of the mind recall.

Summary

- Once the marketing analysis phase is complete, the next stage in the marketing process consists of market segmentation, target market selection and product positioning. It is widely known as STP - Segmentation, Targeting and Positioning, in marketing.
- Market segmentation involves dividing the market of potential customers into homogeneous subgroups. These subgroups may be distinguished in terms of their behaviour pattern, attitudes, demographic characteristics, psychographic profile and the like.
- The market segments are not created by the company, but it exists in the market. The marketer needs to identify the segment and then decides as to which one he will target.
- Mass customisation means production of individually customized goods and services at mass production prices.
- A market can be segmented in five ways. These are demographic segmentation, geographic segmentation, geodemographic segmentation, psychographic segmentation and behavioural segmentation.

- Demographic segmentation is most commonly used base for segmentation. The basis of the segmentation is age, sex, education, income, occupation, marital status, family size, family life cycle, religion, nationality and social class.
- Geographic segmentation is the starting point and the simplest form of segmenting the market. Here, the market is divided into countries, states, regions and cities.
- Geodemographic segmentation combines the geographic and demographic segmentation. It is based on the philosophy that consumers staying in the same area have got similar characteristics and needs.
- Due to the difference in their personality, lifestyle and values, people with the same demographic profile may act in a totally different manner. Psychographics segmentation helps to understand these consumers better with the combination of psychology and demographics.
- In the case of behavioural segmentation, the buyers are divided into different groups on the basis of buyer's purchase decision role, product or brand usage, occasions user status and usage rate.
- In the target market selection process, the company evaluates the market opportunity with the understanding of the customer and analyses the competition. It also checks out its ability to reach the customers in the segment and the costs involved in reaching them. Then the barriers to entry, potential profitability and growth forecasts are taken into consideration in target market selection.
- Once the market segment is identified by the company to be targeted, it needs to be positioned in the mind of the prospective customer.
- Positioning is creating an identity in the minds of the target market. Positioning is not what you do to a product. Positioning is what you do the mind of the prospect. That is, you position the product in the mind of the prospect.

Discussion Questions

1. Discuss the role and importance of STP - Segmentation, Targeting and Positioning, in marketing.
2. Define market segmentation? How do you segment a market? Elaborate with examples.
3. What do you mean by demographic segmentation? Discuss the various variables with suitable examples.
4. Psychographic Segmentation. Elaborate AIO framework and Sri Consulting's VALS model framework

5. What do you mean by target market selection? How does a company choose its market pattern in the process of targeting?
6. Discuss the statement: 'But positioning is not what you do to a product. Positioning is what you do the mind of the prospect. That is, you position the product in the mind of the prospect.'
7. Short Notes:
    a. Mass Customisation
    b. Socio Economic Classification (SEC)
    c. Personailty
    d. Positioning
    e. Geodemographic Segmentation
    f. Buyer's Purchase Decision Role
    g. Psychographic Segmentation
    h. Multi Segment Specialisation
    i. Gender
    j. VALS framework

References

1. B Josheph Pine II, Mass Customization: The New Frontier in Business Competition, 1992
2. Adrian J. Slywotzky and David J. Morrison, How digital is your business? (New York, Crown Business, 2000, p.39
3. Jerry Wind and A. Rangaswamy, "Customerisation: The Second Revolution in Mass Customisation", Wharton School Working Paper, June, 1999
4. Richard L. Oliver, Satisfaction: A Behavioural Perspective on the consumer, Mc Graw Hill, 1997, New York
5. George H. Brown, "Brand Loyalty: Fact or Fiction", Advertising Age June 1952
6. Vijay Prakash Anand, 'The Tata Group : Driven By Innovation', 2011
7. Al Ries and Jack Trout, 'Positioning: The battle for your mind', Warner Books, 1982

[illegible]

(a) Mass Customization [illegible]

[illegible]

[illegible] Segmentation

[illegible]

3. Jerry Wind and [illegible] [illegible]

4. [illegible]

6. [illegible]

Chapter 8

Competition

Chapter Structure

"*Know yourself and know your enemy. You will be safe in every battle. You may know yourself but not know the enemy. You will then lose one battle for every one you win. You may not know yourself or the enemy. You will then lose every battle.*"

- Sun Tzu

Competition: An Overview

Marketing is all about identifying and fulfilling the needs of the customers. Once you understand the needs of the customers and your core competency, you need to understand the competition. Competition is all about current and potential offerings and substitutes that a customer may consider. You need to assess the strengths and weaknesses of the competitors; as it will help out to differentiate your products and services from others. For Tata Nano, although there was no competition at the price point of Rupees One Lac, but a customer might have thought about buying Maruti 800 instead of Tata Nano LX model, which costs almost Rs 2.15 Lacs on road. Now the scenario is different as Maruti Suzuki has stopped the production of Maruti 800 car; while Tata Nano starts at a price point of Rs. 1.6 Lacs. In the case of Mahindra Scorpio, the competition was limited due to rival offerings in the market available for more than Rs. 14 Lacs. In the case of Nirma, the competition was from Wheel and for the multiplexes, the single screen cinema halls were the competition.

Hero Splendor

Once you are already there in the market with your product or service offering, a company needs to be careful all the time as the competition can take the fizz away from you. As it happened in the case of Bajaj Auto, which was the largest two wheeler manufacturer twenty years back. But in the 1990s, with the onslaught of Hero Honda, it slipped into oblivion. In the 100cc category, Hero Honda Splendor still rules the chart. But with the identification of the customer needs, it's back in the business at no. 2 position with clear leadership in above 100cc segment of motorbikes with Pulsar, Discover and XCD. You might also be familiar with Onida and BPL being one of the key players in TV category in India few years back. Then LG became No.1. Now the television category is primarily LEDs and LCDs; which is dominated by Sony and Samsung. So, beware of competition; it cannot make your business, but it may certainly break your business.

All these above trends require the companies to pay keen attention to their competitors. Generally

Successful companies design and operate systems for gathering continuous intelligence about competitors.[1]

But who are your competitors? The competition is not only about the existing companies, who are trying to satisfy the same customer need that you do, but it is also about the potential competitors, who can come up tomorrow. For example, in the camera business Nikon, Canon, Olympus and Minolta were fighting with one other to grab more market share in the camera business. Now, they are fighting it out in the digital camera business. But today, who is the largest camera manufacturer in the world. It's not a camera company, but it is a mobile company. Earlier it was Nokia, now there is Samsung, Apple iPhones and so many other players. It is all due to the advancement in technology that has created a competition beyond the competition. While Kodak and Fuji wass still fighting it out in the market for film, paper and processing, a company called Hewlett Packard so called HP is laughing all the way to the bank with their printer business. Similarly, the business of pagers got wiped out with the advent of mobile technology. Sony's walkman had to give way to Apple's iPod in the personal entertainment category.

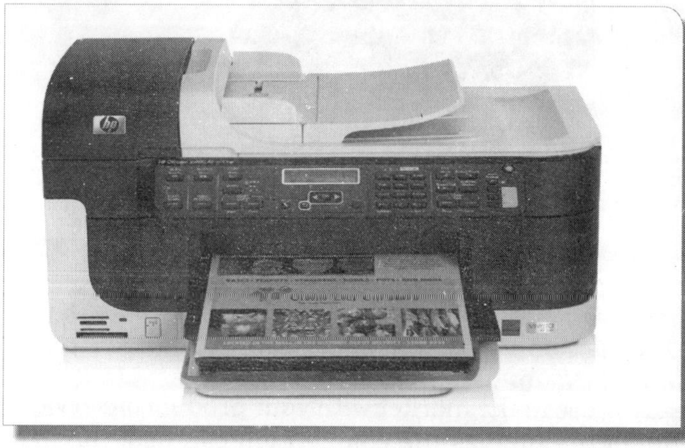

HP (Hewlett Packard)

Flipkart.com

In the era of internet, bookseller like Barnes and Noble in US had to give the way for amazon.com. In India also, Flipkart, Snapdeal, Indiatimes Shopping, Infibeam etc. has become very popular due to better pricing and excellent delivery not only for books, but also for mobiles, electronics, apparels, consumer durables etc. Similarly in cars, most of the body parts and engine is made up of steel. Now aluminum is replacing steel for engine and plastics / fibres are on the way to replace steel body parts. So, Maruti Suzuki will not require the likes of Tata Steel, but it will require the likes of Hindalco, Bharat Aluminium Company (BALCO) and Indian Aluminium Company (INDAL).in the near future.

In today's scenario, you need to see the visible competition and envision the invisible ones. That's why 'new competitor intelligence' is required as told by Leonard M. Fuld in his book 'The New Competitor Intelligence: The complete resource for finding, analysing and using information about your competitors'.[2]

This book was followed by his another book called 'The Secret Language of Competitive Intelligence'. In this book, he said that

'today you need to thoroughly know your competition. Companies like Dell, Wal-Mart, and Google – even a pepperoni company - have rewritten the rule book. Success no longer relies simply on having first-rate products, stellar service, and efficient operations. In this new reality, competitive intelligence, the ability to see through or stay ahead of your competition, is the unspoken, hidden key to success.'

You need to list your competitors and other players, who are offering substitutes of your products. Once you are through with identifying your existing and potential competitors, you need to analyse their capabilities to capture your market. To understand the competitive forces deeper, you need to understand the Michael Porter's Five Forces Framework.

Michael Porter's Five Forces Framework

In the article 'How competitive forces shape strategy' in Harvard Business Review in 1979 and subsequently in 'Competitive Advantage: Creating and Sustaining Superior Performance', Michael Porter has talked about the following five forces for 'getting an analytical grasp on the state of competition and the underlying economics within an industry' (HBR, 1979).

1. The threat of substitute products
2. The threat of the entry of new competitors
3. The intensity of competitive rivalry
4. The bargaining power of customers and
5. The bargaining power of suppliers

Porter says that

'The collective strength of these forces determines the ultimate profit potential of an industry'. The key to growth and survival of any company depends upon understanding these five forces to 'stake out a position that is less vulnerable to attack from head to head opponents, whether established or new, and less vulnerable to erosion from the direction of buyers, suppliers and substitute goods'. The company should solidify relationships with profitable customers, by differentiating the product (through either redesign or marketing), by integrating operations or by gaining technical leadership.[3]

In the market, the strategies for success also depends upon the role, the respective company is playing in the target market. A company can be a leader like Airtel in GSM Mobile services and Reliance in CDMA Mobile Services or a company can be a challenger like Vodafone or a company might be the market follower like IDEA and Aircel or it can be a market nicher. All these players in the mobile service arena need to have different strategies for the success in the market.

Competitive Market Scenario in India

Now, the market is not only competitive, but it has become hyper competitive now. With globalization, almost all the markets across the world have been facing the challenge of hyper competition. In Indian market also, you may find that Chinese products is becoming an integral part in every festival like Holi with their pichkaris, Diwali with their Ganapati and Laxmi idol, colourful Diwali lights and Raksha Bandhan with their rakhis besides different gift products, Toys, Mobiles, MP3 players, Digital Cameras etc. Currently China has become the lowest cost producing country, which is making all the large companies in the world to either source or to have a production facility to take advantages of the benefits.

Similarly India is becoming a small car hub of the world with great domestic demand, low cost and high quality manufacturing facilities. That's why you see Indian cars, besides two wheelers, buses and trucks selling all across the world. Similarly so many business process outsourcing (BPOs) are working in India having businesses from US, UK and other countries. Now your competitive space has also expanded globally and it has become hyper competitive.

In a hyper competitive market, it becomes difficult for a company to sustain its competitive advantage for a long term. Now a company cannot sit back and relax. It has to be on its toes all the time to give the best value for the consumers.

Similarly the passenger vehicles market in India is also becoming a hypercompetitive market with more than 15 leading car manufacturers present in the segment with more than 500 variants of cars. Maruti Suzuki, with almost 37% market share in cars itself has 14 models and over 150 variants ranging from Alto to stylish hatchback Ritz, A-Star, Swift, Dzire, Ciaz sedan to luxury SUV Grand Vitara. If you talk about the mobile manufactures and sellers, you will find more than 20 companies operating in the market besides the Chinese mobiles selling in Indian market. Similarly as of 2010, there are more than 515 channels in the Indian satellite channel space, vying for viewer's attention.

Now let us delve deeper into it by analyzing few market segments, to understand the competition in these markets. We will check out the chocolates, potato chips, noodles, toothpaste, cars and telecom services market in India.

Marketing Insight 8.1

Marketing Insight 8.1

Happy with Surprise Toy, Kinder Joy for Ferrero

Italian co's differentiation strategy helps it beat Nestle's chocolate unit in incremental sales growth

In a small factory on the outskirts of Pune, a handful of employees spends most of its time thrashing out innovative tiny toys. They send the toys to school kids for approval before these are mass-produced. That's still only half the job done. The toys are then sent to Baramati, a rural area some 100 kilometres from Pune, where the company in question, chocolate maker Ferrero India, packs them as a surprise toy inside its Kinder Joy chocolate egg.

Kinder Joy

This surprise factor and other differentiation strategy in packaging and distribution seem to have paid off as Kinder, the German word for children, has helped the Italian chocolate maker beat Swiss giant Nestle's chocolate division in incremental sales growth last year. Ferrero India — which also sells Nutella spread, Ferrero Rocher chocolate and Tic Tac breath mint in the country — added 80 crore year-on-year to its revenues of nearly 341 crore in the year ended August 2012, according to its recent filing with the Registrar of Companies. Nestle India's chocolate division added 69 crore in its kitty last year despite being three times bigger than Ferrero with sales of 1,169 crore in the year ended December. Experts attribute this largely to the firm's differentiation strategy.

"Tic Tac has made its way into stationery shops, while the premium Rocher chocolate packs are available at small kirana stores as well," says an industry source. The ladoo-shaped Ferrero Rocher can be found on the shelves of even traditional mithai shops, which are otherwise considered direct rivals. A Ferrero India spokesperson says, "Innovation and close attention to customer requirements have led to the creation of unique products."

Chocolate Market in India Rs. 5562 Cr. As on Aug., 2012	
Brands	Market Share
Cadbury	67%
Nestle	21%
Ferrero India	6%
Others	6%

Ferrero India was set up about five years ago with headquarter in Bengaluru. After a brief market test in south India, it launched its products at the national level in May 2010. The firm makes Kinder Joy and Tic Tac at its Baramati factory. Officials close to the company say Rocher isn't the big focus of the company yet. Its Indian operations accounted for less than 1% of Ferrero International's revenues of □ 7.8 billion (approx 55,000 crore) last year. Ferrero managed to grow its India business more than 30% in spite of a slowdown in consumer spending as well as having its products priced at least 30% higher than the rival brands. Experts say catering to a niche segment worked in its favour as it largely averted direct competition with existing brands from Nestle and Cadbury. Ashutosh Chakradeo, head of buying and merchandising at HyperCITY Retail, a hypermarket format promoted by retail chain Shoppers Stop, says, "Ferrero Rocher as a product is a 365-day gifting option with an international halo around the brand with its premium positioning." Debashish Mukherjee, partner and Asia foods head at consulting firm AT Kearney, says, Ferrero is catering to two large gaps that existed in the Indian market —"mid-premium gifting space as well as products specifically designed for kids in India."

In fact, Rocher was a favourite gifting option even before Ferrero set up its operations in 2007. Even today, many retailers have the fear of running out of stock. "We have started blocking our orders for Ferrero during Diwali because experience tells us that there is always a greater risk of under stocking the product where demand far exceeds supply," says the head of a supermarket.

Ferrero Rocher

Industry watchers, however, warn that Ferrero will run into tougher competition in India as market leader Cadbury is becoming aggressive in the premium gifting segment by pushing its Swiss chocolate brand Toblerone. The legendary triangular chocolate bar already has 2% share in modern trade within a year of its launch.

Chandramouli Venkatesan, director, India and Asia Pacific developing markets (chocolates), for Mondeleez International, which owns Cadbury India, says Cadbury has been growing by over 30% since the last three years in India as affluent Indians are spending more. "Premium in our category is growing very substantially," he says.

Marketing Insight 8.2

Marketing Insight 8.2

Kurkure, Lays Slipping

PepsiCo's Chips Down, Local Rivals Flourish

Lays Balaji

Top snacks maker PepsiCo Foods has started slipping with a slew of smaller and regional brands eating into the market share of its flagship brands Kurkure snacks and Lays potato chips. Kurkure and Lays, which dominate the . 9,400-crore Indian snacks market, have begun losing share to regional players such as Gujarat-based Balaji, Indore's Yellow Diamond and DFM Foods' Crax in addition to some variants of ITC's Bingo snacks, which are matching the multinational on pricing, variants and regionalisation.

Industry official quoting Nielsen data said both Kurkure and Lays' market shares slipped 2-3% in the April-September period, while some others like ITC's Bingo, Balaji, Parle and even Yellow Diamond have gained. Nielsen data also shows that PepsiCo Foods' (FritoLay India) share in overall western snacks has slipped to 40% last fiscal from 48% in 2009-10.

A PepsiCo spokesperson said the company doesn't comment on market shares, which "fluctuate from quarter to quarter". "This year we have further strengthened our market position in all potato chips, Kurkure, baked snacks and traditional namkeen that we operate in, with more than 25 new launches including new category introductions like Kurkure Monster Paws and Kurkure Puffcorn," the person said.

Officials said the firm is banking on volumes, multiple packs and increased marketing spends to get back its market share. But then its smaller rivals too are widening their product portfolio and reach. DFM Foods, maker of Crax snacks, for example, stepped up its distribution in North India and launched Crax in the western markets last summer. "This has helped in our brand share going up," Mohit Satyanand, independent director atDFM Foods, said.

The salted snacks market in the country has been growing 25% a year, and smaller players have been fuelling category growth as much as bigger ones like Pepsi-Co, ITC and Haldiram's. And they are attracting the attention of private equity players. Mid last year, Sequoia Capital invested close to $30 million in Indore-based snack food maker Prakash Snacks, owner of Yellow Diamond chips. The eight-year-old Indore-based firm sells a range of chips and savoury puffs. PepsiCo has been selling products at prices ranging from Rs 2 to Rs 55 across categories.

Last year, it consolidated its masspriced snacks under a new entity, Lehar Foods, to take on regional brands such as Balaji, Bikanervala and A-Top Foods. It operates on a low-cost model and PepsiCo is hopeful that Lehar Foods will contribute 50% to the firm's foods division FritoLay by 2015. A couple of years back, PepsiCo attempted to buy out strong regional players such as Gujarat-based Balaji Wafers and A-Top Foods, but the talks did not materialise. Meanwhile, the competition is increasing. Biscuits and snacks maker Parle Products extended its portfolio to the traditional salted snacks category with the revamp of its 'Parle namkeens' earlier this month. "Whenever new products enter any category, the dominant player naturally gets impacted," B Krishna Rao, group product manager at Parle Products, said. He said the company was enthused by the product's initial response and hoped to capture 20% share by the end of this fiscal.

Marketing Insight 8.3

No Instant Karma Here

First Mover Maggi still rules the roost, Johnnie-come lately ITC has gained significant ground, and HUL and GSK Consumer still have to get their act right in the fast-growing instant noodles category

Maggi

Some 26 years after Nestle launched Maggi noodles with its captivating two-minute proposition, three big consumer products companies, Hindustan Unilever Ltd (HUL), Glaxo-SmithKiine Consumer Healthcare (GSKCH) and ITC, decided to test the waters.

Almost three years after these three giants got into the fray, Maggi still rules the roost, with more than three-fourths of the 2,500 crore market in the bag, as of September 2012. ITC's Yippee has done well to grab a double-digit share. Top Ramen from Nissin Foods of Japan, which entered the country way back in 1988, has a 4.3% slice of the pie. But the two multinationals, HUL with Knorr and GSK with Foodles, have yet to show any substantial gains.

For a category that is growing at 20% annually, and in a country in which instant foods are beginning to catch on with India's burgeoning middle class, you'd expect plenty of action in noodles. As Devendra Chawla, president, food & FMCG at Future Group, says: "Noodles are no longer considered a processed food; it has become mainstream, a choice rather than a last alternative and has come to be accepted as a part of the regular household menu."

Why then have brands from reputed consumer marketers not been able to make a dent? The biggest shocker is Foodles, which has used the health plank as a differentiator. According to a recent Edelweiss research report, Foodles' contribution has dipped roughly 24% year-on-year and the company has shifted focus to niche multi-grain offering, which earns higher gross margins but does not compete in the mass noodles segment.

Noodle Market in India *As on Sept., 2012, Source: Nielsen*	
Brands	**Market Share**
Maggie	**78.6%**
Sunfeast Yippee!	**10.6%**
Top Ramen	**4.3%**
Knorr	**3.0%**
Foodles	**0.7%**
Others	**2.8%**

HUL, which has extended a soup brand into the category, may be having trouble convincing consumers that Knorr is also a noodles label, say analysts. "The soup imagery of Knorr has made customers think of it as a product that is consumed during winters," says an analyst tracking the foods sector who did not want to be named. An HUL spokesperson declined to comment when contacted, although HUL's annual report for 2011-12 does say: "Knorr soupy noodles managed to double the business during the year as the product has received good response from consumers across all the markets."

ITC, for its part, is pleased as a punch with the share it has garnered so far, and attributes its No 2 position to factors like quality, inter-business synergies and distribution strength. V L Rajesh, executive vice president & head of marketing, foods division, ITC says: "We did few things that are pretty old fashioned really. Our hotels business has some of the most exceptional chefs in India today, and they have played a huge role in shaping our noodle offering." Rajesh adds that ITC's clout with distributors has also helped it reach consumers. "Distributors trust ITC. They know that if there is a product problem, we will take it back or we will find a solution to the problem."

Maggi, meantime, shows few signs of faltering, launching new variants — one of the newer ones is Maggi Masala Damdaar — and pulling out all stops to cement itself in the consumer mind space. In 2012, for instance, it signed on tinsel town superstar Amitabh Bachchan as brand ambassador. "Maggi is growing consumption by upsizing packs with various combo & multi packs," says Chawla.

If Nestle has to worry, it's less about the multinationals — at least for now — and more about regional players who have carved out handsome shares locally. One such marketer is CG Foods. The maker of the Wai Wai brand of noodles claims it is has been able to beat Maggi in the north east. G P Sah, global business head, CG Foods, claims that Wai Wai has a 65% market share in West Bengal and the north east.

Sunfeast Yippee

Sah goes on to claim that Wai Wai is also the second largest noodles seller in India with a 16% share (he pegs Maggi's share at 62%). "Wai Wai sells 20 lakh packs of noodles per day. And I challenge any brand that claims to be second to Maggi, if they have the guts to declare their numbers publicly," declares Sah.

Nissin Foods, which has shuttler Saina Nehwal promoting the brand, is attempting to leverage its early mover advantage and its ability to put out variants like 'cup noodles', 'mug noodles' and a curry variant in the market. "There is a huge opportunity in the Indian market and Top Ramen will develop products aimed at gaining more share. Our closest competition is Maggi, but they have been in the market for a longer time," says a spokesperson for Indo Nissin Foods.

The opportunity is indeed huge, what with instant noodles ceasing to be just a metro phenomenon and become popular in semi-urban and even rural markets. And the likes of ITC, which has made significant inroads into villages, are well placed to gain more ground. "We have the commitment to do what we should to become big in the market," says Rajesh.

Marketing Insight 8.4

Marketing Insight 8.4

Combined Share of Local Brands Slips to 2%

Big Players Brush Away Regional Toothpaste Firms

Colgate

Regional toothpaste brands, including Anchor and Vicco, have almost been wiped out from the . 7,000-crore Indian oral-care market as large players rapidly fill gaps in their network and product range to reach all areas of the country.

The combined share of all the local brands, including Vicco, Ajanta, Anchor, Smyle and Baidyanath — considered a major force just a decade ago — slipped to 2% in calendar 2013 from more than 5% two years ago, industry officials said, quoting data from Nielsen. Nielsen didn't validate the data, citing client confidentiality policies.

Regional players had over 15% share in the toothpaste market some 10 years ago. So what has changed? Big marketers such as Colgate, Hindustan Unilever and the lone Indian player in the big league, Dabur, have widened their reach to almost all rural and urban markets and slashed entry-level prices to . 5 and . 10 — hitting local brands on their home turf. Also, multinationals Procter & Gamble (P&G) and GlaxoSmithKline (GSK) entered the oral-care market recently, increasing competition.

"Pricing for bottom of the pyramid consumers were blurred by several national companies, including Dabur, in the last few years," Rana Banerjee, category head for oral care at Dabur, said. Dabur has 11% market share in the country's oral-care market. Banerjee said its Dabur Red toothpaste is the fastest growing brand in the market with 17% annual growth rate. The brand crossed Rs 200-crore mark last year. Companies such as Dabur and Hindustan Unilever (HUL) have doubled their rural reach over the past couple of years to grow their market share. Market leader Colgate, too, increased its share in the toothpaste segment to 54% last year, from 51% in 2011.

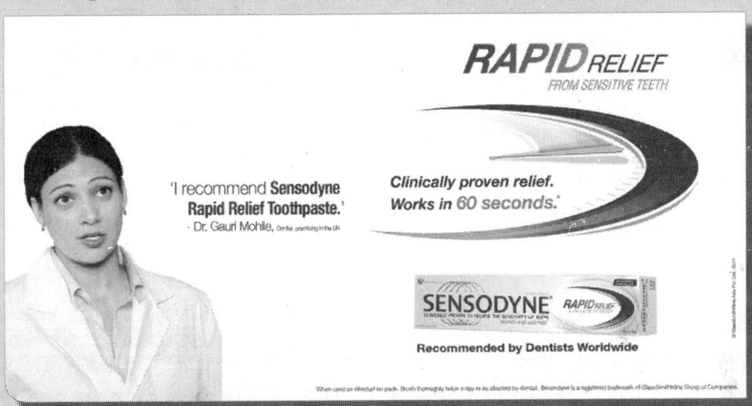

Sensodyne

Big players in the oral-care space also wooed consumers with value-added products that offer extra benefits at a small premium to the basic white toothpaste that most regional players sell. The successful entry of P&G and GSK to the market since 2011 also affected small regional players. GSK's Sensodyne has already gathered more than 2.3% share in the Indian oral care market, while P&G's mass brand Oral B has garnered a market share of 30 basis points in the first six months of its launch.

Jayant Singh, executive vice-president for marketing at GSK Consumer Healthcare, said Sensodyne has crossed . 100 crore in annual revenues and leads the sensitive toothpaste category with a 27% market share. "Localised taste, rising awareness, innovative retail display and aggressive advertising helped us establish brand Sensodyne," Singh said.

Marketing Insight 8.5

Marketing Insight 8.5

Maruti Suzuki Boosts Passenger Vehicle Market Share to 42% in FY14

Maruti S-Cross

NEW DELHI: The country's largest carmaker Maruti Suzuki India (MSI) consolidated its position in the passenger vehicles segment by increasing its share to 42 per cent in a declining market during 2013-14. Its closest rival remained Hyundai Motors India Ltd with a 15.18 per cent share, while Mahindra & Mahindra (10.15 per cent) overtook Tata Motors (7.94 per cent) to the third spot. Japanese major Honda was in fifth place with a market share of 5.36 per cent, just ahead of Toyota's 5.14 per cent.

Domestic sales of passenger vehicles, which includes cars, utility vehicles and vans, declined 6.05 per cent to 25,03,685 units in the previous financial year from 26,65,015 units in 2012-13, according to data from the Society of Indian Automobile Manufacturers (SIAM).

Maruti's market share increased from 39.43 per cent in 2012-13, when Hyundai's was 14.39 per cent, Mahindra's was 11.65 per cent and Tata Motors 11.79 per cent. During FY14, Maruti's passenger vehicle sales grew marginally to 10,53,689 units from 10,51,046 units in 2012-13. Hyundai sold 3,80,253 units in FY14 against 3,83,611 units in FY13. Mahindra's passenger vehicle sales were down 18.14 per cent to 2,54,344 units from 3,10,706 units. Tata Motors sold 1,98,812 passenger vehicles in FY14, a drop of 36.77 per cent from 314,464 units.

Honda Cars India, which had a good year riding on its compact sedan Amaze and the new City model, posted growth of 82.81 per cent to 1,34,339 units. Toyota Kirloskar Motor, which has been hit by labour unrest at its two plants in Bangalore, sold 1,28,811 units in 2013-14, down 22.17 per cent.

In the car segment, Maruti's sales in FY14 grew 3.38 per cent to 8,90,455 units, while that of Hyundai was down 0.86 per cent to 379,555 units. Honda's car sales zoomed 82.17 per cent to 1,33,321 units, while those of Tata Motors fell 38.64 per cent to 1,07,187 units. Toyota Kirloskar's car sales were down 21 per cent at 56,865 units. During the previous financial year, Mahindra's sales of utility vehicles dropped 16.86 per cent to 2,19,421 units.

Marketing Insight 8.6

Airtel, Vodafone and Idea Dominate Indian Telecom Sector

The three GSM incumbents have jointly crossed 70% in revenue market share, Trai data show

Vodafone

At first glance, the telecom regulator's numbers reveal that in the Indian market, Bharti Airtel Ltd, Vodafone India Ltd and Idea Cellular Ltd continue to lead the revenue market share charts. But take a deeper dive into the latest numbers released by the Telecom Regulatory Authority of India (Trai) and it reveals a landmark shift in India's telecom sector: GSM incumbents—Bharti Airtel, Vodafone and Idea Cellular—have jointly crossed 70% in revenue market share.

Idea

Numbers don't lie and this is precisely what they show: These three operators had a 99.6% share of the incremental revenues during the June 2013 quarter. Even if one were to assume that this was a one-off quarter, you still cannot fight the numbers—over the last 12 months, Bharti, Vodafone and Idea, have captured 91.1% of incremental revenues in a 13-player hyper competitive market.

Competitive Strategies

All these competitive market scenario calls for careful planning and implementation of right marketing strategies to sustain and grow in their respective markets. A company requires a right market strategy to do the same. Depending upon the market share in hand and the ambitions in heart, generally a company follows one of these four strategies to conquer the market.

Marketing Insight 8.7

The Great Indian Mobile Phone War

Welcome to the Great Indian Mobile Phone War.

Welcome to the Indian Market, where the homegrown Indian players like Micromax, Karbonn and Lava have waged a war for supremacy against the global behemoths like Samsung, Nokia, Motorola and Apple on the one hand and Chinese ones like Xiaomi, Gionee etc. on the other hand.

According to a recent report from Hong Kong based Counterpoint Research, Micromax became the leading mobile phone supplier brand in India in Q2 2014 for the first time ever by capturing 16.6% market share against Samsung's share of 14.4%. In the same report, it was also pointed out that Micromax has also become the leading feature phone supplier overtaking Nokia for the first time. But in the smartphone category, Samsung still maintains a wide lead with market share of 25.3% against Micromax's share of 19.1%.

Let us get into the data to understand the market scenario better. On the whole, mobile phone category can be classified under feature phone and the smart phone category.

Rank	Mobile Handset Shipments Share (%)	Q2 2014
1	Micromax	16.6%
2	Samsung	14.4%
3	Nokia	10.9%
4	Karbonn	9.5%
5	Lava	5.6%
	Others	43.0%
	Total	100%

Rank	Smartphone Shipments Share (%)	Q2 2014
1	Samsung	25.3%
2	Micromax	19.1%
3	Karbonn	5.9%
4	Motorola	4.3%
5	Nokia	4.0%
	Others	41.4%
	Total	100%

Rank	Feature Phone Shipments Share (%)	Q2 2014
1	Micromax	15.2%
2	Nokia	14.7%
3	Karbonn	11.4%
4	Samsung	8.5%
5	Lava	7.3%
	Others	42.9%
	Total	100%

Source: Counterpoint Research

Micromax

From the above table, we can conclude the following:

1. It is clear that Micromax is leading the sales in the mobile phone category on the whole and feature phone category in particular; while Samsung is still maintaining the lead in the smartphone category.
2. Now, Nokia is dethroned from the leadership position in the feature phone category and is taken over by Micromax.
3. All the tables also feature two more Indian mobile phone players i.e. Karbonn and Lava, besides Micromax.

Moto G

4) Another interesting fact is the entry of Motorola at fourth place with 4.3% market share in smartphone category. In all the tables, top five players have majority market share i.e. around 41 to 43% of the total mobile handset market in India.

On the contrary, a report by IDC suggests that Samsung leads Indian market in the 2nd quarter, but is closely followed by Micromax. Let us not get into the debate of who is no. 1 right now in the Indian market. We should look at the larger picture. The market is getting into hyper competitive mode and it will be difficult for any company to hold their forte. Few years back, Nokia was ruling the charts in India, now it is almost on the brink and hopes are also fading. Similarly Samsung has been quite strong in Indian market, but Micromax is currently giving a tough fight. Even in Chinese market also, Samsung has lost its dominance to Xiaomi, which is also nicknamed as 'Apple of China'. It's very interesting to know that both in Indian and Chinese markets, Samsung is dethroned from the top position by the local players like Micromax and Xiaomi. It is also interesting to note that both these companies are only 5-6 years old in the market.

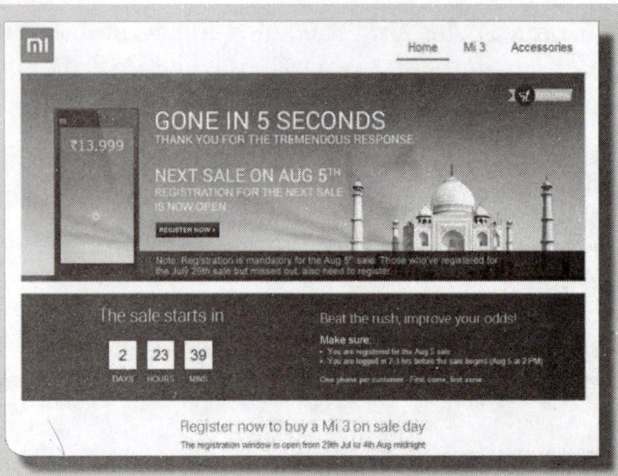

Xiaomi

But, both are following a different strategy. In India, Micromax sources the components from China and assembles the same in India; while Xiaomi has the advantage of in house manufacturing. It means Xiaomi can manufacture a handset at a lower cost than Micromax and thus, the most important edge of Micromax – its killer pricing, may not sustain in the near future or pricing may come at par with its competition. Advantages like strong dealer network and after sales service is also under attack, where Xiaomi and Motorola has gone to the online route by supplying directly through Flipkart and it has done wonders for Motorola. That's why you find Motorola being ranked on No. 4 with 4.3% market share.

Xiaomi also followed the online route and has sold 95,000 smart phones in six flash sales, organised by Flipkart. In the last sale on 26th August, Xiaomi sold 20,000 smart phones, while more than 1 Lac customers registered them selves to buy the same on Flipkart. In all these flash sales, the smart phone on offer Xiaomi Mi3 has been sold within ten seconds. This is the best, Xiaomi could have asked for in Indian market. This is also a warning signal for all Indian players like Micromax, Karbonn, Lava etc. that time has come to pull up their socks to be ready for the war.

As far as after sales service is concerned, companies which are selling online, are not far behind. Motorola already has a wide service network, while Xiaomi is looking for 24 hour turnaround time for its customers.

So, on the whole the macro picture looks very complex and so is the the future of these companies. Now let us talk about the developments, which are taking place in this market right now.

1. Mozilla has recently come out with a $35 Firefox OS smartphone and launched the same in collaboration with Spice named Fire One priced at Rs. 2299/-.

Android One

2. Google is also not far behind. It is launching smart phones under Android One project in India in the price range of $100 . These smart phones are going to be sold in India by Micromax, Karbonn and Spice. The only respite is that both these smartphones are going to be sold, in collaboration with Indian counterparts.

Xiaomi Mi 4

3. Xiaomi has launched Mi 4 at a price point of 1,999 yuan, that is around $322; which is almost half that of the iPhone 5s. Mi 4 is not only bigger than Apple's iPhone, but also rivals iPhone in terms of performance. It is expected to be launched by December in India. Currently Xiaomi is selling Mi 3 here.

4. Apple may be launching iPhone 6 on 9th Sept. This may further fortify its position in India. It has already gained ground in India by offering buyback, exchange and EMI schemes on its iPhone 5s and 5c.

Above are the current developments in this industry, which may impact future of various companies. The silver lining in this scenario is that Indian smart phone market is growing exponentially. In 2013, the market size was around 44 million mobile handsets, while in 2014, it is expected to touch 80 million handsets. It means that there is a lot of scope for all to grow. But all these companies needs to be vigilant all the time to sustain and grow in the market.

Just to add some drama to the story, do you know how big is Xiaomi? According to TrendForce, a Taiwanese market research company, Xiaomi was ranked seventh in the global smartphone market, with a share of 4%, in the January-March quarter this year. Xiaomi sold 26.1 million mobile handsets in the first half of 2014 i.e. around 4 million handsets more than what was sold in India in 2013 on half yearly basis.

So, the mobile handset market scenario looks tough ahead in India. Can we do something to improve the current situation? Yes, we can. In this hyper competitive scenario, all these companies need to follow what I call – the BIG approach.

The BIG Approach

The BIG approach is nothing but Branding, Innovation and Global Marketing.

All the Indian companies need to invest in their branding efforts. On this front, Micromax has taken a lead by earlier roping in Akshay Kumar as the brand ambassador for its feature phones, while they roped in Hugh Jackman for their Canvas series of mobile phones. But somehow, the advertising campaign does not look cohesive and a lot of efforts is still required on this front. Other companies like Karbonn and Lava are too far from the branding effort. Their efforts are mostly concentrated on announcing new phones with attractive pricing tag. Now is the time to wake up or, the consumer may count these mobile handsets third on the priority list, after Global players and Chinese ones.

Karbonn

Another aspect is innovation, which is crucial for the existence of these companies. On this front, these companies are quite in disadvantageous position, as they source all the components of a mobile handsets from China and are fully dependent upon them. That's why Mi 4 can come from China to counter Apple iPhone 5; but it may take long to come something from India to counter the likes of Apple and Samsung.

Every company needs to sustain and grow in the market, to achieve its business objective i.e. profit. Now Global marketing is no more a strategic decision, but a contemporary one. You need to play globally, to remain competitive in the market or you will be wiped out from the market. Tata Motors is a very good example, whose success today is mostly dependent upon its subsidiary Jaguar and Land Rover (JLR). It might be a good strategy for Micromax, Karbonn and Lava to expand globally. In this process, mergers and acquisitions may also help them to achieve nirvana, by integrating their business backward. In turn, it will help these companies to source the components of the mobile handsets.

Thus the BIG approach will help these companies to plan for today and tomorrow. These companies need to cultivate the habit of 'being proactive', as said by Stephen Covey in his book 'The Seven Habits of Highly Effective People'. This will help these companies to understand and anticipate the requirements of the customers better. If they can understand the customers better, they can serve them better.

It will be interesting to watch this space, as to who emerge as the winner in this Great Indian Mobile Phone War. Hope, an Indian company does. Amen....

Market Leader Strategies

The company with the largest market share in the respective market is called the market leader. Due to its sheer size, volume and revenue, the company enjoys a dominant position in its market, with brand preference, loyalty, price preference on the one hand to the distribution and promotional muscle on the other. Generally these companies also enjoy higher profits due to economies of scale as well as price premium.

Market leader leads the market through its product offerings and innovations, through its pricing, through the distribution network and through the promotional campaigns. Airtel, Microsoft, Intel, HP Printers, Reebok, Pepsi, HUL, Amul Butter, Nirma, Hero, Maruti Suzuki are few of the market leaders in India. Reebok and Pepsi leads the respective market segment in India, against Nike and Coke, which are the market leaders in USA.

Amul Butter

In the cars segment, the market is clearly dominated by Maruti Suzuki, while the two wheeler segment is ruled by Hero. It's an irony that Suzuki cars are selling like hot cakes in India, while Suzuki motorcycle is begging for buyers.

In the case of market leader, a company like Airtel has the largest market share and it tries to be better off than other players on the account of all the 4 Ps – Product, Price, Place and promotion. These companies tend to lead the market with innovations. Just to understand this, you may recall that Apple iPhone was launched in India in association with Airtel and Vodafone and then iPhone4 was launched with Airtel and Aircel. Now iPhone5 is also launched in association with Airtel.

Airtel 3G with iPhone 4

But the life is not so cool at the top. You need to innovate constantly with your product or service offerings; otherwise you will be dethroned by the market challenger, as it has happened in the case of general entertainment channel (GEC) segment in India. Star Plus was the market leader for the last few years and then there was a fight among Sony and Zee TV for the second place. Star Plus was sitting cool in the market, with the same kind of erstwhile successful Saas Bahu Programming. 9X came in the market and then there was the launch of NDTV Imagine. Both came and stayed in the market without having a presence. Then the real stunner came called Colors on July 21st, 2008. At that point of time, Star Plus was the leader in the segment and the fight for the second position was still going on between Zee and Sony. Within few months of existence, Colors grabbed the second place with its innovative programming like Balika Vadhu, Uttaran, Khatron Ke Khiladi, Big Boss and satellite premiere of Hindi film blockbusters.

Mahabharat on Star Plus

Now in 2014, Star Plus still leads the pack, but it is followed by Zee TV and Colors. While a relatively new entrant Life OK has also entered the general entertainment channel space and grabbed the fourth position with serials like Devon ka Dev Mahadev, Tumhari Pakhi, Shapath and Savdhaan India. Few of the leading programs now are Diya aur Baati Hum (Star Plus), Jodha Akbar (Zee TV), Saathiya Saath Nibhana (Star Plus), Yeh Rishta Kya Kehlata Hai (Star Plus), Mahabharat (Star Plus), Taarak Mehta Ka Ooltah Chashmah (SAB TV) and Comedy Nights with Kapil (Colors) and Dance India Dance (Zee TV).

CNBC Awaaz **Aaj Tak**

But the case is not the same in the hindi news segment. You still find Aaj Tak being No1 for the last thirteen years, due to being 'sabse tej' in content and programming among the Hindi news channels. Similarly in the hindi business news segment, CNBC Awaaz is on the top for the last nine years.

All these real life scenarios suggest that being on top has not been easy for everybody. It requires a consistent and sustained effort in the form of marketing strategy to keep the position intact. Generally a company can sustain and grow, if it can drive the total market demand or it may increase the market share, even if the market remain equal or it can try to maintain its market share in the current market.

Expanding the total market

Cadbury Dairy Milk

A market can be expanded either though adding new customers or it can be expanded with the increased usage of the product. Being a leader, the first thing a company can do is to expand the market base through new users, new uses and more usage. Once the market is expanded, it will automatically get you the most of additional customers. The same thing is applied successfully in India by the market leader, Cadbury in the chocolate segment. With more than 70% value market share, Cadbury has expanded the chocolate segment through its innovative promotional campaigns like 'Kuchh Khas Hai Zindagi Mei', 'Kuchhh Meetha Ho Jaye', 'Pappu pass ho gaya' and now 'Shubh Aarambh'. With these ad campaigns, Cadbury has not only added new customers, but also expanded the segment by new uses as well as more usage.

Defending Market Share

Before looking out for expanding the market, it's important for the market leader to also defend its market share. How does a company defend its market? A company can defend its market, if it can provide the best value to the customer. The value derived by the customer, can be in terms of pricing or branding or services or product offerings. But one thing is for sure, a company needs to innovate continuously and consistently. A company needs to be market driving, rather than market driven to lead the market. Sony, Apple, Google, Tata etc. are the companies, which are regularly following this principle.

The aim of the defensive strategy is to reduce the probability of attack, divert attacks to less threatening areas and lessen their intensity. The defender's speed of response can make an important difference in the profit consequences. A dominant company can use the six defense strategies summarized below:

1. Position Defense: In position defense, a company tries to fortify its image through branding efforts. Fevicol, Nestle, Amul has used this strategy effectively.

2. Flank Defense: In flank defense, a company tries to protect against potential loss of its market share by strengthening its competitive position there. When Nirma gained market share in the low priced detergent powder category, HUL got its act together to fight out Nirma with Wheel.
3. Preemptive Defense: Preemptive defense means defending a company by launching a strategy to preempt the moves of its competitors. The strategy has been well implemented by Apple, with preannouncements for its products, whether it is iPod or iPhone or iPad.
4. Counteroffensive Defense: Counter offensive defense is activated, when a leader is attacked. The leader comes out with a better proposition in the market to fight out the attacker. In the telecom segment, these moves are used by the competitors against Airtel. Where Airtel has come out with counterww0offensive strategies to hit the competitors hard.
5. Mobile Defense: In mobile defense, a company tries to broaden its marketing or it may diversify its operations. In the case of ITC, the company has moved on from a cigarette company to apparel to food processing to stationery to confectionery and so on. Again in the case of Moser Baer has diversified its activities into solar panel from optical disk manufacturing and video marketing company.
6. Contraction Defense: Sometimes, a company also withdraws from some segments or territories to focus on the core areas. Following this path, Tata Group sold its soaps and detergents business units to Unilever in 1993.

Expanding Market Share

The market leader should not only try to defend its market share, but should also try to expand its market share. But in the era of hyper competition, it becomes very difficult for a company to expand its market share. In some cases, while defending its market share, a company also happens to increase its market share. But this may be a one off case.

On the whole, the market leader should try to expand the market, which in turn will bring more business automatically for the company. But most of the time, we find the leaders like Maruti Suzuki, Nokia, Airtel etc, are struggling to defend their market share.

Market Challenger Strategies

Vodafone

Market challenger companies are those companies, who are occupying a second or third or some lower position in the market like Vodafone (No. 2 Player in GSM Mobile) and try to be in the aggressive bid for increasing the market share. If the companies choose not to aggressively look out for No. 1 position, then those companies can be called as market followers. Market challenger can either attack the Leader like Colors or it can attack the firms of its own size, as it was happening in the case of Sony and Zee or it can attack smaller, regional firms. The market challenger may give discounts, offer cheap prices, provide better service or can launch an intense ad campaign to lure the customers. Here innovation can also help a company to challenge the market leader. In the smart phone category, Samsung is leading the path with the right product portfolio of Samsung Galaxy range of mobile phones.

Market Follower Strategies

Market follower companies prefer to follow the market leader, than to challenge. These companies look out for sustaining their market base with fair share of incremental customers. In the case of capital intensive industries like cement, fertilisers, steel and chemical industries; the scale of product differentiation is minimal. In these industries, the price plays an important role, but the service is not that important. Till the time, you want a decent turnover in the industry with average profits; everything works fine. But if you have stronger ambition, then you need to promote yourself as a market challenger rather being a market follower. For example, in the cement market in India, the market is led by ACC and challenged by Ambuja, Grasim and Ultratech cement. Still you will find other players like Jaypee Cement and Binani Cement trying to make their mark with their celebrity endorsers like Sachin Tendulkar and Amitabh Bachchan respectively.

Binani Cement

Although innovation is essential for any company to survive and grow,

Theodore Levitt's viewpoint is that a strategy of product imitation is as profitable as a strategy of product innovation.[5]

In the case of product imitation, the company does not need to bear the cost of innovation and still has the benefit of selling at a similar kind of profit. It leads to better profitability for the company. But it has been found that the companies, which are market follower generally remains a market follower. All the large and successful companies are those, who are operating as a market leader or market challenger. Again the image of a company is built by the innovation it does, not on the basis of imitation. For example, the brand names of Apple, Sony, Microsoft, Intel, Tata, Mahindra and Mahindra, Nirma, Infosys are respected a lot due to their philosophy of constant innovation and customer centricism.

Market Nicher Strategies

Logitech

Logitech

The strategy of market nicher has also found to be successful. If you cannot be the leader, you become the challenger or else you become a market nicher. Market nicher specialises in catering to a small segment. Generally these segments are also safe as far as competition is concerned, as these are too small for large companies to get attention to. The strategy of market nichers is also advocated by the positioning guru Al Ries and Jack Trout. As market nichers are leaders in their own segment, they can easily expand their operations based on the goodwill and image they have created in the market. Logitech, the famous computer mouse company, has expanded from catering to a niche manufacturer of mice to several computer peripherals like Keyboards, webcams, Speakers, remotes, gaming accessories and laptop accessories.

Intex

In India, a company called Intex Technologies started their operations under the leadership of Mr Narendra Bansal and started selling Ethernet Cards, sourced from Taiwan and China. From being a nicher, Intex has now expanded into six business segments- Computer Peripherals, PC, Mobile Phones, Consumer Electronics, Retail and Enterprise Business. The business segments cover a portfolio of 26 Product Groups spread across 350 items including Mobile TFT-LCD monitors, DVD players, Computer UPS, Mobile Phones (GSM, CDMA, Dual SIM), Desktops, Netbooks, Multimedia Speakers, Home UPS, Cabinets, Headphones and Web Cameras; to name just a few. Now, Intex is the most selling brand in the computer UPS category (IDC Tracker, Q2, 2009) and also enjoys leading market share in many states in India for several other product groups such as Multimedia Speakers, Keyboards, Mouse, Add-on cards, etc.

On the whole, **Consumer orientation and competitor orientation is the two most important aspects for the growth and success of any business.**

Amazon

But there should be a good balance between both the orientations. The priority for any company should always be customer orientation rather than competitor orientation. The same has also been echoed by Jeff Bezos, the founder of the largest online bookstore in the world Amazon.com.

'Amazon.com's mantra has been that we were going to obsess over our customer and not our competitors. We watch our competitors, learn from them, see the things that they were doing good for customers and copy these things as much as we can. But we were never going to obsess over them.'[6] – Jeff Bezos.

Summary

- Competition is all about current and potential offerings and substitutes that a customer may consider.
- According to Michael Porter, the key to growth and survival of any company depends upon understanding these five forces: the threat of substitute products, the threat of the entry of new competitors, the intensity of competitive rivalry, the bargaining power of customers and the bargaining power of suppliers.
- A company requires a right market strategy to counter the competition. Depending upon the market share in hand and the ambitions in heart, generally a company follows one of the four strategies to conquer the market.
- The company with the largest market share in the respective market is called the market leader. In the case of market leader, a company tries to be better off than other players on the account of all the 4 Ps – Product, Price, Place and promotion. These companies also tend to lead the market with innovations. Generally a company can sustain and grow, if it can drive the total market demand or it may increase the market share, even if the market remain equal or it can try to maintain its market share in the current market.
- Market challenger companies are those companies, who are occupying a second or third or some lower position in the market. These companies try to be in the aggressive bid for increasing the market share. These companies may give discounts, offer cheap prices, provide better service or can launch an intense ad campaign to lure the customers. Here innovation can also help a company to challenge the market leader.
- Market follower companies prefer to follow the market leader, than to challenge. These companies look out for sustaining their market base with fair share of incremental customers.
- If you cannot be the leader, you become the challenger or else you become a market nicher. Market nicher specialises in catering to a small segment. Generally these segments are also safe as far as competition is concerned, as these are too small for large companies to get attention to.

- Consumer orientation and competitor orientation is the two most important aspects for the growth and success of any business. But there should be a good balance between both the orientations. The priority for any company should always be customer orientation rather than competitor orientation.

Discussion Questions

1. What do you mean by Competition? Discuss competition in the context of any one product market or service market in India.
2. Discuss the role and importance of competition. Explain Michael Porter's Five Forces Framework in detail.
3. Discuss the various competitive strategies in detail with the right examples.
4. What is the difference between a market leader and a market challenger? Discuss their strategies to succeed in the market.
5. Discuss the difference between market challenger and market follower with an example. Also elaborate their strategies to succeed in the market.
6. What do you mean by a market leader? How do you expand a market to increase your sales?
7. Short Notes:
   a. Market Leader
   b. Competitor Intelligence
   c. Market Nicher
   d. Threat of Substitute Products
   e. Bargaining Power of Customers
   f. Market Challenger
   g. Five Forces Framework
   h. Consumer Orientation vs. Competitor Orientatio

References

1. Leonard M. Fuld, 'The New Competitor Intelligence: The complete resource for finding, analysing and using information about your competitors', John Wiley, 1995

2. Leonard M. Fuld, 'The New Competitor Intelligence: The complete resource for finding, analysing and using information about your competitors', John Wiley, 1995
3. Michael E. Porter, 'How competitive forces shape strategy' in Harvard Business Review, March-April 1979, p. 113-135
4. Philip Kotler and Ravi Singh, 'Marketing Warfare in the 1980S', Journal of Business Strategy (Winter, 1981), p. 30-41
5. Theodore Levitt, 'Innovation Limitation', Harvard Business Review, Sept. – Oct., 1966 p.63
6. Robert Spector, 'Amazon.com: Get Big Fast', Harper Business, 2000, p. 151

Chapter 9

Brand

Chapter Structure

'A brand for a company is like a reputation for a person. You earn reputation by trying to do hard things well.' -

-Jeff Bezos

'And I'm not an actress. I don't think I am an actress. I think I've created a brand and a business.'

- Pamela Anderson

'What's a brand? A singular idea or concept that you own inside the mind of the prospect.' -

-Al Ries

Positioning

Positioning is an important concept in marketing. It plays a crucial role in the success of a product or service in the market. In the era of hyper competition and over communication, it becomes extremely difficult for the company to differentiate its product from competition. In almost all the product categories, there are ten to fifteen companies, which are vying for the consumers' attention. On the top of it, plethora of media vehicles makes the job even more difficult for the marketer to communicate the consumers. That's why it becomes extremely important for the marketer to create a distinct and persuasive image in the minds of the consumer, to stand out from the crowd. Thus, Positioning is all about creating an image or identity in the minds of the customers.

The term 'Positioning' was first coined by Jack Trout in the paper 'Positioning is a game people play in today's me-too market place' in the publication Industrial Marketing. Then it was expanded into the ground-breaking first book, 'Positioning: The Battle for Your Mind', written by Jack Trout with Al Ries.

In this book, they have defined **Positioning as "an organized system for finding a window in the mind. It is based on the concept that communication can only take place at the right time and under the right circumstances"**[1]

According to Al Ries and Jack Trout, positioning is something (perception) that happens in the minds of the target market. It is the aggregate perception the market has of a particular company, product or service in relation to their perceptions of the competitors in the same category. It will happen whether or not a company's management is proactive, reactive or passive about the on-going process of evolving a position. But a company can positively influence the perceptions through enlightened strategic actions.

In marketing, positioning has come to mean the process by which marketers try to create an image or identity in the minds of their target market for its product, brand, or organization. It is the 'relative competitive comparison' their product occupies in a given market as perceived by the target market.

'Products are created in the factory, but the brands are created in the mind.'
– Jack Trout

In Indian market, Amul with slogan 'Utterly Butterly Delicious Amul', Lux with 'The Beauty Soap of Film stars, Fevicol with 'The Ultimate Adhesive', Vodafone with 'Wherever you go, our network follows' and now with 'Zoozoo' are few of the examples of excellent positioning by the respective companies.

Marketing Insight 9.1

Marketing Insight 9.1

How Fevicol went on to enjoy equity that billion dollar cola and soap labels do

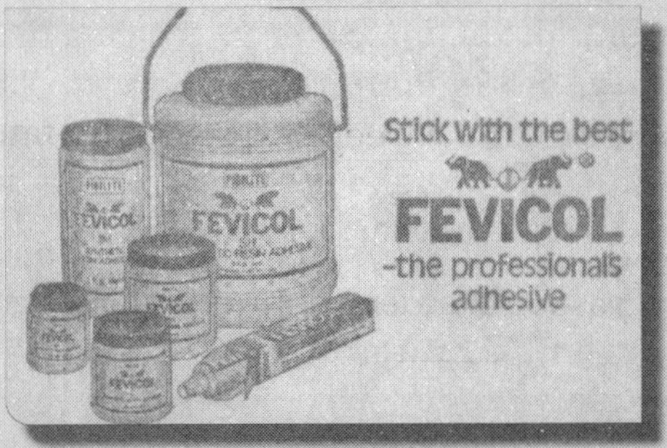

Some 33 years after the Fevicol was launched came the television commercial with the memorable line 'dum lagake haisha,' which took the synthetic adhesive brand from Pidilite Industries into consumer homes and into advertising halls of fame. But over the past five decades a lot more has gone into "the 100% mindshare" that Prabhakar Jain, CEO, global Fevicol division at Pidilite, claims the brand has today.

From warding off competition — both small-scale to multinationals like Hoechst Dyes & Chemicals (which had a similar brand of white glue called Movicol); to creating a durable bond with carpenters; to innovative packaging and retailing that brought the brand within buying distance of households, the Fevicol story is one of progression and case study on how to transform a brand in a low-involvement category into one that enjoys recall and equity reserved for colas, soaps and shampoos.

Today Fevicol is distributed through 1,000 stockists, 60,000 retailers and has a presence across 80% towns of India — not bad for a brand whose core customer is the carpenter. "The carpenters give us valuable feedback because they use the product on a daily basis," explains Jain.

They also participate in what Fevicol calls Champion Day where every member of 'Carpenter Clubs' — in which carpenters are taught to read interior design drawings, and use new electric tools, amongst other activities — is required to undertake one day of social work. "These carpenters earn well, but lack prestige in the society. Through the various activities, we want to help them feel valued," explains Jain.

And then there's the advertising that made the brand a fast-moving consumer product. Ad veteran Piyush Pandey has been handling the brand since his early days at Ogilvy and counts the work done on Fevicol as among the best in his career. He reminisces about the time he first presented to the founders.

What Pandey had created was a radio spot for a brand extension called Fevitite, a 'super-fast' adhesive. "I did the voiceover, took a few of my colleagues and 5-6 people from my sister's theatre group and recorded it." The spot was 'Fevitite ka majboot jod hain...tutega nahi.' Pandey says he was very scared when he presented to the client, "I was only six months old in Ogilvy," he says. When the Parekhs — the founders of Pidilite — heard the spot, they liked it a lot and asked Pandey to make a TVC out of it. Pandey then roped in his friend and editor Raju Hirani to act in the 'Dum Lagake Haisha' ad — way before Hirani went behind the camera to make '3 Idiots.'

When Pandey showed the ad to the Parekhs, he says "they spoke the most beautiful words that I have ever heard in my career to date." The family opened up the purse strings to Pandey and told them to re-shoot the entire commercial for Fevicol as they felt the ad was better suited to the mother brand.

Piyush's younger brother Prasoon Pandey, founder of Corcoise Films, remembers being confronted on the roads of Mumbai by a stranger. "He said you make Fevicol ads, right? I have an idea for you," guffaws Pandey. The elder Pandey gives complete credit to the client team. "Fevicol likes to experiment. They always say let's do something new. They are innovative and not risk averse. They are not formula-driven. And they are really quick at taking decisions, something I have never seen in MNCs," he shares. From being a scared advertising newbie, sent to handle a 'boring' client, Piyush Pandey rode on Fevicol and vice-versa to success.

For the longest time, Fevicol had the imagery of Rajasthan associated with it. However both Pandeys say it was not intentional. "We have grown up in Rajasthan, maybe that is why we found a lot of plots that lent themselves well to Fevicol," says Piyush. Talking about the 'Bus' commercial — which has an overcrowded bus but people don't fall off it thanks to Fevicol — which won a silver Lion at Cannes, Prasoon says they were initially planning to shoot in Film City, Mumbai. "But I had seen such overcrowded buses in Rajasthan. Travelling in a desert, with local people, I just knew Rajasthan would be a good setting for the ad," explains Prasoon.

Other unforgettable commercials against a Rajasthani backdrop from Ogilvy include one with the unbreakable egg (the hen was being fed out of a Fevicol can) and another is the 'moochwali' ad in which a girl sticks a moustache on for a skit — with Fevicol, obviously — only to be stuck with it for a lifetime.

Abhijit Avasthi, national creative director at Ogilvy, recalls creating a radio spot that went: "Woh kaunsi cheez hai job aapke cheezon ko hamesha jode rakhti hai? Bilkul sahi, bas wahi ek hai joh saalon se aapke cheezon ko jod raha hai." (What keeps things stuck together? Absolutely correct! It's the only thing that can keep things stuck for years.) In this spot, the brand name wasn't mentioned even once, but everybody understood that the spot is for Fevicol. "It is like Nike, which has a language of its own. You need not write Nike next to the swoosh. People know what it is," says Prasoon.

Amul

Fevicol

Vodafone

Sometimes it may also happen that more than one company is looking after the same position. In this case, either the company has to employ to say the same things differently or it may look out for points of differentiation. In India, every car manufacturer talks about the fuel efficiency. But Maruti Suzuki and Tata say it differently. Maruti Suzuki runs an ad campaign, where it goes with the saying 'Kitna deti hai?' (How much is the mileage?); while Tata goes directly with their fuel efficiency figures. Now even, Honda advertises its cars like Amaze and City with the class leading fuel economy of 25.8 kmpl.

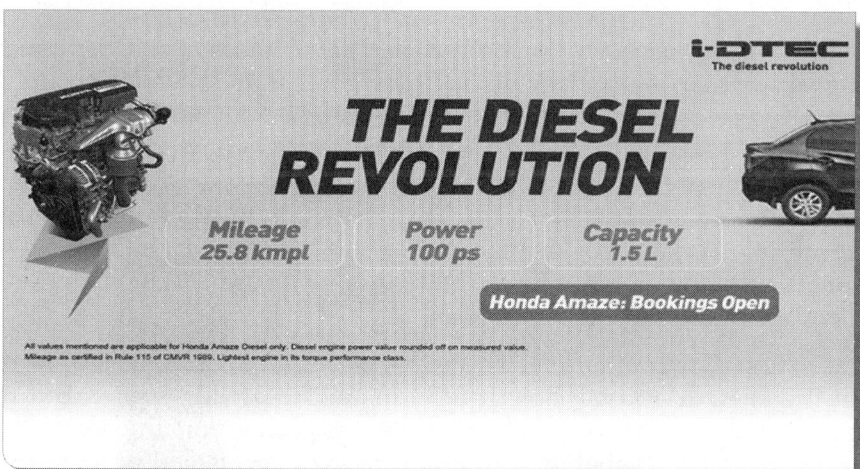

Honda Amaze

Similarly in airline services, Indigo distinctly differentiates itself from other airlines operating in India with its on-time performance and promotes the same with an advertisement with the headline 'Indigo Standard Time'.

Marketing Insight 9.2

Cool Branding Lands IndiGo in Biz Class

Moves from a budget airline to a preferred business carrier through reliability & low cost

In 2006, when global advertising agency Wieden+Kennedy took on the task of building a new, cool airline brand from scratch, their peers laughed. Indian passengers, the conventional wisdom went, cared only about price, and no amount of branding could change that. "Today, they don't ask us that question anymore," says Mohit Dhar Jayal, MD, Wieden+Kennedy Delhi.

Despite launching squarely in the budget airline segment, IndiGo promoter Rahul Bhatia and his agency were clear about their goal: IndiGo would be the third cool international budget carrier after JetBlue and Southwest Airlines of the US. And it's got there. According to aviation expert Rajan Mehra, IndiGo now carries more corporate passengers than leisure travellers. "The mix of corporate and holiday travellers for IndiGo has increased to 60:40," he says. This transition in positioning and perception was the result of a very conscious plan put together by the brand and agency. At the time of launch, print and outdoor media were used to focus on launch markets, with the tagline "Ready for take-off".

The airline's first TV commercial was clearly targeted on a first-time or at least infrequent traveller, describing how IndiGo made the process easier. But quite soon, focus was switched to customer touch points — everything from the design of the safety instruction card, to the availability of a boarding ramp instead of a staircase, to the packaging of in-flight snacks were aimed at being more engaging, while still on-brand. This was the crucial phase when the voice of brand IndiGo would speak directly to the passenger, drawing attention to the high standards of service.

"The real challenge was the transition to the new ideology and clientele because lowcost carriers behave in a certain way. They wear the 'common-man' badge, like say Air Deccan. Once that was overcome, the position only evolved," recalls V Sunil, executive creative director, W+K. The next stage was a subtle switch to target the corporate passenger by emphasising on-time performance.

One of IndiGo's most popular TV commercials in 2010 featured a musical-style depiction of the link between making its processes more efficient and getting its passengers to their destinations on time. A voiceover added: "When we get our work done on time we become the world's most powerful economy on time; on time is a wonderful thing."

Indigo's outdoor advertising of new flights also emphasises their value to the business traveller, focusing on metro routes and frequency. Today, it has companies like Airtel, Coca-Cola, the Tata Group, GSK and the Aditya Birla Group signed up as corporate clients – giving them a premium seat allocation and on-board meal bundled with each ticket purchased. Global brand consultancy firm Wolff Olins feels that IndiGo's high service standards are the key to its share of the corporate travel market. "For a business traveller, IndiGo stands for reliability. It then stands for low cost," says Zia Patel, Wolff Olins India strategy head.

But like all market leaders, there is now tremendous pressure of expectation. Anand Halve, founder of communications consultancy firm chlorophyll points out: "When you start slipping on things, people start noticing. They have a huge lead compared with rivals and so a margin of error too, but not for long." Fresh competition from AirAsia could mean trouble as well. "The biggest mistake that IndiGo could do is to ignore AirAsia. They should not let AirAsia prove that the latter could be better. The focus should be to enrich, extend and deepen the brand," Halve added. No problem, says Wieden + Kennedy. There'll soon be something new that addresses these issues, but "the IndiGoness will not go," says V Sunil.

Indigo Airlines

The differentiation and positioning task consists of three steps[2]:

- Identifying a set of differentiating competitive advantages upon which to build a position,
- Choosing the right competitive advantage and
- Selecting an overall positioning strategy.

Repositioning

Sometimes, a company may also need to change its positioning, if it is not working or if the market scenario has changed. In this case, it may need to reposition itself. Repositioning involves changing the positioning platform to suit the identity of the product in the marketing environment against the competition.

Depositioning

On the other hand, sometimes a company may go for de-positioning to change the identity of competing products, relative to the identity of your own product, in the minds of the customers. Tata Motors generally compare its cars with the leading player in the segment like Vista with Swift and now Manza with Amaze.

Tata Vista Ad – Taking a dig on Maruti Swift

In the ad, Tata Manza is trying to compete head on with Honda's bestseller Amaze, by talking about its big space with 'Bigger is better' headline.

Kingfisher Ad – Taking a dig on Indigo Airlines

To break the growing clout of low cost carriers in India especially Indigo, Kingfisher ran an ad campaign with tagline, 'Why fly low cost carriers, Fly Kingfisher'.

Jet Aiways - Kingfisher - Go Air Hoarding

In airlines industry in India, the cut throat competition has taken the airlines companies far in their advertisement. Few years back, with the Kingfisher airlines hogging the space for being a five star airlines through its advertisements, Jet Airways came out with a campaign called 'We have changed'. To counter this, Kingfisher came up with an advertising campaign – 'We made them change'. Taking it far, Go Air came out with the campaign 'We have not changed; we are still the smartest way to fly'.

Brand

What is a brand? American Marketing Association has defined

Brand as a name, term, sign, symbol or design or a combination of them, intended to identify the goods or services of one seller or group of sellers and to differentiate them from those of competitors.

Under trademark law, the seller is granted exclusive rights to the use of the brand name in perpetuity. Brand is the art and cornerstone of marketing. Perhaps the most distinctive skill of professional marketer is their ability to create, maintain, protect and enhance brands. A brand is essentially a marketer's promise to deliver a specific set of features, benefits and services consistently to the buyers. Brands vary in the amount of power and value they have in the marketplace. At one extreme are brands that are not known by the most buyers. Then there are brands for which buyers have a fairly high degree of brand awareness.[3]

Branding helps the companies to stay ahead in the business than their competition. On the one hand, it helps the customers to differentiate between the different products and on the other hand customers are also loyal to the brand. Most of the time, differentiation between the products are not real. But it is psychological and these differences are created with the right kind of messages projected through right media vehicles to the customers. Branding also helps to fight the price wars. Most of the time, customers are willing to pay 10% to 20% more for a brand. In some categories, it can go up to 30% to 40 %.

The brand needs to be regularly fortified through the real differences - innovations and the psychological differences – image building exercises. Recently, Vodafone's advertising campaign with the character Zoozoo has been so popular with the masses that it has got more that two lacs fans on Facebook. In turn, it helps Vodafone to occupy the top of the mind recall value for the brand Vodafone. Although there is no real differentiator as far as the mobile service is concerned with respect to the competition, yet this campaign has successfully created psychological differentiation. Similarly, Nokia, Colgate, Dettol, Fevicol, Surf Excel, Cadbury's Dairy Milk, Amul Butter, Parle G etc. have all been successful in fortifying their brand images through their communication messages.

Marketing Insight 9.3

Marketing Insight 9.3

Welcome to Rs. 1000 Crore FMCG Club

Welcome to Rs.1000 Crore FMCG Club

Let me ask you few multiple choice questions.

Q1. Name the highest selling consumer goods brand in India?

a) Surf b) Parle G c) Wheel d) Lux

Q2. Name the highest selling brand of Hindustan Unilever limited (HUL)?

a) Wheel b) Lifebuoy c) Surf d) Lux

Q3. Can you name the top 3 consumer products company in India?

a) HUL, Nestle India and GCMMF (Amul)

b) Nestle, HUL and P&G

c) HUL, GCMMF (Amul) and Nestle India

d) HUL, P&G and ITC

Q4. Identify the market size of the largest consumer goods company in India?

a) Rs. 30000 Cr. plus b) Rs. 18000 Cr. plus c) Rs. 39000 Cr. plus d) Rs. 9000 Cr. plus

Q5. Name the FMCG company with the maximum number of brands in Rs. 1000 Cr. club?

a) P&G b) Nestle c) ITC d) HUL

I hope, you got most of the answers right. The answers are given at the end of the article.

Before we move further, let us understand, what do you mean by FMCG. As you know, FMCG means Fast Moving Consumer Goods. Now the question arises, where does the goods move fast. Here, the answer is on the retail shelves. When the goods move fast on the retail shelves, it is known as FMCG.

Now, let us get into technicalities.

Fast Moving Consumer Goods are of low unit value with high volume potential and require frequent repurchase.

These frequent purchases make FMCG move faster on the retail shelves. FMCG generally include a wide variety of frequently purchased products such as toothpaste, shampoo, soap, cosmetics, hair oil and detergents, as well as other non-durables such as plastic goods, CFL bulbs, paper & stationery and glassware. FMCG may also include chocolates, pharmaceuticals, packaged food products and soft drinks.

In 2013, the market size of FMCG industry was Rs. 2.2 lakh-crore in India. The top 10 companies in the FMCG sector are Hindustan Unilever Limited (HUL), Amul, Nestle India, ITC, Procter & Gamble, Dabur, Asian Paints, Cadbury India, Britannia Industries and Marico Industries. While other leading companies in this segment are Reckitt Benckiser, GlaxoSmithKline, Pepsi, Coke, Himalaya, Bajaj, Godrej etc.

According to a news report published in 'The Economic Times' dt. 29th Oct., 2014; Procter & Gamble, one of the top two FMCG firms in the world, has topped Nestle and ITC to become India's third-largest consumer products maker after HUL and GCMMF (Amul) (Kindly check out the table 1 below).

Table 1 : Top 5 Consumer Products Maker in India

Company	FY14 Revenue (In Cr. Rs.)	CAGR %	Major Brands
Hindustan Unilever Ltd.	30053	13.1	Rin, Surf Excel, Wheel, Lux, Lifebuoy, Fair & Lovely, Dove, Pond's and Clinic Plus
GCMMF (Amul)	18143	22.7	Amul
P&G India	9274	23.7	Ariel, Tide, Whisper, Vicks and Gillette
Nestle India	9197	15.5	Maggi, Nescafe, KitKat, Munch and Everyday
ITC – FMCG	8099	22.1	Aashirvaad, Sunfeast, Bingo!, Vivel, Fiama Di Wills, Minto, Candyman, Vivel and Superia

As you can check out from the above table, the top 5 consumer products maker in India are HUL, GCMMF (Amul), P&G India, Nestle India and ITC. The fastest growing company in the list is Proctor & Gamble; while the growth of HUL is the lowest. But you should also keep in mind that HUL is more than three times bigger than P&G India or Nestle India or ITC – FMCG. It is also interesting to find that HUL and Amul, the top two players in this category, are not competing against each other in any segment.

Now, let us talk about Rs. 1000 Crore club and answer the Question 1, 2 and 5. The highest selling consumer brand in India is Parle-G. In 2012 only, it crossed Rs. 5000 Crore mark to become the largest consumer brand in India. It also has the distinction of being the largest selling biscuit brand in the world. Started a long way back in 1939, Parle G has come a long way in redefining the biscuit market in India. Parle-G is a good marketing case to understand, as to how do you stay relevant in the market and also sustain and grow your brand with the changing times. In the last 75 years, its value proposition, affordability, quality has remained unchanged. And that's what Parle-G is promoting through an ad campaign – 'Pehli Wali Baat'. Please Check out the television commercial (TVC) above.

Brand	Sales at MRP (In Rs., 2012 Data)
Parle-G	5010 Cr.
Wheel	3700 Cr.
Ghari	3500 Cr.
Lifebuoy/Lux	2800 – 3000 Cr.
Surf	2900 Cr.

The other highest selling brands in the top 5 list are Wheel, Ghari, Lifebuoy/Lux and Surf. All these brands are owned by HUL, except Ghari which is owned by Rohit Surfactants Pvt. Ltd. (RSPL).While the second and third brand i.e. Wheel and Ghari are fighting out against each other in the low cost detergent powder category. Personal soap category is also making their presence felt at No. 4 slot with Lifebuoy and Lux; while Surf completes the list through its presence in the detergent powder category.

Surf Excel

Ghari Detergent

Lux

It is also very interesting to note that HUL has got the highest number of brands crossing the magic figure of Rs. 1000 crore in sales (FY13), under its belt. The list is pretty long with ten entries i.e. **Rin, Surf Excel, Wheel, Brooke Bond, Lux, Lifebuoy, Fair & Lovely, Clinic Plus, Pond's and Dove. Wheel,** currently the highest selling brand in HUL, took almost three decades to reach Rs. 1000 Cr. mark, while Dove only took two decades after its launch in 1993 in India. Even, Dove has the distinction of being the fastest growing brand in the last few years. It has grown ten times between 2007 and 2013 from a mere Rs. 100 Cr. to become Rs. 1000 Cr. brand. Dove has played its brand extension card well by transforming itself from just a bathing bar to conditioners, deodorants, hair oil, lotions, body and face wash.

Dove

Besides HUL, PepsiCo and Coke have also many brands under their sleeves clocking turnovers of more than Rs. 1000 crore. The list includes PepsiCo's Pepsi Cola , 7Up , Mirinda, Slice Lay's and Kurkure. It also includes Coke's Maaza , Thums Up, Sprite,

Fanta and Limca Mountain Dew, Coke and Kinley. All these brands are doing quite well in India. In this list, there is also the presence of Colgate, Maggi, ITC's Aashirvaad atta and Sunfeast biscuits and so on. The list is pretty long and many brands are on the verge of joining the list.

As long as a company fulfils the needs of consumers and keeps the faith of the consumers in the brand on a sustained basis, the brand can only look upward and Parle-G has been doing the same for the last 75 years and many more years to come.

Disclaimer : The listing of brands are not exhaustive, but only indicative. The revenue quoted for specific brands are applicable to the respective financial year.

Answers:

Q1. b) Parle G

Q2. a) Wheel

Q3 c) HUL, GCMMF (Amul) and Nestle India

Q4. a) Rs. 30000 Cr. plus

Q5. d) HUL

Branding means to create a new brand. With the advent of packaging, brands originated in the 19th Century. But the idea of marking things, people or animals by burning identifying marks on them was an ancient practice. That's why the word "brand" is derived from the **Old Norse brandr** which means **'to burn'**. It refers to the practice of producers burning their mark (or brand) onto their products.[4]

The first registered brand in the world was the red triangle, registered by Bass Beer, England. It was the first trademark to be registered under the British Trade Mark Registration Act 1875, filed as trademark no.1.

Bass Beer

Industrialisation helped the branding exercise to take shape, for the primary function of identifying the goods or services of one seller or group of sellers and to differentiate them from those of competitors; as defined by AMA. Factories started shipping their products with the logo type insignia on the shipping barrels. In USA, Campbell Soup, Coca Cola, Juicy Fruit Gum, Aunt Jemima and Quaker Oats were the first few products, which got branded.

Campbell Soup

Coca Cola

Juicy Fruit Gum

Marketers try to create a unique or special identity to create a positive impression in the minds of the consumers. In 1955, Burleigh B. Gardner and Sidney J. Levy introduced the concept of Brand Image, in their article 'The Product and The Brand'. They said that a brand image can be developed by attributing a personality to, or associating an image with a product or service, whereby the personality or image is branded on the consciousness of consumers. They used projective techniques to help define assets of the brand and to help define a holistic brand image. Two basic points being:

- A reputable brand persists as a stable image over time and
- It is rarely possible for a product or a brand to be all things to all people.

While products and brands have interwoven sets of features, and consumers evaluate them in complex ways, advertising has to be based on attitudes and motives, while management has to play a complementary role to make the task richer.[5]

When a brand is widely known in the market, it acquires brand recognition. When brand recognition builds up so much to create a critical mass of positive sentiments among the consumers, it is said to have achieved brand franchise.

Benefits of Branding

Branding provides a lot of benefits to the consumers as well as companies. Consumers are benefited in the following ways:

- Brand helps identify the product and the company that consumers like or dislike.
- Brand helps consumers in reducing their purchasing time
- Brand helps reduce consumer's perceived risk of purchase
- Incase of difficulty regarding assessing quality of the products, brand helps consumer believe in the product.

Aston Martin Car

Gucci

- Consumers derive psychological reward and pleasure from owning the brand, as it may happen with your Aston Martin Car or Rolex Watch or Gucci handbags and shoes.

Companies are benefited in the following ways:

- Brand helps the companies differentiate their product from competitors' product.
- Brand helps companies in getting repeat orders from the customers.
- Brand helps companies in their price defense against competition. Sometimes, companies also enjoy price premiums on the basis of their brand image.
- Brand helps a company in introducing a new product in the same name. In turn it helps the company with a lesser cost of advertising and promotions.
- Brand attracts partners be it supplier, banker or an advertising agency

- Brand brings loyal consumers to the company. In turn, it brings sustained revenue and market share for the company.

Branding Approaches

There are different branding approaches behind the successful brands. Following are the approaches, in which the companies have branded their products.

Liril

- **Individual name:** In FMCG products, individual names are very popular. In this approach, each brand has a separate name. But the drawback of this approach is that the brands may compete against one another, as it happens in the case of HUL products like Lux, Lifebuoy, Hamam, Liril, Breeze, Pears, Dove and Rexona.
- **Company Name:** Company branding is very popular in India. Right from Tata to Reliance to Godrej uses their family brand name in all their products and services. In the automobile industry also, Tata, Mahindra, Maruti Suzuki, Ford etc are used with their product names to market their vehicles. In FMCG category also, Dabur, Cadbury, Nestle etc. use their company name in the product lineup.

Intel

- **Derived brands:** In some cases, the supplier of a major component of the end product promotes its product through a brand name to gain competitive advantage. Intel is an excellent example, which supplies the heart of the computer ie. micro processor, with a sticker with slogan 'Intel Inside.'

- **Multi brands:** A company may resort to launching more brands in the same market with the probability of getting some extra market share for the company. Multi brands also benefit a company by enabling it to launch different brands for different sets of consumers. That's why HUL sells Surf Excel, Rin as well as Wheel detergent powder in India, while Procter and Gamble India (P&G) sells Ariel and Tide plus in India. In apparels, Levis has launched Denizen and Wrangler has launched Hero Wrangler to occupy the budget conscious consumers.

  The only drawback in this strategy is cannibalization, where the new brand may takeover the market share of the established brand. But it may be helpful for a company, if the net impact on the market share and revenues are in positive.

Sach by Future Group

- **Private Labels:** With the growing clout of retailers in India, private labels are gaining the attention as well as the market share. Private labels are the retailer's own brands, which sells in their retail stores like Tasty Treat food products and Sach endorsed by Sachin Tendulkar in Big Bazaar to Stop apparels in Shoppers Stop.

- **Individual and Organisational Brands:** Tom Peters has advocated personal branding that treat persons and their careers as brands. For example – Sachin Tendulkar, M. S. Dhoni, Amitabh Bachchan, Aamir Khan, Aishwarya Rai etc. Similarly an organisation can also be branded like a product.

- **Country Branding and Place Branding:** Country branding refers to a process in which a country claims a distinct positioning in the minds of its citizens and the global customers.

Omega

Any country that has a strong brand also benefits the products and services that come out of that country. The country, from which a company (product/service/brand) originates, has an effect on the company's perceived quality and likeability in the minds of consumers – this is the country of origin effect (COO). Swiss watches, French wine, Danish designs, Thai hospitality, Italian fashion, the 100% pure New Zealand are some of the well known examples.[6] Similarly places like Champagne, popular for specific quality of wine exclusively produced in Champagne region in France, Aligarh in India for locks have its own branding.

Brand Management

Application of the marketing techniques to a specific product or a brand is called brand management. It enhances the product's perceived value to the minds of the consumers. The brand acts as a implied promise that the level of quality of product or service is going to remain the same for their future purchases. For example, once you walk in to a PVR, you know as to what kind of service you can expect in the multiplex, what kind of seats you will get. The kind of service remains the same all across India in their different multiplexes. On the one hand consistency in a product or service helps the consumers to become loyal for the company. On the other hand, a company can also charge premium for their product or service, with respect to their competition.

The discipline of brand management is almost 80 years old. It started in 1931 at Procter & Gamble PLC based on the famous memo written by Neil H. McElory. The memo was written by Neil for the additional manpower required for his brand team for Camay. He was of the view that all the brands require a concentrated effort, as if it were a separate business. In this way the different brands would be distinguished from others. This memo has such an impact on the marketing and brand management per se, that it is still widely emulated by many FMCG and other companies all across the world.

Brand name

A good brand name should be easy to pronounce, easy to remember and easy to recognise. It should also be protected under trademark laws to gain the present and future advantage from the brand. It should also attract attention and may suggest product benefits or may suggest usage. Naming the brands has been quite an interesting process for different companies. Following are the ways in which companies have given their brand names.

- **Acronym**: A brand name is made of initials such as PVR, an acronym for Priya Village Road show, IDBI, ICICI, HDFC, IBM etc.

Shoppers Stop

- **Descriptive**: A brand name may also describe a product benefit or function like Big Bazaar, Infosys, Shoppers Stop, Airbus, Sleepwell, Videocon etc.
- **Founders' names**: Sometimes brand names are also based on their founders' name like L&T, Disney, Ford, HP etc.
- **Family names:** In India, family surnames are quite popular with big names in business like Tata, Birla, Godrej etc.
- **Religious names:** In India, some times a company may use a brand name based on the religious persona like Maruti (represents God Hanuman), Balaji Telefilms, Shree Ashtavinayak Cine Vision etc. On the global scale, many companies also use Greek gods and goddesses name in their brand name like Apollo, Nike etc.
- **Neologisms**: These brand names are completely made-up words like Wii, Kodak, Exxon etc.
- **Foreign word**: Sometimes a foreign word is also used in a brand name like Volvo or Samsung

- **Geography**: Some brands are named in accordance with their regions and area like Champagne, Cisco, Fuji Film etc.,

In some cases, brand names have become so popular that it denotes the product category itself. This is called **brandnomer**. Bisleri, Xerox, Band-aid, Godrej (Almirah) are few examples of brandnomer.

Brand Strategy Decisions

Quaker Oats

A brand is the most valuable asset to any company. That's why John Stewart, former CEO of Quaker Oats once said

> **'If this business were split up, I will give you the land and bricks and mortar, and I would keep the brand and trademarks, and I would fare better than you.'**

On the similar lines, a former CEO of McDonald's said that

> **'If every asset we own, every building and every piece of equipment were destroyed in a terrible natural disaster, we would be able to borrow all the money to replace it very quickly because of the value of our brand............The brand is more valuable than the totality of all these assets.'**

Brand is the driving force of any business. That's why it needs to be developed and nurtured cautiously in accordance with the business strategy. Following strategic decisions are needed to be made by the company.

Brand Acquisition

Thums Up

Brand can either be built from scratch or it can be acquired. In the world, there are several examples of brand acquisitions. In India, Thums Up brand was bought by Coca Cola, when Coke reentered the Indian market in 1993. Now also, the success story of Thums Up continues with its brand ambassador Salman Khan. Tata Motors acquired Jaguar and Land Rover, while Lenovo, a Chinese company bought the PC and laptop business of IBM. On the one hand, Mittal Steel acquired Arcelor, while Tata steel acquired Corus. Similarly, Bharti Airtel took over Zain's business in Africa,while Godrej acquired Darling Group in Africa. Brand acquisition helps a company to expand and grow. It provides an opportunity to a company to scale greater heights in a short span of time.

Brand Architecture

Brand architecture is all about structure of a brand in the organizational framework. It details the existence of brands and sub brands in the organizational framework with points of similarities as well as differences.

> According to **Rajagopal, Brand architecture may be defined as an integrated process of brand building through establishing brand relationships among branding options in the competitive environment. The brand architecture of an organization at any time is, in large measure, a legacy of past management decisions as well as the competitive realities it faces in the marketplace.**[7]

As far as brand architecture is concerned, there are three levels of branding.

- **Umbrella Brand / Corporate Brand / Family Brand**: Most of the time, companies use umbrella brand or corporate brand or family brand to market their products and services. Tata, Reliance, Kingfisher, Virgin, Maggi etc. Maggi sells right from noodles to sauces to soups to pasta to cooking aids under Maggi umbrella brand. After the split between Mukesh and Anil Ambani, Reliance is using their umbrella brand with different design of their logos to identify their businesses.

Maggi

Reliance
Industries Limited
Growth is Life

Reliance – Mukesh Ambani Group

RELIANCE

Reliance – Anil Ambani Group

- **Endorsed Brands and Sub Brands:** In this branding exercise, brands include their parent brand or umbrella brand like Cadbury Dairy Milk, Maruti Swift, Nestle Kit Kat, Chevrolet Beat, Ford Figo, Sony Bravia etc. The umbrella brands add credibility and recognition for the company.
- **Individual Product Name:** Fast Moving Consumer Goods (FMCG) companies use individual product brand like Lux, Liril, Dove, Lifebuoy, Surf Excel, Rin, Wheel etc. Here the parent company's name is not given prominence, as happening in the case of Hindustan Unilever Ltd. (HUL) to which the above brands belong.

Brand Orientation

Samsung Galaxy S5

In the hyper competitive market, a product's superiority is not a guarantee for its success. A company needs to deliberately orient itself towards strong branding efforts.

> Brand orientation refers to **"the degree to which the organization values brands and its practices are oriented towards building brand capabilities"**[8]

The branding orientation leads the company to a better competitive scenario. In the global market, every company is fighting out with Apple to grab the market share in product categories like MP3 players, tablet computer and smart phones. Even Samsung has come out with Galaxy S5 to beat iPhone 5S and Galaxy tabs to counter iPads, but it seems little difficult for Samsung to get in the leadership position; as the kind of brand orientation Apple has got, right now nobody can beat that.

Brand Image

Bugatti Veyron

Brand image refers to the psychological aspect of a brand. It is a symbolic construct created within the minds of the consumers. It consists of the feelings and images associated with the brand. It is based on the proposition that consumers don't only buy the product, a commodity per se, but they also buy image associations like power, wealth, success, sophistication and identification and association with other users of the brand. That's why Bugatti, Ferrari, Rolls Royce, Maybach, Gucci,

Piaget, Omega, Aston Martin, Bentley can have consumers lining up to buy the products at exorbitant prices with respect to the product and competition.

A good brand image is always positive and unique. It needs to be reinforced by brand communication exercises like advertising, promotion, packaging, customer service, word of mouth and other aspects of brand experience.

Once a brand is widely known in the market, it earns brand recognition. Once the brand recognition reaches a level of positive sentiments among the consumers, it is said to have achieved brand franchise.

Brand Awareness

Consumer's ability to recall brands in terms of its brand name, logo, jingles, tagline etc. is called brand awareness. The first and foremost exercise in marketing is brand awareness, as consumers start considering the brand as one of their choices, when they are aware of it.

Zoozoo - Vodafone

With the emergence of social media in a big way through Facebook, Orkut, Twitter etc., love of a brand or Brand Love is shown through the Brand fan pages as it is happening with Harley Bikes or Zoozoo character of Vodafone.

Brand Promise

The marketer and owner of the brand has a vision of what the brand must be and do for the consumers.[9] Brand promise is a promise from the brand to the consumers to have same amount of trust and confidence on the product or service again and again. It is based on the consumers' brand experience. Brand extensions take the advantage of brand promise by instilling confidence and lessening risk perceived in the product or service for the consumers by the company.

Brand Identity

World's No.1 Brand **India's No.1 Brand**

The brand identity is the outward expression of a brand, including its name, trademark, communications, and visual appearance.[10] Here the brand identity is created by the brand owner in the way, in which owner wants to communicate to its consumers. This is in contrast to the brand image, which is a customer's mental picture of a brand.[10] A brand identity is conveyed through the visual communication in the form of logo, use of specific fonts and colours, signs or symbols and through taglines.

Brand Personality

Brand personality describes brands in terms of human characteristics. Most of the time, it is difficult to differentiate brands on the basis of functional characteristics. That's why companies create brand personality through their communication messages, which makes the brand differentiate from competing brands. Christine Restall of McCann Erickson has drawn a distinction between brand image and brand personality

'In many markets, there are no real differences among the competitors. So you begin to explore a more emotional level and this is where the brand personality comes in. Brand image refers to rational measurements like quality, strength, flavour. Brand personality explains why people like some brands more than others even, when there is no physical difference between them.'

Harley-Davidson

Crask & Laskey's view of brand personality is that it is the sum of intangible assets of the brand. Whereas, Paul Southgate defines personality as 'the human characteristics of the brand in question, whilst taking special care that it is the brand that is being described and not the target customer.' Aaker also believe in brand personality being the set of human characteristics associated with a brand. For example, Harley Davidson motorcycle brand persona is of a macho, freedom-seeking man. While, Coke's personality is real (the real thing!) and Pepsi's is young, spirited and exciting.

Coca Cola

Aaker has gone further and developed a brand personality dimension framework to describe and measure the personality of a brand in five core dimensions, each divided into a set of facets. It is an easy to understand model to describe the profile of a brand using an analogy with a human being. The five core dimensions and their facets are as following.:

- Sincerity (Down to earth, honest, wholesome, cheerful)
- Excitement (Daring, spirited, imaginative, up to date)
- Competence (Reliable, intelligent, successful)
- Sophistication (Upper class, charming)
- Ruggedness (Outdoorsy, tough)

Each facet is in turn measured by a set of traits on a five point scale (1 = not at all descriptive, 5 = extremely descriptive). The ratings of a trait describe the specific brand of interest.

Brand Equity

Brand Equity is an asset to the company. The term brand equity is used to understand the effect of the brand on the customer. How much customer is willing to pay for a particular brand against the competing brand?

According to **Chan Su Park and V. Srinivasan, 'Brand Equity is the added value bestowed on the product by the brand name.'**

According to **David Aaker, 'Brands have equity because they have high awareness; many loyal customers; a high reputation for perceived quality; proprietary brand assets such as access to distribution channels or to patents; or the kind of brand associations (such as personality associations).'**

A powerful brand has high brand equity. Brand equity is the differential effect that knowing the brand name has on consumer response to the product and its marketing. It's a measure of the brand's ability to capture consumer's preference and loyalty. A brand has positive brand equity, when consumers react more favourably to it than a generic or unbranded version of the same product. It has negative brand equity, if consumers react less favourably than to an unbranded version.11

Apple, Google, Coca Cola, Microsoft and IBM are the top global brands in 2013, based on the study by Interbrand; while Colgate, Dettol, Clinic Plus, Lifebuoy and Lux leads the brand listing in India in 2013, on the basis of Brand Equity Most Trusted Brand survey. All these brands have one thing in common that they deliver unique benefits to the consumers. They forge deep connection with the consumers and stay relevant with the times.

Ad agency Young and Rubicam's Brand Asset Valuator measures brand strength on the basis of four consumer perception dimensions.

1. Differentiation – What makes the brand standout,
2. Relevance – How consumers feel it meets their needs,
3. Knowledge – How much consumers know about the brand and
4. Esteem – How highly consumers regard and respect the brand.

Brands with strong brand equity rate high on all of these dimensions. [11]

A brand with high brand equity is a very valuable asset. Brand valuation is calculated on the basis of the total financial value of the brand.11 Following is the list of top ten global brands, according to the Best Global Brands 2015 list by Interbrand. Apple leads the list with a whopping $170 billion valuation, followed by Google at $120 billion and Coca Cola at $78 billion.

2015 Rank	Brand	Region/ Country	Sector	Brand Value	Change in Brand Value
1		United States	Technology	170,276 $m	+43%
2	Google	United States	Technology	120,314 $m	+12%
3	Coca-Cola	United States	Beverages	78,423 $m	-4%
4	Microsoft	United States	Technology	67,670 $m	+11%

2015 Rank	Brand	Region/ Country	Sector	Brand Value	Change in Brand Value
5	IBM	United States	Business Services	65,095 $m	-10%
6	TOYOTA	Japan	Automotive	49,048 $m	+16%
7	SAMSUNG	South Korea	Technology	45,297 $m	0%
8		United States	Diversified	42,267 $m	-7%
9		United States	Restaurants	39,809 $m	-6%
10	amazon	United States	Retail	37,948 $m	+29%

Top 10 Global Brands based on Best Global Brands 2015 list by Interbrand

In India, the leading financial daily, Economic Times' Brand Equity conducts 'Most Trusted Brands Survey' every year. In 2015, Colgate emerged as India's Most Trusted Brand, followed by Tata Salt, Dettol, Dove, Lifebuoy, Horlicks, Samsung, Lux, Maaza and Surf Excel. Among the service brands, Airtel topped the chart, followed by Vodafone, Big Bazaar, State Bank of India, and LIC.

Top 20 Indian Brands based on Most Trusted Brands 2015 List by Brand Equity

Marketing Insight 9.4

Airtel: 'Second insight' on friendship

Airtel

'Har ek friend zaroori hota hai' advertisement is clearly the best Airtel has expressed itself in a long time. The country's largest mobile operator's numerous campaigns in the past 3–4 years — including its around Rs 300-crore rebranding, complete with new logo and signature tune, in November last — failed to match the buzz that Vodafone's Zoozoos, pug and Idea's 'What an idea, Sirji' created.

Taking its friendship theme forward, telecom brand Airtel has released an ad campaign titled 'Jo mera hai woh tera hai', that conveys the new insight that friendship equals sharing.

Crafted by Taproot India, the campaign has at its centre a film that has been released on TV (65 seconds) as well as online (105 seconds on YouTube). The picturisation is vibrant, peppy, colourful and pretty much bursting with youth, and the upbeat mood of the ad is complemented by an anthem that has started creating quite a buzz on the digital space.

Towards the end of 2010, Airtel launched the then new **'Dil jo chaahe paas laaye'** campaign that was centred on its core message of 'relationships'. In mid-2011, the brand took this promise forward in its communication that leveraged its **3G offerings**; the ads focused on internet on-the-go. Both these campaigns were created by JWT.

Then, in August 2011, the brand launched its **'Har ek friend zaroori hota hai'** campaign that was created by Taproot. It positioned Airtel as an out-and-out 'friendship brand'. The task back then was to make the brand more contemporary and youthful. The insight used was that everyone has a different set of friends at a particular time in life, and technology and mobile phones connect a person to all of them. Since then, all of Airtel's campaigns have been inspired by the theme of friendship.

Earlier this year, taking the same thought forward, the brand rolled out a series of ad films introducing consumers to humorous characters that represent different types of friends. Over 20 ad films created by Taproot were released on TV and on the digital medium.

According to Bharat Bambawale, director, global brand, Bharti Airtel, the current campaign embodies the brand's "second insight on friendship", namely, that friendship is all about sharing.

However, friendship as a theme and the concept of sharing things with one's friends is not a new space for a telecom player to explore. Besides, given the larger theme of friendship that Airtel has owned for around a year, was it just a matter of time before the concept of sharing was explored by the agency - somewhat like an obvious insight just waiting to be executed?

While no specific product feature is being highlighted in the campaign as yet, the fact that a large part of this 'sharing' is happening via the digital medium, is something the brand has acknowledged adequately. This has been brought out through the lyrics and picturisation of the film. At the end of the film, the VO (voiceover) says, 'Aur friendship ki sharing ko hamesha on rakhke -- Airtel internet' as the words 'Airtel Internet' appear as a super on the screen.

However, one can't help but wonder that when removed from the context of digital, does the notion of 'friendship equals sharing' fall short? "The notion does not fall short but the extent to which it happens is highest online," responds Dias.

"For today's kids who have grown up in an online world and don't know any other, even if they have nothing to do together they do that 'nothing' online. When we were growing up we just shared play-time with our friends, had a few common interests and did some 'universally teenage' things. We never shared each other's lives '24 by 7' the way it is done today," he elaborates.

In fact, the campaign thought occurred to Dias when he was brainstorming with a team-member on how best to capture the extent to which our lives are shared online. Besides TV and digital, the media mix of the campaign comprises outdoor, radio, print and cinema.

Overall, industry folk find the campaign engaging. According to Minakshi Achan, co-founder, Salt Brand Solutions, Taproot has identified a nice, broad creative territory of friendship for Airtel and the fact that the agency finds new renditions of the same, time after time, is great.

Regarding the 'sharing angle', she feels that while it is a relevant and true insight, it doesn't really say saying anything new about friendship. "Though friendship as a platform is hackneyed, 'Har Friend Zaroori' was a fresh new execution and it connected hugely with everybody. I'm not sure this one has the same currency as the first," she says.

Does the current campaign stretch the friendship theme too far? "Well," she says, "it is the brand's positioning and it does make sense to stick with it, but the execution is the same as the 'Har Friend Zaroori' film so it is a blind spot for me."

Will it work or not? "With the media weights on it, it will certainly be noticed," says Achan. In the opinion of Suraja Kishore, national planning director, Publicis Ambience, the beauty of this campaign lies in the fact that it executes the obvious in the best possible manner. To him, the 'Har Friend Zaroori' campaign was like a montage of all the facets and nuances of friendship. And while the current 'sharing' campaign is not exactly a fresh insight, it extends the previous story forward.

Does the execution adequately convey the insight this time around? "Creatively, it very much seems like more of the same thing. Maybe the approach could've been new; perhaps a new way of expressing the insight," says Kishore. He however adds that every brand that has witnessed resonance with its audience through a previous, successful campaign is faced with this challenge both from a strategic as well as creative point of view.

In 2015, Interbrand presented the third edition of Best Indian Brands, an India focused version of Interbrand's highly acclaimed Best Global Brands study. Tata Group tops the list followed by Reliance, Airtel, LIC and Satate Bank of India. Built on an ISO certified Brand Valuation methodology, this annual study takes into account several parameters Including, but not restricted to the company's finances, the role of the brand and how strong it is in the marketplace. In contrast to other studies and surveys that focus on consumer opinion or perception, Best Indian Brands is based on a foundation of solid data and analysis.

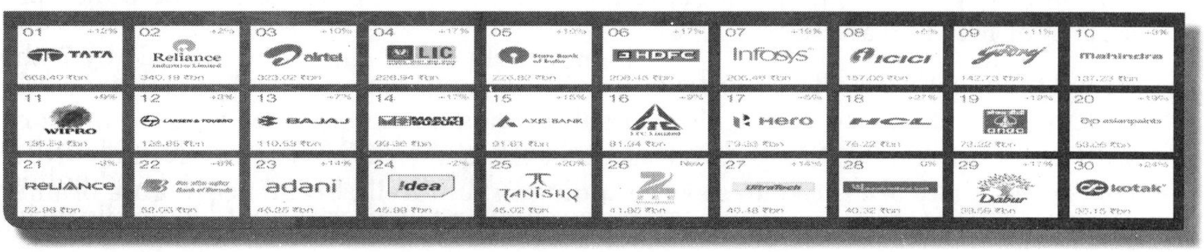

Best Indian Brands 2015 by Interbrand

All the above studies and surveys point out to just one thing. A brand needs to satisfy the consumers by providing best of the products and services. Secondly it needs to forge deep connections with the consumers and stay relevant with the times.

Summary

- According to Al Ries and Jack Trout, positioning is something (perception) that happens in the minds of the target market. It is the aggregate perception, the market has of a particular company, product or service in relation to their perceptions of the competitors in the same category.
- According to American Marketing Association, Brand is a name, term, sign, symbol or design or a combination of them, intended to identify the goods or services of one seller or group of sellers and to differentiate them from those of competitors.
- Branding provides a lot of benefits to the consumers as well as companies.
- There are different branding approaches like individual name, company name, derived brands, multi brands, private labels, individual and organisational brands, country branding and place branding.
- Brand management is the application of the marketing techniques to a specific product or a brand. It enhances the product's perceived value to the minds of the consumers.
- A good brand name should be easy to pronounce, easy to remember and easy to recognise. A brand name can be an acronym or descriptive or neologisms, or, it can be based upon founders' names, family names, religious names, foreign word, geography etc.
- A brand is the most valuable asset to any company. Brand can either be built from scratch or it can be acquired.
- Brand architecture is all about structure of a brand in the organizational framework. It details the existence of brands and sub brands in the organizational framework with points of similarities as well as differences. As far as brand architecture is concerned, there are three levels of branding i.e. umbrella brand / corporate brand / family brand, endorsed brands and sub brands and individual product name.
- Brand orientation refers to the degree to which the organization values brands and its practices are oriented towards building brand capabilities.
- Brand image refers to the psychological aspect of a brand. It is a symbolic construct created within the minds of the consumers. It consists of the feelings and images associated with the brand.
- Consumer's ability to recall brands in terms of its brand name, logo, jingles, tagline etc. is called brand awareness. The first and foremost exercise in marketing is brand awareness, as consumers start considering the brand as one of their choices, when they are aware of it.

- Brand promise is a promise from the brand to the consumers to have same amount of trust and confidence on the product or service again and again. It is based on the consumers' brand experience.
- The brand identity is the outward expression of a brand, including its name, trademark, communications, and visual appearance.
- Brand image refers to rational measurements like quality, strength, flavour. Brand personality explains why people like some brands more than others even, when there is no physical difference between them.
- Brand Equity is an asset to the company. Brand Equity is the added value bestowed on the product by the brand name.
- Brand valuation is calculated on the basis of the total financial value of the brand.

Discussion Questions

1. What do you mean by Positioning? Discuss positioning with relevant examples from India.
2. Define Brand? Discuss the benefits offered by a brand.
3. What do you mean by Brand? Discuss different branding approaches.
4. Define Brand? List the top 5 brands in India and in the world.
5. Which brand do you like most and why?
6. Explain the characteristics of a good brand name. Discuss the ways in which companies name their brands.
7. What do you mean by brand architecture? Discuss the levels of brand architecture.
8. What do you mean by brand image? How is it different from brand personality?
9. Define brand personality. Is there any difference between brand image and brand personality.
10. What do you mean by brand equity? How is it different from brand valuation?
11. Short Notes:

    a. Brand Image b. Brand Equity

    c. Umbrella Brand d. Repositioning

    e. Brand Orientation f. Brand Promise

    g. Brand identity h. Depositioning

References

1. Al Ries & Jack Trout, "Positioning: The Battle for Your Mind,", 2001. p 19 of paperback edition
2. Kotler, Armstrong, Agnihotri, Haque, Principles of Marketing – A South Indian perspective', 13th edition, 2010 pp179
3. Philip Kotler, 'Marketing Management', 11th Edition, Pearson Education, 2004 pp. 418-423
4. MarketingMagazine.co.uk
5. Burleigh B. Gardner and Sidney J. Levy, 'The Product and The Brand', Harvard Business Review, March-April, 1955, pp 33-39
6. MartinRoll, 'Indonesia – The country branding puzzle' http://www.venturerepublic.com/resources/Indonesia_%E2%80%93_The_country_branding_puzzle.asp
7. Rajagopal; Romulo Sanchez, 'Conceptual analysis of brand architecture and relationships within product categories'. Journal of Brand Management: 2004, 233–247.
8. Bridson & Evans, 2004)(Bridson, K., and Evans, J. (2004) 'The secret to a fashion advantage is brand orientation', International Journal of Retail and Distribution Management, 32(8): 403-11
9. Kotler P., Keller K.L, Brady M., Goodman M., Hansen T. (2009). Marketing Management, pp.861
10. Neumeier, Marty (2004), *The Dictionary of Brand.* ISBN 1-884081-06-1, pp.20
11. Kotler, Armstrong, Agnihotri, Haque, Principles of Marketing – A South Indian perspective', 13th edition, 2010 pp 203

Chapter 10

Product

Chapter Structure

- Product
- Product Classifications
- Product Mix
- Product Line and Brand Extensions
- *Marketing Insight 10.1: HUL, Nestle to Extend Knorr, Maggi into Oats*
- New Product Development (NPD)
- *Marketing Insight 10.2: Indian Innovations Relevant in Europe Now: Unilever CEO*
- *Marketing Insight 10.3: Sensodyne Overtakes Colgate in Sensitive Category*
- *Marketing Insight 10.4: Tata Motors is Developing new Products for Domestic Market*
- *Marketing Insight 10.5: Bolt, Zest to go Global*
- *Marketing Insight 10.6: Ford Fiesta, Tata Aria, Nissan Evalia: Launched with Great Expectations but Failed to Deliver*
- Product Life Cycle
- Managing Product and Brand Portfolios
- Summary
- Discussion Questions
- References

"A brand for a company is like a reputation for a person. You earn reputation by trying to do hard things well."

-Jeff Bezos, Founder, Amazon.com

Product

Product, the first P in the Marketing Mix, is the starting point of any marketing activity. A company needs to have some product to sell. If the company is new; then it should develop a product to sell in the market or it can buy the product from a manufacturer and market it subsequently. In the case of an existing product, the company needs to differentiate its market offering.

A Product is anything that can be offered to a customer to satisfy his or her need or want. Whether it's a refrigerator or insurance policy, the product offers a total bundle of benefits to the customers. Typically in marketing, the term product is used for any good or service or any other entity, which can be marketed.

According to Philip Kotler, ten entities can be marketed: Goods, Services, Experiences, Events, Person, Places, Properties, Organisations, Information and Ideas.

Samsung Refrigerator

In case of new products, how should the company develop its product? If the company has launched a new product in the market and competitors are coming up with 'me-too' products, then how should a company react? When the company should expand the product line with brand and line extensions, without diluting the brand? When is the time to cut down the product line? All these questions are answered in this chapter.

A company can offer five levels of product to satisfy the needs of the consumers. These five levels are called Customer Value Hierarchy.[1]

1. Core Benefit of the Product,
2. Generic Product,

3. Expected Product,
4. Augmented Product and
5. Potential Product

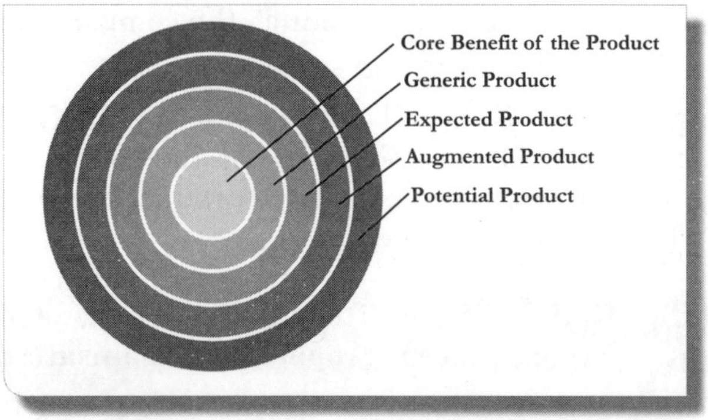

Customer Value Hierarchy: Five Product Levels

Taj Hotel, Mumbai

Generally a customer buys a product for its core benefit. In a hotel service, the core benefit is rest and sleep. Similarly in an air conditioner, the core benefit is the cooling. For an airline, the core benefit is the traveling from one place to another. In hotels, the core benefit is then turned into a basic product by having a bed, bathroom, TV, wash basin, towels. In the third level, the company can offer the customers the expected product by offering him clean bedroom and bathroom. At the fourth level, the company tries to give the customer an augmented product by providing superior experience. The potential product is the fifth and highest level, which can incorporate all the possible benefits, the product can provide today and tomorrow.

Customer value hierarchy is not only about the physical benefits the product offers, but it is also about the psychological benefits to the customer. The psychological benefits come in the form of the brand name of the product. The brand name makes you feel special.

That's why brands have become a crucial aspect in most of the product offerings. You won't see whether Fevicol is used in your furniture, but if you are buying adhesive personally to make the furniture, you will see to it that Fevicol is used. That's the impact of brand on the customers.

In cases, where you can see your brand with you like a watch, the brand has got an impact and in the cases where the brand is not seen after the usage like paint, it still makes a lot of difference.

Fevicol

What is a brand? American Marketing Association has defined

Brand as a name, term, sign, symbol or design or a combination of them, intended to identify the goods or services of one seller or group of sellers and to differentiate them from those of competitors.

Under trademark law, the seller is granted exclusive rights to the use of the brand name in perpetuity. Brand is the art and cornerstone of marketing. Perhaps the most distinctive skill of professional marketer is their ability to create, maintain, protect and enhance brands. A brand is essentially a marketer's promise to deliver a specific set of features, benefits and services consistently to the buyers. Brands vary in the amount of power and value they have in the marketplace. At one extreme are brands that are not known by the most buyers. Then there are brands for which buyers have a fairly high degree of brand awareness.[2]

Product Classifications

Traditionally, products can be classified on the basis of durability and tangibility and use.[3] On the basis of durability and tangibility, products can be classified into three groups:

1. **Non Durable Goods**: Non durable goods are most of the fast moving consumer goods, which is consumed in one or few uses like a shampoo or a chocolate. The company needs to have a large footprint its distribution network to have more and more customers. It also needs to advertise more on Television, as it influences the customers in a passive way. Clinic Plus, Happydent, Lux, Colgate are examples of few of the non durable goods.
2. **Durable Goods**: Durable goods stay a lot longer than the non durable goods. TV, Refrigerator, Clothing and Apparels are all durable goods. The company needs to promote its brand effectively in the market with a good service back.
3. **Services**: Services are non physical and intangible in nature and can satisfy a need. Banking, Couriers, Hotels, Airlines, Multiplexes, Trains, Doctors, Lawyers, Management Consultants are all examples of services. In the era of cut throat competition in the market, the services should not only satisfy, but delight the customer.

On the basis of the use, the goods can be classified into Consumer goods and Business Goods or Industrial Goods.

1. **Consumer Goods Classification**: On the basis of shopping habits, consumer goods can be classified into convenience, shopping, specialty and unsought goods.

Chlor-mint

a) **Convenience Goods**: Convenience Goods are bought frequently by the consumers like Salt, Soap, Potato Chips, Chocolates etc. It can further be classified into Staple, Impulse and Emergency Goods. Staple goods are bought on a routine basis like toothpaste, shampoo, soap etc. Impulse goods are bought on impulse, without any deliberation like Chlor-mint, Lay's Potato Chips and Cadbury Chocolates. Emergency goods are purchased in case of an urgent need like N95 swine flu protection mask. It also happens with the seasonal goods like Umbrella and rain coat in a rainy season and a body warmer in the winter season.

b) **Shopping Goods**: Shopping Goods include electronic appliances, clothing, furniture etc., which require a deliberate decision to buy the product on the various attributes, the product can offer.

c) **Specialty Goods**: Reid & Taylor Suits, Reebok shoes, Apple iPods, Bose Sound Systems are examples of specialty goods. Brand plays an important role in making these goods unique to the customers.

LIC

d) **Unsought Goods**: Many other products are also useful to the customers, but they may not be aware or they will generally not think about buying it. Security systems, fire extinguishers, smoke detectors, insurance, encyclopedias are examples of unsought goods, which needs a direct marketing and personal selling approach to influence the customers to buy the product.

2. **Industrial Goods Classification**: Industrial Goods include Material and Parts, Capital Items and Supplies and Business Services. **Material and Parts** include raw material and manufactured material and parts. Maruti Suzuki requires steel, paint, tyre, steering wheel and several other material and parts for producing its cars. ITC requires farm products like wheat as the raw material for its Aashirvaad Atta; while Tata steel

requires a natural product like Iron ore for producing Steel. Manufactured material can further be classified into Component material like cement, wire, TMT bars and component parts like bearing, steering and tyres. In both the cases, price and service play a crucial role.

Tata Tiscon

Capital items include installations like factories and offices and equipments like generators, assembly unit like Tata Motors's Tata Nano plant in Sanand in Gujtrat, after the fiasco in Singur.

Supplies include Maintenance and repair items like screws, nails, paint and operating supplies like stationery, lubricants, coal etc. Collectively it is known as MRO goods. Business Services include maintenance and repair services for office equipments, housekeeping and business advisory services like Human Resources services, Legal services, consulting services and advertising services.

Product Mix

Most of the companies in India and in the world, deal in many products at a time. It helps the company to differentiate its offering for different set of customers. Product mix, also known as product assortment, consists of all the products a company offers. For example, LG Electronics India deals in 9 categories, while HUL deals with 4 different product lines. Tata Motors deals in 4 different categories with 12 cars in the passenger cars category.

Any product mix consists of several product lines. Product line consists of a group of products, which are closely related and similar in nature and sold to the same kind of customer base. The product mix of any company can further be divided into its width, length and depth.

Generally a company starts small with a single product line and with success, moves on to become a multiple product line company like T-Series, Nirma, Ghadi Detergent and Intex Technologies. Multiple product lines in the company are also known as the width of the product mix. HUL deals with 4 different product lines – personal care, home care, food and drink and water purifier. Earlier it was clubbed under 12 different product lines named - Personal Wash, Laundry, Skin Care, Hair Care, Oral Care, Deodorants, Cosmetics, Ayurvedic Personal and Health Care, Tea, Coffee, Foods and Ice Cream. LG deals in 9 product lines – Television, Home Entertainment (Digital Audio Video), Computer Products, Mobile Phone, Kitchen Appliances - Refrigerator, Microwave Oven and Dish Washer; Home Appliances - Washing Machine, Vacuum Cleaners and Water purifiers; Air Conditioners - Residential and System (Commercial) Air Conditioner, Automotive and Commercial products.

Hindustan Unilever Limited Product Mix

Sl. No.	Personal Care	Home Care	Food and Drink	Water Purifier
1	**Axe**	**Surf Excel**	**Bru**	**Pureit**
2	**Fair & Lovely**	**Active Wheel**	**Kissan**	
3	**Pond's**	**Rin**	**Red Label**	
4	**Lakme**	**Comfort**	**Kwality Walls**	
5	**Pears**	**Vim**	**Knorr**	
6	**Dove**	**Sunlight**	**Taj Mahal**	
7	**Clinic Plus**	**Domex**	**Magnum**	
8	**Lux**	**Cif**	**Annapurna**	
9	**Pepsodent**	**Magic**	**Modern**	
10	**Elle 18**		**Lipton**	
11	**Lifebuoy**		**Brooke Bond Taaza**	
12	**Sunsilk**		**Brook Bond 3 Roses**	
13	**Close Up**			
14	**Vaselin**			
15	**Clear**			
16	**Aviance**			
17	**Rexona**			
18	**Hamam**			
19	**TRESemme**			
20	**Breeze**			
21	**Ayush**			
22	**Liril 2000**			
23	**Tigi**			
24	**Sure**			
25	**Toni & Guy**			

In different product lines, a company offers many items or say brands with distinct characteristics. These are called the length of a product mix. In the case of HUL, the length of personal wash product line goes up to 8 brands with brands like Lux, Liril 2000, Hamam, Breeze, Lifebuoy, Dove, Pears and Rexona; while in oral care, it has two brands: Pepsodent and Close Up.

In product mix, depth refers to different variants offered under the product length. In India, Lux is offered in six variants with different sizes. All these different sizes and variants constitute the product depth. If you take into account the cars manufactured by Maruti Suzuki, then most of the cars are offered in three variants called – Lxi, Vxi and Zxi.

The consistency in the product mix is also important for any company, as it will help the company to leverage the market segment, technology and the distribution channel. That's why you find HUL dealing in more and more FMCG products, while LG is concentrating on consumer electronics.

Product Line and Brand Extensions

When an existing brand is extended to introduce additional items in the same product category, then it is known as Line Extension. For example, Lux launched two fruit extract soaps called Lux Strawberry & Cream and Lux Peach & Cream in March, 2008 under the line extension. In this case, the brand name remains the same, but a new flavour, package size or different form can be introduced by the company.

Under the brand extension, the same brand name is used in a new product category. In 1995, HUL launched Dove brand in the premium personal wash category in India. Now the brand has been extended to shampoos, conditioners and hair oil.

Dove Shampoo

Dove Hair Oil

In the existing product category, an additional brand may be introduced. It is a part of multi brand strategy by many FMCG companies. Ghari Detergent launched MR2 detergent powder for its premium customers, besides having Ghari Detergent powder at the lower end.

Brand \ Product Category	New	Existing
New	Additional Brand	Diversification
Existing	Line Extension	Brand Extension

Product Line and Brand Extensions Grid

Marketing Insight 10.1

HUL, Nestle to Extend Knorr, Maggi into Oats

Kellogg and GSK Consumer too plan to launch masala oats soon

SAGAR MALVIYA MUMBAI 4th Jan 2013

Two of the country's largest food companies, Hindustan Unilever and Nestle India, will soon launch oats, extending their battle in ready-to-cook food category from noodle and soup to the healthy cereal. Hindustan Unilever and Nestle plan to launch oats under Knorr and Maggi brands, respectively, as healthy extensions of their noodle segment this year, two people familiar with the development said. While Nestle didn't comment to an email query, a HUL spokesperson declined to comment on "market speculation".

Oats—a grain that is still considered horse feed in some parts of the world including pockets in India—has already emerged a popular breakfast cereal on the back of increasing demand for health food in metros and big cities.

While PepsiCo's Quaker Oats, which calls itself the World's No. 1 Oats brand, entered India over seven years ago, more than half a dozen food companies including GSK Consumer, Kellogg India, Britannia and Marico have entered the Rs. 200-crore oats market, which is growing more than 40% annually, over the last few years.

Despite a healthy growth rate, the Rs. 600-crore breakfast cereal industry has not made much progress in trying to convince Indians to change their eating habit from oily parathas to healthy options.

That's because when they have had to make a choice, Indians have always preferred health to taste. For example, Nestle's Maggi noodles alone is estimated to be more than Rs. 1,100-crore brand, almost double the size of overall breakfast cereal market. Now, some experts say marketers have found a way to bring taste and health together with flavoured oats.

"A lot of experimentation has taken place in last 2-3 years in breakfast category and with the recent launch of flavoured oats specially with Indian taste the entire story has changed and we seem to have, for once, found the solution to marketers dilemma of 'what's healthy is not tasty and what's tasty is not healthy'," Devendra Chawla, president—Food Bazaar at Future Group, says. Hence, companies are shifting their communication to oats being amenable rather than just healthy to Indianise their offerings.

"While there challenges in changing Indian consumers' food habit, breakfast as an occasion is seeing the maximum change," says Sameer Satpathy, marketing head of Marico, which was the first company to launch masala oat variant. "The organized breakfast market is under penetrated and new entrants will help grow the segment even as competition intensifies," he added.

PepsiCo's Quaker is by far the market leader with share of over 35% ahead of Marico's Saffola and GSK Consumer's Horlicks. Traditionally, companies were focused on South India, which accounts for more than three-fourth of the total market but recently began expanding nationally. Quaker, which has been selling the masala variant since last year, has extended the brand to Indian ready-tocook mixes such as upma and poha this week.

Industry officials said that Kellogg and GSK Consumer too plan to launch masala oats soon. Future Group's Chawla says oats has the potential to grow beyond just a morning snack. "While consumer interest is high, the challenge is to take it beyond breakfast including snacking and meals like noodles and even include kids, which currently is not the case," he says.

The decision of HUL and Nestle to enter the segment is also triggered by their slowing growth. For instance, while HUL's processed food and beverages portfolio has grown at 16.4% CAGR over CY05-FY10, its growth rate has decelerated to 13.2% in the last two years, despite the company being aggressive with its Knorr portfolio.

Similarly, Nestle is expected to post its lowest revenue growth of 11.3% in 7 years in 2012. Anand Mour of ICICI Securities, in a report, wrote that Nestle's low revenue growth is "driven by channel rationalisation, deceleration in growth of food business and competition in noodles segment".

sagar.malviya@timesgroup.com

The company may also go for new brand in a new product category. It becomes a part of the company's diversification strategy. ITC was earlier into Cigarettes. Now it has expanded into food products, lifestyle retailing, personal products, agarbattis, safety matches and stationery with various brands under its belt. In the food category, it has got ready to eat products under the brand 'Kitchens of India', staples like Atta, Salt, Spices and Instant Mixes under the brand 'Aashivaad', snack food like Biscuits under brand 'Sunfeast', potato chips and finger snacks under the brand name 'Bingo!' and confectionery under the brand 'Mint-O' and 'Candyman'. In the case of Lifestyle Retailing, it markets the apparels under 'Wills Lifestyle', 'John Players' and 'Miss Players'. In the personal product category, it has got 'Essenza Di Wills', 'Fiama Di Wills', 'Vivel', 'Vivel Ultar Pro', 'Vivel Di Wills' and 'Superia'. In the incense stick category, it has 'Mangaldeep' Agarbatti and 'Expressions' aromatic candles. In the safety matches, it has 'Mangaldeep', 'Aim', 'Aim Mega' and 'Aim Metro'. In the stationery category, it markets the products under 'Classmate' and 'Papercraft' Brand. Besides these FMCG products, ITC is also into the business of Paperboards and Packaging and Agri-Business, besides hotels under the brand of 'ITC-Welcome Group' and Information Technology under 'ITC Infotech',

New Product Development (NPD)

"The purpose of business is to create a customer, the business enterprise has two– and only two–basic functions: marketing and innovation. Marketing and innovation produce results; all the rest are costs." - Peter F. Drucker.

The successful companies all across the world are those, who constantly try to innovate and deliver the products or services, which the customer wants. Be it Yahoo or Google or Apple or Tata or Reliance; all the successful companies rely heavily on constant innovation and marketing of their products or services. Tata group's products Tata Nano and Tata Swach water purifier are excellent examples of new product development by an established company with the innovation at the core of business philosophy.

Marketing Insight 10.2

Marketing Insight 10.2

Indian Innovations Relevant in Europe Now: Unilever CEO

Our Bureau Bengaluru ET 23 Nov 2012

Paul Polman, chief executive of Unilever, one of the world's largest consumer goods corporations, said innovations that have marked its growth in India, are now more relevant than ever, in recession hit parts of the world such as Europe. **of a pick-up truck by 2017**

Pureit

"Learnings" from India such as lower price points for products in smaller packages or sachets, is gaining acceptance in the European market, where poverty has returned as the local economies continue to reel under recession, the Unilever CEO said. "In UK, we sell some of our best brands at a price point of one pound," Paulman said. "People still want the best brands and now we can make it accessible to them."

Paulman, who was in Bangalore on Thursday to open Unilever's global technology center, also highlighted the success of the affordable water purifying product, Pureit. The product entirely developed in India, is now being sold by Unilever in at least 15 other countries, where according to him, it has become a popular brand.

Polman, who took over the reigns of the Anglo-Dutch corporation in 2009, said that developing markets including India will contribute at least 75% of revenues by 2020. Currently, these geographies that include India and China make up about 55% of its global revenues of about euro 46 billion. Last month, Unilever had reported its third quarter revenues euro 13.4 billion, aided by strong sales from emerging markets including India.

In India, Unilever operates as Hindustan Unilever Ltd, country's largest FMCG company, listed on BSE and having revenues of around Rs. 21,000 crore. Polman, who is known for pushing sustainable business practices within Unilever, said that it is possible to grow responsibly by giving back to the society rather than just taking from it. "You can be successful, grow both top and bottomline and still be very responsible to your consumers," Polman said. "The more we can do that, others will follow." Polman was in India to formally launch Unilever's global technology centre.

The centre is being tasked with providing IT services and also helping Unilever to find new ways of using technology to improve its business.

The 220,000 sq ft centre, the largest such facility for the company globally, currently houses 1,400 people but the headcount expected to go up as more global support functions are done out of here. Some of Unilever's existing IT services vendors such as Infosys and Accenture will continue to support the company and will have their staff based at the new centre. Unilever recently shut four of its plants and cut close to 800 jobs in the UK.

A company needs to develop new products constantly to remain in the growth and profit mode. According to Booz, Allen and Hamilton, a company can develop six categories of new products.[4]

1. **New to the World Products**: New products, which create an entirely new market.
2. **New Product Lines**: New products introduced by any company to enter into an established market for the first time.
3. **Additions to existing product lines**: New variants, sizes, flavours can be added to existing product lines.
4. **Improvement and revision of existing product**: Improved and revised products replace the existing products to give more value or improved performance.
5. **Repositioning**: Existing products can be targeted to new market segments.
6. **Cost reductions**: New products, which provide similar benefits at a lower cost.

Most Companies rarely innovate, some innovate occasionally and a few innovate continuously. In the last category, Sony, 3M, Dell, Sun Microsystems, Oracle and Microsoft are the stock price gain leaders in their respective industries.[5] Among Indian companies, Tata, Reliance, Mahindra & Mahindra are leading the innovators list.

Marketing Insight 10.3

Sensodyne Overtakes Colgate in Sensitive Category

Within two years of its launch, GSK brand becomes top-selling sensitive toothpaste

RATNA BHUSHAN & SAGAR MALVIYA NEW DELHI I MUMBAI

ET 7th Nov 2012

Just two years after its launch in the country, GlaxoSmithKline's Sensodyne has overtaken Colgate Sensitive to become the top-selling sensitive toothpaste brand in modern retail outlets and pharmacies that account for most sales in this category.

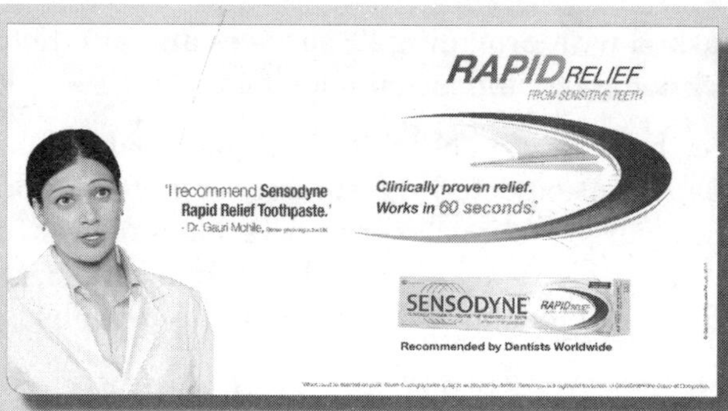

Sensodyne

"India had very low levels of awareness on the condition of tooth sensitivity. Over the past two years, Sensodyne has invested in creating awareness both through media and through dental detailing which has led to good category growth," Jayant Singh, executive vice-president, marketing, at GlaxoSmithKline Consumer Healthcare, said. He said Sensodyne has already crossed the . 100-crore sales mark.

Oral care giant Colgate Palmolive, which controls about 53% of the country's toothpaste market, has been selling its Sensitive brand in India since the last seven years. While Sensodyne has taken a lead in modern retail and pharmacies, in overall market the two brands have similar share, industry officials said quoting Nielsen data. The sensitive toothpaste segment accounts for less than 10% of the country's Rs. 5,400-crore toothpaste market at Rs. 470 crore, but is growing at 50% a year.

GSK Consumer Healthcare, which also makes Horlicks milk food drink and Foodles noodles, plans to spend Rs. 35-40 crore on advertising this year, up from Rs. 25 crore last year. Hindustan Unilever, the second-largest toothpaste maker, recently expanded its Pepsodent Expert Protection range to tap the rising demand for premium products. "Over the last few years we have seen the premium segment of the oral care category grow well ahead of the market," a HUL spokesperson said. "This is largely on account of improved consumer awareness and their growing prosperity."

Colgate Sensitive Pro-Relief

Colgate too has aggressively marketed premium products, and analysts say the market leader is not facing any big risk. "We don't see an immediate risk for Colgate as the category is not very big in Colgate's portfolio. And Colgate being market leader in oral care, if the segment interests the company, it will grow faster benefiting all the players involved," Nitin Mathur, consumer research analyst at Espírito Santo Securities, said.

In the globalised world, the customer needs are ever changing. The technology is also progressing at a lightning speed. The competition is hotting up with world becoming a globalized market. Earlier there were just two cars – Hindustant Motor's Ambassador and Premier Padmini. Then, with the introduction of Maruti 800 in 1983-84, Indian market is flooded with more than hundred models from various manufacturers and is witnessing a revolution in the automobile industry. Every year, all the companies are launching new and new cars to sustain their growth. In 2009 only, within a time span of just ten months, till October, 2009, 36 new cars have been launched in different market segment. All these cars, which has been launched in the market falls somewhere between the six categories of new products discussed earlier.

Marketing Insight 10.4

Marketing Insight 10.4

Tata Motors is Developing new Products for Domestic Market

April 23, 2014, 14:05 IST by CarTrade Editorial Team

Tata Nexon

Tata Motors seems keen at tapping into new segments with new products which are yet in development stage. Putting all rumours to rest, in a new development, some details are finally out on the Tata Motors' entry level premium SUV which the company is developing in collaboration with its British subsidiary, JLR. Tata's new SUV will be juxtaposed to Toyota's popular premium SUV, Fortuner, an expected price tag ranging between Rs 20 lakh and Rs 25 lakh is being considered for the SUV. Reports suggest that the SUV will be brought to life by 2016-17 and will mark its global debut by then.

Besides an entry level premium SUV, Tata is also developing a replacement of Indicae V2 hatchback, conceived on XO platform. The hatchback will be priced between Rs 3 lakh to Rs 4 lakh and could be launched in India by 2015.

Tata's first premium SUV codenamed Q5 will be a seven seat vehicle offered in 5+2 layout. Under the leadership of Karl Heinz Servous, Project Director for Joint Projects, a team of 45 engineers is working meticulously on the SUV. Underpinning the Freelander 2 SUV, Q5 will be a largely modified version of the former built to suit Indian driving conditions. Freelander is conceived on Ford's EUCD platform, this platform is also used by Volvo for S80. A source close to development opines that Q5 will vary immensely from Freelander, differences will be visible largely in form of new additions and modifications. The SUV could be offered under Tata badge, however a joint badging option is also being pondered.

Tata currently offer SUV's in its present line-up, but this would be first highly priced product from Tata Motors. In China, JLR and its Chinese partner Chery could launch a sub-brand and Q5 could be made available under this brand.

Coming back to the new hatchback from Tata based on XO platform, it will be an alter ego of Vista varying immensely from the outgoing model on mechanical front. The new hatchback will compete with cars in mini hatchback segment including Maruti's Wagon R. Tata will begin production of Vista's reskinned version effective 2015 at its Sanad manufacturing unit where the company currently manufactures Nano. Looking at the low demand for Nano, production capacity at Sanad plant is being wasted with only 1000-2000 units of Nano being produced every month. By producing the new hatchback at the plant the company could make use to the production capacity which is 20,000 units a month.

Tata is also bringing a new hatchback christened Bolt, previewed at 2014 Auto Expo. The production of new Bolt was scheduled to take place at Ranjangaon plant that it shares with Fiat, now fresh reports suggest that Bolt will be rolled out at Tata's manufacturing unit located near Pune.

The development of new products ranges from product modifications to an original product. Either the product development will be incremental or it will be a breakthrough like a Walkman or an iPod or an iPhone or an iPad or Tata Nano. Thus, new product projects fall somewhere along a continuum, with breakthrough products on extreme and incrementally altered or improved products on the other.[6]

Breakthrough versus Incremental Product Development

Breakthrough	Incremental
• New to the World Performance Features • Huge advance in performance • Dramatic cost reduction	• Improvement in existing product • Derivative of existing product platform • Exploits existing form of technology
• High Risk	• Lower risk
• Infrequently occuring	• More frequent
• Costly to do	• Less costly
• Targeted to new or existing markets	• Taregeted to existing or adjacent martkets
Marketer's Key Responsibility	
• Envision the market • Create demand • Educate the market	• Listen to the existing market • Accommodate current demand

Breakthrough product introduces new products with cost reduction and creates the demand in the market. Incremental product development tries to improve the product offerings, so that the existing demand can be served. If breakthrough product development represents innovations to the core, incremental product represents innovation at the margin.

Stages in New Product Development

New product Development (NPD) process passes through various stages to reach its customers. These stages are as following:

1. **Idea generation and screening**
2. **Concept development and testing**
3. **Physical product development and testing and**
4. **Commercialisation**

The nature of the new product development process generally differs with the product to product across different industries. In a pharmaceuticals company like Ranbaxy, NPD process will be different from a software company like Microsoft or an automobile company like Maruti Suzuki or a consumer electronics company like LG or an FMCG company like Dabur or Nirma. In a pharmaceuticals company, the development of a drug starts with thousands of compounds, years of extensive clinical trials and innumerable failures to get an effective and commercially successful drug. Similarly in the software business, after the software development, a beta version is issued to test the product. Once all the problems are rectified in the beta version, the final version is launched.

Marketing Insight 10.5

Bolt, Zest to go global

MURALI GOPALAN Business line

May 15, 2014:

Tata Motors is putting in place an aggressive global script for its passenger car business which will kick off with the launch of the Bolt and Zest next month.

"The capabilities within Tata Motors are immense and we have all the resources needed to make the best-in-class vehicles. One of the key things we did last year was to look at all our products and craft them into portfolios to take us to the next level of becoming a global player," Ranjit Yadav, President, Passenger Vehicles Business Unit, told *Business Line* in London this week.

The Tata Motors board accepted the plan and the team is now readying a pipeline of products running all the way till 2020. From Yadav's point of view, it is increasingly clear that the days of being a local player are long gone and going global is an imperative.

Tata Zest

This is where the Tata Motors European Technical Centre at Coventry near London is playing a vital role in tandem with the operations in Pune and Turin, Italy. The focus has been to build cars with an emphasis on top-class design, ease of driving and connectivity. All these functions are part of the company's Horizonext strategy unveiled last year. The Bolt and Zest are the first two products that have emerged from this strategy. Following the India launch, Tata Motors will take them to markets where it already has operations like South Africa and Indonesia, a recent addition.

The company is also in the process of launching its passenger vehicles in Algeria and this again could be a potential market for these two cars. "It is clear that you cannot operate in your local markets alone and need more countries for scale and volume. Our first play is emerging markets and progressively other regions as well," Yadav said.

Over the last six months, more than 200 dealerships have been revamped and the new look will coincide with the launch of these two cars.

The Bolt and Zest will also signal a new brand repositioning for Tata Motors in reaching out to personal buyers. The focus lately has been more on the taxi segment but things have changed with the Nano Twist positioned as a smart city car, and the Bolt and Zest adding to the momentum . Going forward, Tata Motors will launch compact SUVs, which are gaining ground in emerging markets.

(The writer was in the UK on an invitation from Tata Motors.)

Swift Dzire

In an automobile company like Maruti Suzuki, the NPD process passes through new design and engine for the car, to test run to corrections based on the feedback and then to the final product like Maruti Suzuki Swift. The hugely successful Swift is based on an extensive research on the needs, trends and the suggestions made by Maruti Suzuki's existing customer base in India. Maruti Suzuki invested Rs. 440 Crores in the Swift project. It sent 25 Indian Engineers and Designers to Europe for 6 Months to study the trends. Then they went to Japan for 18 Months to design and develop the Swift. Based on the European styling, Japanese quality and precision and Indian engineering capability; Swift became a huge success in India. The new Swift Dzire is also based on the same platform by adding a boot in the car. Both Swift and Swift Dzire have been so successful in Indian market that the customers are waiting for weeks together to get the delivery of their favourite vehicle. Recently this car has celebrated its fifth anniversary. The attractiveness of this segment has led Tata Motors to launch Indigo Manza to compete with Swift Dzire.

Failure of New Products

Product and brand failures occur on an ongoing basis to varying degrees within most product-based organizations. This is the negative aspect of the new product development and marketing process. In most cases, this failure rate syndrome ends up being a numbers game. There must be some ratio of successful products to each one that ends up being a failure. When this does not happen, the organization is likely to fail, or at least experience financial difficulties that prohibit it from meeting profitability objectives. The primary goal is to learn from product and brand failures so that future product development, design, strategy and implementation will be more successful.

A product is a failure when its presence in the market leads to:

- The withdrawal of the product from the market for any reason;
- The inability of a product to realize the required market share to sustain its presence in the market;
- The inability of a product to achieve the anticipated life cycle as defined by the organization due to any reason; or,
- The ultimate failure of a product to achieve profitability.

Failures are not necessarily the result of substandard engineering, design or marketing. Sony's Beta format was a clearly superior product to VHS, but their decision to not enable the format to be standardized negatively impacted distribution and availability, which resulted in a product failure. Apple has experienced a series of product failures, with consistent repetition as they continue to fight for market share.[7]

In India, Tata Sierra, Rajdoot 350, Maruti Omni with High Roof, Maruti Versa are the examples of product failures.

Marketing Insight 10.6

Marketing Insight 10.6

Ford Fiesta, Tata Aria, Nissan Evalia: Launched with great expectations but failed to deliver

By *Ketan Thakkar*, ET Bureau | 5 Apr, 2013, 06.50AM IST

MUMBAI: With one Ford Fiesta being sold every two minutes in 2012 in Europe, the US carmaker Ford Motor Co. harboured a lot of expectations on the car doing well in India, when it was launched in India a couple of years ago, emboldened by the success of Figo, its popular hatchback in the market. Fiesta, was touted as the big rival, was expected to threaten leaders in the sedan space such as Honda City, Hyundai Verna.

Tata Aria

Today, the sale of Fiesta is lagging behind its peers and does not make up for tenth of highest selling sedan Hyundai Verna in the mid-size segment. ET learns Ford has sold just 1957 units on Fiesta for the entire fiscal year of FY-13, which is an average of 163 units a month, as against Hyundai Verna, which sold about 4,800 units to 5,000 units a month.

Fiesta is not alone. Models such as Tata Aria, Nissan Evalia and General Motor's Chevrolet Sail hatchback were launched with a lot of expectation, but could not deliver the desired result. Aria, Fiesta and Evalia are yet to achieve 10% of what they intended, according to vendors. GM however managed to achieve 50-60% of it targeted volumes for its hatchback Sail by selling an averaging of 1,200 units a month.

Nissan India was targeting to sell at least 2,000 units of Evalia every month. However, its monthly sales over the past six months have averaged at little over 200 units. Tata Aria, despite introducing entry level 'Pure' variant and offering steep discounts, had touched a low of four units in the month of February. All these models are of strategic importance to each of these manufacturers.

All these models are of strategic importance to each of these manufacturers. They were either aimed at expanding the portfolio or targeted to bring in additional volumes from the growing segments. Experts say the reasons for lukewarm response are very specific for all these models. Tata Aria was positioned as a premium crossover. Experts say somehow premium and Tata don't go well together, as the company over the years has delivered value for money models. Ford Fiesta was hit due to its premium pricing.

Nissan Evalia's van-like looks didn't invite much attention and Chevrolet Sail, the highest selling car brand in China, has got hit due to no major differentiator versus best-selling Maruti Suzuki Swift or Hyundai i20 and the overall market environment, too, made it difficult for these models.

Car	Units Per Month		Year of Launch
	Internal Target	FY13 Avg Sales	
Tata Aria	2,500 – 3,000	Less than 100	Oct. 2011
Ford Fiesta	3,000 – 3,500	Less than 200	Jun. 2011
Nissan Evalia	3,000 – 3,500	Less than 250	Sept. 2012
GM Sail	2,250 – 2,500	1,150 – 1,200	Nov. 2012
Source : Industry Sources and SIAM Data			

According to Pradeep Saxena, executive director at marketing research firm TNS Automotive all these models have failed to come in the consideration set of prospective buyers on various front. For some of these models it was an issue of value proposition (Fiesta and Aria), Chevrolet Sail is a me-too offering with nothing additional in a highly competitive space and for some it was just about creating enough awareness (Evalia, Aria and Sail).

Yamaha Rajdoot 350

On the global platform, Cadillac Cimarron, Pontiac Fiero, Chevrolet Corvair, Ford Edsel, IBM's PCjr—introduced in March 1985, Apple's Newton, Apple's Lisa, Coleco's Adam, World Football League, Women's National Basketball Association, World League of American Football, United States Football League, Burger King's veal parmesan, Burger King's pita salad, Polaroid instant home movies etc. had failed earlier.

The reasons for the failure can be attributed any of the following:

- Faulty concept
- Faulty product design

- Overestimated market size
- Incorrectly positioned product
- Iineffective promotion, including packaging message
- Incorrectly priced—too high and too low
- Misleading market research that did not accurately reflect the actual consumer's behavior for the targeted segment
- Conducted marketing research and ignored those findings
- Key channel partners were not involved, informed, or both and
- Lower than anticipated margins

Using these potential causes of a product or brand failure may help to avoid committing those same errors. Learning from these lessons can be beneficial to avoid some of these pitfalls and increase the chance for success when you launch that next product or brand.

Maruti Eeco

Maruti Versa

Taking a cue from the failure of Maruti Versa, Maruti relaunched Versa as 'Eeco'in 2010 with a cheaper price tag by almost Rs. 1 lac and making some changes in the engine and interiors. Now the failure in Versa has turned around with success in Eeco for Maruti Suzuki. Similarly a company can relook at their product and marketing strategies to increase the chance of success.

Product Life Cycle

New product development process is just the starting point of the product life cycle (PLC). In the life of business, product life cycle passes through four stages: introduction, growth, maturity and decline. While plotting on a diagram, it takes the shape of a bell; leading to call it a Bell shaped PLC Curve.

1. **Introduction:** In the introduction stage, initial sales growth is slow, but marketing and promotional expenses are high, leading to negative or no profit. The company tries to create product awareness and induces trial for the product.
2. **Growth:** In the growth stage, sales starts picking up, leading to rising profits. The company tries to maximize market share, resulting in increase in profits.
3. **Maturity**: Sales reach to its peak in this stage and then it starts declining. Profit also starts declining. At the end of the stage, the company struggles to keep it market share intact.
4. **Decline**: In the decline stage, sales as well as profit go down.

Stages of the Product Life Cycle

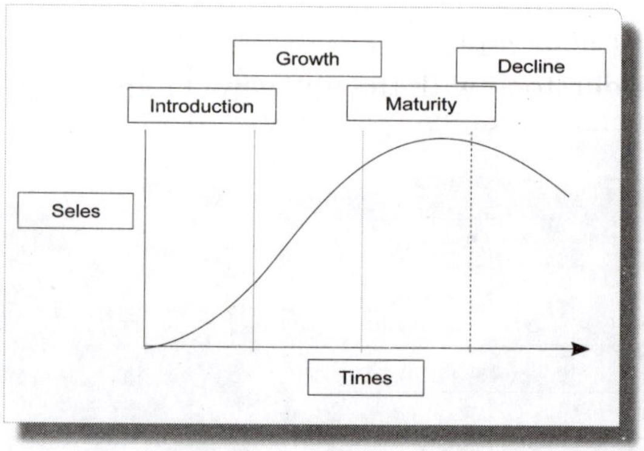

(Theodre Levitt, 'Exploit the Product Life Cycle', Harvard Business Review, Nov.-Dec., 1965, pp. 81-94)

Generally all the products pass through these four stages, but in some cases the PLC curve may be different. For example, in 2009, the demand for N95 masks had gone up tremendously in India with swine flu outbreak. But the demand had fallen sharply with the improvement in curbing it. This also happens in the case of Fads, the fashion that becomes hit among the people instantly and then it peaks and after that it declines very fast.

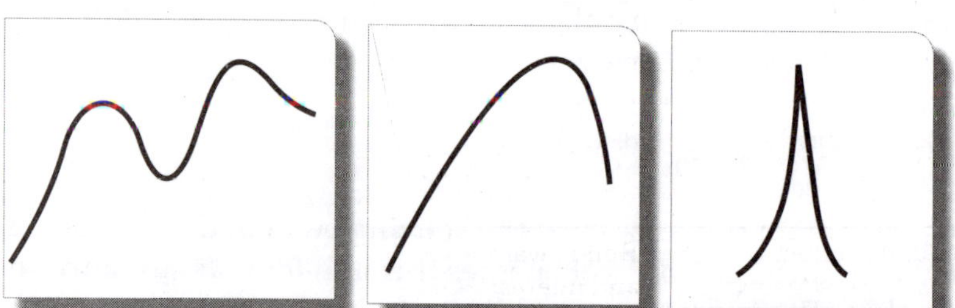

1. Style 2. Fashion 3. Fad

With the new usage of the product also, the sales and profit cycle shows a different scalloped pattern like plastics, nylon and fiber.[8]

Sometimes, a product grows rapidly, reaches its peak and then fell to a petrified level. The petrified level is sustained by the replacement market of early adopters and new market for late adopters. Another PLC pattern is found in the case of new drugs, where the drug reaches its peak and then declines, again the company pushes the product and it produces a second cycle.[9]

Strategies for Different Stages of Product Life Cycle

As far as product strategy is concerned, PLC process helps a company to strategise its marketing mix. In the introduction stage, the company may focus on the core benefits through the basic product, can add product line extensions in the growth stage. Expand the brand in the maturity stage and prune the product or brand mix in the decline stage.[10] The same can also be understood with the following table:

Charactris-tics/ PLC	Introduction	Growth	Maturity	Decline
Sales	Low sales	Rapidly rising sales	Peak sales	Declining sales
Costs	High cost per customer	Average cost per customer	Low cost per customer	Low cost per customer
Profits	Negative	Rising Profits	High Profits	Declining profits
Customers	Innovators	Early Adopters	Middle Majority	Laggards
Competitors	Few	Growing Number	Stable number beginning to decline	Declining Numbers
Marketing Objectives				
	Create product awareness and trial	Maximise market share	Maximise profit, while defending market share	Reduce expenditure and Milk the brand
Strategies				
Product	Offer a basic product	Offer product extensions, service, warranty	Diversify brands and item models	Phase out weak products
Price	Charge cost plus	Price to penetrate market	Price to match competition	Cut price
Distribution	Build selective distribution	Build intensive distribution	Build more intensive distribution	Go selective : phase out unprofitable outlets
Advertising	Build product awareness among early adopters and dealers	Build awareness and interest in the mass market	Stress brand differences and benefits	Reduce to level needed to retain hard core loyals

Sales Promotion	Use heavy sales promotion to entice trial	Reduce to take advantage of heavy consumer demand	Increase to encourage brand switching	Reduce to minimal level

(Source : Chester R. Wasson, Dynamic Competitive Strategy and Product Life Cycles, Austin Press, 1978; John A. Webber, Planning Corporate Growth with Inverted Product Life Cycles, Long Range Planning, October, 1976; Peter Doyle, The Realities of the Prodyucty Life Cycle, Quaterly Review of Marketing,Summer, 1976)

In the above table, as it is shown; in the introduction stage, a company always focuses on creating product awareness and trial. Then, it leads to maximizing market share in the growth stage. In the maturity stage, the objective of the company is to maximize profits, while defending its market share. In the decline stage, the company needs to reduce the expenditure and milk the brand. As far as product strategy is concerned, in the beginning, the company offers a basic product, which goes on to offer product extensions in the growth stage. In maturity, it needs to diversify brands and item models and in decline, it can phase out the weak models. The company offers cost plus pricing in the introduction stage, while it may offer prices to penetrate market and go on to offer competitive prices in the maturity stage. In the decline stage, it needs to cut the price. On the distribution front, a company can go for selective distribution to intensive to again selective distribution in the decline stage. In the beginning, advertising and promotional efforts are intended to create awareness and induce trial, which go on to brand building exercise in the growth and maturity stage. In decline stage, the advertising and promotional efforts are reduced with the declining sales.

Managing Product and Brand Portfolios

The concept of PLC is important for the success and longevity of the company. The company should always take a cue from it and formulate its marketing strategy. In the era of cut throat competition, many companies try to put their eggs into different baskets to minimise the risk. It means that through a product portfolio, a company can counter most of the attacks in the market. For example, Maruti Suzuki has got a product portfolio of 13 different cars. As the market is very competitive with players like Hyundai, Tata Motors, Chevrolet, Fiat, Honda, Ford, Mahindra & Mahindra etc; Maruti is always trying to better its car offerings or trying to launch a totally new car in the market. In 2009, it has launched Ritz and Estilo and now in 2010, it has launched all new Wagon R. In the same way, its competitors are not far behind. Tata has launched Nano and Indigo Manza, while Hyundai has launched new facelifted Santro, i20 Diesel and i20 Automatic, Verna Automatic and facelifted Sonata.

The different cars sold under the Maruti stable are under different life cycle. The erstwhile highest selling car, Maruti 800 has been phased out and Alto 800 has taken its place. Swift and Swift Dzire are enjoying the growth phase, while Zen Estilo has also been phased out. Now with the growing demand of Compact SUV, Maruti Suzuki is launching S Cross and also bringing IV 4 concept. Sedan SX4 is also getting replaced by Ciaz.

Maruti Suzuki Ciaz

The company can also put some life into its products through line extension. Brand extension can also help in getting to a new category, through the same brand image. But it should be used carefully. Companies like ITC has gone further and added additional brands in several product categories and also diversified in other businesses to sustain and enhance the business growth.

Summary

- A Product is anything that can be offered to a customer to satisfy his or her need or want. The product offers a total bundle of benefits to the customers. Typically in marketing, the term product is used for any good or service or any other entity, which can be marketed.
- A company can offer five levels of product to satisfy the needs of the consumers. These five levels are called Customer Value Hierarchy. These are - core benefit of the product, generic product, expected product, augmented product and potential product.
- Brand is a name, term, sign, symbol or design or a combination of them, intended to identify the goods or services of one seller or group of sellers and to differentiate them from those of competitors.
- Traditionally, products can be classified on the basis of durability and tangibility and use. On the basis of durability and tangibility, products can be classified into three groups: non durable goods, durable goods and services. On the basis of the use, the goods can be classified into Consumer goods and Business Goods or Industrial Goods.

- Any product mix consists of several product lines. Product line consists of a group of products, which are closely related and similar in nature and sold to the same kind of customer base. The product mix of any company can further be divided into its width, length and depth.
- When an existing brand is extended to introduce additional items in the same product category, then it is known as Line Extension. Under the brand extension, the same brand name is used in a new product category. In the existing product category, an additional brand may be introduced.
- A company needs to develop new products constantly to remain in the growth and profit mode. Most Companies rarely innovate, some innovate occasionally and a few innovate continuously.
- The development of new products ranges from product modifications to an original product. Either the product development will be incremental or it will be a breakthrough. Breakthrough product introduces new products with cost reduction and creates the demand in the market. Incremental product development tries to improve the product offerings, so that the existing demand can be served.
- Product and brand failures occur on an ongoing basis to varying degrees within most product-based organizations. The reasons for the failure can be attributed to faulty concept or faulty product design or overestimated market size or incorrectly positioned product or ineffective promotion, including packaging message or incorrectly priced—too high and too low etc.
- New product development process is just the starting point of the product life cycle. In the life of business, product life cycle passes through four stages: introduction, growth, maturity and decline.
- As far as product strategy is concerned, PLC process helps a company to strategise its marketing mix. In the introduction stage, the company may focus on the core benefits through the basic product, can add product line extensions in the growth stage. Expand the brand in the maturity stage and prune the product or brand mix in the decline stage.

Discussion Questions

1. What do you mean by Product? Explain the Customer Value Hierarchy with an example.
2. Define product in Marketing? How do you classify a product based on its durability, tangibility and use?
3. What do you mean by Product Mix? Discuss the width, length and depth of a product mix with an example.

4. Define Brand? Discuss Product Line and Brand Extensions Grid.
5. Discuss the role and importance of new product development. Explain the various stages of new product development with an example.
6. Explain the various stages in product life cycle. Discuss the strategies for different stages of product life cycle.
7. Short Notes:
   a. Marketing Mix
   b. Line Extension
   c. Growth Stage
   d. Length in Product Mix
   e. Unsought Goods
   f. Customer value Hierarchy
   g. Potential Product
   h. Breakthrough versus Incremental Product Development
   i. Failure of New Products

References

1. Theodore Levitt, 'Marketing Success through Differentiation: of Anything', Harvard Business Review, Jan.-Feb., 1980, pp. 83-91
2. Philip Kotler, 'Marketing Management', 11th Edition, Pearson Education, 2004 pp. 418-423
3. Patrick E. Murphy and Ben M. Enis, 'Classifying Products Strategically', Journal of Marketing, July, 1986, pp. 24-42
4. Booz, Allen and Hamilton, 'New Product Management for the 1980s', Booz, Allen and Hamilton, 1982
5. Thomas Kuczmarski, Arthur Middlebrooks and Jeffrey Swaddling, 'Innovating the Corporation: Creating values for customers and shareholders', NTC, 2000
6. Marketer's Toolkit', Harvard Business School Press, 2006, pp.105-106
7. Tim Berry, Product And Brand Failures: A Marketing Perspective, http://articles.mplans.com/product-and-brand-failures-a-marketing-perspective/#ixzz1Pswy1bHg

8. Jordan P. Yale, 'The strategy of Nylon's growth', Modern Textiles Magazine, Feb., 1964, p.32

9. William E. Cox Jr., 'Product Life Cycles as Marketing Models', Journal of Business, Oct., 1967, pp. 375-384

10. Alvin J. Silk, 'What is Marketing', Harvard Business School Press, 2006, p. 107

Chapter 11

Services Marketing

Chapter Structure

Our mission remains inviolable: Offer the customer the best service we can provide; cut our costs to the bones and generate a surplus to continue the unending process of renewal."

-Joseph Pillay, Former Chairman - Singapore Airlines

Ultimately, only one thing really matters in service encounters - the customer's perceptions of what occurred."

-Richard B. Chase and Sriram Dasu

Services Marketing

Theodore Levitt said '....**There is no such thing as service industries. There are only industries, where service components are greater or less than those of other industries. Everybody is in the service industry....**'

Airtel

The above statement talks about the emergence of the service sector in a big way. In fact, services are everywhere and it has become an indispensible part of our lives. Day do day, we use an array of services like talking on a phone, taking a bus / train to the college / office, sending an application / letter by courier, booking an airline ticket or a hotel, taking out money from an ATM, going to a multiplex to watch a movie, having fast food, sipping a hot cuppa of coffee at a café joint and taking a radio taxi back home. All of these activities are possible due to service providers like Airtel / Vodafone, DTDC / DHL, Yatra / Make My Trip, ICICI Bank / SBI, PVR / Fame, Mc Donalds / Pizza Hut, Starbucks / Café Coffee Day, Meru Cabs / Flash Cabs, Indigo / Jet Airways etc.

Marketing Insight 11.1

Marketing Insight 11.1

Trip Advisor Survey: IndiGo is Preferred Airline Third Year in a Row

IndiGo scores over rivals due to its on-time performance, in-flight maintenance, landing and take-off quality and time taken to deliver baggage.

Budget carrier IndiGo has emerged as the preferred airline in domestic skies among 2,500 respondents surveyed by travel site TripAdvisor. The respondents preferred IndiGo over other airlines due to its on-time performance, in-flight maintenance, landing and take-off quality and time taken to deliver baggage.

The respondents rated full-service carrier Jet Airways best in its ground handling services, website experience, check-in process at the airport, cabin crew appearance, in-flight experience in food, entertainment and comfort in terms of enhanced leg space. National carrier Air India, however, emerged as the least favourite airline for the third consecutive year.

According to the as many as 53 per cent of the respondents said they would prefer to fly Tata-SIA airways prior to experiencing AirAsia India. Though 48 per cent of the respondents held AirAsia's entry into the Indian market will bring down fares temporarily. Emirates was voted as the best international airline, followed by German carrier Lufthansa and Singapore Airlines.

The findings of the survey showed that while most passengers (37 per cent) are comfortable with paying consolidated fares, nearly a quarter (24 per cent) of the respondents said that they would like to pay a basic fare and then pay for additional services as per need. Another 14 per cent of the respondents said that unbundled fares suit the needs largely of solo or overnight business travelers who travel with minimum luggage but are not appropriate for a family going on a holiday.

The high air fares have meant that an increasing number of travelers now feel that airlines are not transparent when it comes to costs. Nearly half the respondents (50 per cent) said domestic airlines are not transparent about all the costs including booking a flight for example cost of - meal, extra baggage costs, etc compared with 42 per cent last year.

Growth of Service Sector Economy

In India also, service sector is growing at a rapid pace. It has gone up from a meager share of 15% in GDP contribution in 1950 to a 55% share in GDP in 2007.[1] In USA, service account for close to 79 percent of GDP. By 2014, it is estimated that nearly four out of five jobs in the United States will be in service industries. Services are growing even faster in the world economy, making up 64 percent of gross world product.[2]

Although service sector has come up in a big way in the recent years; yet its' existence is not a new thing for the world. It has always been existed since ages. In India, if we go by the historical facts, we find the mention of doctors (Vaidya), Money Lenders (Sahukar), Midwives (Dai), Masseurs (Champi), Transporters, Dharamshalas and Sarais in the literature. In the modern time, the list of services is getting bigger and bigger with the complexities in life as well as the growing needs for different kind of services to make life easy. Many forces are also transforming our economies, making them more service oriented. They include government policies, social changes, business trends, advances in information technology and globalization.[3]

Defining Services

Marketing, on the whole, can be divided into goods marketing and services marketing. Although according to Philip Kotler, besides goods and services, a marketer also markets eight other entities like Events, Experiences, Persons, Places, Properties, Organisations, Information and Ideas; yet it is generally clubbed together and is widely known as goods and services. In marketing, services marketing essentially deals with the products, which are intangible in nature. Services are created through a direct interaction between the service provider and the customers.

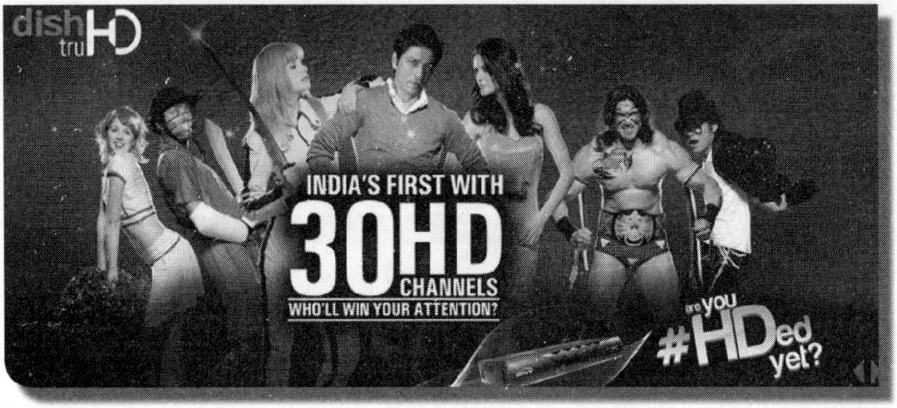

Dish DTH

Goods are physical, tangible articles, while Services are non physical and intangible in nature and can also satisfy a need like goods. Financial services - Banking, Telecom, DTH, Courier, Hotel, Airline, Multiplex, Train, Doctors, Lawyers, Healthcare and Management Consultancy are all examples of services. With the advancement in the economy, a country moves from a goods producing country to a service oriented country. For example, USA, which is one of the most developed countries in the world, is having a 21% - 79% mix of goods and services.

Services can be defined as following:

'A service is any activity or benefit that one party can offer to another, which is essentially intangible and does not result in the ownership of anything. Its production may or may not be tied to a physical product.' – Kotler, Armstrong, Saunders and Wong

'Services are economic activities that create value and provide benefits for customers at specific times and places as a result of bringing about a desired change in – or on behalf of – the recipient of the service.' – Christopher Lovelock

Characteristics of Service Industry

Services have unique characteristics, which differentiate it from goods. This means that management and marketing of services require a different approach than goods marketing. Following are the four unique characteristics of services.

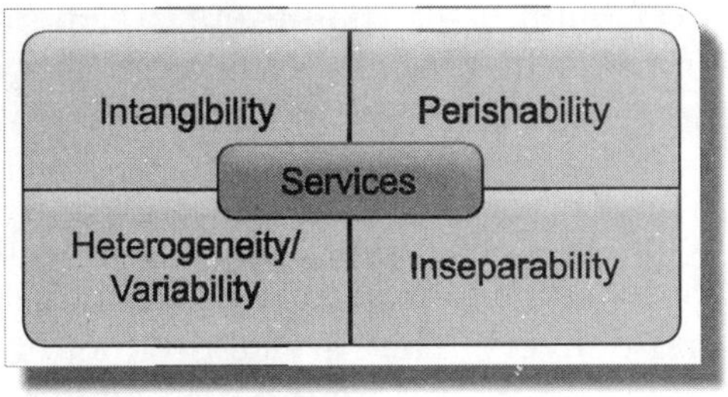

1. **Intangibility**: Services are intangible. Intangibility of a service implies that a customer cannot see, touch or feel the service product. The characteristics of intangibility make the job difficult, for both the customer as well as the marketer. Without buying the product, it is pretty difficult for the customer to either believe in the product or comprehend the product. A service like insurance, hotel, restaurant, medical care, or consultancy cannot be fully understood, without availing the same. That's why the service product takes the form of concept selling; where the customer needs to immerse himself into buying the services. It also leaves no scope of impulse purchases.

   As there is no concept of ownership, possession or acquisition for the customer after the service transaction, it becomes difficult for the customer to understand the value. On the marketer side, it becomes difficult to convince the customer about the value proposition of the same.

2. **Perishability:** Unlike goods, services cannot be stored for future sales. Services need to be transacted during the given time. Otherwise, it will lose its value. For example – A six a.m. Indigo flight from Delhi to Mumbai needs to fly at that point of time, whether there are 30 passengers or 150 passengers. Indigo Airlines will forever lose the vacant seats in the said flight. Similarly the seats for say, 6.40 pm show of Dhoom 3 at PVR Multiplex, Ambience Mall, Gurgaon can only be sold at or before the show. The multiplex cannot recover the revenue from vacant seats afterwards. In a B-School, if only 40 students take admission in a particular session against the capacity of 60 students; then the revenue from the 20 students will be lost for forever.

PVR Pictures

The characteristics of perishability also points out to a characteristics of simultaneous production and consumption in services. Unlike goods, where the goods are first manufactured, sold and then consumed; the services are produced and consumed simultaneously.

3. **Heterogeneity or Variability:** Services also have the unique characteristics of heterogeneity or variability or say non standardization. The service product is never consistent in quality and delivery. The service product is never the same for all its customers. It happens due to human beings being involved in the service delivery. A customer may receive differentiated service from different employees of the bank or even from the same employee in different time frames. For example – Mr. Roy works with ICICI Bank and an entrepreneur Mrs. Gupta goes to the bank almost every day for some banking transaction or the other. She regularly meets Mr. Roy, who helps her in doing the transaction. But today, Mr. Roy is not in a good mood, as he had a fight with his wife in the morning over some personal issue. Today again, Mrs. Gupta is there in the bank for some work. But Mr. Roy is not the same today and he does not greet Mrs. Gupta and also not interested in doing the transaction. Now the bank and the employee is the same, then also the service can vary and it will vary more with the change in person or the location, that's why service industry suffers from this curious characteristic of heterogeneity or variability. Similarly in a B-School, the same subject can be taught by four different faculty members and the delivery will be quite different from one another.

   There is another aspect also related to variability. As the services are delivered with customer being the part of the delivery; customer also affects the same. For example, in a B-School, all the students will not receive the same level of education and training from a faculty member; as their own background like education, IQ level, attitude, mood and personality may be different from their classmates. Although companies are trying hard to create the processes to deliver similar service quality, but still there may be heterogeneity at the end.

Arijit Singh, Aashiqui 2 Fame Singer

4. **Inseparability**: Services are inseparable. The service provider and the customer need to be present at the time of service delivery. An artist can only perform in a single place at a given point of time. During surgery, a surgeon as well as the patient should be present for the service delivery. It also means that the services cannot be replicated and made available in many places simultaneously. For example, many times an artist suffers from the plenty. Arijit Singh, Aashiqui 2 fame singer is wanted for the New Year party in Mumbai as well as in Delhi. But he can only present in one location, leaving the other. That's why; the service marketer concentrates on bringing both together under one roof, the customer as well as the service provider.

Service Offerings

The term service is quite general in concept and it includes a variety of services. It is not only the business organizations, which offer services, but a lot of private, not for profit organizations and governments also offer services. Following are the few of the services offered by different organizations:

Private, for profit business organisations	Private, not for profit business organisations	Governments
Hotels, Restaurants	Colleges	Postal services
Telecom Services	Schools	Hospitals
Airlines	Hospitals	Schools, Colleges, Universities
Banks	Temples, Churches, Mosques, Gurudwaras	Fire services
Insurance companies	Museums	Police
Management Consulting	Foundations	Military
Medical practices	Orphanages	Courts
Legal Practices		Electricity
Real Estate companies		Water supply
Courier services		Municipal services
Stock Broking services		Train
Advertising		Museums
Private security agencies		Zoo
Multiplexes and Single Theatres		
Photography and Videography		
Retailing – Wholesale and Retail distribution, Dealers, Agents, Clearing & Forwarding Agents		
Architects		

Private, for profit business organisations	Private, not for profit business organisations	Governments
Teaching		
Beauty Parlours, Health Clubs, Slimming Centres, Gymnasiums		
Event Management, Catering, Tent House, Decorators		

The same services can either be offered by any of these three types of organizations. For example, a restaurant can be managed by either private, for profit business organization or by private, not for profit organization or by the government.

Classification of Services

Services can be classified in many ways. Following are the most popular ones.

1. **Degree of Tangibility**: On the basis of the tangibility, service offerings may be categorized on the following basis.

Accenture

   a. **Pure stand alone services**: In the case of pure stand alone services, the services cannot be touched, felt or seen, like consultancy, physiotherapy, counseling, babysitting etc. Arthur Anderson, Accenture, TCS, Infosys falls into this category, where these companies offer pure stand alone services.

Marketing Insight 11.2

Marketing Insight 11.2

Innovation from TCS helps Ferrari Retain Pole Position in Formula One

Tata Consultancy Services

Tata Consultancy Services, the leading IT services, business solutions and outsourcing firm today announced that it received the Innovation Award from Ferrari for its ability to use technology services to spur innovation in one of the most competitive and technologically advanced arenas of automobile engineering. Stefano Domenicali, Ferrari Racing Department Director, presented the Innovation Award to TCS officials.

The citation for the Innovation Award highlights the innovation provided by team TCS and ability to work closely with the Ferrari in a model of collaboration and cultural integration. "TCS has won the Innovation Award for their zeal and proactive attitude, the excellent involvement in the activities of design and the contribution in the selection of IT technologies supporting innovation. Tata Consultancy Services (TCS) is an outstanding example of technological leadership and a model of cultural integration and exchange", said Mario Almondo, Operations Director of Scuderia Ferrari.

"This is no ordinary recognition. We are delighted that TCS' ability to innovate and help Ferrari dominate the Formula One racing has been recognized by Ferrari," said S Ramadorai, Chief Executive Officer and Managing Director, TCS. "The F1 car is the most advanced automobile in the market and this award is a tribute of the work of our team of engineers who are helping as a seamless unit with the engineering and technology team from Ferrari," he added.

b. **Hybrid**: Hybrid, as the name suggests, is a combination of services and goods. These kinds of services are inclusive of the product, like the restaurant, where a customer gets a tangible good in the form of say a Masala Dosa or a burger and gets it served at his table. Restaurant chains like Moti Mahal, Nirula's, Café Coffee Day, Pizza Hut etc. falls into this category.

c. **Tangible goods with accompanying service**: In this case, services are bundled as a part of components of goods in the total marketing mix. Cars, two wheelers, appliances are the various categories, where the product is sold and bundled with after sales service promise. In India, Maruti Suzuki is the leader in four wheeler category and its leadership position owes a lot to the after sales service, it provides in multiple locations all across India.

In the following table also, based on the tangibility, the types of services can be understood. On the one hand, products like salt and detergents fall on the higher tangibility side, while Consulting, Life insurance, and Internet Banking falls on the pure services side. In between lies the hybrid services like Fast food restaurants, where the service offering is bundled with a tangible product.

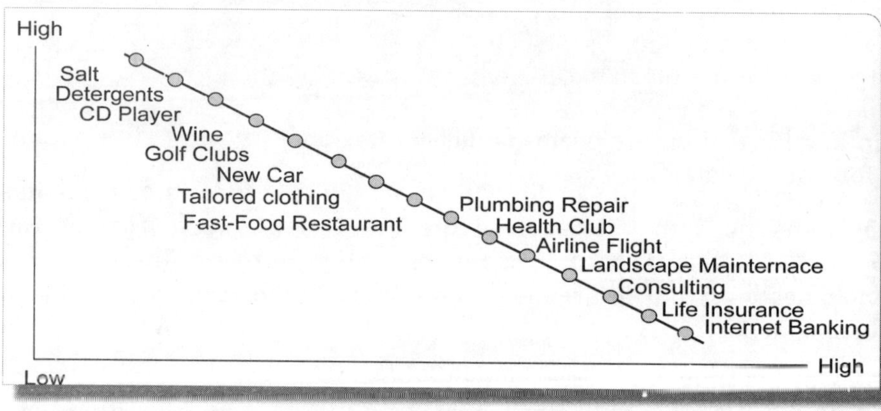

The aspect of tangibility is also discussed by Zeithamal, through his 'Product-Service Continuum'. In the figure below, the goods and services have been categorised and differentiated on the basis of difficulty of evaluation. While buying services, it is pretty difficult for a customer to assess the quality. It happens more so in the case of pure stand alone services. At the left side of the figure, Zeithamal has talked about the goods, which are high in search attributes. The same can be evaluated before making the purchase decision like Clothing, Jewellery, Furniture, Motor Vehicle. At the middle are the goods and services, which can be evaluated after making the purchase like restaurant meals, haircut etc. The same is high in experience attributes. At the right side are the services, which is difficult to evaluate even after consumption like computer repair, education or surgery. These are the services, which is high in credence attributes.

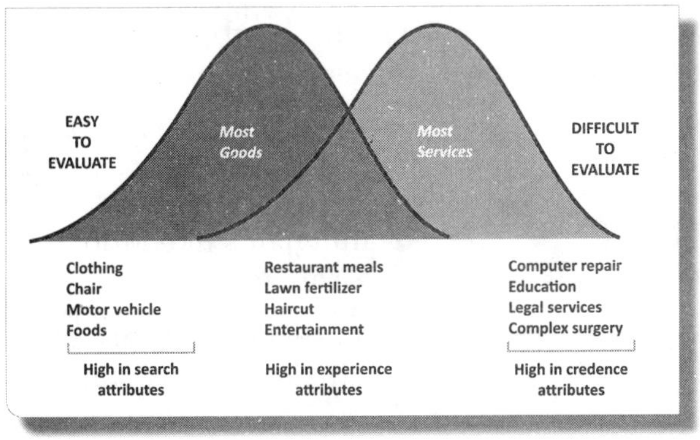

Product-Service Continuum
Source: Adapted from Zeithaml

All the above factors make the service purchase decisions a bit risky. That's why a customer relies more on word of mouth and the aspect of people, process and physical evidence of the services. This also makes customers loyal to one service provider. On the marketer side, it becomes extremely difficult to pull the customers away from the competition.

2. **Process Perspective:** From the process perspective, Christopher H. Lovelock has classified services into four broad categories.[4] The nature of the service act in the first two categories is tangible in nature, while the other two is based on intangible actions. Tangible actions are performed on people's bodies or to their physical possessions; while intangible actions are performed on people's mind or to their intangible assets. These four broad categories are as follows:

	Who or what Is the direct recipient of the service?	
Nature of the Service Act	People	*Possessions*
Tangible Actions	*People processing* (Sarvices dirracted at people's bodies): ❑ Barbers ❑ Health care	*Possession processing* (Services directed at physical Possessions): ❑ Refueling ❑ Disposal/recycling
Intangible Actions	*Mental stimulus processing* (Service directed at people's minds): ❑ Education ❑ Advertising/PR	*Information processing* (Services directed at intangible assets): ❑ Accounting ❑ Banking

a. **People Processing**: In the case of people processing, as the services are directed at people's bodies, customers must physically enter the service system to avail the services. For example- A barber can only cut the hair, when the customer is present at the time of service delivery. Similarly, a surgery can only be done, if the patient is present in the operation theatre. Just by booking a flight from New Delhi to Mumbai, you cannot reach Mumbai from New Delhi. You need to be present there and then only services can be availed.

DTDC

b. **Possession Processing**: In the case of possession processing, a customer can avail the services without being physically present there; as the service is directed towards the physical possession. For example, if a car needs to be serviced, the car needs to be present at the service location, not the owner or driver. Similarly, you can send a package from New Delhi to Mumbai, by just availing the services from DHL or DTDC. Thus customers are less physically involved with this kind of services.

c. **Mental Stimulus Processing**: In the case of mental stimulus processing, services are directed at people's mind like education, news and information, psychotherapy, professional advice, entertainment etc. In this case, the customer may be physically present at the site or he may be off site. But, still the services can be transferred. For example, a faculty member can teach a class in IIM Kolkata or a similar class can also be transmitted on an educational TV broadcast or may be supplied on CD/DVD. In both the cases, the customer's mind can be processed. The possibility of services being available at a later date or time benefits this kind of services being inventoried. In this case, it is also essential that a customer is mentally present to receive the service benefit. Otherwise the services will not get transferred. But in people processing, the services can be availed by the customer, if he is just physically present. For example, a passenger can sleep during his flight from New Delhi to Mumbai and then also he can reach his destination.

d. **Information Processing**: In the case of information processing, services are directed at intangible assets. These services are dependent on effective collection and processing of information like law, marketing research, medical diagnosis, accounting and management consulting.

3. **Degree of Contact:** Services can also be classified into two categories on the basis of the type of contact that the service providers have with their customers.

a. **High Contact**: As the very name suggests, in the high contact service, the service provider have high degree of contact with the customers. All the services under people processing comes under this. It also includes services under mental stimulus processing. Some examples are surgery, beauty care, counseling, teaching etc.

b. **Low Contact**: In the case of low contact, service providers interact very little with the customers and most of the processes are automated like banking through Automatic Teller Machines (ATMs), coin operated weighing machines at railway stations, vending machines for Cold Drinks, Snacks, Magazines etc. Internet based services like online retailers, multiplex ticket booking, internet booking of railway tickets etc. also fall under this service category.

Services Marketing Triangle

Service marketing is a game of promises played among the three entities called the company i.e service firm, the customer and the employees. On the basis of interaction between these entities, the success of the service firm lies in effective implementation of three types of marketing to create and deliver the services:

1. External Marketing
2. Internal Marketing and
3. Interactive Marketing.

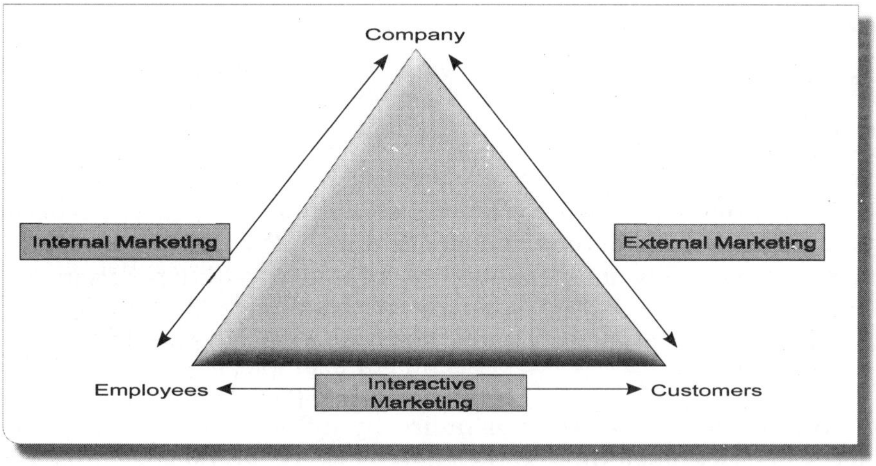

All these three types of marketing are required, as the services are very different from goods. In goods, external marketing is very important, where the company markets the goods to the customers. But besides external marketing, internal and interactive marketing is also required to create right kind of service environment and delivery. Internal marketing means that the service firm should orient its employees to deliver the service in best possible manner. For the same, the service firm needs to focus on hiring, training and motivational aspects of its employees. On the other hand, interactive marketing means that service quality is dependent upon the interaction between the service provider i.e. employees and the customer. That's why the employees should master the skills required to understand and serve the customer well.

Now let us check out the marketing tools, which help a service firm to effectively implement its marketing plan.

Service Marketing Mix

The four characteristics of services make marketing of services different from marketing of goods. To fulfill the marketing objectives of a service firm, it requires additional marketing tools and practices. Apart from the traditional marketing mix i.e. 4 P's like product, price, place and promotion, **Booms and Bitner** has suggested another three Ps, besides 4 Ps; totaling it to 7Ps of Marketing in the case of services and for knowledge based economy.[5] These P's are:

1. **Product,**
2. **Price,**
3. **Place,**
4. **Promotion,**
5. **People,**
6. **Process and**
7. **Physical Evidence**

The first 4Ps are equally important for the goods as well as services. The first P – product becomes a service product, while price, place - distribution and promotion become equally important. As services are different from goods due to its characteristics of intangibility, heterogeneity, inseparability and perishability; it requires additional Ps in the marketing mix to fulfill the marketing objectives in the target market. All the first 4Ps have been discussed in detail in the 'Product' Chapter. That's why we will now discuss the additional 3Ps. These are as following:

5. **People**: All people, who directly or indirectly influence the perceived value of the product or service, including knowledge workers, employees, management and consumers comes under the 5th P of Marketing. In any service, the use of appropriate staff and people are of utmost importance for its success. As we have seen earlier in this chapter that services marketing triangle is based upon not only on the company i.e service firm and the customers, but also on the employees, who are an integral part

of the service delivery. It in turn, leads to interactive marketing between the customers and the employees. We have also seen the impact of the same in the earlier example of Mr. Roy, an employee from ICICI Bank in the heterogeneity characteristics. That's why a service firm needs to be very careful in selecting the right kind of staff and should also provide right kind to training to make the service delivery better.

As the customers interact with the employees only, the employees become the face of the company. You may deal and interact with Mr. Roy, but you are not dealing with Mr. Roy, but with ICICI Bank. The image of ICICI Bank in the eyes of the customers, when they deal with the bank is dependent upon the attitude, behavior and response of the employee, who is providing the service and not Ms. Chanda Kochhar, who is the MD and CEO of ICICI Bank.

Marketing Insight 11.3

Now, Banking on Tablets to Win Customers

ICICI Tab Banking

Using a 'tablet' to open bank accounts seems to be catching on. After ICICI Bank's advertising blitzkrieg with Bollywood icon Amitabh Bachchan on how an account can be opened in a jiffy, Axis Bank and Kotak Mahindra Bank too have jumped on the 'tablet banking' bandwagon.

These banks are working on rolling out of their tab banking initiative, not just for account opening but also for putting through transactions, in a bid to win more retail customers.

Apart from opening current and savings bank accounts, ICICI Bank has started using tablets to offer mortgages in cities such as Mumbai, Pune and Surat, where customers can apply and get loans sanctioned on the same day, according to Rajiv Sabharwal, Executive Director at ICICI Bank.

Banks are taking to 'tab banking' to reach out to potential customers across the country, thereby reducing the turnaround time and costs to the bank.

Power of mobility

Says Jairam Sridharan, President of Consumer Lending for Axis Bank: "Everyone is trying to explore the power of mobility. Mobile has the power to do doorstep banking, and that has always been the way of getting sticky customers. Also, consumers are increasingly becoming more comfortable going digital."

"We piloted it (tablet banking) about 10 months ago with our high-end and priority customers and are gauging their experience.

"We will look at going full-fledged as the costs are just a tenth of branch banking," said KVS Manian, President - Consumer Banking, Kotak Bank. Using a tablet equipped with mobile and Internet connectivity, the bank's executive fills account-opening details, clicks the customer's picture and takes the relevant KYC (Know Your Customer) documents without the customer having to visit the bank branch. This brings down the percentage of re-work from 7 per cent to 1 per cent, ICICI Bank said.

For better bonding

The tablet is a fully loaded device which has application forms, bank's videos explaining products and their features.

Sabharwal said, "Tab banking is an effort to harness technology to ease the documentation process, thereby eliminating rejections due to incomplete account opening form or KYC mismatch.

"...We also wanted to open multiple channels for our customers and allow them to choose the channel they prefer. Our effort is to enhance the customers' experience and improve our bond with them." In addition, under tab banking, the bank plans to offer tractor loans to farmers and integrate the tablet with the Aadhaar card issued by the Government to be used as e-KYC.

On similar lines, Axis Bank recently introduced Aadhaar-based eKYC mode of account opening aimed at covering NREGS beneficiaries and pensioners in Andhra Pradesh.

This will offer paperless account opening services within a day through Micro-ATMs — a biometric handheld device.

So far, ICICI Bank has opened half a million accounts in about eight months. Going forward, it plans to add one lakh accounts every month. At present, 10,000 tablets are in circulation in 13 cities. The bank hopes to double this number in the next three months. With increased adoption of smartphones, more banks are likely to take to tab banking, going forward.

6. **Process**: In the case of process; procedures, mechanisms and flow of activities helps the marketer to satisfy the consumer in a better way. For example – Dominos Pizza serves its customers not only through its restaurants, but also with its 30 minutes guaranteed home delivery in India. Mc Donald's serves its customers with freshly made burgers and French fries within two minutes of the order due to its streamlined process. Starbucks wishes to serve its walk in customers within three minutes with a hot cuppa of coffee.

Marketing Insight 11.4

Marketing Insight 11.4

Starbucks' India Operations Fastest Growing in its History

Starbucks Coffee

With 40 stores in 17 months of its operations, India is the fastest growing market in the history of the Seattle-based iconic American coffee chain Starbucks, according to a company statement. The US-based coffee chain, which had sewed up an equal joint venture with Tata Global Beverages, opened its first outlet in Mumbai in October 2012.

"With 40 stores in four cities (in 17 months) and nearly 1,000 partners, India is the fastest growing market in Starbucks history," Tata-Starbucks chief executive Avani Davda was quoted as telling Starbucks annual shareholders meet. Tata Starbucks currently has presence in Mumbai, Delhi, Pune and Bangalore and has its coffee plantations in the Coorg area of Karnataka. Starbucks globally operates over 20,000 stores across 64 countries, serving over 70 million customers per week.

Starbucks chairman, president and chief executive Howard Schultz told shareholders that the company would continue to reinforce the ongoing investments in 200,000 Starbucks partners (employees), including US $ 250 million in their healthcare benefits and USD 234 million in bean stock in fiscal 2013. He said the company recorded record revenue of US $ 14.9 billion, up 12 per cent and record earnings per share of US $ 2.261, up 26 per cent, taking its net profit to US $ 2.5 billion, a rise of 23 per cent in fiscal 2013.

Process becomes extremely important, as it helps to minimize the negative impact of heterogeneity. Whether Mr. Roy is happy or not happy, the customer should always be happy at ICICI Bank. That's why ICICI Bank and other service firms have processes, which binds the employees to work under a time and service quality framework. That's why, in a service firm like banks, there are time stipulated for availing the services. The same is also replicated by e-governance measures in several states; where a time frame is stipulated. For exam – a birth certificate to be issued say, within 15 days after the application is made for the same.

7. **Physical Evidence**: Physical evidence deals with the direct sensory experience of a product or service that allows a customer to measure whether he or she has received value. Through physical evidence, a service marketer gives intangible services, a tangible character by using certificates, tickets, logos etc. For example, if you travel first class on an aircraft, you expect enough room to be able to lie down. Again, once you walk into a restaurant, you expect a clean and friendly environment. All these factors are very important in giving the right value to the consumers. A five star hotel should be better in all the respects, with a three star hotel. Sometimes the norm for the categorisation is decided by the association of respective firms or the govt. authority or a professional body. In Rajdhani trains, passengers pay much more than other trains; but they also receive the benefits in terms of good food and faster trains, thus saving time for them. Then, there are trains like Palace on Wheels, which takes the experience to a different level for their passengers and it conveys that luxurious expression through its physical evidence by offering the best through the royal ambience inside the coaches and service, which are offered inside the train.

   All the above 3Ps helps a marketer to effectively implement the marketing plan for services, besides using the traditional 4Ps.

Quality Gaps Model

V. Zeithamal, L. Berry and A. Parasuraman have conducted intensive research on service quality and identified ten dimensions used by customers in evaluating service quality. They also found a high degree of correlation between several of these variables. Then, they consolidated all these variables into five broad dimensions.[6] These are:

1. Tangibles – Appearance of physical elements.
2. Reliability – Dependable and accurate performance.
3. Responsiveness – Promptness and helpfulness.

4. Assurance – Credibility, security, competence and courtesy.
5. Empathy – Easy access, good communication and customer understanding.

After a thorough understanding of the service quality, V. Zeithamal, L. Berry and A. Parasuraman identified four potential gaps within the service firm that may lead to the fifth gap – the perceptions gap and the sixth and final gap – the service quality gap. The Perceptions Gap is the difference between what customer expected and what they perceived was delivered, while service quality gap is the difference between what customers expect to receive and their perceptions of the service that actually is delivered.[7]

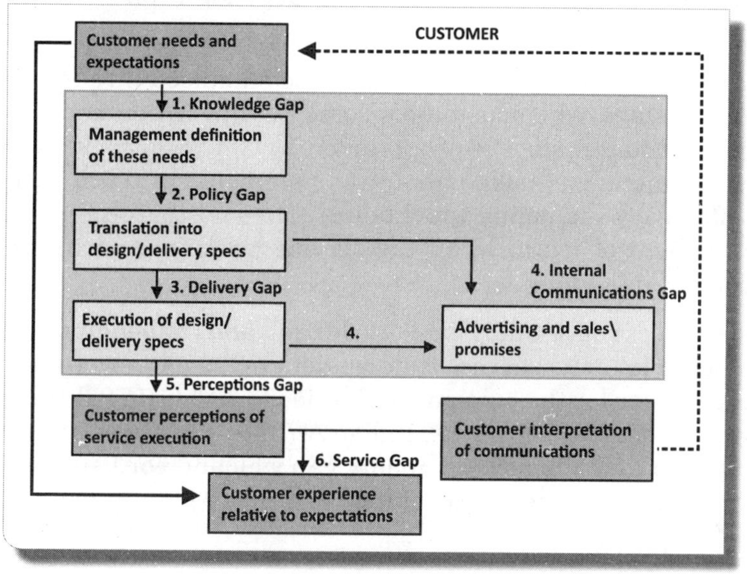

Services Quality Gaps

1. **Gap 1 – The Knowledge Gap** is the difference between what service firm believes customers need and the actual customers' needs and expectations.
2. **Gap 2 – The Policy Gap** is the difference between service firms' understanding of customers' expectations and the quality standards for service delivery.
3. **Gap 3 – The Delivery Gap** is the difference between specified service delivery by the service firm to actual service delivery.
4. **Gap 4 – The Communications Gap** is the difference between what the company communicates and what it actually delivers to its customers.
5. **Gap 5 – The Perceptions Gap** is the difference between the actual deliveries to the customer to what customers perceive they have received.

6. **Gap 6 – The Service Quality Gap** is the difference between what customers expect to receive and their perceptions of the service that actually is delivered.

The Gaps Model provides an insight to the service firms to plug the gaps to create a better service experience for the customers. Out of all these service gaps, the last gap - service quality gap is the most critical for a service firm.

A service firm should try to close or narrow the gap for being successful in the market and this can also be achieved if the service firm provides the services in the range of desired and adequate service levels, as customers perceive it. This is also known as the **zone of tolerance.**[8] The size of the zone of tolerance is dependent on many factors including competition, price etc.

The service experience for the customer can also be enhanced through betterment of the **"service encounter"** stage, when customers come directly in contact with a service.[9] The concept of service encounter stage is propounded by G. L. Shostock. Taking this concept further, Richard Normann has talked about the **"moments of truth"**, which showed the importance of effectively managing touchpoints. He said that 'the perceived quality is realized at the moment of truth, when the service provider and the service customer confront one another in the arena.[10]

Thus, managing services successfully is a very difficult and challenging exercise for service firms. Unlike goods, a lot of its success is dependent on its employees, who can make the service experience better for the customers. Service firms like ICICI Bank, Airtel, DTDC, Café Coffee Day, McDonalds, Starbucks, Indigo Airlines etc. are very successful today, as they have managed to plug the service quality gap well and consistently been delivering services better than the customers' expectations.

Summary

- A service is any activity or benefit that one party can offer to another, which is essentially intangible and does not result in the ownership of anything. Its production may or may not be tied to a physical product.
- Goods are physical, tangible articles, while Services are non physical and intangible in nature and can also satisfy a need like goods.
- There are four unique characteristics of services like intangibility, perishability, heterogeneity and inseparability.
- Services can be classified in many ways. On the basis of the tangibility, service offerings may be categorized as pure stand alone services, hybrid and tangible goods with accompanying service

- The aspect of tangibility is also discussed by Zeithamal, through his 'Product-Service Continuum'. The goods and services have been categorised and differentiated on the basis of difficulty of evaluation.
- From the process perspective, Christopher H. Lovelock has classified services into four broad categories - people processing, possession processing, mental stimulus processing and information processing.
- Services can also be classified into two categories on the basis of the type of contact that the service providers have with their customers – high contact and low contact.
- Service marketing is a game of promises played among the three entities called the company i.e service firm, the customer and the employees.
- Apart from the traditional 4 P's like product, price, place and promotion, Booms and Bitner has suggested another three Ps i.e. people, process and physical Evidence, thus totalling it to 7Ps of Marketing in the case of services and for knowledge based economy.
- After a thorough understanding of the service quality, V. Zeithamal, L. Berry and A. Parasuraman identified four potential gaps within the service firm that may lead to the fifth gap – the perceptions gap and the sixth and final gap – the service quality gap.

Discussion Questions

1. Define Service Marketing. Discuss four unique characteristics of services with examples.
2. What is so distinctive about services marketing that it requires additional 3Ps.
3. Why is it so difficult to define services?
4. What distinguishes high contact service from Low Contact ones? Explain how the nature of a customer's experience may differ between the two?
5. 'Service Marketing is a game of promises'. Explain the statement.
6. What do you understand by 'Services Marketing Mix'? Discuss in brief, the 7Ps of marketing mix.
7. Discuss the quality gap model in the context of services.
8. Why do you require additional 3Ps in Marketing?
9. Discuss the four broad processing categories of services and provide examples for each.

10. Short Notes:
    a. Intangibility
    b. Heterogeneity or Variability
    c. People Processing
    d. Mental Stimulus Processin
    e. Service Quality Gap
    f. Product Service Continuum
    g. Physical Evidence

References

1. Source: "CIA – The World Factbook – India". CIA. 2007-09-20. Retrieved 2007-10-02.
2. Source: "CIA – The World Factbook – India". CIA. 2007-09-20. Retrieved 2007-10-02.
3. Lovelock, C., Wirtz, J., Chatterjee, J., "Services Marketing", Pearson, 2011
4. Christopher H. Lovelock, "Classifying services to gain strategic marketing insights," Journal of Marketing, 47, Summer 1983: 9-20
5. Bernard H. Booms and Mary J. Bitner, "Marketing strategies and organization structure for service firms", in J. H. Donnelly and W. R. George, eds. Marketing of Services. Chicago: American Marketing Association, 1981, 47-51
6. V. Zeithamal, L. Berry and A. Parasuraman, Delivering Quality Service. New York: The Free Press, 1990.
7. V. Zeithamal, L. Berry and A. Parasuraman, " A conceptual model of service quality and its implications of future research", Journal of Marketing, 49,Fall 1985, 41-50; V. Zeithamal, L. Berry and A. Parasuraman, "Communication and control processes in the delivery of services", Journal of Marketing, 52, April 1988, 36-58
8. V.A. Zeithamal, L.L. Berry and A. Parasuraman, "The Behavioral Consequences of Service Quality", Journal of Marketing, 60, April 1996, 31-46; R. K. Teas and T. E. Decarlo, "An Examination and Extension of the Zone of Tolerance Model: A Comparison of Performance based models on Perceived Quality", Journal of Service Research, 6, No. 3, 2004, 272-286
9. L. Shostack, "Planning the Service Encounter", in J. A. Czepiel, M. R. Solomon and C. F. Suprenant, eds. The Service Encounter. Lexington, MA: Lexington Books, 1985, 243-254
10. Richard Normann, Service Management: Strategy and Leadership in Service Businesses, 2NDeD. Chichester, UK: John Wiley & Sons, 1991, 16-17

Chapter 12

Price

Chapter Structure

- Price
- Setting the Price
- *Marketing Insight 12.1: Ford's EcoSport to Kick up Dust-er with Pricing*
- *Marketing Insight 12.2: With Moto E Priced at Rs. 6,999, Motorola Aims to Disrupt Micromax and Co's Low Cost Strategy*
- *Marketing Insight 12.3:* Rs 5 Price Point becomes a Magic Word for Marketers Across Products
- Adapting the Price
- Changing the Price
- *Marketing Insight 12.4: Food Firms Give up Popular Price Points on Rising Costs*
- *Marketing Insight 12.5: Hidesign Changes Pricing Strategy; Affordable Products Soon in Multi-Brand Stores*
- Summary
- Discussion Questions
- References

"""Price is the money; you pay for any product or service. The name may be different like airfare, tuition fee, college fee, hotel tariff, insurance premium, interest charges, rent, lease rental, retainer fee, consultancy fee, salary, commission, wage, toll or honorarium; but it means the same."

- David J. Schwartz

Price

Price, the second P in the marketing mix, has a great relevance in business.

Price is the only element in marketing, which produces revenue. It is the monetary amount a buyer pays for a good or service.

That's why, price communicates the value proposition.

When a company wants to modify its marketing mix, price is the only factor in the marketing mix, which can be adjusted in the short run.

All the other factors like product, place and promotion; may take a longer time to change. For example – General Motors (GM) cut the price of its Spark cars on 12th Oct., 2007 by a whopping Rs. 53000/- by just announcing in a press conference. Similarly, Reliance cut its mobile tariffs to 50 paise per minute, reacting to the offer given by Tata DoCoMo's 1 paisa per second.

In the era of hyper competition, pricing is the easiest way to react in the market. After Tata DoCoMo's offer of per paisa per second tariff rate in mobile services, almost every company in the mobile service segment like Airtel, BSNL, MTNL, Vodafone, Idea, Aircel, Reliance and Tata Indicom, has reduced their tariff rates. Now, MTS is offering half a paisa per second tariff for local as well as STD.

Price is the money; you pay for any product or service. The name may be different like airfare, tuition fee, college fee, hotel tariff, insurance premium, interest charges, rent, lease rental, retainer fee, consultancy fee, salary, commission, wage, toll or honorarium; but it means the same.[1]

Earlier the process of buying and selling was done through the barter system. The barter system was followed by monetary units. In both the process, there were no set prices. It was decided through the negotiation process between the buyers and sellers.

With the advent of organized retailing and mass manufacturing, the companies have been setting fixed prices. There are government regulations in India to quote the maximum retail price (MRP) for any packaged product. The government is only interested in fixing the MRP, so that no consumers are cheated with a higher price under any circumstances. But, a retailer or a reseller or a dealer is free to charge a lower price than the MRP. While shopping on few websites like Priceline.com or Ebay.in, you can choose your own price to buy the product or services. In unorganised retailing also, you can bargain the price in the shop or you can bargain the price with local roadside vendors.

Setting the Price

The Pricing strategy plays a key role in the success of any business. Once a company develops a new product, it needs to fix the price. For example, Tata launched its midsized C segment car Indigo Manza on 14th Oct., 2009 and fixed the price between Rs. 4.8 Lacs to Rs. 6.75 Lacs, which is almost similar to its direct competitor Swift Dzire. Recently Ford has also priced its compact SUV Ecosport quite competitively against Renault Duster. The pricing is so competitive that Ford is even aiming at buyers of compact sedans such as Maruti Suzuki Dzire and Toyota Etios.

Marketing Insight 12.1

Ford's EcoSport to Kick up Dust-er with Pricing

Ford's EcoSport to Kick up Dust-er with Pricing xport strategy helps co price its new compact sports utility vehicle at Rs. 6-9 lakh

Ford Ecosport

US automaker Ford plans to aggressively price its compact sports utility vehicle EcoSport, taking on hatchbacks like the Hyundai i20 and Suzuki Dzire in its bid to expand the SUV market and challenge French carmaker Renault's bold opening gambit. ET learns that the initial launch price of the compact EcoSport SUV will be Rs. 5.9-6 lakh, much lower than Renault Duster's launch price of Rs.7.19 lakh. Higher variants will command a higher price, but Ford has worked out the pricing in such a way that the topmost EcoSport variant, at around Rs. 9 lakh, will still be cheaper than the Duster's Rs. 11 lakh.

The EcoSport's pricing is likely to intensify competition in the SUV segment and also force hatchback makers such as Hyundai and Maruti to change tack quickly. The highest Dzire/ i20 variant is likely to cost more than the base version of an EcoSport, giving buyers an opportunity to buy an SUV (even if it is a compact one) than a premium, costly premium hatchback or a compact sedan. For instance, the highest version of a Maruti Dzire costs Rs. 7.5 lakh while the i20's premium version costs about Rs. 7.79 lakh. Duster's customers have included buyers of mid-size sedans such as Honda City, Volkswagen Vento and Hyundai Verna, but the EcoSport, being a B segment compact SUV, will aim at buyers of compact sedans such as Maruti Suzuki Dzire and Toyota Etios.

E Duster rattled the SUV market veterans, primarily M&M, by launching the Duster at an initial price of Rs. 7.19 lakh. It has become Renault's best-selling vehicle, averaging 4,000-5,000 units a month, and one of the reasons behind the scorching pace of SUV growth this year along with M&M's XUV 500. Though M&M has seen its market share falling to 47%, its volumes have grown over 30% this fiscal to over 2.4 lakh units. A senior official at Ford India while declining to give specific pricing told ET that scale enables companies to deliver that level of efficiency, which helps in bringing value for the consumer through aggressive pricing. Despite the excise duty hike for SUVs this budget, Ford is reportedly expected to fall in compact car category and the company will pay only 12% excise duty on EcoSport.

EcoSport will be positioned in the untapped compact sub-4 metre SUV space, occupied by M&M's Quanto, launched six months ago, and Premier's Rio. While M&M's Quanto averages around 2,000 to 2,500 units a month, Rio sells less than a hundred units a month.

The attractive price offering has been possible due to the strong exports strategy at the heart of it, just like Figo, a source said. Today, 30% of Figo's production is exported. ET learns that 40-45% of EcoSport's expected annual production of 1.5 lakh units will be shipped out of India, with Chennai acting as an exports hub to over 40-50 countries. The local plant will produce 380 variants for markets across the globe.

The export-led strategy works well in favour of the Indian customers. International benchmarks help Indian customers to avail of advanced features such as Bluetooth Sync, rear parking sensor and hill climb assist in some of its top-end variants, which are standard features with the EcoSport globally. In addition, the vehicle will come with 1-litre EcoBoost petrol engine that promises to be fuel efficient, delivering mileage of over 15-17 km a litre. The vehicle will also be available in 1.5-litre diesel engine and 1.5-litre petrol engine with automatic transmission.

"Scale brings in efficiency, it helps companies deliver capacity and get a better rate from the vendors and suppliers; it helps you keep your cost in check in high inflationary scenario and that's what global manufacturers really get to the table, that's what Ford has got to the table, with its ability," the Ford official quoted earlier added.

iPhone5

A company may also need to price the product, when it enters new markets or a new geographical area. Most of the multinational companies face the challenge of pricing the product in different markets. Apple also had to juggle a lot while pricing its iPhone4 in India and ultimately, it decided the price of Rs. 31,000/- for an 8GB version and Rs. 36,100/- for a 16 GB version; while it costs $199 for an 8GB model and $299 for a 16 GB model in USA. But, somehow this pricing has not gone down well with the Indian customers and that's why in the initial phase mere 20,000 units of iPhone have been sold in Indian market; while it is successful in most of the foreign markets.

Apple took a lesson from the iPhone4 and it launched iPhone5 with an EMI offer. It worked wonders for Apple and now it is selling more than 4,00,000 units every month with sales growth of 400%.

Moto G

On the other hand, Motorola was also facing a tough time in the Indian market and nearly closed down its Indian operations. But today, with the success of Moto G, Moto X and Moto E, it has truly made a comeback. The exclusive deal with Flipkart helped in creating a big hype and the value

Marketing Insight 12.2

With Moto E Priced at Rs. 6,999, Motorola Aims to Disrupt Micromax and Co's Low Cost Strategy

Moto E

Motorola has finally unveiled the Moto E and India will be the first country to get a taste of the latest budget effort from the one-time mobile giant. The phone is priced at an unbelievable Rs 6,999, which makes it great competition to the Indian low-cost smartphone brigade.

After facing a tough time in the Indian market ever since smartphones broke out on the scene, Motorola has been on the sidelines and nearly folded its Indian operations. With very limited resources, the company kept its India business alive and ticking, but if you had asked us this time last year if Motorola will be a force to reckon with, we would have laughed you off.

Cut to the present and three phones later, Motorola has well and truly made a comeback. It started with the Moto G earlier this year, which now is the most successful launch in the company's history. The exclusive deal with Flipkart helped in creating a big hype and that sumptuous price tag helped win buyers. But the Moto G did better than we expected. It looks more polished than phones in this price range and had very good specs too. This was how you did budget phones.

Then the Moto X, which puts most quad-core smartphones, priced nearly twice its price to shame. It's a superbly built handset, which fits perfectly in your hand and has sensible software additions with stock Android UI. Most importantly, the Moto X arrived with Android KitKat, which immediately set it apart from competition. Moto G changed the budget landscape and the Moto X is trying to do the same with the mid-range segment. It's currently available for under Rs 20,000 with the right exchange offer from Flipkart.

And now it's the turn of the Moto E. With a price tag of Rs 6,999, there's great reason for every one of the Indian manufacturers to be worried. Motorola has come right at their throat with this pricing, given the decent specs and the guarantee of the latest software. It also comes with features that are eye-catching to the average buyer: scratch-resistant glass, splashproof body and a multitude of colours.

If the Moto G and Moto X threw a challenge to the budget and mid-range segment, Moto E is going after the lowest rung of the ladder. We had expected a price closer to the Moto G, but Motorola has pulled off a great coup. It certainly makes things interesting for the low-cost players such as Micromax, Karbonn and others, who have made great strides in establishing market share, but haven't been able to build a reputation as reliable brands with good after sales service and product quality. In fact, at this price tag the Moto E doesn't even have competition from any of the bigger international brands, so it's clearly holding a great advantage.

The Moto E will be a big obstacle for these brands; it could end up making Motorola a force to reckon with once again, and no one's laughing now.

Price produces revenue for the company. The revenue in turn helps the company to fund the firm's current value creation activities and generate a profit. It also helps a pharmaceuticals company like Ranbaxy or a technology company like Intel or Microsoft to support research that leads to future value creation. As the customer is interested in getting the value for his money, the price should be set in relation to the value delivered and perceived by the consumer. In case the price is lower than the value received, the company may lose the potential profit, while in the other case the company may lose customers.

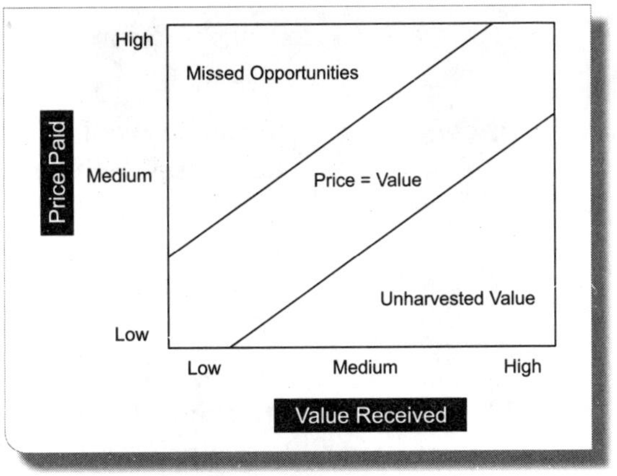

Price is consumer's incentive to buy and company's incentive to sell. It is very crucial for any company, as too high a price will reduce the demand and too low a price will increase the demand, but will reduce the profit margin. That's why you need to think a lot, while pricing your product. A company may set the price on the basis of the following six steps:

- Pricing Objective
- Demand
- Costs
- Competition
- Pricing Method
- Final Price

Pricing Objective

Here the company may be guided by the objective, it sets for the market. Few of the common objectives are:

- **Market Share:** For a large company like Reliance and Tata, the objective of market share is very important, as it produces several strategic benefits for the company. The ad campaign like 'Kar Lo Dunia Mutthi Mein' and subsequent pricing of the handset and mobile service at a downpayment of just Rs.500/- led Reliance to have a leadership share in the mobile service category. This type of pricing is called Market Penetration Pricing, by pricing the product as low as possible.
- **Profit Maximisation**: A company can also look for maximizing its profit in the short run or in the long run.
- **Unit sales Maximisation**: A company like Reliance or Tata DoCoMo may look forward to subscribing more and more people to the network or LG may try to sell the highest number of LED TV in India.**Discourage competition** - A company can also go for modest profits to discourage the entry of competitors in the market.

Rolex

- **Exclusivity**: Bentley, Rolls- Royce, Rolex may price their products higher to create a perception about exclusivity of the product. When a company launches a new technology, then they set a higher price to 'skim' the market. The consumer electronics Sony regularly follows the policy of Market Skimming pricing. When it launched High Definition television for the first time in 1990, the price was $43,000. Now the same product costs a mere $600.
- **Partial Cost Recovery**: In the case of nonprofit and social organisations, the pricing is based on the partial cost recovery like in the government colleges and hospitals.

Spencer's

- **Slashing the Price of a Staple Item**: This strategy of 'Loss Leader' is regularly applied by retailers like Big Bazaar and Spencer's in India, where they sell one staple item like Atta, Wheat, Rice or Sugar at a lower price to drive the traffic to their store. The losses are made up from stimulating the other profitable sales in the store.
- **Trial Purchases**: A company may price the products lower to induce the trial purchases.

The objectives may differ from company to company and situation to situation, but the companies, which use price as a strategic tool, are the companies, which will be successful in the long run. The market forces or the cost should not drive the strategy of pricing.

Demand

Once the pricing objective is clear, a company needs to determine the demand for the product or service. Generally, the price and the demand are inversely related - The higher the price, the lower the demand and the lower the price, the higher the demand. This is called Price elasticity of Demand. Once plotted on a graph, it is a downward sloping curve, as it is seen in the below figure.

Inelastic Demand Curve

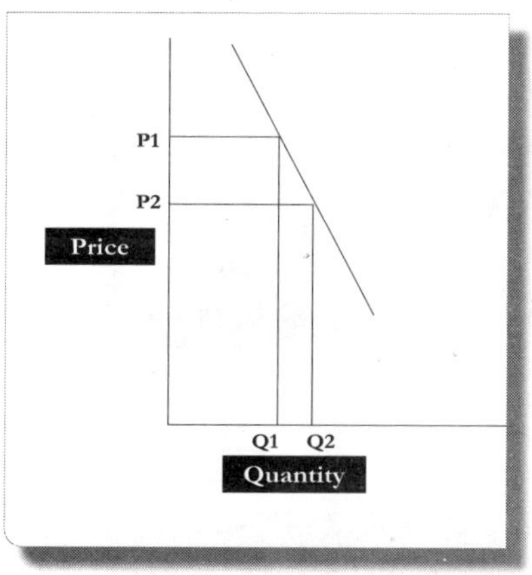

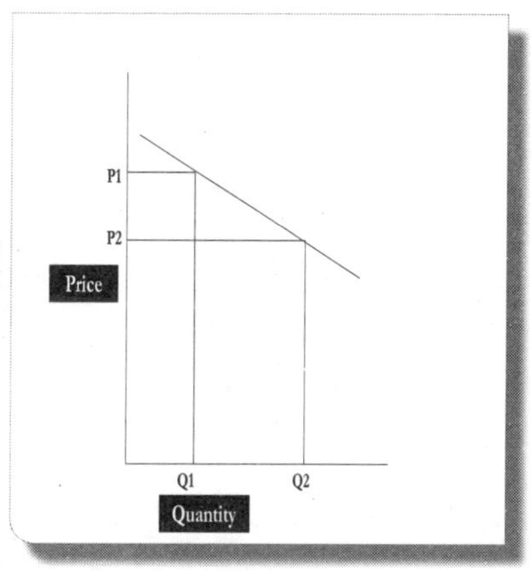

Elastic Demand Curve

But in the case of prestige and exclusive goods like Bentley or Rolls Royce cars, or perfumes like Christian Dior, Ralph Lauren, the higher price may lead to more demand, as some customers assume it to be of superior quality.

In the case of frequently bought FMCG products, the customers are very price sensitive. But in the case of infrequently bought items like LCD TV or Air Conditioner, they will be less price sensitive. Sometimes, a company can charge a higher price and still sell more, when the company can convince the customer that the Total Cost of Ownership (TCO) is lower than the competing brands. HP advertises on the principle of low cost of ownership for its PCs, by showing downtime cost to the company for its competitors PCs.

Generally companies try to estimate their demand curve by doing a statistical analysis or price experiments or by a survey. In the statistical analysis, the past data is analysed to understand the trends in the demand by doing longitudinal (over a period of time) or cross sectional (different locations in the same period). A price experiment was conducted by Bennett and Wilkinson, where they systematically varied the prices of several products sold in a discount store and observed the results.[2] Similarly customers can be enquired about the quantity they will buy at different price points.

It is important to understand price elasticity of demand for the pricing strategy. In the case of inelastic demand, where the impact of price change is not much; the company can change the prices. But in the case of elastic demand, it may hurt the company to increase the prices.

Costs

Besides the demand, a company also needs to estimate the cost. Costs are internal to the company, while demand is an external factor. Demand shows the way as to how much maximum a company can charge its customers. While costs helps to find out how much minimum price can a company can afford.

Maruti Alto

In any business, there are different types of costs. Fixed Cost is the cost, which does not vary with production. For example, fixed cost like plant and machinery remains the same, whatever the number of units are produced. But variable costs vary with the production. For example, for producing one Tata Nano, five tyres are required and if you want to produce two Tata Nanos, then you require ten tyres. Total Cost is the sum of the fixed and variable cost and average cost of the product is taken out from total costs divided by no. of units produced. A company should try to keep the production level at the optimum, where the average cost of production per unit is least.

Once a company goes on producing the same product for a longer duration like Maruti Suzuki manufacturing Alto or Hero manufacturing Splendor, then the company can reduce the average costs with accumulated production experience. It is also called Experience Curve or learning Curve. Maruti Suzuki still sells its Alto at a price lower than the price ten years back or Hero still sells its bike at a similar price of 1999 and makes a handsome profit, in spite of increase in raw material and component prices.

- **Activity Based Cost Accounting: Retailing:** In the age of organized retailing, the real profitability of dealing with different retailers, the manufacturer needs to use activity based cost (ABC) accounting instead of standard cost accounting.[3] ABC accounting takes real costs into consideration on each of its customers. Besides the other costs, it also takes overhead cost into account.
- **Target Costing:** Generally in the learning curve, you can reduce the cost of production with your scale and your experience. But if you are offering a new product in the market, then how do you do that? You do it by the cumulative effort of your engineers, designers and your suppliers. This way you can reduce the cost and offer the product at a lower price than your competitor like the Japanese companies do. They call it Target Costing. They at first decide the price to sell it and then go backward to the target cost, on which they want the product.[4]

Taking a cue from the target costing, Ratan Tata announced a car to be made for Rs. 1 Lac in 2003 and made it possible in the form of 'Tata Nano' in 2009. The success of Bajaj Auto can also be attributed to target costing, when Rajiv Bajaj decided to sell its bike Bajaj Boxer at four to six thousand rupees cheaper than Splendor, the largest selling bike in India.

Competition

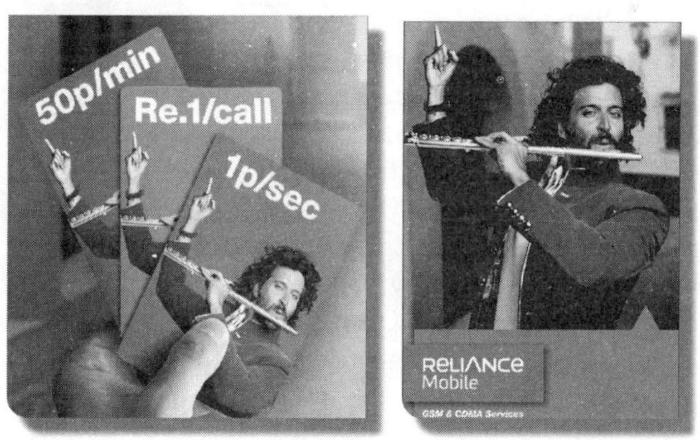

Reliance

Competition plays an important role in setting the price. In few segments like Mobile Services, the competition is so tough that the companies react to the price change within hours and days. When Airtel launched the lifetime prepaid validity card for Rs. 999 on

23rd Dec., 2005, Hutch launched its lifetime scheme on 26th Dec., 2005 and Reliance on 27th Dec., 2005. It was then followed by Idea and MTNL. In Oct., 2009, with Tata DoCoMo's offer of one paisa one second, Aircel started offering the same and Reliance came out with 50 paisa per minute call rate for local or STD calls. Now, Airtel, Vodafone, Idea, MTNL and BSNL have been offering similar plans for their customers.

Although the price is decided on the basis of the cost and demand factors, the competitive prices and offers are very important to sustain the business. If the differentiation is big enough, then you can relax with your premium pricing. But if the difference is not understood, then the company may offer similar pricing or better pricing than the competitor.

Pricing Method

On the basis of the customer demand, cost of the product and the price set by the competitor, the company can select a pricing method. There are several ways to select the price.

a. **Full Cost or Markup Pricing** :Full Cost or Mark up pricing is the most elementary and desirable way of pricing by the company. The company just needs to calculate its cost and then it has to decide the margin or the mark up it wants, and price is decided. But the market is not that easy to let you decide your price. Most of the time, the customer and competition will drive you to go for a different pricing altogether.

b. **Target Return Pricing:** In the similar way, a company may decide its return on investment (ROI). On the basis of the ROI, the company can decide its target return pricing.

c. **Perceived Value Pricing:** In the case of perceived value pricing, price is decided on the basis of perceived value from the product by the customers. The value can be understood with the help of a survey, focus groups, conjoint analysis, statistical analysis of the past data and through own judgement. Most of the time, leading companies prices their product higher than their competitor on the basis of higher perceived value; as the perceived value with the company is higher than the competitors, on account of better performance, warranty offered, customer care and brand value. Companies like DuPont and Caterpillar generally go for perceived value pricing.

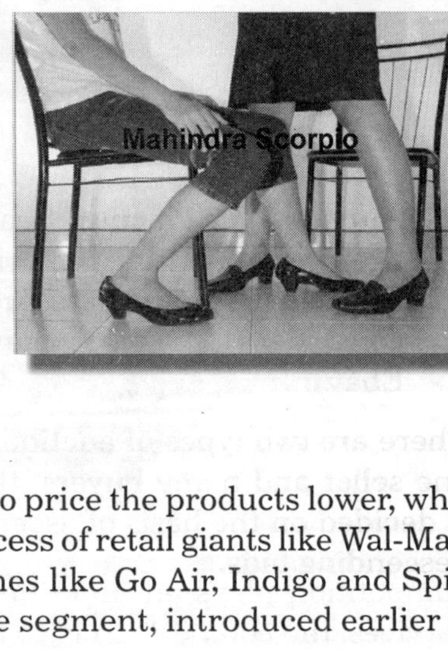

d. **Value Pricing**: Value pricing is an age old technique to price the products lower, while giving a high quality product to the customer. The success of retail giants like Wal-Mart, Big Bazaar, Vishal are a proof of that. Low cost airlines like Go Air, Indigo and Spice Jet also follow the value pricing method in the airline segment, introduced earlier by

Captain Gopinath of Air Deccan. Bata also follows the value pricing for its footwear products in India. Wal-Mart follows the philosophy of value pricing through Every Day Low Prices (EDLP), where it charges constant low prices. Another method is High-low pricing, where the prices are temporarily lowered for a specific period than the EDLP level. On the other days, the retailer charges a higher price.

e. **Follow the Crowd or Going Rate Pricing**: It is largely based on competitors' prices. Most of the commodities like cement, steel, paper, fertilizer, TMT bars are sold at a similar price. If there are some differences in the price, it is minuscule. Although the going rate pricing is based on the collective wisdom of the industry, it cannot be the best option for many companies.

ebay.in

f. **Auction Type Pricing** – Sealed Bid Auction has been quite popular with the government agencies for getting the price from their suppliers. In the Business to business (B2B) segment also, it's quite prevalent. Now it is also becoming popular for Business to consumer (B2C) or consumer to consumer (C2C) segment through Priceline.com or Ebay.in.

There are two types of auctions: English Auction and Dutch Auction. When there is just one seller and many buyers, the English auction takes place, where the highest bidder is decided on the basis of ascending bids. In Dutch auctions, it is decided on the basis of descending bids.

Groupon

g. **Group Pricing**: Group pricing is quite popular in the western countries, where through Internet, buyers join groups to purchase the products at a lower price. In India, snapdeal.com was a popular website offering upto 90% discounts on group buying. But now it has become a full fledged online shopping site. Mydala.com with the tagline of 'We bargain you gain' is another website promoting group buying. Groupon is another very popular website, which is present in many countries across the globe, besides India

Final Price

Pricing methods help a company to select a price from a range of prices. While selecting the final prices, a company must consider the following:

a. **Consumer Psychology and Pricing:** Many customers feel that if they are buying an expensive product, they are buying a better quality product. In status symbol and ego sensitive products also, price becomes an indicator of quality. Again, if the price happens to be an odd number and falls on say 99 or 95 or .95, then the consumers might feel it being cheaper. Bata pricing with Rs.99.95 or Rs 134.95 or a book priced at Rs. 295 or an LED television priced at Rs. 29990 makes pricing attractive to the customers.

Many companies also like to keep their maximum retail price (MRP) higher than the actual price in the market i.e. market operative price (MOP). It leads the customers to beleive that the product is of high quality and now it is available for a lower price. In the case of Sony, actual prices may only be lower by 5%, while in the case of LG it can be 10-15% below the MRP. In the case of new cars in demand, there is often lesser or no discount, while there will be more discount on the models, which are not so much in demand.

Marketing Insight 12.3

Rs 5 Price Point becomes a Magic Word for Marketers Across Products

Fair & Lovely

Aamir Khan's 'paanch matlab Coca-Cola' advertising campaign may have been a marketing disaster, but the Rs 5 price point has become a magic word for marketers across products, from Wheel detergent and Kurkure snacks to Bharti Airtel calling cards to Fair & Lovely and Gillette blades. Affordability, along with convenience of coinage and single-serve usage, is making thousands of middle class consumers buy Rs 5 packs of anything from snacks, biscuits and chocolates to detergents bars, mobile calling cards and shaving blades. Today, Rs 5 is perhaps the most-in-demand price point.

"We do everything we can to protect the Rs 5 price point," says Vidur Vyas, marketing director, foods, of PepsiCo India. He says Rs 5 price point contributes 45% to the overall foods sales of the maker of snacks such as Cheetos, Kurkure, Lays, Uncle Chipps, Lehar namkeens and Aliva biscuits. He says that this price point allows first time consumers to experience the category at an affordable price. It also allows individual consumption and in many cases, portion control. Another benefit is that of convenient coinage, which works both for consumers and retailers, says Vyas.

Most telecom players now offer Rs 5 recharge plans. And almost two-thirds of sales in the Rs 11,300-crore biscuits market take place at sub-Rs 10 price points. Neeraj

Chandra, COO and VP of Britannia Industries, attributes the success of the price point to single serve consumption and convenience.

"The Rs 5 has that much buzz because of the convenience it offers," he says. Britannia sells popular brands such as Good-Day and Cream Treats at Rs 5 packs. Chandra says that packs sold for less than Rs 10 are core category drivers. While it's a volume driver, the Rs 5 price point may not be a profit booster. Analysts say that consumer goods companies take a hit on margins at the Rs 5 price point, hoping that they will be able to offset it through volumes off take.

"The Rs 5 price point is a convenient transaction point but it also highlights that companies don't have flexibility to pass raw material hikes," says Anand Mour, VP (FMCG and Retail) at brokerage firm Indiabulls Securities. "It amounts to commoditisation of brands, because in the past when marketers have deviated from prices points like Rs 5 and Rs 10, they have seen volume decline."

The Idea Cellular daily pack priced at Rs 5 a day (or the ‹Idea Daily Decrement› as it›s called), offers free local minutes, night calling minutes and free local/national SMS at just Rs 5. The daily pack is valid only till midnight on the day of recharge. Other telecom service providers Tata Docomo, Bharti Airtel and Vodafone too hopped on to the Rs 5 bandwagon about five months ago with recharge options at that price point. Llyod Mathias, president, corporate monitoring, at Tata Teleservices says the Rs 5 price point phenomenon is an indication of the democratisation of the category. "Many categories have been able to become mass only due to lower price points to remove entry barriers," he says.

According to Mathias, telecom is all-pervasive with 55-60 % penetration. More than 90% of the subscription base use prepaid cards. And bottom-of-the-pyramid users are using small denominations to cap their daily expenditure and restrict use of phones. With this subscription base growing rapidly, service providers have looked at low denomination offers, he says.

Brand consultancy Interbrand India managing director Viren Razdan says the strategy emerged as marketers saw potential in "the emerging market within the emerging market of India". A multitude of brands across categories have used the 'magic five' formula to drive trials, engage consumers and demolish basic entry-level barriers. "The Rs 5 price point also justifies a one time, controlled consumption experience," he says. He adds that low value packs, the bedrock of the sachet revolution, has pulled in brands and categories, like Coca-Cola and PepsiCo, which invested heavily in the Rs 5 for 200 ml strategy, however, hard it pushed their profitability.

For the country's largest consumer products firm Hindustan Unilever, which straddles the pyramid across prices from soaps and detergents, to ice-cream and soups, detergent bars at Rs 5 is a core price point. "Currency price points such as Rs 5 and Rs 10 are an important element to provide value to consumers and make our brands affordable and accessible," says a company spokesman.

HUL has successful price points at Rs 10 for Wheel detergent powder and Rs 5 for Wheel bar. "As we go down the pop strata into smaller towns and villages, most consumers ask for a 'brand-currency point' combination. This strengthens price point awareness and discourages any tendency to overcharge the consumer," the spokesman says. But unlike packaged foods, in personal care categories like shampoo and skin creams, the Rs 5 price point is not critical.

In shampoo, for example, it's rare. Here, it's the 50-paise, Rs 1, Rs 1.50, Rs 2 and Rs 3 packs, which are preferred by consumers for single or double use requirements. HUL's Rs 1 Clinic Plus, for example, is big at the mass end. And the Rs 3 pack is important for top-end shampoos like Dove, Pantene, Clear and Head & Shoulders. In creams, HUL's Fair & Lovely at Rs 5 is a key price point. In toothpastes, while most players sell packs at Rs 5, it's not a big category in terms of consumer off take and marketers have a presence here more to generate trails and drive category penetration.

b. **Gain and Risk Sharing Prices**: In the case of software, generally the prices are too high. In those cases, the software development company may guarantee the expected returns or expected profits or expected efficiency for the buyer company with the usage of the software. Here, the seller company might bear the risk in selling and the method is known as gain and risk sharing prices.

c. **Impact of Other Marketing Activities**: Besides the price, depending upon the quality of the product and the advertising and promotions, a company can charge a premium price or, it can go for competitive pricing. Most of the times, consumers are more concerned about the quality, service, customer support, delivery and other aspects.

Indigo Airlines

d. **Company Pricing Policies**: Different companies in different sectors have different pricing policies, while selling the product. In the banking sector, with more usage of ATM and other facilities like online banking or mobile banking, most of the banks are charging penalty for not maintaining average quarterly balance (AQB). In the same way, most of the Low Cost Airlines charge a cancellation fee on their tickets. Dell uses a technique called 'Cost Forecasting' to price its products based on consumer demand and the company's own cost.

e **Pricing Impact on Other Parties**: While a company decides its pricing it needs to take into consideration its distributors, dealers and retailers, besides the competition and the government regulations.

Adapting the Price

Based on different factors like geographical cost and demand, purchase timing, delivery frequency, guarantees, service requirement, a company may adapt its pricing.

1. **Geographical Pricing**: In the case of automobile, the consumers are charged differently based on the locations. The difference can also be attributed to the difference in excise duty and road tax structure in different states.
2. **Price Discounts and Allowances** : In the distribution channel, most of the companies give discounts for early payments, bulk purchases and off season buying. Price discount is also a regular phenomenon in the case of consumer durable and cars purchases. In FMCG goods also, all the big retailers like Big Bazaar, Spencer's etc give regular discounts.
3. **Promotional Pricing** : Time to time, companies also employ various pricing techniques to increase the sales.
    - **Loss Leader pricing**: This strategy of 'Loss Leader' is regularly applied by retailers like Big Bazaar and Spencer's in India, where they sell one brand at a lower price to drive the traffic to their store. The losses are made up from stimulating the other profitable sales in the store. But this kind of philosophy might hurt the brand, on whose discounts are given. For example, if Big Bazaar gives substantial discount on say Aashirvaad Atta, then the brand 'Aashirvaad' will take a beating.
    - **Cash Rebates**: Cash rebates are given by the Car companies to increase the sales of those cars, which are not selling much. In the month of December also, they give a lot of discount on almost all the cars; as consumers are interested more in buying the next year model, which in turn affects the resale value of the car.
    - **Low Interest financing**: As an incentive to the consumer, a company can provide low interest financing or zero interest financing. Bajaj auto generally sells its bike at a lower rate of interest, while Mercedes and BMW also follow the same strategy. With the increase in petrol price, almost passenger car companies are offering their petrol models at lower rate of interest than their diesel models. In consumer durables category also, most of the companies offer zero interest financing.

Chevrolet

- **Warranties and Service Contracts**: Warranties and service contracts can also be utilized to make the product more attractive to the consumers, as it is successfully done in the case of Chevrolet Spark and Beat. Chevrolet offers 3years / 100000 Km warranty on all its cars in India.

4. **Differentiated Pricing**: Sometimes companies follow differential pricing strategy across different market segments. In the case of low cost airlines, different fares are charged from different customers. If you buy the tickets early, you get it cheaper or you will pay a higher price. It is also known as Time pricing.

- **Product Mix Pricing**: To maximize profits, a company needs to price its products in a different way, when the product is a part of product mix. Due to demand and cost interrelationships and varying degree of competition, the pricing becomes a difficult exercise.

Intel

- **Product Line Pricing**: Most of the companies deal in multiple products under single product line. That's why they need to form a policy of pricing, so that the profits of the company can be maximized and pricing can suit different market segments. It is equally applied to a FMCG company like HUL selling Lux to Dove, to a technology company like Intel to price their products properly for their different microprocessors. For a typical desktop, Intel has got six microprocessors to choose from, right from the lowest priced Intel Atom to Celeron to Pentium to Core 2 Duo to Core 2 Quad to Core i3 to Core i5 to the highest priced Core i7 processor.

- **Optional Feature Pricing**: This strategy is regularly used by car manufacturers to price their cars at a lower price for the basic model and the better equipped models at a higher cost a lot. Even Suzuki Swift Lxi Petrol model starts from Rs. 3.99 Lacs and goes up to Rs. 5.20 Lacs for the Diesel Vdi model. Ultimately consumers end up buying better equipped models at the higher price.

Gillette

- **Captive Product Pricing**: The utility of some products are dependent upon captive or ancillary products, like shaving razors require cartridges and a printer also require cartridges. In this case, a leading company in printer, HP often prices its printers at a lower cost and prices cartridges at a higher prices. Similarly Gillette also prices its razors at a lower price and makes it up by selling a cartridge at a higher price.
- **Two-Part Pricing**: Two part pricing involves fixed fee and a variable usage fee. In the case of mobile post paid and telephone services, generally a monthly fee is charged and then on the basis of the usage, a variable fee is charged. In the case of Discotheques also, there is a cover charge and then there is the variable payment, if ordered something more than the cover charge.
- **By-Product Pricing**: In the case of petroleum and vegetable oil, the production also results in a byproduct. Depending upon the usage and prices of these by products, the pricing of main products can be lowered.
- **Product Bundle Pricing**: Many companies try to sell a product bundle to the consumer for making the offer attractive by giving more value to the consumer. For example, one product may be bundled with an ancillary product like Hand

Wash with Hand Wash Refill pack or in some cases the bundle may be totally different like selling a television, Microwave oven, Refrigerator together in the wedding season or, in some cases products may be offered with services like Nokia Handset with Airtel connection.

Changing the Price

Companies also need to respond in the situations, when the prices are needed to be changed. The price change can either be on the company's initiative or reaction to the changes in the competitors' price.

- **Price Cuts**: Many companies go for price cuts to gather more market share or to sell the unsold inventory due to excess plant capacity. Chevrolet cut the prices for Spark by Rs. 53000/- to capture more market in the entry hatchback car segment. Similarly, Mobile service providers are regularly cutting their tariffs to survive in the hyper competitive market.

Koutons

But the company should be careful as not to get in to the low quality trap. Brands like Koutons, Priknit and Cotton County have fallen into low quality trap, with almost year round discounts on their apparel products. The company should also avoid fragile market share trap, where the customers switch their products frequently on the basis of the price cuts by different companies. In shallow pockets trap, a company like Tata or Reliance can cut the prices and can sustain themselves for a longer period of time due to their deep cash reserves.

- **Price Increases**: Increase in prices leads to more profitability for any company. In normal circumstances, every company wants to increase their prices. Generally a company increases its price by a small amount, so that it is below the just noticeable difference (jnd) for the customer. FMCG companies like HUL, Colgate tend to reduce the quantity of the product, rather than increasing the price. For example, Maggi still sells for Rs. 10, but now it weighs just 90 gms instead of 100 gms earlier. The company may also go for larger packaging to sell at a lower price or it may remove few of the product services. The company may also offer a fighter brand to counter the competitors' low pricing and to increase its market. For example, Levi's has launched Levi's Signature and Wrangler has launched Hero Wrangler to fight the competition with a lower priced offering under these brands.

Price changes directly affects the customers, competitors, dealers, retailers and the government. Customers perceive price cuts in FMCG as a welcome step, while with respect to other costlier products, they might think about the low quality of the product. Price increase is thought out favourably in the market for a costlier item; but in the case of FMCG or services like mobile, it can be affect adversely in the hyper competitive market.

Marketing Insight 12.4

Food Firms Give up Popular Price Points on Rising Costs

Parle, ITC, Cadbury among firms vacating currency-friendly price tags such as 1, 5 & 10

Parle Top

Packaged food and confectionery makers are increasingly giving up popular price points such as 5 and 20 for more inconvenient prices such as 6 and 22 because they could no longer reduce pack sizes to manage rising input costs. "Adopting unconventional price points is inevitable for food companies," says BK Rao, group product manager at the country's largest biscuits maker Parle Products, which has increased prices of Top biscuits from 5 to 6 and from 20 to 22. "There is a limit to which a brand can reduce pack weight to balance for the increase in input cost, otherwise consumers would not enjoy the mouthfill or pleasure which they used to have from those packs," Rao says. Parle Products has also increased prices of its two top-selling candies, Kismi toffee and orange candies, from 25-paise to 50-paise, and is now planning to launch a 2 pack for Melody toffee to move up from the current 1 price and Eclairs from 50 paise to 1. The country's fastest growing food company, ITC plans to gradually increase price points across product segments such as Sunfeast biscuits, Bingo! wafers and its confectionery range from 5 to 6-7 and 50 paise to 1 by launching newer variants. "However, we would move higher price points by providing enhancement, either in taste or pack weight," says Chitranjan Dar, divisional chief executive (food division) at ITC.

Cadbury Eclairs

"While trade and consumers want convenient price points, it is only due to currency issues... consumers actually may not have a problem paying little more for a differentiated product," he says. Last November, the consumer affairs ministry made it mandatory for consumer goods firms selling 19 product categories including biscuits, tea, coffee and cereals to sell their products only in specified standard weights and sizes.

Cola makers, Coca-Cola and PepsiCo, have already increased prices of 300-ml returnable glass bottle to an unconventional price point of 13 in some markets. Homi Battiwalla, category director (colas, hydration and mango-based beverages) at PepsiCo India, says the company has adopted unconventional pricing only for 300-ml bottles which is sold more in restaurants than in traditional trade. "Unconventional price points do have a bit of resistance from trade and customers since currency becomes an issue." Battiwalla, however, says it will be difficult to retain currency-friendly price points in the current scenario of commodity inflation. Top confectionery maker Cadbury recently launched a 2 Éclairs variant, which is now promoted heavily against the 1 conventional pack. Devendra Chawla, president (Food Bazaar) at the country's top retailer Future Group, says brands' decision to adopt unconventional price points will depend on the elasticity of the category and its penetration.

Competitors can react differently in the case of price changes. Generally smaller companies or the companies, which are new in the market, tend to go for price cuts to take away the customers from the leading companies. For example, Chevrolet cut the price of Spark car to take the customers away from Maruti Suzuki models like Alto, Estilo and A-Star and Hyundai's Santro. Similarly, Tata DoCoMo, a new player in the GSM segment, is trying hard to get more and more customers from leading companies like Airtel and Vodafone by offering per paisa per second call rate and 'Diet SMS' in the form of tariff of per paisa per character. In this case, Airtel, Vodafone and other players have tried to match their Offers. In other cases, a company can maintain the price or can maintain the price with better value to the customer or can increase price or it can improve quality.

Levis Denizen

To cater to the masses, premium brands also adopt a model to introduce products at a lower cost. Many companies have been doing it successfully. These companies launch a fighter line to remain in the competitive arena like Levi's has launched Denizen, while Wrangler has launched Hero Wrangler. Similarly Jet Airways launched JetLite to cater to price conscious customers. Premium international leather accessory-maker Hidesign is also making way for introducing affordable products to increase its product portfolio in the entry-to-mid range price points targeting Indian multi-brand outlets (MBOs).These products will compete with various private labels and other accessory-makers who generally provide deep discounts; while the exclusive outlets will keep only the premium products.

Marketing Insight 12.5

Marketing Insight 12.5

Hidesign Changes Pricing Strategy; Affordable Products Soon in Multi-brand Stores

Premium international leather accessory-maker Hidesign is looking to increase its product portfolio in the entry-to-mid range price points targeting Indian multi-brand outlets (MBOs).These offerings will compete with private labels (of MBOs) and other accessory-makers who provide deep discounts.

According to Dilip Kapur, Founder and President of Hidesign, its standalone stores, however, would stock mostly premium and high-end offerings. New offerings, he said, are for the "price-sensitive customer" at MBOs like Shoppers Stop, Westside, and Lifestyle, among others. "We are not creating a sub-brand or lowering the price. But we will increase the product basket. For example, if there was one bag between Rs. 1500 – Rs. 2,000, we will now have two more at the same price. Our exclusive outlets will mostly stock premium products," he told Business Line.

Hidesign

Globally, Hidesign is retailed at premium multi-brand retail outlets like John Lewis, Selfridges and House of Fraser in the UK, Myers and David Jones in Australia, Stuttafords in South Africa, Parksons in Vietnam and Robinsons in South-East Asia. Based out of Puducherry, the company's product bouquet includes handbags, clutches, briefcases, wallets, sling bags, laptop cases and brief cases.

The reason for this differentiated strategy – different products across multi-brand outlets and standalone stores – is because of the extended discount sales impacting demand for premium accessories.

Hidesign, traditionally, is not known for deep discounts. As other brands compete through discounted offerings, high-end and international names are known to take the hit if they are averse to such schemes. "If premium brands offer deep discounts then it impacts their image. Hence, it makes sense to have differentiated offerings," said a competing accessory-maker who did not wish to be named.

Hidesign's new products would be priced around Rs. 1,000 - Rs. 1,500 at the entry level. Offerings are normally priced between Rs. 1,100 and Rs. 2,700 for smaller products like wallets; handbags cost between Rs. 3,500 and Rs. 14,000 while laptop covers, briefcases and so on are priced upwards of Rs. 6,500.

According to Kapur, the brand will look to set up a new manufacturing facility in Guwahati (Assam) at an estimated investment of Rs. 4 crore. Expected to be operational over the next four to five months, the unit is likely to cater to demand in the eastern region. The company has three plants in Puducherry and one in Baddi (Himachal Pradesh).

Summary

- Price is the money; you pay for any product or service. The name may be different like airfare, tuition fee, college fee, hotel tariff, insurance premium, interest charges, rent, lease rental, retainer fee, consultancy fee, salary, commission, wage, toll or honorarium; but it means the same.
- The Pricing strategy plays a key role in the success of any business. Once a company develops a new product, it needs to fix the price.
- Price produces revenue for the company. The revenue in turn helps the company to fund the firm's current value creation activities and generate a profit.
- Price is consumer's incentive to buy and company's incentive to sell. It is very crucial for any company, as too high a price will reduce the demand and too low a price will increase the demand, but will reduce the profit margin.
- A company may set the price on the basis of these six steps i.e. pricing objective, demand, costs, competition, pricing method and final price.
- A company may price a product depending upon its objective of market share, profit maximization, unit sales maximization, discourage competition, exclusivity, partial cost recovery and trial purchases.
- Demand shows the way as to how much maximum a company can charge its customers. In the case of inelastic demand, where the impact of price change is not much; the company can change the prices. But in the case of elastic demand, it may hurt the company to increase the prices.
- Costs help a company to find out how much minimum price it can afford.
- A company may calculate the cost based on activity based costing or target costing.
- Although the price is decided on the basis of the cost and demand factors, the competitive prices and offers are very important to sustain the business.
- On the basis of the customer demand, cost of the product and the price set by the competitor, the company can select a pricing method, which can be full cost or markup pricing, target return pricing, perceived value pricing, value pricing, follow the crowd or going rate pricing, auction type pricing and group pricing.
- While selecting the final prices, a company must consider consumer psychology and pricing, gain and risk sharing prices, impact of other marketing activities, company pricing policies and pricing impact on other parties.

- Based on different factors like geographical cost and demand, purchase timing, delivery frequency, guarantees, service requirement, a company may adapt its pricing. A company may adapt it for geographical pricing, price discounts and allowances, promotional pricing, differentiated pricing and product bundle pricing.
- The price change can either be on the company's initiative or reaction to the changes in the competitors' price. The price can either be cut or it can be increased.

Discussion Questions

1. Define pricing? Discuss the steps in setting the price for a product or a service.
2. What do you mean by price? Discuss the various pricing objectives with examples.
3. Discuss the role of demand and costs in pricing.
4. Explain the impact of competition in pricing. Discuss the various pricing methods with examples.
5. Discuss the points a company must consider, while selecting final price.
6. Discuss the factors on which a company may adapt its price.
7. Short Notes:
   a. Captive product pricing
   b. Target costing
   c. Full cost or markup pricing
   d. Loss leader pricing
   e. Follow the crowd or going rate pricing
   f. Consumer psychology and pricing
   g. Product bundle pricing

References

1. Referred from David J. Schwartz, 'Marketing Today: A Basic Approach', 3rd Edition, Harcourt Brace Jovanovich, 1981, p.271
2. Sidney Bennett and J. B. Wilkinson, 'Price Quantity relationships and Price Elasticity under In Store Experimentation', Journal of Business Research, Jan., 1974, p. 30-34

3. Robin Cooper and Robert S. Kaplan, 'Profit Priorities from Activity Based Costing', Harvard Business Review, May-June, 1991, p. 130-135

4. Japan's Smart Secret Weapon', Fortune Magazine, Aug. 12, 1991, p.75

Chapter 13

Place

Chapter Structure

"A Marketing Channel performs the work of moving goods from producers to consumers.

It overcomes the time, place and possession gaps which separate goods and services from those, who need or want them."

- Philip Kotler

Place

Place, the 3rd P in marketing, is very critical for the success of any business. Place is all about reaching out to the customers. It is also known as a marketing channel or trade channel or a distribution channel.

Marketing channels are sets of interdependent organisations involved in the process of making a product or service available for use or consumption.[1]

It is a set of mechanisms or the network via which a firm goes to the market. It serves mainly four functions as shown in the figure. :

1. Demand Generation,
2. Demand fulfillment,
3. After Sales Service and
4. Info / Feedback for Strategy Development

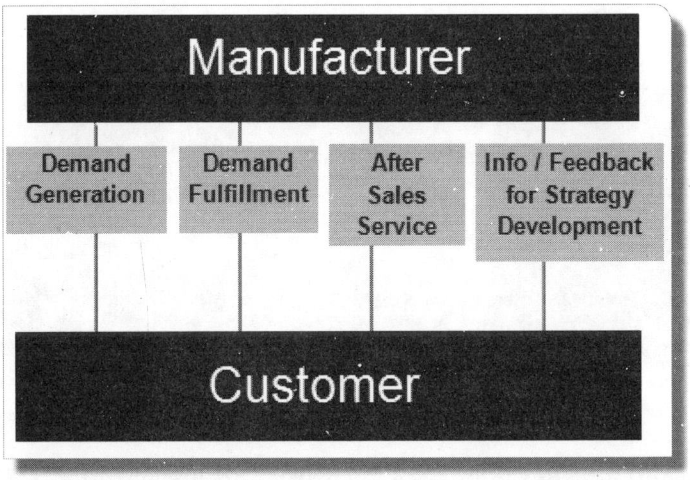

(Figure from - Robert J. Dolan, 'Going to Market', Harvard Business School Publishing, 1999)

The marketing channel helps to generate the demand for the company. The company then, fulfills the demand and also provides after sales service through them. It also helps in giving the information and feedback to the company from the customers.[2]

For example, the leading car manufacturer in India, Maruti Suzuki has 802 dealers in 555 towns and cities across India to sell its 14 brands of cars with more than 150 variants. It has also got 2740 service points across more than 1335 towns and cities in India with more than 353 Maruti True Value outlets in 208 cities.

HUL Sales and Distribution in India

Similarly the leading FMCG Company, Hindustan Unilever Limited (HUL) caters to seven million outlets, with 59% of these outlets located in the rural area. HUL directly services over 1 million stores and has a network of 7000 stockists and distributors.

HUL Sales and Distribution in India is divided into three categories:

1) Modern Trade
   a. Organised Retail
   b. Self Service Stores
2) General Trade
   a. Wholesaler
   b. Family Grocer
   c. Marginal Retail
3) Rural Trade
   a. Multi Purpose Retail

Wheel

HUL sends its products from factory to Clearing and Forwarding (C&F) Agents for the distribution. There are two types of C&F Agents. One who has invested money in buying the products from HUL and the other who has not invested any money. The C&F agents without investment are just a forwarding agent and a transporter for the company. The goods are then supplied to the Stockist or Distributors, who in turn supply to the retailers. The Stockist also supplies to retail chains like Big Bazaar, Spencer's and Army's Canteen Stores Departments (CSD).

The sales and distribution channel in HUL is managed through e-CRM software called 'UNIFY'. The company links this software with all the stockists. It gets up to date record of inventory positions of all the stockists. Once the inventory level falls below the minimum requirement, the software itself orders for the goods and then HUL sends the goods to the stockists.

Marketing Insight 13.1

Marketing Insight 13.1

Dabur India, Hindustan Unilever's Tech Route to Rural Markets

Dabur

With urban consumers cutting back on their spending spree, fast-moving consumer goods companies have redoubled efforts to tap into rural India in 2012-13. In their latest annual reports, Dabur India and Hindustan Unilever (HUL) have both highlighted why the rural markets are so critical and what they are doing to better their rural sales.

HUL's decade-old Project Shakti received a technology boost in 2012. About 40,000 Shakti Ammas were equipped with a basic smartphone. These smartphones had specifically designed software enabled them to take and bill orders, manage inventory and receive updates on promotional schemes run by the company. This improved their efficiency The Shakti workforce rose to 48,000 in 2012, up by around 3,000 from the year before. Project Shakti equips women with the basic entrepreneurial skills and facilities needed to set up and market FMCG products.

If HUL depended on its Shakti Ammas to connect with consumers, Dabur India embraced the idea of getting rural folk to sample products and experience the benefits for themselves. The idea was to get word-of-mouth advertising of product benefits.

The company made the most of fairs and melas around the harvest seasons when purchasing power is high. It also conducted school health camps to boost its toothpaste and chyawanprash portfolio and beauty pageants, to showcase its ayurvedic beauty products.

That's not to say the company ignored the power of the mobile phone. Dabur's rural sales force used mobile phones to report sales. Phones were equipped with maps showing the demographics and market potential of each locality, to improve rural coverage. Over two years, Dabur's rural strategies saw it doubling the villages under its coverage to 30,091.

For any FMCG company, the efficiency and reach of its distribution systems is the most important tool to improve profits and drive sales. In this regard, HUL has a giant coverage reaching out to over 2 million outlets. To improve connect and with its distributors, HUL set up a helpline for its distributors and retailers to address problems or questions quickly.

Dabur, meanwhile, armed more than half of its urban sales force with hand-held devices to generate data, which is then used to decipher buying patterns and customise selling strategies. IT has also been used to provide information to, and generate feedback from doctors on Dabur's formulations and ayurvedic products.

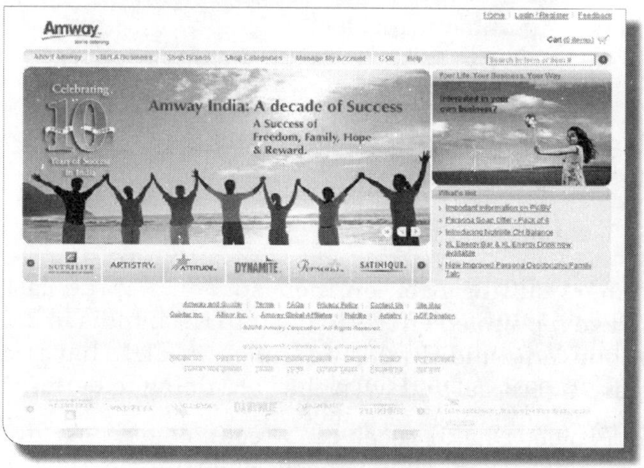

Amway

In the market, different companies follow different ways to reach the market. While Maruti appoints its dealer network, its service network and its True Value dealers network; HUL sells its products with the help of millions of retailers. A company like Eureka Forbes, Asia's largest direct sales organization, sells its Water Purifiers, Vacuum Cleaners, Air Purifiers and Security Solutions through 7000 direct sales force touching 1.5 million Indian homes. Similarly in India, Amway sells its products through 4.5 Lacs Amway Business owners.

On the whole, marketing channel intermediaries can be classified into following three categories.:

1) Merchants,
2) Agents and
3) Facilitators.

Merchants buy, take title to and resell the goods from the company, like wholesalers and retailers. Agents do not take title to the goods and just help the company in forwarding the goods to the stockist or distributors. They are also known as brokers, manufacturer's representatives and sales agents. Facilitators help a company in the distribution process. These include warehouses, transportation companies, banks, advertising agencies etc.

Most of the companies do not prefer to sell the products directly, but with the help of marketing channels. Marketing channels are used by a company, because many companies lack the financial resources to distribute the products on their own. For example, Maruti Suzuki may require an additional investment of more than Rs. 2000 cr. to manage its dealer network. Sometimes it is not just feasible to sell the products directly like Chlormint, which sells through millions of retailers. These channels also help in breaking the bulk and create assortment for the consumers. This is particularly important in the case of rural areas, where the goods are sold in small quantities. From the business perspective also, by concentrating on manufacturing, a company can earn more than it can earn into direct retailing or direct selling.

Marketing Channel Levels

For any company, successful value creation needs successful value delivery. A company needs to design the distribution network and then it needs to manage this network.

A company can decide its way to reach the customers. In some cases, the company has a choice to decide; but in some cases there are no choices. When a company reaches its customers directly, then it can be called a **Zero Level Channel**. It is also called a direct marketing channel. Companies like Eureka Forbes, Amway, Dell, Tupperware, Avon, Bata does their business directly. It also includes door to door sales, telemarketing, TV marketing, internet selling and manufactured owned stores. Home Shop 18 sells its products on Television and also sells it online. Similarly, Eureka Forbes sells its products directly to the customer through its sales force. Bose sells its sound systems through its 15 showrooms across India. Many products are also sold through infomercials on various television channels in India in the late night. Customers can order the products through phone and get the home delivery.

Eureka Forbes

One level channel includes one intermediary between the company and the customers. For example, all the two wheeler and four wheeler companies like Hero Honda, Bajaj Auto, Maruti Suzuki, Hyundai, Chevrolet etc. have dealers in between the company and the customers. In **two level channel**, a wholesaler and a retailer deals with the company on the one side and customers on the other. In **three level channel**, there are three intermediaries – Distributor, Wholesalers and Retailer. In certain products, there is the existence of multi level channel. In case of HUL also, there are three and more intermediaries depending upon the point of sales to the customers, like C&F Agents, Stockist and then to retail outlet. Sometimes, there is a wholesaler in between the stockist and retail outlet. In the case of food grains and vegetables also, sometimes there are three to six level channel involved.

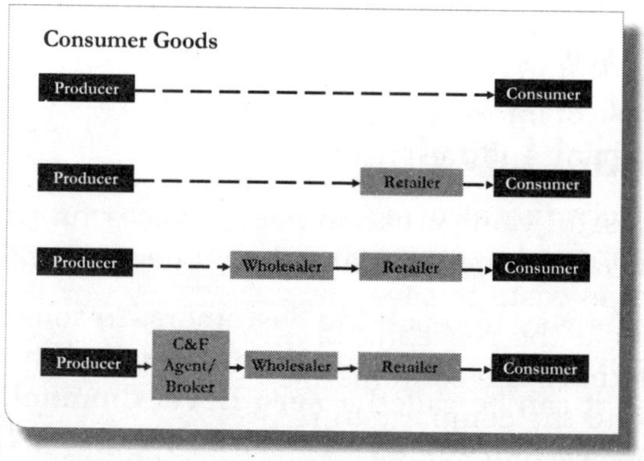

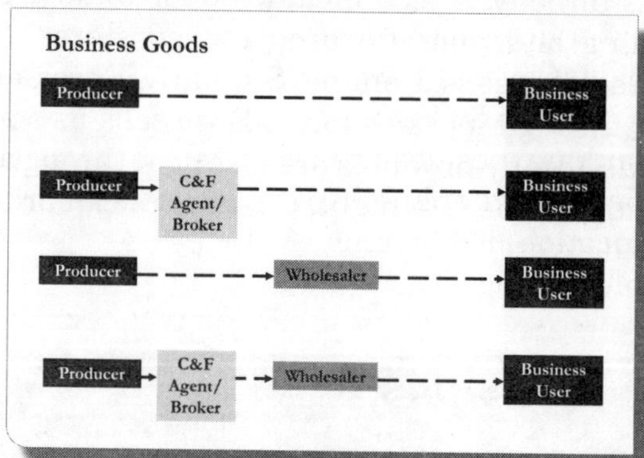

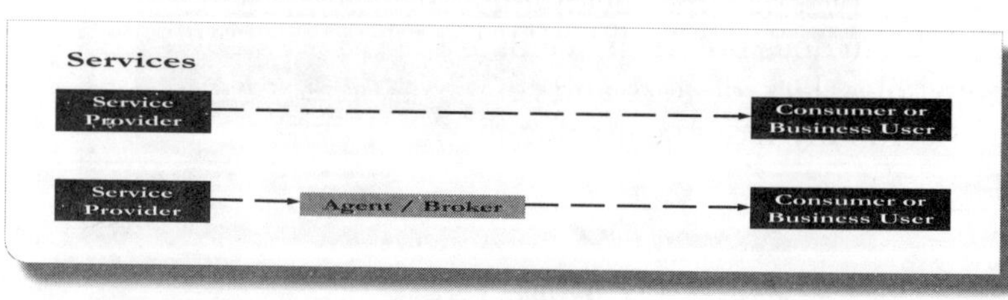

In the case of industrial marketing also, a similar structure exists in the market. Either the manufacturer sells its products directly or it can sell through a distributor. As the products are technical in nature, sometimes, the distributor is assisted with the manufacturer's representative or manufacturer's sales branch.

Channel Functions and Flow

A Marketing Channel performs the work of moving goods from producers to consumers. It overcomes the time, place and possession gaps which separate goods and services from those, who need or want them.[3]

As far as the flow of goods, title and promotion are concerned in different channel levels, there is a forward flow. But in the case of payment, it goes backward to the company from the customer. In the case of information, negotiation, finance and risk taking, it flows both ways between the company and the customer with the intermediaries in between.

There are reverse flow channel also, in which the product moves back to the company. For example, Nokia has launched a campaign called 'Take Back' in India to make consumers aware about recycling e-waste to save environment. The customers are encouraged to dispose their handsets at the recycling bins set up by Nokia at its Concept stores and priority dealers. Sometimes the containers go back to the company for reuse. In resale, products also go back to the company to refurbish it. In the case of Maruti True Value, Maruti sells refurbished second hand cars bought from their owners.

Besides the products, services also need to be distributed. Services like Banking, Insurance, Stock buying, travel etc. have found a new platform like Internet and Mobile technology to reach out to more and more customers. Now, all the banks have ATMs, Net Banking and Mobile Banking, besides the Branch Banking. Similarly Insurance, Stocks and Travel plans can be booked online. Now service delivery has become easier due to technology. Even in education, it's making an impact through online education through Internet and Video Conferencing.

Channel Design Decisions

Channel design decisions are crucial for any company, whether it's new or it's old. In the case of a new company, it becomes even tougher to get the products on the shelves of the retailers. The problem does not lie in deciding the channel design, but the problem lies in convincing the wholesalers, dealers and retailers to carry your product. In case of an old and established company like Maruti Suzuki, the company might be spoilt with choices for the dealers.

Yellow Diamond

A company needs to understand as to what kind of marketing strategy it wants to implement, whether it will be a Push strategy or a pull strategy. In the case of low cost, low involvement, impulse products; push strategy works better. The company just needs to push its products through the marketing channel by its sales staff. Sales staff is supported by the trade promotion schemes. On the other hand, pull strategy works better in high involvement products like consumer durables and automobile. In this strategy, manufacturer advertises the products heavily to induce customers to ask for the products. It may also happen that in similar kind of product, two different companies are following opposite strategies. For example, Lays potato chips sells through a pull strategy, while Balaji or Yellow Diamond potato chips are sold on the basis of a push strategy in western India.

The length of the Channel can be decided on the basis of the following:

A) **Analysing customers' desired service output levels**

1) **Size of the Market**: Larger market requires longer channel to serve the customers, while shorter channel is required for small market.

2) **Service Requirement**: If the product requires a service back up like a car or a bike, the channel should be zero or one level.

3) **Lot Size**: A customer may require the product in lot size of one, while a business customer may require the same product in bulk quantity. Depending upon the requirement, the channel length is decided.

4) **Product Variety**: Most of the companies deal in wide assortment of products. Then, the availability of all the products becomes essential at the retail outlet.

B) **Establishing Objectives and Constraints**: Channel objectives are also taken into consideration, while deciding the role of intermediary. FMCG product does not require any support, that's why the length can be longer. While products needing service support like construction equipment, machineries require to be sold directly by the company or by the agent. Perishable products like vegetables are sold directly to the customers in the rural areas, but gets into a one to two level channel in the urban areas.

C) **Identifying Major Channel Alternatives**: There are several channels options available with any company to market its products like Distributor, Dealer, Wholesaler, Retailer, Sales Force, Agents, Direct Mail, Telemarketing and Internet. It depends upon the company as to which channel it wants to sell its products through. Eureka Forbes sell it's Water Purifiers through direct selling and Kent RO Water purifier sells the product through distributor, direct marketing dealers and showrooms. In the same way, Avon sells its cosmetic range through direct selling network, while Revlon, Lakme, Pond's sell its cosmetics through a regular channel involving stockist, wholesalers and retailers.

At each channel level, a company also needs to decide the number of intermediaries. There are three distribution strategies available to the company.

Pizza Hut

Pizza Hut

1) **Exclusive Distribution**: Exclusive distribution strategy is generally followed in the case of two wheelers, four wheelers, consumer electronics, men's and women's apparels besides other products. A company can provide the best customer experience through its exclusive distribution network. BMW, Mercedes, Porsche, Maruti Suzuki, Hero Honda, Gucci and Bose try to give the best of sales and service support to the customers. Fast food companies like McDonalds, Pizza Hut and Domino's Pizza also go for exclusive distribution through their franchisees.

2) **Intensive Distribution**: Intensive distribution is just the opposite of Exclusive distribution. A company tries to sell its products through many channels to get more market share. It works well in the low cost and low involvement products. Most of the convenience goods are sold through a wide variety of different retail

outlets. The distribution setup of HUL is based on intensive distribution. Mobile service providers like Airtel, Aircel, Vodafone, Reliance, Tata etc. are also following the strategy of intensive distribution.

Marketing Insight 13.2

Chemists Turn Key Sales Partners for FMCG Cos

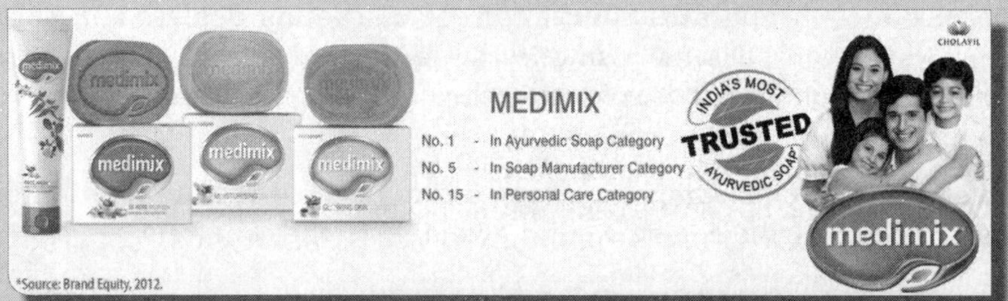

Medimix

When Chennai-based Cholayil hired a medical representative earlier this month to push its Medimix soap, it surprised most conventional marketers and also confirmed the increasing importance of chemists as a sales channel for consumer goods companies.

Chemists account for about 9.1% of overall FMCG sales in the country, or some 45% higher than modern retail, according to a study by market research firm Nielsen. And sales through this channel are growing faster than through traditional trade as more and more people trust their neighbourhood chemists to choose personal care and healthcare products.

No wonder, from Cadbury India to Hindustan Unilever to L'Oreal India, most FMCG companies bet on chemists to push their premium personal care and healthcare products. "It's about time marketers started writing their own prescriptions to win with chemists," Ranjeet Laungani, VP at Nielsen India, says.

Nielsen estimates chemist channel to swell to an FMCG market worth $6 billion by 2016 and $12 billion by 2020 from its current size of $3 billion. Over 75,000 chemists joined the FMCG world last year, mostly in towns with less than 10 lakh people. L'Oreal, world's largest cosmetics and beauty care firm, says chemists are its biggest sales channel in the country, contributing more than 20% to its total sales. "When it comes to premium personal care products, consumers tend to take the advice of chemists more seriously," Satyaki Ghosh, director of consumer products at L'Oreal India, says.

The same goes with healthy products too. Cadbury, maker of Bournvita malt drink, believes chemists drive growth in this category. "First time users of milk food drinks

The same goes with healthy products too. Cadbury, maker of Bournvita malt drink, believes chemists drive growth in this category. "First time users of milk food drinks generally buy from chemists due to their high credibility," Narayan Sundararaman, director – powdered beverages, gum & candy, at Cadbury India, says. A spokesperson of its rival GlaxoSmithKline Consumer Healthcare, maker of Horlicks and Boost, says chemists are gaining importance as products get more specialised. About 30% of malted beverage drink sales come from chemist channels, while for traditional consumer products like shampoos, the percentage is about 15%-18%.

Devendra Chawla, president, Food Bazaar, at India's largest retailer Future Group, does not think so. "While modern trade is fast becoming a launch pad for FMCG products, for value-added personal care and health categories, brands rope in chemists as a channel first within general trade for mass dissemination...," he says. And it's not just categories such as diapers, deodorants and milk food drinks that chemists stock. Nielsen finds that chemists are increasingly stocking impulse-buying products such as salty snacks, chocolates and biscuits.

Bhavesh Dedhia, proprietor of Apple Medical Store in a Mumbai suburb, says it works. "While pharma products have higher margins, consumers tend to buy chocolates or snacks while they shop for medicines," he says. Marketers say chemists demand higher margins on FMCG products. "The terms of trade and margins are generally higher in the case of chemists as space for consumer products is limited in their stores," Anil Chugh, senior vicepresident at Wipro Consumer Care and Lighting, says.

3) **Selective Distribution**: Selective distribution is about choosing the middle path to sell your goods. Selective distribution is about selling the products in few places, rather than all the places. In the consumer electronics category, apparels category, PCs, Laptops Netbooks and Mobile category, companies prefer to go for selective distribution. Companies like Sony, LG, Levi's, Wrangler, HP and Acer generally go for selective distribution by having their own brand shops like Sony World or LG Best Shop or Samsung Plaza; or selling through big retailers like Big Bazaar, Croma, e-Zone, Reliance Digital or selling through retailers or resellers.

Marketing Insight 13.3

Tata Group's Croma Store Hits 101 Mark as Retail Battle Heats Up

When Cyrus P Mistry inaugurated a Croma store in Mumbai's Prabhadevi area last month, it was a milestone of sorts— it was the 101st Tata-owned Croma store in the country and the second time that a Tata Group chairman was doing the honours.

The event, however, is being widely seen as Mistry's growing focus on the salt-to-steel conglomerate's electronics business, which is locked in competition with billionaire Mukesh Ambani's Reliance Retail in the Rs 40,000-crore consumer durables market.

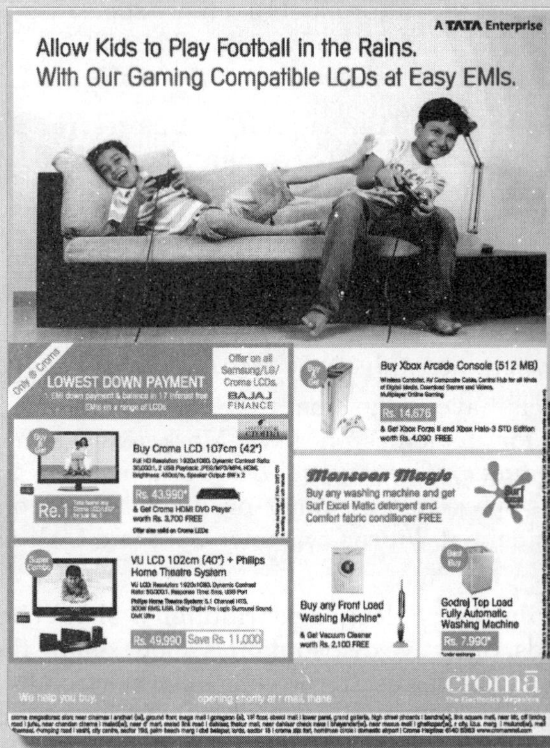

Croma

In 2013-14, Reliance Retail's consumer electronics business reported Rs 3,044 crore revenue, according to a presentation the company made to analysts, narrowing the gap with market leader Croma, which, people familiar with the details say, could post about Rs 3,200 crore during the period. In 2012-13, Croma had reported Rs 2,500 crore in revenue compared with Reliance Retail's Rs 2,160 crore. Croma declined to comment on revenue projection.

Reliance, which operates 284 stores in the electronics space across three formats—Reliance Digital, Digital Xpress and Digital Xpress Mini—aims to overtake Croma in sales in 2014-15, according to a company executive. The company plans to set up about 2,000 stores across the three formats this fiscal, with focus on growing the number of Digital Xpress and Digital Xpress Mini stores in small towns.

The Reliance executive said the larger store base is expected to have a cascading effect on its revenue. In contrast, Croma plans to open 10-12 stores this fiscal and consolidate its presence in its existing 16 markets. To maintain its lead, the company plans to push per sq ft sales by focusing on mid-to high-end models.

Ajit Joshi, chief executive and managing director of Infiniti Retail, which operates Croma, said the retailer has per sq ft sales of about Rs 40,000 on an annualised basis—the highest in the industry.

"Our target is to control 20 per cent of the total consumer durables business in each of the cities we operate. We would achieve this with deeper penetration in existing cities, rather than expanding into newer cities," Joshi said. Another area Joshi is betting on is online sales, with Croma.

Consumer durable makers say both Reliance Retail and Croma are competing hard and bargaining for the best deals and promotions. And Mistry, they say, is taking keen interest. For instance, when Panasonic global president Kazuhiro Tsuga was in India last year, he met with Mistry and Joshi to explore ways to grow the business through the Croma chain of stores, including launch of exclusive models and even those not yet in available in India.

According to a senior Tata Group executive, Croma, along with Tata Motors-JLR and Titan, has become a priority for Mistry and Tata Sons. "Croma has fared well and posted its first-ever cash profits last year. The group has realised that Croma is providing a lot of equity to the group after Titan in the consumer space and can grow further," the executive said.

A senior executive at Samsung said both groups have realized that the potential in durable retailing is huge and that it is unlikely that any foreign electronics retailing chain will enter India any time soon.

"The mom-and-pop store model in durable retailing is fast diminishing since higher investment is required for inventory and large retail space for display. It is here that national chains such as Croma and Reliance have an advantage and regional retail chains too emulating the same model", he said.

According industry data, the penetration of television in India is 32 per cent, followed by refrigerators at 20 per cent. It is abysmally low for air-conditioners (2 per cent) and microwave ovens (1 per cent).

For companies like Samsung, LG, Sony and Panasonic, Croma and Reliance together account for 8-9 per cent of their sales. A senior Sony India executive said the average selling price in Croma and Reliance is amongst the highest in the industry.

Besides the types and number of intermediaries, a company should also decide the role and responsibilities of its channel partners with respect to price policy, conditions of sale and distributors' territorial rights. It helps to build a long term relationship with its channel partners. In the case of exclusive dealerships and franchisee, these rights and responsibilities in black and white becomes more important.

D) **Evaluating Major Channel Alternatives**: Channels of distribution may be evaluated on such primary criteria as cost of distribution, coverage of market (penetration), customer service, communication with the market and control of distribution networks. A detailed cost analysis of distribution is the first step in evaluating various channel alternatives on a sales-cost basis.[4]

The decision that a company should go with wholesalers or it should have its own branch office depends upon the costs involved into that. Generally costs can be calculated from the published sources and through market information network.

Companies generally try to move towards lower cost channels. Among all the channel alternatives, Internet is the lowest cost channel, while Direct Sales Force is the highest. In between channel like Telemarketing, Retail Stores, Distributors, Value Added Partners exists.

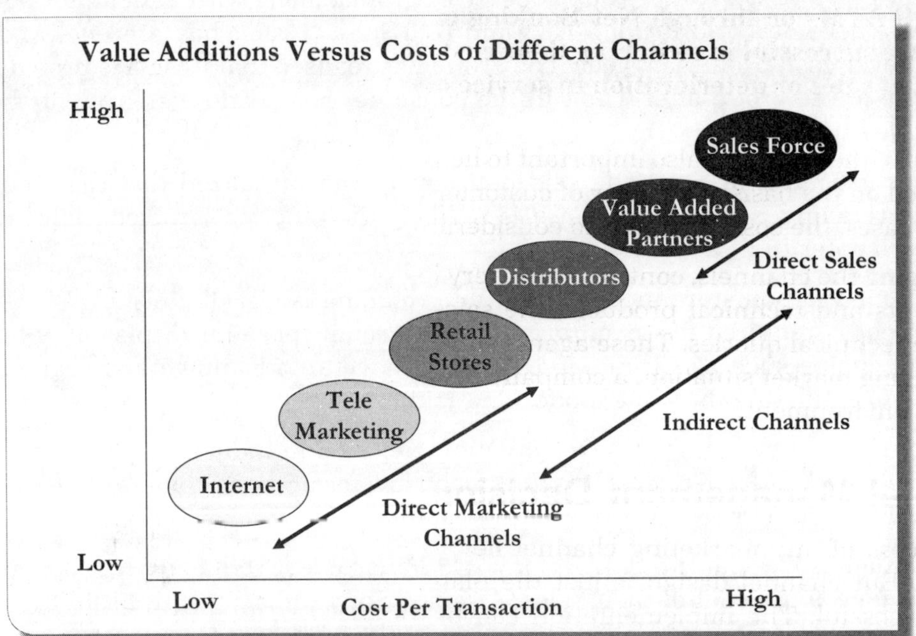

(Source : Oxford Associates, adapted from Dr. Rowland T. Moriaty, Cubex Corp.)

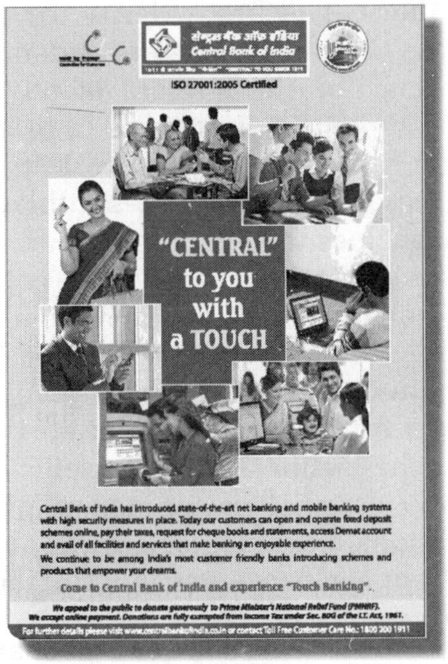

Central Bank of India

For example, a bank can deliver its services to the customers with branch banking, through ATMs or through Net Banking or through Mobile Banking. Companies those are successful in switching their customers to lower cost channels, assuming no loss of sales or deterioration in service quality, will gain a channel advantage.[5]

Coverage of the market is also important to help you out in decision making. Coverage can be decided on the basis of number of customers or on the basis of a geographical area. In both the cases, the cost is taken into consideration for channel decision making.

In managing the channels, control is also very important. Mostly in the cases of industrial equipments and technical products, the sales agents need to be intelligent enough to solve the technical queries. These agents should also handle the promotions carefully. In the changing market situation, a company needs to be adaptive responding to a changed business environment.

Channel Management Decisions

The success of any marketing channel lies in the foundation of right channel design decision. But channel design is just the planning part; it needs right implementation to be successful. The implementation can be taken care of, with the help of channel management decisions. It includes right from, selecting a channel member to training them to motivating them and to evaluating them on their performance. In case, the performance is not as expected, the modifications are done by the company in the channel arrangements.

- **Selecting Channel Members**: The first priority for any company is choosing the right channel members. As the business is dependent upon the marketing channel partners, it becomes crucial for the success of any company to select the best channel partner. All the companies whether it's a product manufacturing company like Colgate or Onida or a service company like IMS or Career Launcher, needs a good channel partner to succeed. Generally all the companies advertise through newspapers and trade magazines to look out for channel partners. If the company is known and successful, it becomes quite easy for the company to find them. But in the case of a new company launching a new product, then finding a channel partner can be tough. In both the cases, the parameters for choosing a channel partner should be very clear for the company as well as the channel partner. In some businesses, like opening a McDonald's franchisee, the location becomes more important than in any other business. As the business is dependent on the footfalls it can get. The company can evaluate any channel partner on the basis of business experience, financial capabilities, locational advantages, growth and profit record, experience of the promoters. In the case of exclusive distribution, these parameters become more important for the company.

Kirloskar

- **Training Channel Partners**: Once the channel partner is selected, they need to be trained as they are the face of the company. All the companies have intensive training programmes for its dealers to tell them about their sales and service capabilities, product knowledge, expected service quality and operational procedures to follow. For example, LG Electronics India regularly trains its sub-dealers, direct dealers and service franchisees. The training tries to facilitate performance, improve knowledge, skills and attitude of its dealers and sales staff. The training is given both through online and offline methods, which covers functional, technical and behavioural aspects. Similarly Kirloskar Brothers Limited (KBL) makes the customers and dealers aware of the fundaments and working principles of Centrifugal Pumps, enabling them to operate and maintain the equipments more efficiently. The training program is designed by KBL to offer best possible theoretical as well as practical knowledge to their valued customers and dealers.

Marketing Insight 13.4

Mom & Pop Stores upgrade Staff

Mom & pop stores, those family-run neighbourhood outlets for everything under the sun, are adding value to their staff in order to stand up to organised retail giants. Mom & pop stores, those family-run neighbourhood outlets for everything under the sun, are adding value to their staff in order to stand up to organised retail giants. Training courses for staff like sales associates are in. Besides retail selling skills, the grooming process covers basic English and personality development.

B S Nagesh, founder of Trrain, a retail staff training firm, says such initiatives have become imperative as organised retail and bigger brands have well-trained staff -- and mom & pop stores cannot afford to lag in this regard. "Requests for training are coming from even smaller towns and cities where big brands and modern retail have emerged only in the last few years," says Nagesh.

For instance, Panda Travel Mart, a luggage chain store in Bhubaneswar, had decided to train its staff as part of its modernisation. Shiba Prasad Panda, Panda's MD, says, "The training process has helped instil confidence in our sales associates. They have been able to use their retail skills effectively which eventually will translate into higher sales for us."

There are other benefits. Value-added staff is giving a new touch to upgradation works at neighbourhood stores and unorganised retailers. Apart from revamp, several stores have changed their formats by opting for open shelves. This gives better display for combo offers and discounts during festive seasons, just like at modern retail chains.

Nagesh says that producing a conducive retail environment with trained staff can go a long way in improving sales. Proof of that is Me n Moms, a Mumbai-based retail chain that sells mother- and baby-care products. Naresh Khattar, its CEO, says training undertaken six months back has helped produce a more conducive retail atmosphere which is now gradually increasing footfalls. That staff training is gaining wide recognition is evident from the tremendous response to Trrain's programmes, says Ameesha Prabhu, its CEO. Several small shops and retail associations from different localities in Mumbai are showing interest in undertaking staff training, she says.

But the biggest challenge for the retail sector, including mom & pop stores, is the high rate of attrition. A survey done in February by Tata Consultancy Services and the Retailers Association of Indian revealed that about 33% of the respondents faced an attrition rate of about 100% every year. Such a high rate is coming in way of many retailers signing up for staff training programmes.

- **Motivating Channel Members**: As the channel members are as important as your customers, a company needs to make them happy. Just like anybody, channel members are also needs to be motivated. On the one hand, the company tries to train them for their better performance and on the other hand, the company provides them incentives, higher margins, premiums, display allowances, advertising allowances and special deals.

  While managing the relationship with the channel members, a company can use coercive power or it can use reward power or legitimate power. A company can also use expert power or referent power. In the case of coercive and legitimate power, the relationship can turn sour and it may not be productive in the long run. But the widely used reward power works the best to get the cooperation from the channel members. In the case of expert power, the channel member looks forward to the company for its expertise and becomes dependent, if the expertise is ever changing. When a company is highly respected like Sony, LG, Apple, Maruti Suzuki, then they have referent power. The channel members feel proud to be associated with it. In turn, it makes the channel partners cooperate with the company. This is the highest authority a company can possess.[6]

  The most advanced supply distributor agreement is distribution programming, which can be defined as building a planned, professionally managed vertical marketing system that meets the needs of both manufacturers and distributors. The manufacturer establishes a department within the company called distributor relations planning. Its job is to identify distributor needs and build up merchandising programmes to help each distributor operate as efficiently as possible.[7]

- **Evaluating Channel Members**: Channel members are evaluated on the basis of their sales, inventory level, service support, delivery time performance, complaint redressal, promotional program implementation and training performance. If the performance of the channel member is satisfactory, then it is rewarded for its efforts and if the performance falls below mark, it is advised to make necessary changes in the processes. In case of channel members, where the problems are beyond rectification, they are removed and the company appoints a new channel member.

- **Modifying Channel Arrangements**: With the changing times, the company needs to modify its channel arrangements. The product line can expand, the consumers buying pattern can change, the new competition can come up, a new distribution channel can emerge or the demand of the product can change by getting into the later stages of product life cycle. All these factors can lead the company to change its channel arrangement.

When Intex started their operations in 1996, they had just one product – Ethernet card. Now the product has expanded to 26 product groups with more than 300 stock keeping units. Now their marketing channel consist of 2 mother warehouses, 2 regional offices, 28 branches, 57 service centres, 183 service franchises and more than 2000 channel partners. Similarly with the growing usage of Internet, all the retailers are trying to follow a brick and click model, where they sell their merchandise in their stores and they sell it online also. Kishore Biyani's Future group is a good example of the same. They target their customers through a brick model with Big Bazaar, Pantaloons, E-Zone, Home Town etc. and follow the customers online through their click model i.e. www.futurebazaar.com and www.ezoneonline.in . From time to time, a company needs to track the changes in the market and on this basis; they need to modify their channel members.

Channel Conflict

With more competition in the market, channel conflict arises among most of the channel members. In the cases of selective distribution and intensive distribution, the channel members are always at loggerheads. Now a typical retailer faces the competition not only from the competitors to sell its products, but also from the other retailers or resellers or dealers. A retailer faces competition from its neighbourhood stores, exclusive brand shops and organized retailer. For example, a Sony retailer faces competition from Sony World, other stores selling the Sony product and the organized retailers like e-Zone and Croma. A company needs to manage the channel conflicts in such a way that ultimately it should lead to more sales.

- **Causes of Channel Conflict**: Vertical channel conflict happens when wholesalers and retailers come into conflict. While in the horizontal conflict, it may arise at the same level. Like in case of bikes, it may happen that one Hero Honda dealer is giving more discount to the customer than another Hero Honda dealer. Multi channel conflict arises, when the company has more than two channels, as discussed above in the case of Sony. These kinds of conflicts are quite common. Many times, the conflict arises due to differences in perception by the company and the channel members. The company may be optimistic about the current and future sales, but the channel members may not be. The channel members can also be affected by the product and pricing policies of the company, which may lead to conflict. Sometimes, a conflict may arise between the sales force and the dealers for over promising the customers.

- **Managing Channel Conflict:** Sometimes channel conflict may be constructive, but most of the time, it's destructive in nature. The best way for a company is to manage it at the channel level. Ultimately a channel as well as a company seeks more profits in selling the product. The four strategic alternatives available for resolving conflicts between channel members are bargaining, boundary, interpenetration and super organizational strategies.[8]

LG

The bargaining strategy involves both the parties to look out for mutual benefit and in return to be ready for some give and take. For example, LG can say that it will increase the inventory level of its dealers by 50%, but will also give credit from the earlier 30 days to 60 days. The boundary strategy is meant for resolving conflict through diplomacy. The diplomat should be fully aware with the situation and should know what to negotiate. In the interpenetration strategy, the conflict is resolved through frequent informal interactions. A dealer council helps to remove horizontal channel conflict as well as a vertical channel conflict. Here the company needs to talk to the channel members to understand their mutual benefit and implement strategies, which are useful for both of them. Lastly, if the conflict is not resolved, then super organisational strategy of counciliation, mediation and arbitration works for the company. In some cases, government authorities also interfere in solving the matter; as Telecom Regulatory Authority of India (TRAI) looks after the mobile telephony and Drug Controller looks after the pharmaceutical industry.

Summary

- Place is all about reaching out to the customers. It is also known as a marketing channel or trade channel or a distribution channel.
- Marketing channels are sets of interdependent organisations involved in the process of making a product or service available for use or consumption. It serves functions like demand generation, demand fulfillment, after sales service and info / feedback for strategy development.
- Marketing channel intermediaries can be classified into categories like merchants, agents and facilitators. Merchants buy, take title to and resell the goods from the

company, like wholesalers and retailers. Agents do not take title to the goods and just help the company in forwarding the goods to the stockist or distributors. Facilitators help a company in the distribution process.

- A company can decide its way to reach the customers. When a company reaches its customers directly, then it can be called a Zero Level Channel. It is also called a direct marketing channel. One level channel includes one intermediary between the company and the customers. In two level channel, a wholesaler and a retailer deals with the company on the one side and customers on the other. In three level channel, there are three intermediaries – Distributor, Wholesalers and Retailer. In certain products, there is the existence of multi level channel.
- As far as the flow of goods, title and promotion are concerned in different channel levels, there is a forward flow. But in the case of payment, it goes backward to the company from the customer. In the case of information, negotiation, finance and risk taking, it flows both ways between the company and the customer with the intermediaries in between.
- Channel design decisions are crucial for any company, whether it's new or it's old. In the case of a new company, it becomes even tougher to get the products on the shelves of the retailers. In case of an old and established company the company might be spoilt with choices.
- The length of the channel can be decided on the basis of analysing customers' desired service output levels, by establishing objectives and constraints, by identifying major channel alternatives and by evaluating major channel alternatives.
- A company may go for exclusive distribution or selective distribution or intensive distribution.
- Companies generally try to move towards lower cost channels. Among all the channel alternatives, Internet is the lowest cost channel, while Direct Sales Force is the highest. In between channel like Telemarketing, Retail Stores, Distributors, Value Added Partners exists.
- The success of any marketing channel lies in the foundation of right channel design decision. It includes right from, selecting a channel member to training them to motivating them and to evaluating them on their performance. In case, the performance is not as expected, the modifications are done by the company in the channel arrangements.
- With more competition in the market, channel conflict arises among most of the channel members. In the cases of selective distribution and intensive distribution, the channel members are always at loggerheads.
- Sometimes channel conflict may be constructive, but most of the time, it's destructive in nature. The best way for a company is to manage at the channel level. The four strategic alternatives available for resolving conflicts between channel members are bargaining, boundary, interpenetration and super organizational strategies.

Discussion Questions

1. What do you mean by Place? What are its functions in Marketing?
2. Define marketing channel. Discuss marketing channel in detail with examples.
3. What do you mean by marketing channel? Discuss the different marketing channel levels.
4. What is the difference between merchants, agents and facilitators? Discuss the channel functions and flows.
5. Discuss the various parameters on which channel length is decided, with examples.
6. How do you select, train motivate and evaluate a channel partner?
7. What do you mean by channel conflict? How do you resolve a channel conflict?
8. Short Notes:
    a. Place
    b. Channel flow
    c. Single level marketing channel
    d. Merchants
    e. Channel conflict
    f. Training channel partners
    g. Selective distribution
    h. Major channel alternatives

References

1. Louis W. Stern and Adel I. El-Ansary, 'Marketing Channels', Prentice Hall, 1996
2. Robert J. Dolan, 'Going to Market', Harvard Business School Publishing, 1999
3. Philip Kotler. 'Marketing Management', Pearson Education Indian Reprint, 2004
4. Subhash C. Jain. 'Marketing Planning and Strategy', South Western Educational Publishing, 1999
5. Lawrence G. Friedman and Timothy R. Furey, 'The Channel Advantage: Going to Marketing with multiple Sales Channels', Butterworth – Heinemann, 1999
6. John R. P. French and Bertram Raven, 'The Bases of Social Power', in Studies in Social Power, ed. Darwin Cartwright, University of Michigan Press, 1959, pp. 150-167
7. Philip Kotler, Marketing Manangement, Pearson Education, 2004, p. 519
8. Louis W. Stern and Adel I. El-Ansary, 'Marketing Channels', Prentice Hall, 1988, pp. 290-298

CHAPTER 14

Promotion-Integrated Marketing Communications

Chapter Structure

- Promotion - Integrated Marketing Communications (IMC)
- Communication Process
- Six Ms Models for Communication Planning
- Indian Advertising Industry
- Consumer Response Hierarchy Models
- Integrated Marketing Communications (IMC)
- Tools of IMC
- *Marketing Insight 14.1: Difference between Above the Line (ATL) and Below the Line (BTL)*
- *Marketing Insight 14.2: Krrish 3 May Net $3 m from Off-screen Action*
- *Marketing Insight 14.3: Amazon Raises Stakes with High-Decibel Ad Pitch*
- *Marketing Insight 14.4: Celebrity Ad Fever*
- *Marketing Insight 14.5: Ad Wars Rage Again*
- *Marketing Insight 14.6: Companies Offer Freebies to Beat Slowdown Blues*
- *Marketing Insight 14.7: White Goods Cos in Shop-Floor Push for Sales*
- *Marketing Insight 14.8: Digital Advertising Spend to Grow the Most in 2014*
- Monitoring, Evaluation and Control
- Summary
- Discussion Questions
- References

"Unless your campaign has a big idea, it will pass like a ship in the night"

- David Ogilvy

Half the money I spend on advertising is wasted, and the problem is I do not know which half."

- Lord Leverhulme, British founder of Unilever and Philanthropist

"For a business not to advertise is like winking at a girl in the dark. You know what you are doing but no one else does."

- Stuart H. Britt, US advertising consultant

Promotion - Integrated Marketing Communications (IMC)

Integrated marketing communications deals with the fourth P of marketing i.e. Promotion. Promotion is the coordination of all the efforts, the company undertakes to aware and persuade the consumers to buy goods and services. Once the product is developed in accordance with the needs of the customers, it needs to be priced attractively and then it needs to be available at the point of purchase. But, the customer will ask about your product in the market, only when he or she is aware about it. Again, awareness or communication to the customer is not everything. It should be in such a way that the customer chooses your product over competitors' product.

Promotion is termed as communication by Robert Lauterborn, from the perspective of the consumer. Earlier it was known only as marketing communications, as the media vehicles were few and doing promotion was simpler before 1980s. Now with the growing complexity, a company needs to integrate all the marketing communications activities to get the maximum reach to the target audience with minimum resources. That's why it is called Integrated Marketing Communications now.

Communication Process

Today customers are communicated through various communication channels like Print Advertisement, TV Commercials, Posters, Leaflets, Point of purchase Materials, Hoardings, Video Films, Directories, Sales Meeting, Fairs and Trade Shows, Online Shopping, Telemarketing, Catalogue Marketing, Contests, Seminars etc. This process of marketing communication passes through nine major components, as shown in the following figure.

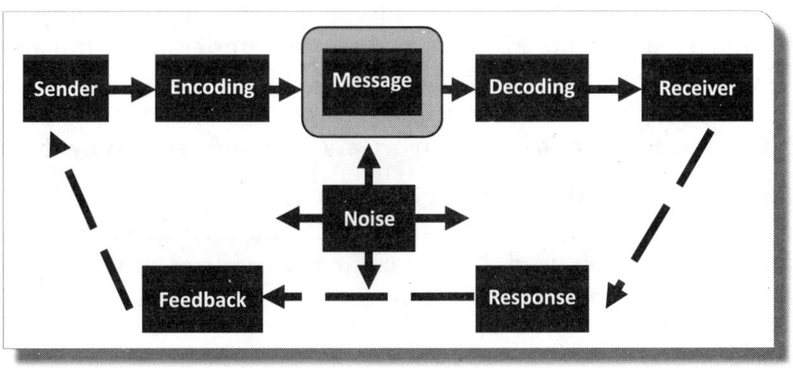

Communication Process

There are two major parties – **Sender and Receiver** in the communication process and two communication tools – Message and Media. In the process, four communication functions are involved – **Encoding, Decoding, Response and Feedback.** Besides these, there is **noise**, which falls in the process of communication. Through this model, the communication exercise can be done effectively. The sender i.e. the company needs to know, whom they want to reach. On the basis of the audience, the massage is designed and right media vehicle is chosen to communicate the message. The message should be in such a way that can be decoded by the audience easily. Through feedback and response, the company can modify its message and communication channel to be more effective.

Six Ms Models for Communication Planning

As a marketer, you need to communicate the customers in such a way, to make them purchase your products. This kind of communications planning requires six M's to be taken care of. The first three Ms are meant for the strategy part and the other three are meant for the Implementation part.[1]

Strategy Part

1. **Market** To whom the communication is addressed?
2. **Mission** What is the objective of the Communication?
3. **Message** What are the specific points to be communicated?

Implementation Part

4. **Media** Which vehicles will be used to execute on the goals?
5. **Money** How much will be spent in the effort?
6. **Measurement** How will impact be assessed after the campaign?

The first M – Market makes you understand as whom is your communication addressed to? It covers not only your customers, but also covers the distribution channel through which your products are sold. Mission makes you understand the objective of the communication. The third strategic issue is the message. A customer will be interested in knowing about your product and features, while your wholesalers, retailers will be keen to know the discounts, terms of trade, delivery and the pull created by the advertising.

Once a company is through with the strategic part, it needs to implement its communication through Media, Money and Measurement. A company needs to finalise, as to which communication vehicles to be used. Now, a company requires multiple vehicles to reach the target audience. Some of these communication vehicles are one way vehicles, while others are two way vehicles.

With reference to the below diagram, it is clear that communication vehicles like Television, Magazine, Newspapers and Radio fall among the mass communication vehicles, while Direct Mail, Catalogues, Infomercial, E-mail and Telemarketing offers two way communication to the marketer. In the case of telemarketing, it becomes instantaneous, while in the case e-mail, is' almost instant. But in the case of Direct mail, catalogue and infomercials, it has a time lag in response.[2]

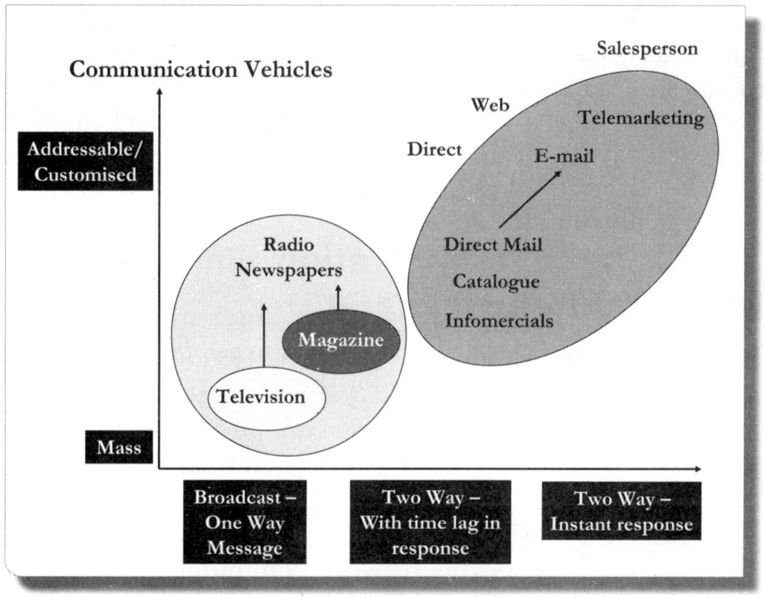

Source: Robert J. Dolan, 'Integrated Marketing Communications', Harvard Business School Notes, 2000, Note 9-599-087

Besides selecting the media vehicle, a company also needs to budget the communication effort, as to how much money the company wants to spend. The budget for the promotion needs to be carefully earmarked by the company taking into several things into consideration. The company needs to look out for the benchmark expenditure in the industry for advertising. Sometimes budgets are set in accordance with a percentage of previous year sales figures or expected sales figure of the next year.

Aircel

It also needs to take product life cycle stage into consideration. Generally new products require larger advertising budgets, while products in other stages require relatively lower budgets. It also takes market share, competition and clutter into account to finalise the budget. In a competitive market of mobile services, even a new company like Aircel is advertising heavily to beat the clutter with the celebrity endorser in India - M. S. Dhoni. For Aircel, ad to sales ratio is quite high than Airtel, being in the introduction stage and being in a highly competitive industry.

Indian Advertising Industry

The Indian media and advertising industry was worth Rs 21,602 crore in 2009, as compared to Rs 21,380 crore in 2008. According to the survey conducted by Zenith Optimedia, part of the French advertsing conglomerate Publicis Groupe SA, the Indian advertising pie is expected to be worth about Rs 23,631 crore in 2010 and Rs 25,892 in 2011.

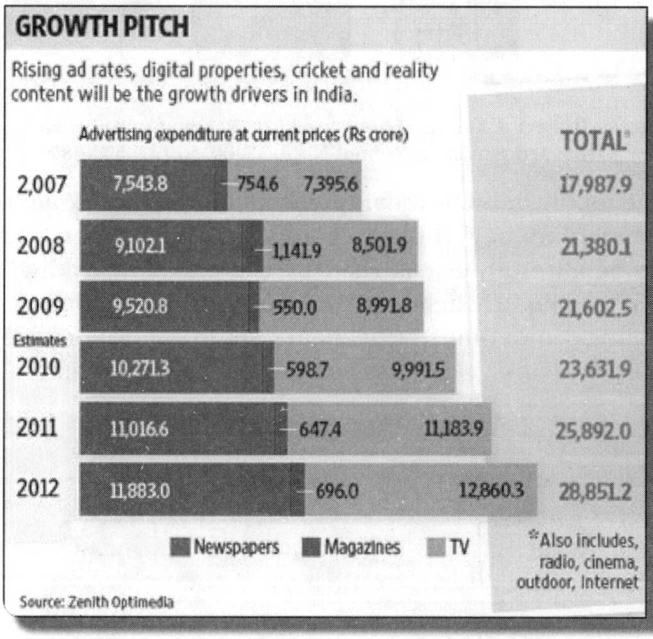

Source: Zenith Optimedia

The Indian economy withstood the test of global slump and grew at 6-7% in 2009. While on the contrary, ad expenditure fell 23.1% in central and eastern Europe, with drops as steep as 42% in Russia, 44% in Latvia and 48% in Ukraine in 2009. Zenith Optimedia has forecast a 5.7% ad spending growth in central and Eastern Europe in 2010, and 8.5% in 2011.

Newspaper advertising, which grew 5% in 2009, is likely to see 7-8% annual growth in 2010-11 in India. Rising literacy levels and better distribution in the regions are steadily improving the reach of newspapers. The survey also predicts a healthy 11-12% growth for television in India riding on the digital wave and advertising opportunities offered by the new larger than life entertainment formats. Sports are gaining popularity due to the success of the Indian Premier League (IPL) and the Commonwealth Games. The study stated that Internet advertising in India will be driven by social media. The survey pegs Internet advertising growth at an annual 25% in the coming three years.

At least two other advertising surveys have predicted 12-13% growth for Indian advertising. A recent Pitch-Madison report has also predicted the ad industry to grow at 13% growth in 2010-11.[3]

In India, newspapers and Television is running neck to neck, as far as advertising pie is concerned. But in the near future, the television is going to take the lead from the newspaper, as shown in the above table.

If we go back, we find that during 2004-05, the advertising expenditure was Rs. 6378 Cr. Overall the companies spent 1.26% of their revenue on advertising. Out of Rs. 6378 Cr., FMCG companies spent Rs. 2363 Cr. (6% of their revenue on advertising), Banking spent Rs. 519 Cr. and Automobile industry spent Rs. 714 Cr. Generally a FMCG company in India invests 6% to 15% of their sales turnover on the promotions. Following table gives an overview of advertising budget during 2003-04 and 2004-05 by leading companies of India.

AD BUDGETS				
	Ad spend in Rs Cr		Ad spend of % of sales	
	2003-04	2004-05	2003-04	2004-05
Hind. Lever	759.09	835.98	7.51	8.42
ITC	265.72	220.53	4.15	2.90
Ranbaxy Lab	182.26	201.72	5.01	5.44
Tata Motors	123.60	172.37	0.96	1.01
Dabur India	154.95	171.79	14.31	14.01
Hero Honda	124.46	147.48	2.13	1.99
Bajaj Auto	129.32	143.87	2.71	2.50
Colgate Palmolive	147.65	136.84	15.74	14.23
Reckitt Benck	102.17	124.41	16.21	16.43
Nestle India	136.12	121.26	6.36	5.44
ICICI Bank	68.68	116.26	0.76	1.24
Reliance Ind	220.64	114.56	0.43	0.17
GlaxoSmith	97.92	101.45	12.30	11.78
Britannia Industries	114.66	101.09	7.96	6.37

Advertising Budget of Leading Advertisers

Once the money is invested by the companies on the communication efforts, it needs to be monitored. Monitoring helps in more efficient utilisation of resources by continuing or modifying advertising plan with respect to the desired result.

In advertising, advertising agencies play a key role in creating, planning and handling advertising for their clients. The clients include for profit organisations, nonprofit organisations and government agencies. According to Economic Times - Band Equity Agency Reckoner 2010; following is the list of the top 10 advertising agencies in India.

Top 10 Advertising Agencies in India

Ranking	Company Name	Website
1	Ogilvy and Mather	www.ogilvy.com
2	James Walter Thompson	www.jwt.com
3	Lowe Lintas	www.lowelintas.in
4	Mc Cann Erickson	www.mccannworldgroup.com
5	Mudra India	www.mudra.com
6	Leo Burnett	www.leoburnett.com
7	DDB Mudra	www.mudra.com
8	Draft FCB Ulka	www.draftfcb.com
9	Redifussion YR	www.rediffusionyr.com/
10	Contract	www.icontract.in

Source: Economic Times - Band Equity Agency Reckoner 2010

Consumer Response Hierarchy Models

The ultimate goal of a company is to motivate customers to buy your products. The consumer goes through different stages before landing on to the actual purchase. The stages can be understood more clearly by the following consumer response hierarchy models.

1. AIDA Model given by E. K. Strong,
2. Hierarchy of Effects Model given by Robert J. Lavidge and Gary A. Steiner and
3. Innovation Adoption Model given by Everett M. Rogers.[4]

Through a consumer response hierarchy model, a company seeks cognitive, affective and behavioural response. A company at first tries to make the consumer aware by putting information in the consumer's mind, then it tries to change the attitude and then it seeks the consumer to act and buy the product. The most commonly used model is AIDA model.

It says that a company needs to get the attention of the consumer about the product. Attention leads to generation of interest and then to desire, which ultimately leads to action, by the purchase made by the consumer.

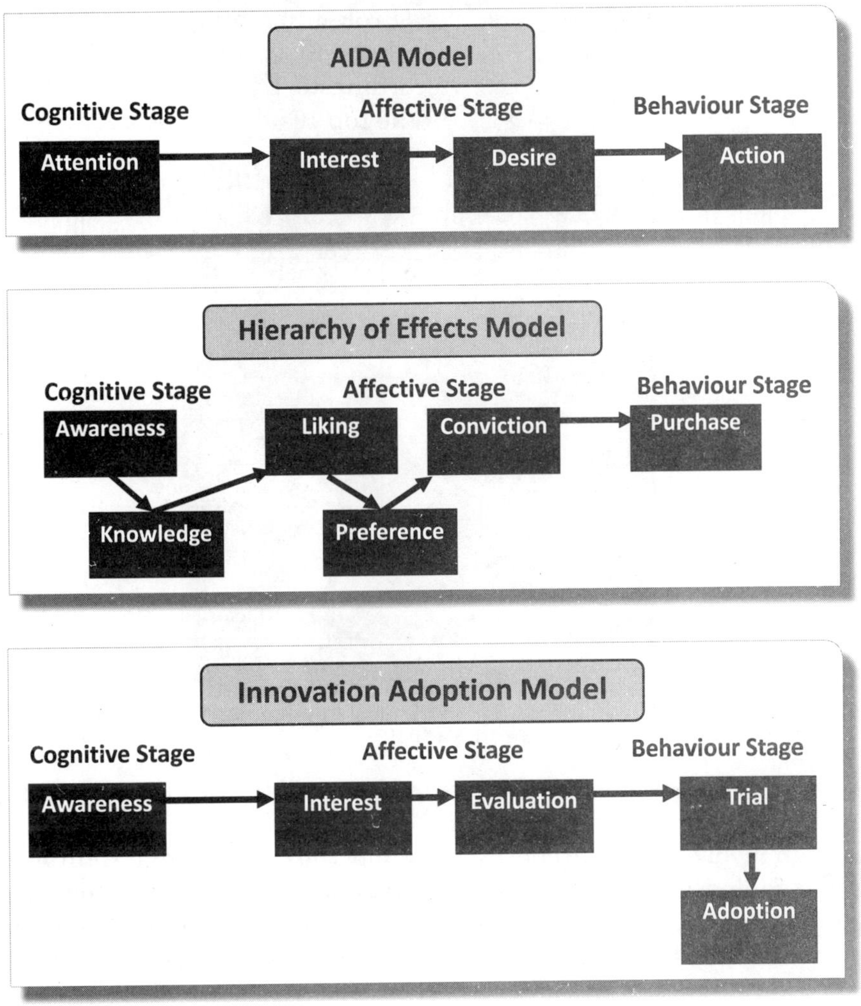

Consumer Response Hierarchy Models

Similarly in the Hierarchy of Effects model, Levidge and Steiner have talked about two stages in the cognitive process i.e. Awareness and Knowledge, which leads to liking, preference and conviction in the affective stage, which in turn leads to purchase by the consumer. Taking the model towards the innovation, Rogers has given the model called Innovation Adoption Model. This model starts with awareness and goes on to interest and evaluation in the affective stage and finally it goes for trial and adoption.

Vadilal

While AIDA model can be widely applicable to almost all the products, it suits more to the low involvement and low cost purchases like Potato Chips, Ice Cream, Soft Drinks etc. For costlier and high involvement purchases, generally the consumer goes through six stages of Levidge and Steiner model like consumer durables. An innovative or a technological product requires the benefits to be clearly understood by the customers, that's why an actual purchase happens in the process of interest, evaluation, trial and then adoption.

Integrated Marketing Communications (IMC)

The fourth P of Marketing is Promotion, as termed by McCarthy. Promotion is the coordination of all the efforts, the company undertakes to aware and persuade the consumers to buy goods and services. Robert Lauterborn calls promotion as communication from the perspective of the consumer. Now it is widely known as Integrated Marketing Communications. Earlier it was known only as marketing communications, as the media vehicles were few and doing promotion was simpler before 1980s. Now it has become more complex. Today, a company needs to integrate all the marketing communications activities to get the maximum reach to the target audience with minimum resources.

Earlier advertising was restricted to mass media vehicles like newspapers, magazines and television. Now there are so many options to choose from like Websites, Posters, Leaflets, Point of purchase Materials, Hoardings, Video Films, Directories, Sales Meeting, Fairs and Trade Shows, Online Shopping, Telemarketing, Catalogue Marketing, Contests, Events, Demonstrations, Seminars etc. besides Print Advertisement in newspaper and magazines and TV Commercials (TVC). A marketer becomes confused to choose the right media vehicle among the plethora of choices available to promote a product. Here IMC can come to the rescue to formulate right kind of strategy for the company.

'IMC recognises the added value of a comprehensive plan that evaluates the strategic roles of - Advertising, Direct Response, Sales Promotion and Public Relations - and combine those principles to provide clarity, consistency and maximum communications impact' - American Association of Advertising Agencies.

Don Schultz, referred as the **'father of integrated marketing communications'**, is of the view that **IMC deals with all the Sources of brand and company contact that a customer or prospect has with a product or service. It takes 'Big Picture' approach to planning marketing and promotion programmes and coordinating the various communication functions. It requires that a company develop a total marketing communication strategy that recognizes how all of a firm's marketing activities, not just promotion, communicate with its customers.**

naukri.com®
India's No 1 Job Site

Naukri.com

IMC builds the most effective platform to promote a product or service through its integrated usage of communication tools for selling soap or selling services to a job seeker. In both the cases, the promotional requirements are different. The promotional requirements of HUL are different from Naukri.com. In the case of HUL, all the FMCG products are meant for mass consumption and distribution, which in turn makes HUL depend more on TV Commercials than the other media vehicle. On the other hand, in the case of Naukri.com, the users can only be internet literates, who can surf a website to find a job (now they also provide SMS messaging for the jobs). That's why most of the communication is done to target online people through ad banners on leading websites Yahoo.com, Rediff.com, Sify.com etc. Here the revenue of Naukri comes from the companies, who place their job requirements and from the peoples, who have gone for premium services. Besides giving a lot of emphasis on

Internet marketing, it also advertises with 'Hari Sadu' Campaign on television to attract the people associated with the companies, who are using or may use their services, besides their target job seekers.

Market Revolution

Zee TV

In the last twenty years, there have been a lot of developments, which have changed the overall structure of the marketing. This marketing revolution has made the advertising too expensive and less cost effective. Earlier there was just one television channel – Doordarshan in India and then DD Metro was launched in 1985. After that, satellite television came into India with Zee TV being launched in October, 1992. Now there are more than 500 TV channels in India. The fragmented customer base has led the companies to move towards lower cost and more targeted communication vehicles. Again in the last few years with the grand success of Big Bazaar in Indian market, there has been tremendous growth in the organized retailing. The growth in organized retailing has led to shift in the market power from the companies to the retailer. Now companies like ITC with its snack Bingo! or, Pepsi's Frito-Lay with Lay's potato chips cannot afford to lose customers by not selling into big retail chains.

Companies are also relying more on database marketing to hit the customers directly. Internet has also changed the promotions arena with more and more people logging on to various websites. These changes have led the companies to make advertising agencies more accountable for the results. In turn, Advertising agencies are looking forward to IMC to bring efficiency and effectiveness in the promotional campaigns.

Advantage IMC

There are several advantages of Integrated Marketing Communications in the ever changing world. The biggest advantage is that it creates synergy among the various promotional tools. When the consumers are less responsive to traditional advertising, it tries to reach through different tools like Internet Marketing, PR and other tools. It also tries to create interactivity in the sales and promotional messages through the usage of technology. As there have been decline in the audience size for many media, it helps to develop more efficient and effective marketing communications program. Many companies try to indulge customers in the teaser campaigns through Internet.

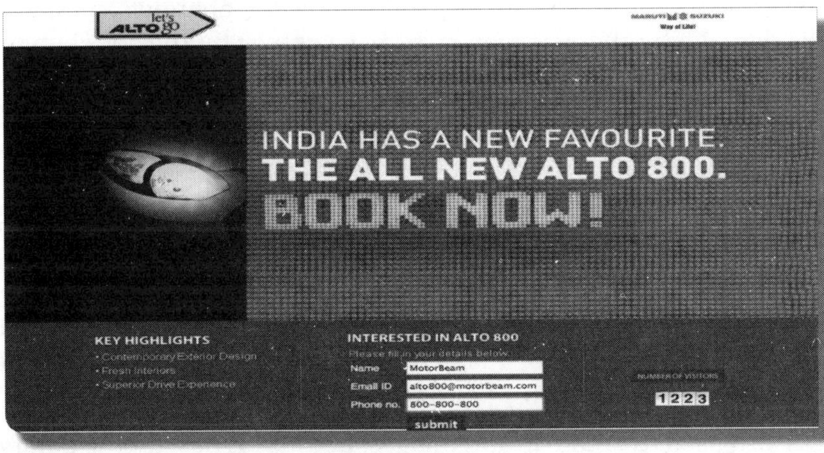

Alto 800

Maruti created a teaser page on its website for Alto 800, to create a curiosity around the product prior to its launch. Bollywood has also been effectively using Internet as a platform to promote its films like Ghajini, Blue, London Dreams, Wanted, Dev D etc.

Tools of IMC

Integrated Marketing Communications uses six tools to reach its target markets and to build its brand equity. These tools are also called elements of Promotional Mix. These tools are:

1. Advertising
2. Sales Promotion
3. Public Relations
4. Direct Marketing
5. Personal Selling and
6. Digital Marketing

All these tools help a company to promote its products efficiently and effectively.

Advertising

'Advertising is defined as any paid form of non personal presentation and promotion of ideas, goods or services by an identified sponsor.' (G. E. Belch and M. A. Belch / AMA)

Advertising is a paid medium, as a company needs to pay for the advertising space in the newspaper or magazine or it needs to buy time on the TV channels. Sometimes, ad space or the time is donated by the newspaper or magazine or by the TV channel or by radio for public service announcement. Advertising is non personal in nature, as it uses mass media like TV, Print and Radio to transmit the message to large number of people at the same time. Again the payment is made by some identified sponsor like HUL, Nirma, LG, Intex etc.

Advertising works best in the case of mass consumer products, when the message can be transmitted to crores of people at the same point of time in India. As it reaches more people, it also becomes a very cost effective medium for the advertiser. For example, in programmes like Balika Vadhu or Big Boss or Khatron Ke Khiladi, the ad cost ranges from Rs. 1.5 Lacs to Rs. 2.5 Lacs for 10 Seconds. It might sound costly, but with respect to viewership it will be less than even 1 paisa for one viewer.

Advertising is also used to create brand images, because it has got the ability to persuade consumers through the advertisements. By attracting consumers', it can help generate sales. Advertising includes Print Advertisement, Television Commercials (TVC), Directories, Billboards, Hoardings, Banners, Posters, Brochure & Booklets, Audio Visual Material, Display Signs and POP Displays.

The objective of any advertising campaign differs from company to company. Sometimes it is aimed at generating immediate response or action from the consumer or sometimes is meant to develop awareness about the product or service or a positive image over a longer period. Most of the FMCG products like Soaps, Toothpaste, and Shampoo are meant for consumer's immediate response. But in the case of cars, the objective of the advertising campaign is to achieve both the goals of influencing the customers to buy and have a positive image around them.

Marketing Insight 14.1

Marketing Insight 14.1

Difference between Above the Line (ATL) and Below the Line (BTL)

Gillette

Above The Line (ATL) and Below The Line (BTL) advertising are two terms that are bandied around often these days in the advertising world and often have the lay person confused as to what they stand for. It might be worth our while to begin this by defining what constitutes the metaphoric 'Line'. To quote Michael John Baker from The Marketing Book , the terms 'Above The Line' and 'Below The Line' came into existence way back in 1954 with the company Proctor and Gamble paying their advertising agencies a different rate and separately from the agencies who took on the other promotional activities.

What are ATL and BTL activities? They seem simple enough. Above The Line (ATL) advertising is where mass media is used to promote brands and reach out to the target consumers. These include conventional media as we know it, television and radio advertising, print as well as internet. This is communication that is targeted to a wider spread of audience, and is not specific to individual consumers. ATL advertising tries to reach out to the mass as consumer audience.

Below the line (BTL) advertising is more one to one, and involves the distribution of pamphlets, handbills, stickers, promotions, brochures placed at point of sale, on the roads through banners and placards. It could also involve product demos and samplings at busy places like malls and market places or residential complexes. For certain markets, like rural markets where the reach of mass media like print or television is limited, BTL marketing with direct consumer outreach programmes do make the most sense. Says Raghu Khanna, CEO, CASHurDRIVE, "When budget is issue and the brand wants to have a consumer connect BTL has better ROI."

Other BTL activities could include roadshows, or moving hoardings with the ad of the product, and vehicles with promotional staff interacting with people demonstrating the product and distributing literature on the product. BTL advertising is advertising that uses less conventional methods of advertising that the specific channels of advertising that may or may not be used by ATL advertising to promote products and services. According to Iya Malhotra Bhatia, Marketing Professional, "BTL is a preferred tool when test marketing a product, sampling and also in case of a targeted campaign in related to another bigger phenomenon. Also when TG is very niche, BTL makes more sense."

Hyundai Grand i10

BTL promotion might include direct mail promotional campaigns, PR and sales promotions which are handled directly by the company itself or outsourced to specifically PR agencies and sales promotion agencies and may or not be related to the advertising campaign. BTL advertising might include email campaigns, telemarketing, etc with targeted groups of potential clients. Says Megha Ghosh, Account Director, Client Services at Encompass, "BTL is preferred on several occasions but the foremost would be when you need to have a personal interaction with the consumer."

Says Kapil Taneja, Regional Head, North, FUN Cinemas (Esselgroup company), "Sometimes BTL is preferred over ATL due to budget issues, the need to physically display the product, to conduct a hand on product contest as well as for new launches and teasers campaigns." Companies prefer adopting BTL as a means of reaching out to their target consumers when their product is something they need to engage the consumer in a touch and feel experience with.

Some people would consider ATL and BTL antiquated terminologies in an era which uses the internet and lightening speed changes in modes of communication to reach out to the consumer. "When you are communicating with a niche audience BTL is better. However, digital media has more or less broken these boundaries of ATL versus BTL as digital communication can address both at the same time.," says Namrata Rana, Director, Futurescape.

Interestingly, there is a new phrase called Through the Line, or TTL, which integrates both ATL and BTL activities. BTL communications from brands is rapidly becoming a dying form of reaching out to the audience with agencies and clients going adopting the Integrated Communication approach.

To end with a quote O&M's Piyush Pandey, from a previous interview, on the two forms of brand communication, Below-the-line is extremely important, but then when wasn't it? It is just that till now it was taken a bit for granted and not too many innovations were made. I am glad the industry is planning to revolutionise this game. It is not a question of mass media versus below-the-line. It is an era of mass media plus below-the-line."

Advertising to Consumer Markets

As marketing can be classified between the consumer and business markets, the advertising efforts for both the markets differ. As far as advertising to consumer markets is concerned, it can be classified on the basis of geographical area and on the basis of the demand structure. On the basis of geographic area, it can be divided on a national basis, regional basis and on a local basis in India. In India, most of the areas can be covered with Hindi and English newspapers, magazines, radio and satellite channels. This kind of National Advertising is meant to inform or remind the customer again and again to create or reinforce the advertiser image, so as to generate purchases for the advertiser. Similarly in some states like Tamilnadu, Karnataka, Andhra Pradesh and Kerala; Tamil, Kannada, Telugu and Malayalam newspapers, magazines, radio and satellite channels respectively are very popular. In almost all the states in India has got their own regional channels and print publications. Consumer Advertising is also done on a local basis for a metro city or a town. This is meant to create local demand for the goods and services for local retail stores primarily.

INSDAG 'Steel for Life' Ad

On the basis of demand, the advertising is done either for a primary demand or a selective demand. In primary demand advertising, the whole industry or product class is promoted. For example, Institute for Steel Development and Growth (INSDAG) launched a campaign to promote the usage of Steel through its 'Steel for Life' Campaign in India.

Marketing Insight 14.2

Krrish 3 May Net $3 m from Off-screen Action

Krrish 3

Actor Hrithik Roshan's upcoming superhero sci-fi film Krrish 3 has signed a two-year licensing and merchandising deal with Mumbaibased Dream Theatre, which manages licensing rights for global brands like Angry Birds, Power Rangers and Noddy. Krrish 3, which is slated for a Diwali release, is expected to generate sales of close to $3 million from merchandise, digital activation including online games and animation-related licensing alone, Afsar Zaidi, chief executive of Carving Dreams, a talent management and entertainment firm that represents Roshan, told ET.

Brand Licensing Industry	
India	$ 300 Million
USA	$ 120 Billion

Dream Theatre manages licensing rights for global brands like Angry Birds, Dream Works Animation, Power Rangers, Noddy, Discovery Kids and Power Rangers in India. Set up by Turner Broadcasting-promoted Cartoon Network's former top official Jiggy George, this is the first time Dream Theatre will work on a local brand. Krrish 3 will be released in five versions — two animated Krrish movies titled Kid Krrish, which will be aired on kids' television channel Cartoon Network before the cinematic release of the actual movie. ET had reported on the various versions of the movie in April 2013. Two more animated Kid Krrish movies will be aired also on the same channel after Krrish is released in theatres, in 3D format. The first of the animated Kid Krrish movies will release in July on Cartoon Network.

Jiggy George, chief executive of Dream Theatre, said, "The partnerships with the movie and animation allow us to extend the lifecycle of the Krrish brand... this is the first time such an experiment is being done in India." Zaidi said: "The brand licensing deal will focus on aspects no other film has looked at so far." He added content was still being created and that overall marketing budgets of the movie were in the process of being finalised, but added Krrish will be the 'most marketed' film of the year. Krrish's overseas distribution have been acquired by Eros International for an estimated 20 crore, while the music rights of the film have been acquired by T-Series for 6 crore.

NECC Ad

Similarly Tea Board, Coffee Board, Coir Board, National Egg Coordination Committee, World Gold Council etc. advertises to promote the usage of primary demand. In these campaigns, individual brands are not promoted, but only the primary product is promoted. Sometimes a company may promote the primary product, when it has the largest market share. For example, Cadbury India is trying to replace the usage of Sweets to Chocolates through its 'Kuchh Meetha Ho Jaye' campaign in

India. With more usage of Chocolates instead of sweets, Cadbury is going to be benefited more than its competitors, as it has got more than 70% market share.

Marketing Insight 14.3

Amazon Raises Stakes with High-Decibel Ad Pitch

Online retailer earmarks Rs. 100-150 crore for advertising on TV, print and online in FY15, almost double that of its Indian rival Flipkart

Amazon

Amazon.com, the largest online retailer in the world, has launched an advertising blitzkrieg in India with a budget that not only dwarfs all its local peers but is also comparable with the country's largest retailer Future Group's ad spends. Amazon India, which started marketplace operation just about a year ago, plans to spend Rs. 100-150 crore on advertising this fiscal year, a person with direct knowledge of the company's marketing initiatives told ET.

India's largest e-commerce firm Flipkart's annual advertising budget is estimated at about Rs. 75 crore while Future Group's Big Bazaar is expected to spend an unprecedented Rs. 250 crore this year. Email queries ET sent to Amazon India did not elicit any response as of press time. Amazon is currently running a high-decibel ad campaign across media platforms including television, print and online. "We have chalked out different strategies for different mediums," said the person quoted earlier.

The Seattle-based company has shelled out Rs. 25-35 crore to become one of the largest television advertisers during the ongoing Indian Premier League, using the popular cricket tournament to unleash its first ever television commercial in the country.

"We are using television to primarily tell consumers that we have started our services in India and highlight our unique selling propositions (USPs) like one day delivery or the wide range of products that we have," the person said. The company is using the print medium to advertise various promotional offers like special weekend discounts, while its online ads are mostly product specific and are being used to increase the traction on the website. The outdoor campaign — a gigantic Amazon box that is used to deliver products —has been put up in business hubs and key locations across several cities. "The box provides a strong visual mnemonic for the brand," the person said.

Online retailing has emerged one of the most visible segments on television and print over the last couple of years with e-commerce firms such as Flipkart, Myntra, Jabong and Quikr advertising aggressively. While these companies refused to share their ad budgets, retail experts estimate that these firms spend anywhere between Rs. 25-75 crore a year. In comparison, top department store chain Shoppers Stop's annual advertising and marketing spends are approximately Rs. 84 crore, according to Vinay Bhatia, its customer care associate and executive vice-president for marketing, loyalty and analytics.

Big Bazaar, the top retail chain the country, recently initiated a Rs 100-crore campaign, its most expensive campaign so far, according to company insiders. Amazon India has not been adverting much till recently as it focused on building the back-end infrastructure to carry online retailing in the country. "We started our operations in India about a year ago and we spent the first 10 months in only strengthening our backend," the Amazon person said.

Now, the online retailer has started focusing on building its bran d in the country as well. Taproot India, owned by Japanese advertising conglomerate Dentsu Aegis Network, is Amazon's creative agency in India.

Globally, Amazon media account moved to IPG agency Initiative from WPP agency MindShare. Initiative's verticals Interactive Avenues and Rapport are handling the digital and outdoor advertising, respectively. Both Taproot and Initiative Media declined to comment on Amazon's account.

Advertising to Business & Professional Markets

Advertising is not only effective for the consumer market, but it is also effective for business market as well. On the whole, business markets can be classified into three categories. A business advertiser can advertise to businesses or it can advertise to professionals or it can target the trade channels. For example, industrial goods, equipments, office equipment and computer companies like L&T, Kirloskar, Thermax, HP, Xerox, Canon etc. regularly advertise their products for their business buyers.

Kirloskar Brothers Limited

Many companies also advertise to professionals like Doctors, Lawyers, Professors etc to encourage them to recommend the products or services for the end user. A business entity also advertises to the marketing channel members like Distributors, Wholesalers and Retailers to keep, promote and sell the products.

Marketing Insight 14.4

Marketing Insight 14.4

Celebrity Ad Fever

Relaxo

By September this year, 37 fresh brands had joined the celebrity endorsement bandwagon that closed 2011 with an impressive 706 brands. Going by the advertisers' appetite, the numbers will only grow.

Several brands that have already been using celebrities are increasing their numbers in their ads. Besides, in addition to Bollywood and cricket celebrities endorsing brands, now television actors are swelling the celebrity ad numbers. The sports celebrity spectrum for advertising has expanded beyond cricket to other sports. Even e-commerce portals are signing on celebrities for endorsements. "There was a time when celebrities were used to break the ad clutter. That's no longer true," admitted Satyaki Ghosh, director – consumer products division, L'oreal India, which uses film celebrities in its advertising.

Sometimes, celebrity ads can also leave people scratching their heads, bemused. "Salman Khan endorsing a brand of rubber chappals is just plain stupid," grumbles Mumbai-based homemaker Anita Desai, 53, who watches a lot of television. Several marketers and ad professionals agree with her. But the fact that people have noticed and registered the Relaxo ads with Salman Khan is moot. "While urban consumers may dismiss such advertising as silly, Ram in rural India may not," Trivikram Thakore, marketing director, Fashionandyou.com, pointed out.

This fashion e-commerce portal has signed on one-film (Rockstar) actress Nargis Fakhri as a brand ambassador. Myntra.com has signed on actor Chitrangada Singh and Yepme.com has roped in Kangana Ranaut. Desai observed that while celebrities draw attention to the ads and brands, they don't necessarily induce purchase. "If something new is endorsed by a celebrity, I would try it out." On the use of TV actors for endorsements, she said: "We see them in serials daily and are familiar with their screen characters. In ads too, we recognise them as their screen personalities."

On whether bringing in celebrities – who at the upper end charge Rs. 10-15 crore for a campaign – can influence buying decisions, Thakore said, "People will buy based on what a brand and product offers. But when product clutter leaves very little left to differentiate, using a celebrity can catch attention. And if many celebrities are used simultaneously, like Pepsi did with Indian cricketers Dhoni, Kohli, Harbajan, Raina versus football sensations Drogba, Torres and Lampard in its 'Change the Game' ad campaign, it makes for high impact."

D'damas

Ashish Mishra, head of Water and Interbrand India operations, added: "There are more celebs in ads simply because today there are more celebs. An increasing number of brands, with their urgency to register themselves quickly in a short rope business environment, are resorting to the celebrity fillip. Celebrity surely gets a fillip; whether the brand does too is a very different matter, of course." Tim Lindsey, CEO of the UK-headquartered D&AD, which awards and trains the international design, advertising and creative industries, said, "Celebrity advertising is mostly lazy advertising. However, using a celebrity over a period of time to build a brand can be effective."

One such brand is L'Oreal, which has endorsement deals with 12 celebrities internationally. In India, it uses Aishwarya Rai and Sonam Kapoor for its hair care brands and Freida Pinto for its make-up range. "L'oreal Paris is about glamour. Our brand ambassadors are stars in their own right. We have long term relationships with them, something consumers connect with," said Ghosh. While L'Oreal has had Aishwarya Rai on board for close to 12 years, it has had Sonam Kapoor for four years and Frieda Pinto for three. Ghosh said that using celebrities successfully involves an entire science behind the advertising process including product quality and values, production value, story board, advertising relevance to the consumer and media planning.

Some brands that have already been using celebrities to tell their stories are now adding on even more. Nescafe, which uses film actor Deepika Padukone and TV actor Purab Kohli in its ongoing campaign, brought in funnyman Vir Das and film producer Karan Johar in different ads. Its current ad has added on music (team) biggies Shankar, Ehsaan and Loy to Padukone and Kohli. Fast Relief, the painkiller ointment, uses sportspersons Zaheer Khan, Sushil Kumar and Mary Kom in its latest ad.

As the growing clutter of celebrity ads jostle for attention, the outcomes are bound to be mixed. "Except in cases where the celebrity tells the brand story effectively, this ad format can be expensive and deliver poor economic outcomes . There is also the danger of the celebrity being bigger than the brand and taking attention away from it," said Lindsey.

Marketing Insight 14.5

Ad Wars Rage Again

Dettol Kitchen Gel

The days of no-holds-barred advertising wars between major brands are gone – or are they? A recent flurry of full-page ads with competitive claims, and TVCs in which brands take sly potshots at each other are keeping the spirt of marketing warfare alive.

2013: Reckitt Benckiser Vs HUL

Reckitt Benckiser launches Dettol Kitchen and follows it up with a TV ad comparing the cleaning product with HUL's Vim. HUL appealed to the Calcutta High Court for a stay order, saying the ads were untrue, but was denied. It then hit back with ads on front pages of mainline dailies claiming Lifebuoy works better than Dettol antiseptic liquid – HUL's ad says it has been 'issued in public interest'

2012 Hyundai Vs Maruti Suzuki

Traditional Japanese and Korean rivalry came to the fore again when Korea's Hyundai Motor went ballistic with its marketing campaign 'Trendsetter V/s Follower' on claims of a much-superior small car EON over the newly launched Alto 800 from Maruti Suzuki

Micromax Vs Samsung

Micromax took a not-so-subtle dig at Samsung, with its latest ad campaign styled as a 'sequel' to Samsung's GalaxyY TVCs. The films brought out the product features through dialogue delivered by spunky kids, ending with the same question: "Aapke paas nahi hai, Uncle?" Micromax responded with a series of films that pick up where the Samsung ads end — the last few words spoken in the Samsung ads are the first words in the Micromax ads. The plot, theme, script and appearance of the ads have been crafted to look similar to the Samsung ads, so much so that at first glance, one assumes it is a sequel to the Samsung campaign.

The Times of India Vs The Hindu

TOI launched 'the Wake Up!' campaign last year, featuring Chennai readers being put to sleep by a newspaper full of boring news. In an attempt to hit back hard Hindu told its readers to 'Stay Ahead of the Times' by reading news that was relevant to current affairs instead of Bollywood and celebrity gossip. Television commercials as well as print ads kept the battle between the two publications going.

Micromax

Micromax Vs Apple

Micromax took a jab at iPhone with the tagline "i (can afford this)", for its A 70 smartphone, priced at 8,000. When Apple launched the iPhone 4S, Micromax went a step further, releasing new ads for the A75 model that used the tagline "i (can afford this) Phone 4S(ure)".

2011: Ford Vs Other Car Companies

Ford India 'Swap the drive' campaign in 2011 challenged multiple players. Through this campaign, Ford engaged directly with owners of nine competing car brands, who were given the opportunity to swap their vehicles with models for a week-long test drive. The company then created ads that showed these consumers' comparisons of their own vehicles vs Ford's, prominently featuring the names of rival brands such as Maruti Swift, Maruti Dzire and Toyota Fortuner.

2010: Hindustan Unilever Vs P&G

In HUL's Rin commercial, a pack of Tide Natural, the brand owned by rival Procter & Gamble, was prominently displayed with a voiceover "Tide se kahin behtar safedi de Rin." And HUL's Clinic All Clear Shampoo spoofed P&G's Head & Shoulders, when it showed Bollywood actress Bipasha Basu searching for a girl with zero dandruff. One girl who does have dandruff mentions the name of her shampoo, making a muted reference to Head & Shoulders.

2009: NESTLE Vs CADBURY

Nestle launched a spoof on a Cadbury ad with tag line, "Khao bina tareekh dekhe" directly challenging Cadbury which had advertised its brand with a tagline "Meetha hai khana aaj pehli tareekh hai".

2008: COMPLAN Vs HORLICKS

In September 2008, GSK's Horlicks showed Horlicks as a better and cheaper option than Complan, in terms of nutritional value and market price.

21st March 2013 ET Team

Sales Promotion

Sales promotion is a very effective tool in the promotional mix. It helps to induce the sales on the consumer side as well as the marketing channel or trade side. Sales promotion is a variety of short term incentives to encourage trial or purchase of a product or service. Consumer-oriented sales promotion efforts are targeted towards the ultimate user. It contains free samples, rebates, Gifts, Contests, More quantity, Low interest financing, Fairs & Trade Shows, Demos and Lotteries. While Trade-oriented sales promotion is targeted towards marketing channels like Distributors, Wholesalers and Retailers. It includes volume discounts, promotional and merchandising allowances, price deals, free offers, sales contests etc.

Marketing Insight 14.6

Companies Offer Freebies to Beat Slowdown Blues

From gyms to smartphones, consumers wooed with discounts to spur demand

Samsung Galaxy

Sign up for three months and get the 4th month membership free, screams an ad from Talwalkars. The fitness chain is not the only one luring consumers using the good old marketing mantra of discounts. Beauty salons have announced "happy hours", while aspirers of high-end mobile phones are flashing iPhones and Samsung Galaxy phones, thanks to equated monthly instalment (EMI) schemes and cash-back offers on some of these iconic brands.

Consumers never had it so good in a long time. From consumer electronics and automobiles to hotels and real estate, freebies and discount schemes are being offered in a more innovative way than before — all that to spur demand at a time when the consumer sentiment is low. While Standard Chartered is offering a 5% cash back on EMI transactions for the iPhone 4 for a limited period, there is a 15% cash back on select Samsung Galaxy phones on a 12-month EMI programme. Six-month and 12-month EMIs, said Vijay Sales' managing partner, Nilesh Gupta, are driving sales of high-end mobile phones. Others like Sony Xperia Z are throwing in free accessories.

Discount schemes in the consumer durables and consumer electronics sector, where growth has been flat, are different, largely because it's a longterm purchase. Onida is offering zero down payment, zero interest rate and no processing fee, free installation and exchange benefits of up to Rs 10,000. There are certain airconditioning brands offering free installation, which is like an indirect discount of around Rs 1,500-2,000. Even on low-value items such as cookware, Sunflame is offering Rs 1,000 discount on select products.

A top consumer durables company CEO, who didn't wish to be identified, said the industry is facing one of its worst periods as most consumer goods companies, be it in auto or durables, had planned extra capacities based on the bullishness after comfortably tiding over the slowdown of 2008-09. Discounts and schemes help in clearing inventory and driving revenues, which are either flat or negative, except for mobile phones, he said. To cash in on the ongoing IPL cricket season, Sony had launched a special EMI scheme on Bravia flat panel televisions, wherein consumers could purchase Bravia with a down-payment of Rs 2,999 and 9 EMIs per month, with zero processing fees. Others are also making competitive offers.

In automobiles, where EMIs are popular, Volkswagen launched a unique scheme which offers a new Vento in a tradeoff for an old car. All the consumer pays is Re 1 and nothing at all for one year. Select Skoda dealers were offering a Fabia hatchback free on the purchase of a Rapid sedan, albeit the customer would get the Fabia after five years. In the luxury segment, BMW is offering up to 100% finance on ex-showroom and consumers have the option to pay 50% of the loan in three years on the BMW 5 Series and the 3 Series. Besides, there is no service and maintenance cost for three years or 60,000 km. Similarly, Mercedes has introduced flexible finance options which include complimentary maintenance.

Tanishq

Mahindra & Mahindra, on the other hand, is offering benefits of up to Rs 70,000 on Xylo. "When competition heats up, we usually see more competitiveness in pricing...

discounts are a regional phenomenon and it depends on the inventories or the demand in a given market," said Pravin Shah, chief executive, automotive division, M&M.

Discounts and freebies, primarily the preserve of FMCG companies, are now being used across categories to free up inventory and turn non-peak hours more profitable. So, Lakme Salons have announced "happy hours" during week days from 10 am to 3 pm wherein a customer gets a discount of 20% on a bill value of Rs 400.

The fact that even gold, silver and petrol prices are down would bolster the low consumer sentiment. So select jewellers are wooing consumers even before Akshaya tritiya in May. Geetanjali jewellers, for one, is offering branded watches worth Rs 4,000 free on a purchase of Rs 15,000 on its diamond jewellery brand. Sales by retail chains for their clothing line is also a common sight.

With inflation sliding to a three-year low and if rate cut talks by the RBI materialize, consumers could definitely feel the balm. Besides food, clothing and accessories, what could perhaps be the icing on the cake for the consumer is that dream home which has moved out of reach. Staring at dismal sales, real estate companies have realized they have to offer value to lure consumers back. So when L&T launched a scheme at around Rs 15,000 per sq ft some time back at Mumbai's Powai, while the prevailing prices were in the region of Rs 20,000 and above, they were immediately able to sell a substantial part of the project. Apart from value offerings, some like Shapoorji Pallonji offered a project in Kandivili, a western suburb of Mumbai, at Rs 11,650 per sq ft under a 20:80 scheme. The scheme entails that a consumer makes a down payment of 20% and the rest is tied through a bank loan with the developer bearing the interest component, either till possession or for a fixed period. Bombay Dyeing has launched a variation of this 20:80 scheme, which enables an individual to pay just 20% and the balance at the time of possession.

Besides, developers are reconfiguring their pre-launch schemes. Earlier, these were offered two to three months before the project was launched, but now that is being done for periods of up to two years, with a discount. Some are even allowing the first transfer of property before the mandatory lockin of two to three years without charging a transfer fee. Others are throwing in cars as well. Delhi also has a spattering of such schemes, the only difference being that developers generally allow re-sales without charging transfer fees. "Low residential sales due to increase in prices over last two years has encouraged developers to resort to innovative payment plans like 20:80 or take loan with principal & interest assigned to developer until possession. Some are offering kitchen or household items as part of package, special discounts are also encouraged for those who are willing to pay full payment or 50% to 70%...," said Sanjay Dutt, executive MD, South Asia, Cushman & Wakefield.

And for those who were planning to give this year's holiday season a miss, think again. Taking a cue from FMCG companies, MakeMyTrip is offering a BOGOF (buy one get one free) on domestic airline tickets, albeit on the base fare only, at a time when the holiday season has just started. Similarly Swisstours is offering up to 50% discount on mountain railways and free entry to nearly 400 museums along with free travel for children under 16. Cox & Kings on the other hand is giving customers cash back of Rs 10,000 per couple if tickets are booked before a certain deadline. Hotels are not far behind either with several hotel chains including Oberoi Hotels offering schemes which throw in additional nights free.

Big Bazaar

Most of the FMCG and Consumer Durable and Automobile companies like Dabur, Priya Gold Biscuits, Proctor & Gamble, Electrolux, Videocon, Onida, Samsung, Maruti, Chevrolet etc go for consumer as well as trade promotion offers. While pharmaceutical companies give more emphasis on trade related sales promotion schemes towards Chemist Shops and Doctors.[6] Organised retailers like Big Bazaar, Reliance Digital, Spencer's etc. also come out with promotional schemes from time to time.

The sales promotion schemes should be used carefully by the company, as it has a negative impact on the brand image. Generally every year, leading apparel companies like Park Avenue, Arrow, Zodiac, Blackberry come out with the Stock Clearance Sale once in a year in the rainy season or twice in a year. On the contrary, brands like Koutons, Cotton County, and Priknit sell their apparels through discount offers almost all round the year. This leads to erosion in the brand image of these companies.

Cotton County

In marketing, the terms - promotion and sales promotion are often confused. Promotion is the part of the marketing mix, while sales promotion is a part of promotional mix. Promotion includes advertising, direct selling, personal selling, public relations, internet and interactive marketing besides sales promotion. Sometimes the term promotion is used alternatively for sales promotion.

Marketing Insight 14.7

Marketing Insight 14.7

White Goods Cos in Shop-Floor Push for Sales

Focus on training sales attendants at places where actual purchases take place

Panasonic

Actor couple Kajol and Ajay Devgn may well be cajoling you to buy Whirlpool fridges and washing machines on television, but the US appliances maker is increasingly betting more on inconspicuous shop-floor attendants and sales representatives to boost its sales in India. Whirlpool's ratio of spending on below-the-line activities versus mass-media advertising was 70:30 last calendar year, while it was 50:50 in 2011. Close to 90% of below-the-line budget goes into shop-floor activities.

And Whirlpool is not alone. Most consumer durable and appliance makers including Videocon, LG, Samsung and Panasonic are steadily increasing their investments on shop-floor activities such as sales promotions, in store branding and product demonstration as they find it a highly effective way to push sales.

"Unlike, say, toothpaste, consumers of appliances are not frequent buyers. If we invest on advertising but don't do enough on the point-of-sale, it would be harakiri," Shantanu Dasgupta, vice president of corporate affairs and strategy, South Asia, at Whirlpool, says. "Even as overall A&P (advertising and promotions) budgets remain tight due to a low demand scenario, absolute spends on BTL will actually increase in 2013," he adds.

Videocon, the country's third largest durable maker, has tripled spends on BTL activities over the last two years, and now almost half of its Rs. 200-crore marketing budget goes into BTL activities. "Most of the marketing spends are invested on in-store branding and shop demonstrators who can explain technology and brand's edge over competitors," CM Singh, chief operating officer at Videocon, says.

The country's estimated Rs. 40,000-crore consumer electronics industry reported flat volume growth last year, with white goods such as refrigerators, ACs, washing machine and microwave ovens reporting fall in sales. The reasons for this included a slowdown in consumer spending and substantial price increases due to rising input costs and devaluation of the rupee. However, the industry is expecting a 5% volume growth in sales this year after five straight years of bleak demand, as there has been no substantial price hike this year with commodity prices having stabilised.

To make the most of this expected revival in demand, white goods makers are focusing more on the shop floor, retail point-of-sale activation and training sales attendants at places where actual purchases are clinched. "The focus on product demonstration at the shop floor is a growing trend across industry, whether it's audio video products, home appliances or smart devices," Mahesh Krishnan, senior VP — consumer electronics at Samsung India, says.

Japanese consumer electronics major Panasonic, which increased its marketing budget to Rs. 400 crore this fiscal from Rs. 350 crore last, too is spending almost half of it offline including shopfloor activity and road shows.

"Product has become the hero and differentiation is key to success, which can be addressed more through BTL," Panasonic MD Manish Sharma says, adding that focus on experiential marketing is on a continuous upswing. LG now spends around 45-50% of its overall budget on BTL line activation, while Godrej Appliances plans to spend almost 40% of its Rs. 130-crore marketing budget on BTL this fiscal.

Public Relations

Public relations (PR) is gaining importance day by day as a communication tool in the promotional mix. The importance of Public relations has been well written by Al Ries with Laura Ries, one of the famous authors of 'Positioning – The Battle for Your Mind', in their book 'The Fall of Advertising and the Rise of PR'. In the early 1900s, Edward Louis Bernays, the founding father of modern public relations, along with Ivy Lee has defined Public Relations as

'the Management function which evaluates public attitudes, identifies the policies and procedures of an individual or organisation with the public interest and executes a programme of action to earn public understanding and acceptance.'

In Encyclopedia of public relations, 2005, Robert L. Heath has defined PR as,

'a set of management, supervisory, and technical functions that foster an organization's ability to strategically listen to, appreciate, and respond to those persons whose mutually beneficial relationships with the organization are necessary if it is to achieve its missions and values.'

Public Relations is a variety of programmes systematically designed and distributed to promote or protect a company's image or products. PR tools consist of Press Kits, Seminars, Speeches, Publications, Lobbying, Company Magazine, Events, Sponsorships, Donations and Annual Reports.

Philip Kotler has coined a term called PENCILS of PR, where he talks about publications, events, news, community involvement, identity tools, lobbying and social investments; as the tools of modern PR.

Public Relations always generate a 'buzz' around a new product or service. Generally the consumers are less skeptical toward the PR exercises. It also involves low cost, as there is no direct expenditure to buy the time or space in a channel or a publication. When Tata Motors showcased its Nano Car on 10th January, 2008 at the 9th Annual Auto Expo at Pragati Maidan, New Delhi, almost all the leading newspapers, magazines, TV channels etc. from India and across the world covered the presentation. The amount of coverage, it got from the channels and publications is unthinkable and

Dabangg 2

worth thousands of Crores. On the same lines, in Bollywood, Aamir Khan always looks out for innovative means of PR for his upcoming films, whether it's Ghajini or 3 Idiots. Taking a cue from this, even Salman Khan did a lot of activities for creating the right buzz for his film 'Dabangg'. On the eve of release of music of Dabangg, one of the leading television news channel devoted more than 20 minutes of its program for the event. In another smart move the music has been launched in Delhi instead of the usual Mumbai, probably owing to the fact that the notion of dabangai is more pronounced in Delhi and up the hinterland as compared to Mumbai and the adjoining areas where it is more of the Bhaigiri. Again, Salman Khan was almost on all the channels to promote his film.[7] It was a similar case for its sequel 'Dabangg 2' also.

Sometimes, Public Relations and Publicity are used intermittingly. But PR has a broader objective than the publicity. Publicity refers to non personal communications regarding an organisation, product, service or idea not directly paid for or run under identified sponsorship. It also includes News story, Editorial or announcement about an organisation and/or its product or services through news releases, press conferences, feature article, photos, films and videos. But there is a difference. Publicity is not always under the control of the organisation and is sometimes unfavourable. The film reviews, which you see in Times of India, Hindustan Times or on the websites like Rediff or on Bollywood Hungama becomes a part of the publicity; as the reviewers are not under the control of the film production companies. It happened also in the debacle of 'Chandni Chowk to China', where everybody wrote the film off and it generated a bad publicity for the film.

The public relations and publicity space has also changed with the technological advancements like Internet and Mobile technology. Now there are more people, who are blogging, besides the celebrities and experts. Anybody can voice their opinion through blogs or through websites like Mouthshut.com. Now you can also find online communities for various products and services on Facebook, Orkut or Twitter. A company needs to utilize these developments in technology to become efficient and effective marketer.

Direct Marketing

With the success of Eureka Forbes, Aquaguard, Amway, Dell, Tupperware and Avon, direct marketing is becoming popular for many companies. In direct marketing, companies communicate directly with their target customers to generate a response and/or a transaction. Direct marketing is much more than direct mail and mail-order catalogs. It involves a variety of activities, including database management, direct selling, telemarketing, and direct-response ads through direct mail, the Internet, and various broadcast and print media.[5] Recently Hypercity Retail India has launched its catalogue shopping retail format called Hypercity – Argos.

With more importance on touch and feel by the Indian consumers, direct marketing companies are also taking the route of opening their representative stores to build reliability about their products. On these lines, Dell has opened its exclusive stores to offer the advantages of Dell's direct model with the additional benefit of retail availability to browse touch and feel the product. Dell's channel model is also making it possible for the Indian customers to see the products on the retail shelves and then place an order for the preferred model with the choice to customise the looks and configuration of the unit. On the similar lines, Hypercity –Argos has also launched their first store in Mumbai. After referring the catalogue, they can collect their products from the nearest store or have it home delivered. Thus, consumers can shop in three ways: by placing their orders over the phone, visit the stores or browse the entire range online at www.hypercityargos.com.

Dell Ad

Direct marketing companies regularly advertise their products through direct response ads with mass media vehicles like Newspaper, Magazines, Radio and Television. Dell regularly advertises in computer and technology magazines like Digit, Chip, PC World and business magazines like Business World, Business Today besides through Times of India, Economic Times and Hindustan Times. Direct market companies are also gaining ground with usage of Mobile, Internet and online payment.

Personal Selling

Personal selling involves two way communications, as the seller gets into face to face interaction with the buyer. The buyer may be a single person or there may be many buyers at the same point of time. Here the seller or sales representative from the company makes a presentation and answers queries of the buyers. If the buyer is convinced, the sales representative gets the order for the product. As it gives an immediate feedback, the personal selling is a powerful tool in the promotional mix. It happens through sales presentation at home or offices, in Sales meetings and through Fairs and Trade Shows. Hindustan Unilever also sells its water purifier 'Pureit' through a direct marketing and personal selling exercise. The only drawback is that it's an expensive tool to promote a product, as you need to manage a sales force to get the desired results. But it is also the most flexible way of marketing communication with great results.

Digital Marketing

In the last twenty years, the consumer behaviour has changed a lot with the proliferation of Internet all across the world. The advancement in technology has led to create a separate space of digital marketing as the promotional medium among the other tools available under IMC. Earlier it was limited to Internet marketing. Now, it has expanded too much.

> According to Wikipedia, **"Digital marketing is marketing that makes use of electronic devices (computers) such as personal computers, smartphones, cell phones, tablets and game consoles to engage with stakeholders. Digital marketing applies technologies or platforms such as websites, e-mail, apps (classic and mobile) and social networks. Social Media Marketing is a component of digital marketing. Many organisations use a combination of traditional and digital marketing channels."**

Facebook Twitter

In other promotional tools, the communication is one sided. Here the consumer can interact and can give feedback or response to the company. It has become almost mandatory for every company now to promote itself through a website on the internet. Internet is a unique promotional tool, as it can also execute all the elements of the promotional mix. Internet itself can promote a product. It can also be used as a medium for advertising. For example, on www.indiatimes.com, an advertiser gets options like Shosh – Sttlilng, Slug Specs, Shosh – Flash Frame Spot, Video Banners, Monster Banner, Leader banner and Pop Ups to name a few. Internet also acts as a direct marketing tool by having a consumer response form on the web page or through a link. Tata Indigo Manza, Tata Indica Vista, ICICI Prudential, Dell, ICFAI Business School, Tata AIG advertises regularly through banner ads on rediff.com, indiatimes.com and yahoo.com, with either a consumer response form or once clicked, it leads to a consumer response form.

Marketing Insight 14.8

Digital Advertising Spend to Grow the Most in 2014

Given the current economic scenario, growth in advertising spends this year will continue to be modest. Advertising budgets are projected to grow by 11.6 per cent as opposed to 10 per cent (from Rs 38,598 crore to Rs 43,065 crore) last year, according to the 'This Year, Next Year 2014' report released by the WPP group's media planning and media buying arm, Group M.

This year's growth may ostensibly appear higher than last year's but actual growth, according to C.V.L. Srinivas, CEO, South Asia, Group M, will be lower, at nine per cent. How come? "Almost 2.5 per cent of the growth will be due to ad spends by various political parties in the forthcoming election campaign," Srinivas added.

The biggest beneficiary of advertising spends this year will be digital advertising which is expected to grow by 35 per cent over last year at Rs 3,042 crore. TV advertising which grew by 13.8 per cent last year is expected to grow by 12.8 per cent this year, while print is expected to witness eight per cent growth vis-Ã -ẏis four per cent in 2013.

Group M also launched M Trends, which listed the likely trends that would dominate the media in 2014. One such is 'adversioning', which will enable brands to engage in micro-targeting and micro-messaging. Thus, a brand which caters to say, just the states of Gujarat and Maharashtra, can advertise on a nationally broadcast TV channel and yet micro-target only the markets of Gujarat and Maharashtra, while the rest of India would watch another commercial. M Tends also predicts further growth of the vernacular media not only in TV and print but also in digital.

The current controversy over TV ratings - TAM ratings may not be available thanks to a cabinet decision - could well lead to a period of ratings darkness this year. This will definitely create confusion in the industry as TV viewership rating is the only metric on the basis of which advertisers decide their TV spends. However M Trends says there could be light at the end of the tunnel, as new low cost technologies could emerge that offer alternative measurement metrics.

Internet also helps in sales promotion efforts of the company. Whenever a company likes to give a short term incentive to the consumer, internet also becomes one of the ways to reach consumers. Many companies also send their offers to the consumer mail boxes. Internet also helps in Public relations and publicity exercises. Many companies and PR firms use Internet to build a public relations campaign. Now with the increased use of community websites like Facebook, Orkut, Twitter etc, consumers are connected through the Internet. That's why even Bollywood is also using Internet for promoting its films.

Besides internet marketing, digital marketing also include mobile marketing through SMS and MMS, Social Media marketing using Facebook, Twitter etc., Search Engine marketing Or any other form of digital media.

Monitoring, Evaluation and Control

Once the promotional plan is implemented, it needs to be monitored and evaluated. The objective of the company is matched with the outcomes from the promotional campaigns. The objective may be awareness or it may be enhancing the brand image or it can be more sales. Whatever may be the result, the company can take necessary efforts in making it more productive. It is done by changing either the creative strategy or the media strategy or by both.

Under the creative strategy, a company can modify its message and can promote it in a different way or it can use different media vehicles to promote the product or service in the right way. Taking the control, a company can achieve its promotional objectives with tools of Integrated Marketing Communication to create awareness and / or to encourage sales of the products and services.

Summary

- Integrated marketing communications (IMC) deals with the fourth P of marketing i.e. Promotion. Promotion is the coordination of all the efforts, the company undertakes to aware and persuade the consumers to buy goods and services.
- The process of marketing communication passes through nine major components. There are two major parties – Sender and Receiver in the communication process and two communication tools – Message and Media. In the process, four communication

functions are involved – Encoding, Decoding, Response and Feedback. Besides these, there is noise, which falls in the process of communication.

- As a marketer, you need to communicate the customers in such a way, to make them purchase your products. This kind of communications planning requires six M's to be taken care of. The first three Ms – market, mission and message, are meant for the strategy part and the other three –media, money and measurement, are meant for the implementation part.
- Communication vehicles like Television, Magazine, Newspapers and Radio fall among the mass communication vehicles, while Direct Mail, Catalogues, Infomercial, E-mail and Telemarketing offers two way communications to the marketer. In the case of telemarketing, it becomes instantaneous, while in the case e-mail, is' almost instant. But in the case of Direct mail, catalogue and infomercials, it has a time lag in response.
- The consumer goes through different stages before landing on to the actual purchase. These stages can be understood more clearly by the various consumer response hierarchy models like AIDA Model given by E. K. Strong, Hierarchy of Effects Model given by Robert J. Lavidge and Gary A. Steiner and Innovation Adoption Model given by Everett M. Rogers.
- IMC deals with all the Sources of brand and company contact that a customer or prospect has with a product or service. It takes 'Big Picture' approach to planning marketing and promotion programmes and coordinating the various communication functions.
- There are several advantages of IMC in the ever changing world. The biggest advantage is that it creates synergy among the various promotional tools.
- IMC uses six tools to reach its target markets and to build its brand equity. These tools are also called elements of Promotional Mix. These tools are: Advertising, Sales Promotion, Public Relations, Personal Selling, Direct Marketing and Internet and Interactive Marketing.
- Advertising is defined as any paid form of non personal presentation and promotion of ideas, goods or services by an identified sponsor. Advertising includes Print Advertisement, Television Commercials (TVC), Directories, Billboards, Hoardings, Banners, Posters, Brochure & Booklets, Audio Visual Material, Display Signs and POP Displays.
- In direct marketing, companies communicate directly with their target customers to generate a response and/or a transaction. It involves a variety of activities, including database management, direct selling, telemarketing, and direct-response ads through direct mail, the Internet, and various broadcast and print media.
- The advancement in technology has led to create Internet as the promotional medium among the other tools available under IMC. Interactive Media through Internet, Interactive TV, Kiosks and CD-ROMs allows for two way information flow.

- Internet is a unique promotional tool, as it can also execute all the elements of the promotional mix. Internet itself can promote a product. It can also be used as a medium for advertising.
- Sales promotion is a variety of short term incentives to encourage trial or purchase of a product or service. Consumer-oriented sales promotion efforts are targeted towards the ultimate user. It helps to induce the sales on the consumer side as well as the marketing channel or trade side.
- Public Relations is a variety of programmes systematically designed and distributed to promote or protect a company's image or products. PR tools consist of Press Kits, Seminars, Speeches, Publications, Lobbying, Company Magazine, Events, Sponsorships, Donations and Annual Reports.
- Personal selling involves two way communications, as the seller gets into face to face interaction with the buyer.
- Once the promotional plan is implemented, it needs to be monitored and evaluated. The objective of the company is matched with the outcomes from the promotional campaigns.

Discussion Questions

1. Define Integrated Marketing Communications? Discuss its tools with examples.
2. What do you mean by promotion? Discuss the promotional mix in marketing.
3. Explain the process of Communication. Discuss six M's models for communication planning.
4. Write a note on Indian Advertising Industry.
5. Discuss the consumer response hierarchy model–AIDA Model, Hierarchy of Effects Model and Innovation Adoption Model.
6. Discuss the advantages of IMC in this dynamic business environment, with relevant examples.
7. Define Advertising. Discuss the difference between advertising to consumer markets and business markets.
8. Define Public Relations. Discuss the difference between publicity and Public Relations.
9. What do you mean by sales promotion? Discuss trade oriented sales promotion with relevant examples.

10. How Internet can be used as a promotional tool? How can it be used to execute all the elements of the promotional mix?
11. What is the difference between direct marketing and personal selling? Discuss the success of a direct marketing company in India.
12. Short Notes:
    a. Personal Selling
    b. Direct Marketing
    c. AIDA Model
    d. Communication Process
    e. Consumer response hierarchy models
    f. Publicity
    g. IMC

References

1. Robert J. Dolan, 'Integrated Marketing Communications', Harvard Business School Notes, 2000, Note 9-599-087
2. Robert J. Dolan, 'Integrated Marketing Communications', Harvard Business School Notes, 2000, Note 9-599-087
3. Anushree Chandran, 'India's ad industry to grow 9% in 2010: study', livemint.com, April 14, 2010
4. AIDA – E. K. Strong, 'The Psychology of Selling', McGraw Hill, 1925, p.9; Hierarchy of Effects – Robert J. Lavidge and Gary A. Steiner, 'A Model for Predictive Measurements of Advertising Effectiveness', Journal of Marketing, Oct., 1961, 61; Innovation Adoption – Everett M. Rogers, 'Diffusion of Innovation', The Free Press, 1962, pp.79-86
5. Philip Kotler, Marketing Management, Pearson Education, 11th Edition, 2004
6. Philip Kotler, Marketing Management, Pearson Education, 11th Edition, 2004
7. Enkayaar, Bollywood Trade News Network, 'Dabangg and the Art of marketing of a film redefined', August 7, 2010

CHAPTER 15

Rural Marketing

Chapter Structure

“The soul of India lives in its villages”

- Mahatma Gandhi

Hindustan Unilever is excited with the opportunity to continue to serve the 800 million consumers in rural India and be a part of this great journey into the future.”

- Mr. Harish Manwani, Global COO, Unilver

Rural Marketing

Rural India

India's rural markets offer unprecedented opportunities for marketers due to its vast size and demand base. Out of the 121 crore Indians, 83.3 crore live in rural areas; that accounts for 68.84% of the total population.[1] If we compare the same on global level, then we find that India's rural population comprises of 12% of the world's population; while it is twice that of Western Europe's population.

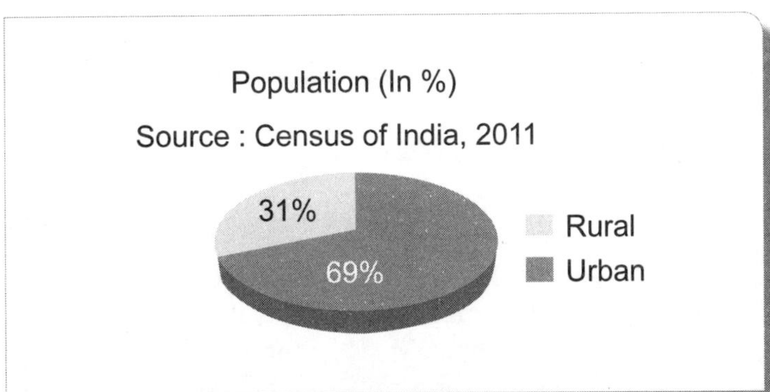

Population (In %)

In India, the rural population is spread over 3,200 small towns and 6,27,000 villages. The market is so huge that close to a third of FMCG and durable sales is contributed by rural markets. LIC sells more than 55% policies in the rural areas. Maruti's sells around 28% cars in the rural markets. Even more than 50% mobile subscribers of BSNL live in small towns and villages. TV penetration has also gone high with penetration level reaching to

39.8% in 2010 from 31% in 2007. Two wheelers penetration has also gone up to 13.9% from 9.5% in the same period.

Life Insurance Corporation of India

In the last few years, Kisan Credit Card has also led the rural market to grow by providing tremendous liquidity through its 41 million cards, compared to 22 million credit plus debit cards circulation in urban areas. All of these facts make the India's rural markets, a very lucrative proposition for the local as well as global companies.

Marketing Insight 15.1

Marketing Insight 15.1

Gearing up for Rural Ride

With their breadand-butter metro markets showing no signs of a demand pick-up, car companies are increasingly focusing more on non-metro, semi-urban and rural markets. Big volume carmakers like Maruti, Hyundai and GM currently get upwards of a quarter of their total sales from rural markets.

With rural and semi-urban demand for cars ruling at 19-25% in sharp contrast with the industry average of negative growth, carmakers are stepping on the gas to drive further into hinterland markets. Hyundai Motor India (HMI), for instance, has been steadily pushing its retail footprint into rural markets. The result: In 2012, 25% of the company's total sales volume came from rural markets. Bo Shin Seo, CEO & MD, Hyundai Motor India (HMI), said, "Hyundai has a strong network of touch points across the country. Our rural market strategy is to penetrate these markets by engaging customers to sustain growth and increase volumes. Our objective is to make our products easily available to firsttime buyers."

To achieve that objective, the company is looking to increase its access footprint. "In 2013, we will increase our sales and service network in these markets," said Seo. "Our target is to increase the dealership network from the current 355 to 385, rural sales outlets from 264 to 350 and sales branches from 173-190."

To achieve that objective, the company is looking to increase its access footprint. "In 2013, we will increase our sales and service network in these markets," said Seo. "Our target is to increase the dealership network from the current 355 to 385, rural sales outlets from 264 to 350 and sales branches from 173-190."

Same is the case for General Motors India, which has also been pushing into hinterland markets along with its new diesel focus. Like Hyundai, a healthy share of GM India's total sales come from rural markets. "Rural market's share in GM India's total sales is around 28-30%. And the growth in rural markets is approximately around 25%," said P Balendran, spokesman, GM India. "We are increasing network, doing road shows, etc, to improve our rural presence and we are running additional schemes for these markets in lieu of corporate discounts in metros," he added.

In Maruti's case, company officials announced earlier this month that its rural sales were up 19% this year. Maruti started its rural focus five years ago and since then, sources say, much of its market share gain has been on the back of sales in rural and semi-urban markets. Rural markets' share in Maruti's total sales has also increased sharply from around 4% in 2008 to around 28% now.

Mahatma Gandhi National Rural Employment Guarantee Act

India's rural markets are also important due to the fact that the growth rates in the rural markets are higher than the urban market growth. Again, recessionary trends do not affect the rural markets as much as it affects the urban markets. Further, with the income level rising in the rural areas on its own, due to increased activity and due to infusion of a lot of public money in terms of government schemes like Mahatma Gandhi National Rural Employment Guarantee Act (MNREGA), Swarnjayanti Gram Swarozgar Yojna (SGSY), Pradhan Mantri Rozgar Yojana (PMRY) etc., rural markets presents a tremendous business opportunity for an Indian marketer. Now, rural markets are also not solely about agriculture and have made a transition from thatched- roof houses and muddy roads to factories and cell phones, says a study by Credit Suisse. In rural India, manufacturing is also booming, as almost 75 per cent of the new factories have come up there during the last decade; contributing to 70 per cent of all new manufacturing jobs created. It has also been found that the income generated in the rural areas convert more into consumption, than savings as in the urban areas.

Defining Rural Markets

Most of India's rural population resides in villages that contain between 500 and 5,000 inhabitants. Even there are villages, where less than 500 people reside. As per the Census of India 2011, the rural sector means any place which meets the following criteria,

- A population of less than 5,000
- Density of population less than 400 per sq km and
- More than 25 per cent of the male working population is engaged in agricultural pursuits.[2]

According to the Planning Commission, a town with a maximum population of 15,000 is considered rural in nature.

The National Sample Survey Organisation (NSSO) defines rural as follows:

- An area with a population density of up to 400 per square kilometer,
- Villages with clear surveyed boundaries but no municipal board and
- A minimum of 75% of male working population involved in agriculture and allied activities.

NABARD defines all locations as rural, which contain a population up to 10,000.

Thus, the approaches for defining rural are quite different in all these institutions. Private companies such as FMCG and Consumer Durables also define rural on their own criteria.

Difference between Rural Marketing and Agricultural Marketing

Sometimes rural marketing is confused with Agricultural marketing. But it is different than agricultural marketing.

Agricultural marketing deals with marketing of agricultural produce from the rural areas to consumer as well as business market. Rural marketing deals with marketing of goods and services to the rural population.

Evolution of Rural Marketing in India

In the recent years, the rural markets of India have caught the fancy of MNCs and local companies alike. Now every company wants to play the rural game. Be it MNCs like Coke or Pepsi, LG or Samsung, Hindustan Unilever or P&G, Honda or Ford or local companies like Ghadi or Nirma, Britannia or Parle, Hero or Bajaj, Tata or M&M; now rural marketing is indispensable for all of them equally. But the scenario was different earlier. If we check out the evolution of rural marketing in India, we can classify the timeline into three distinct phases.

Phase 1: Prior to the 1960s

Prior to 1960s, rural marketing was in nascent stage and can be understood more in terms of Agricultural marketing. It was primarily about marketing the agricultural inputs and selling the rural products in rural as well as urban areas. Due to poor connectivity, poor infrastructure and poor communication, it was very difficult for the companies to market their products in rural areas.

Phase 2: 1960 to 1990

During 1960 to 1990, the growth of rural marketing was quite good. The credit for the same does not go to the marketers, but the credit goes to the two revolutions, which started taking shape in the beginning of the phase and made a long term impact on the rural India. These revolutions are Green Revolution and White Revolution. With the usage of high yielding varieties (HYV) of seeds and the increased use of chemical fertilizers and irrigation, green revolution made India self sufficient in food grains, with the increase in productivity due to the adoption of these new techniques. Norman Borlaug has been hailed as the Father of the Green Revolution, but M. S. Swaminathan is known as the 'Father of the Green Revolution in India'.

At the same point of time, another revolution was taking place in India in the area of milk production. Just like what green revolution did for food grains, white revolution did for milk production. India became the largest milk producer in the world from being milk deficient nation. The credit goes to Dr. Verghese Kurien, who is also known as the 'Father of the White Revolution'.

Amul Ad on Dr. Verghese Kurien

Both these revolutions along with governmental efforts through agencies like KVIC (Khadi and Village Industry Commission), Weavers Societies and handicrafts emporia brought the prosperity in the rural areas; which in turn created demand for FMCG and durable products besides the agricultural inputs. In FMCG and durable products, Nirma, Hindustan Lever (now known as Hindustan Unilever), Philips, Murphy, Usha etc. were popular; while in the agricultural inputs category, Escorts, Mahindra and Mahindra, Eicher, Shriram Fertilisers (now known as DCM Shriram Consolidated Ltd.), Indian Farmers Fertiliser Cooperative Limited (IFFCO)

Phase 3: After 1990

The real growth in the rural marketing has come only after 1990s, after the liberalization and globalization of the Indian economy. Specifically in the last fifteen years, the growth in the rural marketing has been tremendous. It is all due to increased spending by the government in rural areas with an act like Mahatma Gandhi National Rural Employment Act (MNREGA); which aims to guarantee the 'right to work' and ensure livelihood security in rural areas by providing at least 100 days of guaranteed wage employment in a financial year to every household, whose adult members volunteer to do unskilled manual work. All these governmental initiatives brought a lot of money to the rural markets, which ultimately created demand for various products. Overall also, the income of the masses has risen, which also led to increase in demand in rural areas.

Hero Splendor

Mahindra Bolero

Besides the income factor, the sheer size of rural markets also made companies to look after the rural markets in a more serious way. This seriousness can also be seen by the initiatives like Hindustan Unilever's Project Shakti and Operation Bharat, ITC's E-Choupal, Tata Motors' Neev, Titan's Goldplus etc., which has met with a great success in the rural markets. Companies like LG, Samsung, Nokia, Micromax, Maruti, Hyundai, Hero, Bajaj, Honda, LIC are leaving no stones unturned to grab more market share for their respective products. These companies are also coming out with innovative products to suit the rural masses.

Marketing Insight 15.2

Marketing Insight 15.2

Tata Companies' Rural Marketing Initiative

At a time when recession-hit multinationals are looking at India to capitalise on growing urban consumerism, the Tatas are delving deeper into the hinterland by increasing their focus on the burgeoning rural Indian market.

"A large part of the rural Indian market is under-penetrated and presents good opportunities," said Siddhartha Roy, Economic Advisor, Department of Economics & Statistics, Tata Group, while addressing a media roundtable. "The Indian rural market has gone beyond consumer products and agri-input marketing. Total rural income, which is now at around $572 billion, is estimated to reach $1.8 trillion by 2020-21," Dr. Roy added. He further said that India's retail FMCG market could grow from $10 billion presently to $100 billion by 2024-25. The rural market is now flush with funds, and, according to Mr. Roy, it " needs to be tapped." Real rural wages have gone up 7.7 per cent annually over the last five years.

Mr. Roy said that the consumer pattern seen in early 2000s in smaller towns was now being seen in rural areas . Several government-sponsored projects are responsible for this. Considering the vast potential of the rural market, at least four Tata Group companies are well-positioned to take advantage. These include Tata Motors, Titan Industries, Tata Chemicals and Tata Teleservices.

Two years ago, Tata Motors started a rural marketing initiative called 'Neev', which is yielding results. Neev has helped the company sell 1,500 more small commercial vehicles (CVs) per month in six states, and would cross 2,000 units in November. Sales through Neev today account for 8 per cent of the company's national sales volume of small CVs. "Through Neev, we sold more than 13,000 vehicles in the last two years. We will go national by end-2013 and estimate incremental sale of 70,000 units by then which will add $500 million to turnover,'" said Sandeep Kumar, Head-Sales & Marketing, Small Light and Intermediate CV, Tata Motors.

Goldplus, promoted by Titan Industries' Jewellery Division, sells jewellery in rural areas in four states. With 31 showrooms, it is focusedon creating awareness and educating rural customers about gold. "Starting from one store in Erode in 2005, we are aiming for a turnover of Rs. 800 crore in 2012-13," said N. Vaideeswaran, Head – Retail (Goldplus), Titan Industries.

Tata Chemicals is scaling up farm services and expanding its footprint in Bihar and West Bengal. Tata Teleservices wants to increase internet penetration and targeted value-added services to capitalize on increased mobile phone usage amongst rural households.

Rural Markets are Different

Rural markets are different form urban markets in many ways. Let us check the rural employment patterns from the figure below:

Rural Employment Patterns (Male)

Sector	Year – 1987 (% share in employment)	Year – 2004 (% share in employment)
Agriculture	75	67
Transport & Communication	2	8
Trade & Hotels	5	7
Construction	4	7
Manufacturing	7	8

It is clear from the above table that two third of the population is dependent on agriculture and its allied activities, while other people are dependent on transport and communication, trade and hotels, construction and manufacturing.

Now let us check out the rural income trends from the figure below:

Rural Income Trends

Annual Income (at 1998-99 prices, In Rs.)	1989-90 (% Households)	1998-99 (% Households)
<= 35,000	67.3	47.9
35,001 - 70,000	23.9	34.8
70,001 – 105,000	7.1	10.4
105,001 – 140,000	1.2	3.9
>140,000	0.5	3.0

It is obvious from the table that almost half of the population was earning equal to or less than Rs. 35,000/- per annum in 1998-99. Now if we check out the overall population below Rs. 70,000/- per annum, then this figure rises to almost four fifth of the total rural population. Thus on an average, in rural areas, most of the population is earning less than Rs. 6,000/- a month and almost half of the population was earning less than Rs. 3,000/- a month. This figure has improved in the last fifteen years and now being reduced to around two third of the population under Rs. 6,000/- per month bracket.

Dr. C. K. Prahalad

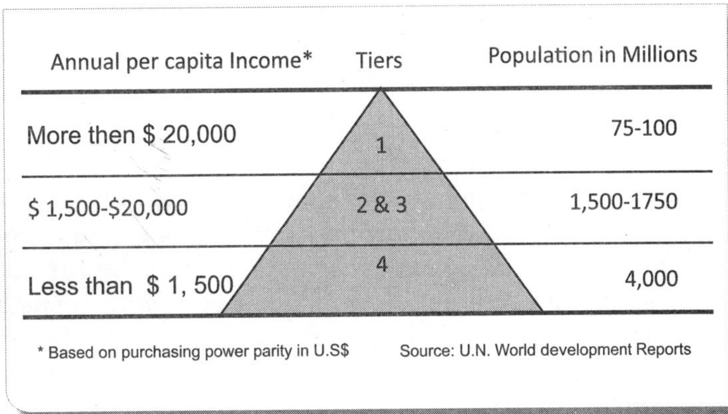

The World Economic Pyramid

The income bracket is the same as was discussed by Dr. C. K. Prahalad in his book 'The Fortune at the Bottom of the Pyramid' in 2004. As can be seen from the World Economic Pyramid above, four billion people lie in tier 4 at the bottom of the pyramid; who earns less than $1500 in a year. At the rate of Rs. 62 to a dollar, that translates into Rs. 93,000/- per annum. According to C. K. Prahalad, Tier 4 markets represent an exceptional opportunity for the marketers. The same is the case in rural India.

Thus, most of the rural population has a very low disposable income. The income is also generated on a day to day basis, as most of them work as daily wage worker or earn through trading, retailing or any other activity. This leads to the philosophy of 'Earn Today, Spend Today'. Thus rather than buying in bulk, they buy in small quantities for day to day consumption. Most of the rural households have also minimal storage space, which makes it better for them to buy in lesser quantity. Another characteristic of the rural markets is that demand for consumer durables, two wheelers, cars etc. are also seasonal in nature. Rural customers generally buy during post harvest period, marriages, festivals and on special occasions. All of these characteristics make rural marketing very different from urban marketing.

Rural Marketing Mix

Now the question arises, will the marketing mix i.e. 4Ps – product, price, place and promotion; which we generally use for urban marketing, be effective in the rural marketing scenario also. The answer is primarily yes, because whichever market, you market your products; you will require these tools. But in the rural market scenario, these tools can be seen from a different angle, as given in the table below.

4Ps - Tools	4As - Challenges
Product	Acceptability
Price	Affordability
Place	Availability
Promotion	Awareness

Marketing Mix in Rural Context

As far as the product is concerned, acceptability is a challenge for the rural marketer. Due to low disposable income, provide affordable goods and services is a challenge. Again, as far as place is concerned, making the product available in 6,27,000 villages is a big challenge. Promotion is also not easy with respect to rural markets, as most of the population is illiterate in many states in India. Creating awareness in the rural masses is also no mean a simpler task. Now let us check out these challenges and how companies are countering this.

Nokia 1100

1. **Acceptability:** The most important challenge for the rural marketer is to develop and design a product or service, which will suit the rural consumers to gain acceptability. Many times companies pass on their products, what has been working in the urban markets and fail. The companies, which are successful, are also the companies, which develop and design their products on the needs of the rural customers. LG customised and developed a television set called Sampoorna, a made for rural-urban range of low priced colour TVs, which was positioned just above the black and white TVs of the same size. This became a mega success and helped LG penetrate the rural markets.[3] Nokia also came out with 1100 series of mobile phones for the rural population with an inbuilt flashlight and dust resistant keyboard. To cater to the rural masses, Micromax also came out with a mobile phone X1i, with a month long battery back-up in 2008. Tata launched a water purifier called Tata Swach for Rs. 999/- targeting the rural and bottom of the pyramid customers. Coke came out with a solar powered eKOCool solar cooler to provide a chilled Coca Cola to their customers in rural areas.

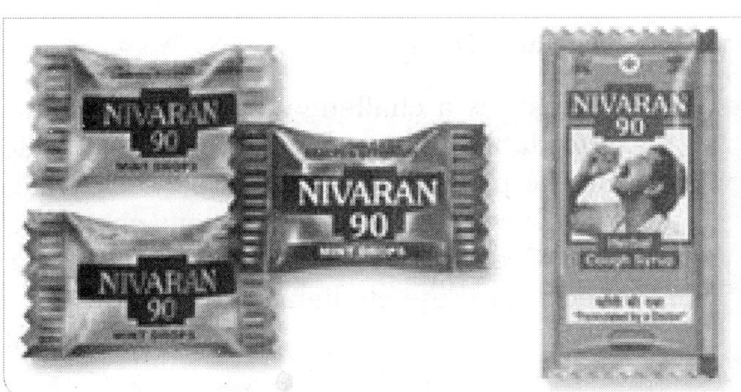

Nivaran Cough Syrup

Chik Shampoo

Marketing Insight 15.3

Coke's New Rural Push

As the first rays of the winter sun hit the small solar panels perched on the roof of Roop Devi's kirana store in a remote village in Bareilly, Uttar Pradesh, a direct current compressor motor whirrs into life. It refrigerates a small, opaque, boxstyled cooler inside her shop. A few hours later Devi opens the box and makes her first sale — an ice-cold bottle of Coke.

It's just another Coke sold, except that the sale has been made in a village that doesn't have any electricity. As the thirsty villager gulps down the fizzy chill gushing out of the bottle, Coca-Cola India moves another step closer to prying open the market in 80,000 Indian villages that do not have any electricity. Of these, 25,000 have little chance of being connected to the power grid in the conventional way.

Coca-Cola India first toyed with the idea of a low-cost solar powered cooler when its president and CEO Atul Singh visited a rural market in Uttar Pradesh in the summer of 2009. Shops there served him warm Coke. When Singh returned, he charged two young Coke engineers, Chandan Samanta and Sunil Gulati, now aged 35 and 40, respectively, with the task of figuring out a low-cost solution. Three-and-a-half years later, 400 such boxes deployed across many villages are delivering a five-fold increase in sales.

Coke is convinced that the new business generated more than pays for the cost of the solar cooler. It plans to distribute 1,000 boxes free to woman entrepreneurs in Madhya Pradesh, UP, Himachal Pradesh and some parts of West Bengal by 2013. The number will go up to 4,000-5,000 in the next 3-4 years. Moreover, at least 22 countries in the Coke universe have lifted 400 such boxes from Coca-Cola India and are adapting it to their markets.

And Samanta and Gulati have become celebrities – their project was showcased at the global all business unit president's meet this April and again at Coca-Cola's shareholder's meet in May, both at Atlanta. "It helps when we can decode the consumer's voice, not just for launching new products, but also newer packages, price points' etc," says India CEO Singh.

"Solar cooler is one such example of an innovation based on local insights and ground realities." Adds Asim Parekh, Vice President - Technical, India & South West Asia, Coca-Cola India: "These (cooler) boxes are bringing first time customers who never tasted our beverages before. The model is helping create a market in areas where Coke was not present at all." As dusk descends, Devi plugs in her solar lantern in the 'cooler box' to generate power for one of the few lights in the village. The light keeps her business going till late in the night. Customers often walk in to plug their mobile phones into the cooler to charge-up the battery. "I no longer need to shut shop just because it is sunset," says Devi. The light facilitates longer hours, helping her earn more income. "When people line up to use the mobile charger, they stay longer and buy more food and beverages while they wait," she adds. "The mobile charging ports are often used by shopkeepers to attract customers," adds Coke's Parekh. "Some allow them to charge their cellphones if they buy something from the shop, others are allowing it free."

Coke is happy giving away the box — named eKOCool solar cooler — free to vendors in villages without power supply. "On the overall scheme of things, the model has turned out to be sustainable as it is increasing Coke's presence considerably in rural areas," he adds. "Most of India's population still lacks access to electric grid. Renewables has to be a central part of India's energy solution," says Vijay Govindarajan, Professor at Tuck at Dartmouth and author of the NYT and WSJ Best Seller Reverse Innovation.

"It is little surprise that Coca-Cola has innovated a solarpowered cooling system for rural markets. Eventually the rich world will adopt this and other renewable energy innovations — when it is time to replace existing assets. This is classic reverse innovation." The company is already working on version 2 of the eKOCool that can cool 100 bottles. The current version can store only 50 bottles. "When we launched, we thought we will sell only 6-12 bottles. Now, women shopkeepers are saying a capacity of 50 is not enough," company officials say. Coca Cola India collaborated with Mumbai-based Western Refrigeration to create the eKOCool solar cooler. The boxes are now also exported to Africa, New Papua Guinea as well as South Africa. In Turkey these boxes are being mounted on trolleys to ferry these bottles on sea beaches.

2. **Affordability:** In rural markets, affordability is a key factor in the success of a product or service. Due to low disposable income, customers prefer to buy the products, which are available in small packs. That's why you will find Chik shampoo for 50 paise, parachute coconut oil for Re 1, Parle G biscuits for Rs. 2, Colgate toothpaste for Rs. 5 and even a cough syrup Nivaran 90 is available in sachet for 50 paise. Even Moov and Itchguard are selling in small sachets for Rs. 10. Almost all the FMCG products are sold in small sachet to make it convenient and affordable for the rural buyer.

Parle-G

But the factor of affordability is not about buying cheap products. It is all about buying products, which is value for money. Although in the FMCG and OTC (Over the Counter) category, small sachet or, packs, or, packets does the trick; yet in the other cases the company needs to understand the customers and provide right value. In rural areas, LG is the leader in durables category, but it's not a cheap product.

Marketing Insight 15.4

Project Shakti

Project Shakti is a rural distribution initiative of Hindustan Unilever Limited (HUL) that targets small villages populated by less than 5,000 individuals. It is a unique win-win initiative that catalyses rural affluence even as it benefits business. Project Shakti benefits business by significantly enhancing HUL's direct rural reach, and by enabling HUL's brands to communicate effectively in media-dark regions. It also impacts society by creating livelihood opportunities for under privileged rural women. Project Shakti impacts society in two ways - the Shakti Entrepreneur programme creates livelihood opportunities for underprivileged rural women.

The Shakti Entrepreneur (SE) programme recognises that while micro-credit plays a key role in alleviating poverty, its ability to do so depends on the availability of investment opportunities. Shakti contributes by creating profitable micro-enterprise opportunities for rural women. Armed with microcredit, rural women become Shakti entrepreneurs: Direct-to-home distributors in rural markets. This micro-enterprise offers low risks and high returns. The products distributed are some of the country's most trusted brands of consumer goods, and include a range of mass-market products especially relevant to rural consumers.

Moreover, HUL invests its resources in training the entrepreneurs, helping them become confident, business-sawy professionals capable o f running their own enterprise.The SE is also called as 'Shakti Amma' — 'Shakti' means 'power/empowered' and 'Amma' means 'mother' inTelugu the language spoken in Andhra Pradesh where Project Shakti was first piloted in 2000. Project Shakti has proved to be a great success for HUL and for rural impoverished women in India. The project started in a few pilot villages in Andhra Pradesh in 2000. In 2002 it expanded to two states and by the end of 2004 had grown to over 13,000 Shakti women entrepreneurs in 12 states. Today there are about 45,000 Shakti Ammas across 15 states in India, selling products to over 3.3 million households in 135,000 Indian villages in 2012

In 2010, HUL rolled out the Shaktiman initiative through Project Shakti. Through the Shaktimaan initiative, men in the Shakti Amma families distribute HUL products to villages adjoining the respective Shakti village. Through the Geographical Information System, villages around the 'Shakti' families are tracked and based on this they are allotted five to six villages. They go to these villages and sell HUL products. The Shaktimaan have also been given bicycles to ensure smooth travelling between villages.

HUL now has over 26,000 Shaktimaans (through the Project Shakti network) across the country now. The revenue earned by the Shaktimaan further augments the household income of the 'Shakti' family. Shaktimaans are covering about five to six villages adjoining the Shakti village. The revenue earned by the Shaktimaan further augments the household income of the respective 'Shakti' family.

Through Project Shakti and Shaktimaan, HUL reaches over 100,000 villages across 15 states in India and over 3 million households every month. HUL works closely with various NGOs, banks and both state and local government departments, who recognise the potential for economic growth by encouraging women to become entrepreneurs.

On an average, a SE earns Rs.700-Rs.l ,000 a month, and since most of them live below the poverty line, this earning is significant, often doubling the household income. With the roll out of Shaktimaan initiative, Shakti families have an opportunity to further augment their income. HUL is also evaluating various opportunities to further strengthen the income of Shakti Ammas.

HUL has continuously endeavoured to augment the income of its Shakti Ammas. In 2011, HUL partnered with the State Bank of India to bring banking services to low-income people in small Indian villages through the Shakti Ammas. The Shakti Ammas are already trusted by local communities and make them a friendly and accessible way to promote access to banking in rural communities and thus promote financial inclusion.

3. **Availability**: One of the biggest challenge for a marketer is to reach the rural markets, as it is very expansive and spread across 6,27,000 villages. Although in the last few years, due to government's initiative like Pradhan Mantri Gram Sadak Yojana (PMGSY), many villages have got good connectivity with all-weather road built up under this scheme; yet it lacks good infrastructure and connectivity. In this area, the companies which have been able to reach the faraway villages, are also the companies, which is

successful in rural markets like Hindustan Unilever Limited (HUL), Ghadi, Velvette, Cavin Care, Nirma, Dabur, ITC, P&G, Colgate, LG etc.

DSCL Hariyali Bazaar

To counter the challenge, many companies have devised innovative ways to reach the rural masses. HUL's Project Shakti, Colgate's Bicycle Entrepreneurs, Coke's hub and spoke distribution model, LG's separate vertical for rural markets; are just few of the examples to cater the rural markets. Here, one can also learn from CavinKare, which is the second largest selling shampoo brand in India with their Chik shampoo or Kanpur based Ghadi Detergent powder, or from Velvette International, which markets Velvette shampoo and Nivaran 90 cough syrup. These small players have made it big, by just having the right strategies for distribution with products in small sachets for as cheap as 50 paisa. The organized retailing is also coming in the rural areas with DSCL Haryali Bazaars, M & M Shubh Labh Stores, TATA / Rallis Kisan Kendra, Escorts Rural Stores, ITC Choupal Sagar, Godrej Agrovet's Adhar Stores, Triveni Khushali Bazar and Warna Bazaar in Maharashtra.

Marketing Insight 15.5

Marketing Insight 15.5

ITC E-Choupal

ITC is helping out the rural households with their popular E-Choupal model, where it helps farmers to get all the information about the weather as well as the market price of the food grains they are producing. E-Choupal' makes use of the physical transmission capabilities of current intermediaries – aggregation, logistics, counter-party risk and bridge financing – while disinter mediating them from the chain of information flow and market signals.

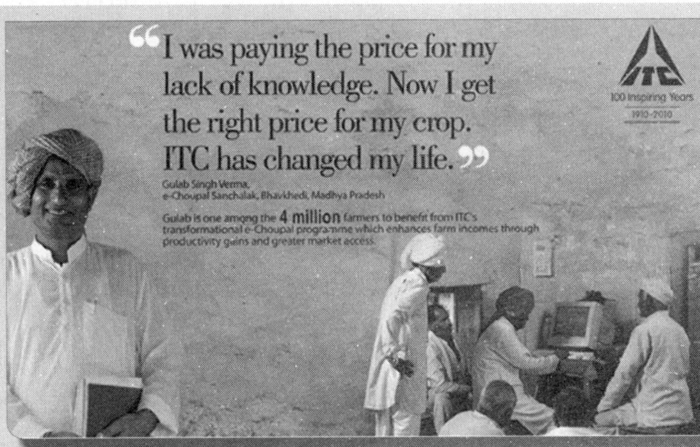

With a judicious blend of click & mortar capabilities, village internet kiosks managed by farmers – called sanchalaks – themselves, enable the agricultural community access ready information in their local language on the weather & market prices, disseminate knowledge on scientific farm practices & risk management, facilitate the sale of farm inputs (now with embedded knowledge) and purchase farm produce from the farmers' doorsteps (decision making is now information-based). While the farmers benefit through enhanced farm productivity and higher farm gate prices, ITC benefits from the lower net cost of procurement (despite offering better prices to the farmer) having eliminated costs in the supply chain that do not add value.

4. **Awareness**: A company also needs to promote its products correctly. It should choose the right media vehicle like advertising on Doordarshan and on regional satellite channels besides the general entertainment satellite channels. Panchayat Televisions are also a popular medium in Tamilnadu. In Tamilnadu, even the government has distributed more than 72 lacs TV sets to the poor people. Direct to Home (DTH) services like Tata Sky, Airtel DTH, Dish TV, DD Direct has come up as a boon for advertisers, as they can reach in every nook and corner of India due to their presence.

   Besides the television, print media vehicles like newspapers, magazines etc. can also help in enhancing awareness and it's good that literacy rate is picking up in many states. Besides the Television, Van campaigns, wall paintings, road shows and edutainment films are also popular in the rural areas. Even 42,000 Haats (periodic markets) and 25,000 Melas (exhibitions) also works in promoting your products and services.

   As the large parts of India are still inaccessible, a lot of companies are trying to mix and match the media platforms to reach the customers. For example – HUL relies a lot on its own company organized media, while LG uses vans and roadshows. Coke uses TV, cinema as well as radio to reach the rural customers, while Ghadi Detergent also uses the mix of TV, print and radio.

LG

It has also been found that to some extent, awareness can fill the gap of availability in the rural markets. Sometimes we find the popular sachet packs from HUL, Colgate, Ghadi are available in the remotest villages; it is not due to wide distribution network. But it is the pull factor of the brand, which brings the rural retailer to feeder towns to get the products. So, if the feeder markets are served well and companies can promote the products effectively, the company can still reach to the remotest of its customers.[4]

Although there are several challenges in the rural markets, yet there is so much opportunity for the marketers that if you correctly harness it; they can create a big business out of it. The same has been done by many companies in India, which are very successful in the rural markets. HUL is one of them and same has been echoed by Mr. Harish Manwani, Global COO, Unilver at HUL's AGM Speech 2012 titled 'Rural India – An Emerging Powerhouse'. While concluding his speech, he said -

'Hindustan Unilever is excited with the opportunity to continue to serve the 800 million consumers in rural India and be a part of this great journey into the future.' – Mr. Harish Manwani, Global COO, Unilver[5]

Summary

- India's rural markets offer unprecedented opportunities for marketers due to its vast size and demand base. Out of the 121 crore Indians, 83.3 crore live in rural areas; that accounts for 68.84% of the total population. The rural population is spread over 3,200 small towns and 6,27,000 villages.

- As per the Census of India 2011, the rural sector means any place, which meets the following criteria - a population of less than 5,000, density of population less than 400 per sq km and More than 25 per cent of the male working population is engaged in agricultural pursuits.
- Sometimes rural marketing is confused with Agricultural marketing. But it is different than agricultural marketing. Agricultural marketing deals with marketing of agricultural produce from the rural areas to consumer as well as business market. Rural marketing deals with marketing of goods and services to the rural population.
- The evolution of rural marketing in India can be classified into three distinct phases - phase 1 : prior to the 1960s, phase 2 : 1960 to 1990 and phase 3: after 1990.
- Rural markets are different form urban markets in many ways. Most of the rural population has a very low disposable income. Rural customers generally buy consumer durables, two wheelers, cars etc. during post harvest period, marriages, festivals and on special occasions.
- In the rural market scenario, the marketing mix – 4Ps can be seen from a different angle in terms of 4As i.e. acceptability, affordability, availability and awareness.
- The most important challenge for the rural marketer is to develop and design a product or service, which will suit the rural consumers to gain acceptability.
- In rural markets, affordability is a key factor in the success of a product or service. Due to low disposable income, customers prefer to buy the products, which are available in small packs.
- One of the biggest challenge for a marketer is to reach the rural markets, as it is very expansive and spread across 6,27,000 villages. To counter the challenge, many companies have devised innovative ways to reach the rural masses. HUL's Project Shakti, Colgate's Bicycle Entrepreneurs, Coke's hub and spoke distribution model, LG's separate vertical for rural markets; are just few of the examples to cater the rural markets.
- A company also needs to promote its products correctly. It should choose the right media vehicle like advertising on Doordarshan and on regional satellite channels besides the general entertainment satellite channels; print media vehicles like newspapers, magazines etc. Van campaigns, wall paintings, road shows and edutainment films can also be popular and effective in the rural areas.
- Although there are several challenges in the rural markets, yet there is so much opportunity for the marketers that if you correctly harness it; they can create a big business out of it.

Discussion Questions

1. Define rural marketing? Discuss the evolution of rural marketing in India?
2. What do you mean by rural marketing? How is it different from Agricultural marketing?
3. What steps should a company take to counter the challenges posed by the rural markets?
4. Discuss the rural marketing mix in detail.
5. Discuss the 4As in rural marketing?
6. Can government initiatives help rural marketing in India? Analyse the statement.
7. How rural customers are different from urban customers.
8. Discuss the innovation strategies adopted by any one Indian company and any one MNC to penetrate the rural markets.
9. Discuss the strategies adopted by rural marketers to create awareness about a product or a service.
10. Short Notes:
    - a. Affordability
    - b. Agricultural Marketing
    - c. Acceptability
    - d. Project Shakti
    - e. E-Choupal
    - f. Sachet Marketing

References

1. Census of India, 2011
2. http://india.gov.in/people-groups/community/rural-indian
3. Rajan R. V., "Don't Flirt with Rural Marketing", Productivity & Quality Publishing, Chennai, 2013.
4. Rajan R. V., "Don't Flirt with Rural Marketing", Productivity & Quality Publishing, Chennai, 2013.
5. Manwani Harish, 'Rural India – An Emerging Powerhouse' at HUL's AGM Speech 2012

Chapter 16

International Marketing

Chapter Structure

NXG, Passion Pro, Passion Plus, Super Splendor, Glamour, Glamour PG Fi, Achiever, CBZ X-Treme, Hunk, Karizma, Karizma ZMR and Pleasure scooters between the price range of Rs. 32000/- to Rs. 91000/-. It's not that only automobile companies are having many choices for the customers.

Even in FMCG products, a company like HUL offers 8 types of personal soaps – Breeze, Lux, Lifebuoy, Liril, Hamam, Dove, Pears, Rexona and Dove; 4 types of detergent powders – Surf Excel, Rin, Wheel and Sunlight; 4 types of skin care – Fair & Lovely, Pond's, Vaseline and Aviance; and 2 types of toothpastes – Pepsodent and Close Up.

Market Positioning

Once the market segment is identified by the company to be targeted, it needs to be positioned in the mind of the prospective customer. Positioning is creating an identity in the minds of the target market. Positioning as a concept, in marketing was popularised by advertising professionals **Al Ries and Jack Trout** through their bestseller book "**Positioning - a battle for your mind**". This concept was first published in 1969 by Jack Trout in the paper '**Positioning is a game people play in today's me-too market place**' in Industrial Marketing. Al Ries and Jack Trout said that

'Positioning starts with a product. A piece of merchandise, a service, a company, an institution or even a person.... But positioning is not what you do to a product. Positioning is what you do the mind of the prospect. That is, you position the product in the mind of the prospect.'

"Economic globalization constitutes integration of national economies into the international economy through trade, direct foreign investment (by corporations and multinationals), short-term capital flows, international flows of workers and humanity generally, and flows of technology."

- Jagdish Bhagwati

Tata Bolt

Positioning is all about how does the customer perceive your product? For example, when Tata launched their first car - Indica, their tagline was 'More car, per car' and Tata Motors tried to give more value to the consumers through lower price, more space, more features

International Marketing

Before we get into defining international marketing, let us check out few facts and figures:

- McDonalds, an American company sells more burgers and fries outside the USA than within.
- Tata group earns more than two third of its revenue not from India, but from abroad.
- Suzuki, a Japanese automobile manufacturer, sells more cars in India than in Japan
- Dr. Reddy's laboratory, an Indian pharma company earns more than 80% revenues from abroad.
- Infosys earns more than 97% of its income from abroad.
- Aditya Birla Group operates in 36 countries and earns more than half of its revenue from abroad.

Aditya Birla Group

All these above facts and figures suggest that marketing has become international. In our day today life, if we check out the products and services we consume; we find that most of the products and services, we consume daily are international products. Here we are not talking only about the foreign MNCs, which are present in India like Unilever, McDonalds, Pizza Hut, Starbucks, Colgate, Ariel, Samsung, Apple, Hyundai, Ford etc., but the homegrown Indian MNCs, which are selling products internationally like Tata, Bajaj, Dabur, ITC, Airtel, Micromax etc. Can you believe that Tata Group is present in 182 countries across the globe? Mahindra Group is present in more than 100 countries across the globe. Even Bajaj sells its two wheelers in more than 50 countries. Thus, the markets have become truly international.

Marketing Insight 16.1

Marketing Insight 16.1

Starbucks is Here, Almost Starry-Eyed

Iconic coffee chain hopes the thrill of holding a Starbucks coffee in hand and aggressive pricing will lure Indians to its swanky outlets

Starbucks

Starbucks expects its Indian business to eventually rank among its top five markets, CEO Howard Schultz said on Friday as the coffee chain entered one of its last untapped markets. "India represents one of the most significant opportunities that we have in all of Starbucks. India should be one of the largest markets in the world for Starbucks. I would say one of the top five over time," he said in an exclusive interaction with ET.

Schultz, the son of a US soldier who grew up in public housing in New York, added that a lot of thought had gone into setting Indian prices at levels that are competitive, a significant departure in business practice for a brand that has globally positioned coffee drinking as an elite experience. "We don't want price to be a barrier. People are surprised, but this will give us a competitive advantage in the market." A cup of coffee at Starbucks will cost anywhere between . Rs. 95 and Rs. 155 depending on the size while iced coffee and blended beverages will be Rs. 115 –Rs. 200. These prices are at a moderate premium to that of largest local rival Cafe Coffee Day, which has around 1,350 coffee chains. It sells a cup of coffee for about Rs. 80 and cold coffee and beverages for less than Rs. 150.

"While Starbucks has maintained its premium positioning, such pricing will come with its own set of negatives. India is a price-sensitive coffee market. Starbucks generally sells a coffee cup for $3 in most markets while India's price at $1.5 will be considered premium," said a senior official in a rival company. "We welcome Starbucks and feel the entry will help grow the coffee market in India," said K Ramakrishnan, president (marketing) at Cafe Coffee Day. Starbucks, whose Indian unit is a joint venture with Tata Global Beverages, plans to open two additional stores in Mumbai next week — before coming to New Delhi early next year.

Indian Coffee Market Worth $230 million

These plans appear to be less ambitious than the ones announced earlier this year. At a press conference announcing the joint venture, officials had talked of investing Rs. 400 crore over time and establishing 50 stores by the end of calendar 2012. The Seattle-based company spent at least a decade trying to figure out when and how it would enter the world's seventh-largest coffee producer before opening a two-level store decorated with locally sourced teak furniture in tony Horniman Circle in south Mumbai. India, Asia's third-largest economy, is the 61st country that Starbucks has entered, an indication of the difficulty it had in finding a local partner.

"The store is perhaps one of the most elegant stores that we ever designed in history, which will overnight put us in a position that no other coffee store exists like this in the country," Schultz said. The Indian market is worth $230 million and is expected to grow at a CAGR of 13-14% over the next five years.

Experts feel that cafes are profitable globally because consumers are attuned to a takeaway culture that adds margins with very little cost. However, India is a contrast where most office-goers and students order a cup a coffee to relax and use cafes as a place where they can sit for hours. Further, India's expensive real estate demands higher per-square-feet realisation from every customer.

Schultz isn't perturbed though. "That's something they said to us in almost every market outside the US, especially in Japan. And 80% of our business (in Japan) is now takeaway. I think people will take Starbucks coffee away. There is a great pride in holding a Starbucks coffee," he said, adding that their partner Tata's clout will come handy in terms of infrastructure and real estate acquisition. There are some strong local touches on the menu too: Murgh Tandoori Kebab, Konkan Twist and something totally unheard of in most cafes — Elaichi Mawa Croissant.

Defining International Marketing

International marketing means marketing across borders. When a company expands its operations beyond the national boundaries, it is said to be doing International Marketing. Sometimes the term global marketing is also used to denote International Marketing.

Keegan has defined global marketing from a strategic point of view and said **'Global or, transnational marketing focuses upon leveraging a company's assets, experience and products globally and upon adapting to what is truly unique and different in each country.'** [1]

American Marketing Association (AMA) has defined **'international marketing as the multinational process of planning and executing the conception, pricing, promotion and distribution of ideas, goods, and services to create exchanges that satisfy individual and organizational objectives.'**

In the AMA definition, only the word multinational has been added to differentiate marketing from international marketing. International marketing is nothing but, just marketing internationally. If we check out the similarities, there are many similarities. Both in domestic marketing and international marketing, a company needs to identify and fulfill the needs of the customers. In accordance with the needs of different customers, a company needs to do research and development to come out with innovative products to suit the need. It has also been found that the products or services, which are successful in domestic markets, are sold across the border to replicate its success there. Colgate, Dove, Lux, Gillette, McDonalds, Starbucks are few of the examples, which replicated its success in hundreds of countries.

Ford Ecosport

Just like a domestic marketer, an international marketer can only be successful, if he caters to the needs of the customers with the right kind of products or services, with attractive pricing. The products or services also need to be widely available and the communication needs to be effective. Once the product fits these parameters, customers will be more than willing to buy the product. The same has been proved again and again. Whether it is Ford Ecosport or Mercedes S class, there are customers all across the world, which are ready to buy it.

Wheel

Ala

In international marketing, a company sells its product in many countries. As the customers are varied, a company tries to develop a product in accordance with the local needs of a specific country. Once that product is successful, the company replicates the success in other countries, which has similar profile of customers. For example – Unilever, an American MNC launched Wheel detergent powder in India through its subsidiary Hindustan Unilever Limited (HUL), after facing a tough competition from Nirma in the lower segment. Once Wheel became successful in India, Unilever plc transported the business principles (not the product or the brand) to create a new detergent market among the poor in Brazil. The detergent brand Ala has been a runaway success in Brazil. Even more importantly, Unilever has adopted the bottom of the pyramid as a strategic priority at the corporate level.[2] Ford Ecosport was launched in Brazil and now it is selling in India and other countries.

Multinational Corporation (MNC)

Multinational Corporation (MNC) is a term widely used in international marketing. MNC simply means a corporation or a company, which operates in more than one country.[3] Aditya Birla Group, Asian Paints, Coca-Cola, Unilever, Dell, DHL, P&G, GE, Microsoft, Dabur, Google, Ford, Honda, Suzuki, ICICI, PepsiCo, Tata Motors, TCS, Tata Steel, LG, Samsung, Apple are few of the examples of MNCs.

International Marketing vs. Domestic Marketing

As we have seen earlier, both in domestic marketing and international marketing, a company needs to identify and fulfill the needs of the customers. Just like a domestic marketer, an international marketer can only be successful, if he comes out with the right kind of products or services with an attractive price tag. The product or service also needs to be widely available and the communication needs to be effective. But there are a lot of differences also, which makes it a very complex exercise.[4] Following are the differences:

1. **Currency**: Each country has its own monetary system and that's why each one has a separate currency also. Thus, the exchange value of the currency is different from that of other. For exam. In India, currently the exchange rate for US Dollar (USD) to Indian Rupee (INR) is around 62, while the exchange rate for USD to Nepali Rupee is around 100. Due to the difference in currency, a company needs to quote the rates in currency, which is acceptable to the other party. All across the world US Dollar is the widely accepted currency. As the exchange rate changes every moment, a company bears the risk of changes in the exchange rate. Although there are measures through which you can hedge the currency, but still the risk lies with the company. Recently with the value of Indian Rupee going down, IT companies in India has benefitted a lot.

Marketing Insight 16.2

Marketing Insight 16.2

Culture Customisation: Wrangler, McDonald's and Starbucks

How international brands such as McDonald's, Starbucks and Wrangler jeans are wooing Indian consumers with localised versions.

Wrangler

Wrangler jeans are getting a makeover in India and going up-market in the process as parent VF Corp customises the all-American denims for the country's motorcycle-riding population and adds features to suit local needs. VF Corp hopes the strategy will add $1.1 billion in revenue to its Asia-Pacific business over the next five years.

India, with its burgeoning middle class, is a fast-growing market for international brands that want to capitalise on opportunities in Asia's third largest economy. McDonald's Corp recently announced its first vegetarian-only restaurant in the country in what many industry watchers say is a sign of how lucrative the market is and how much multinationals are tailoring to local demands.

Coffee chain Starbucks Corp also customised its menu for its first Indian store to include more local flavors.

"In India, they understand the western heritage that is appropriate for the brand because the Indian consumer is open to the film industry," VF Corp Chief Executive Eric Wiseman said in an interview, adding that many Indians are familiar with Westerns, unlike consumers in China.

China and India are the two hot destinations for American retailers, with the Chinese market much bigger. But many note that a large English-speaking population exposed to Hollywood and American pop culture makes the Indian shopper easier to target.

"The Wrangler position in India ... is targeted at the premium customer. The brand is aiming to tap into the potentially large segment of young consumers there whose lifestyles relate to jeans and motorcycles," Wiseman told Reuters. A study by Wrangler in India found most people travel by two-wheelers in the country, as opposed to their American counterparts who drive cars.

Taking into account traffic and climatic differences, VF Corp came up with features like water-repellant material to safeguard mobile phones and wallets, and making the fit of the jeans more motorbike-riding friendly. The new line of jeans costs about 15 per cent to 20 per cent more than the average pair of Wrangler denims, Wiseman said.

From Horses To Horsepower

Wrangler was first sold in the US in 1947 as "cowboy" jeans and is still a popular choice for heavy-duty wear. The price for a standard pair of Wrangler regular fit jeans for men starts at about $19, according to the company's website, making them an affordable buy. Globally, the brand fetches VF Corp about $1.5 billion in revenue annually. In India, it currently brings in less than $50 million (approx Rs 260 crore), CEO Wiseman said.

"It is critical to get local, local, local," said Michael Silverstein, senior partner at The Boston Consulting Group, and co-author of the "$10 Trillion Dollar Prize," a book about the emerging Chinese and Indian middle class. Silverstein estimated there are roughly 300 million Indians who can buy a pair of jeans for the equivalent of about $20. That is almost equal to the population of the US.

Wiseman said Wrangler is developing more products along the same lines that will be introduced in India in the coming seasons.

Experiments in localisation are still rare for clothing companies, mostly because they often do not have the scale or distribution capacity, said Peter Wahlstrom, an analyst with Morningstar. VF Corp is among the few companies that manufactures much of its own merchandise so it has more control over gathering raw material and distribution.

Its India business is expected to grow at a rate of 22 per cent annually, while the Asia-Pacific region is expected to increase by 17 per cent.

2. **Culture**: Culture is a major factor of differentiation. Edward Taylor has defined culture as 'that complex whole, which includes knowledge, belief, art, morals, law, custom and any other capabilities and habits acquired by individuals (as members) of society'. Each country is unique and the requirements for their customers also tend to be different. This makes the marketing exercise very complex. For each market, the company needs to take into consideration the concerned market to formulate and implement the right strategy.

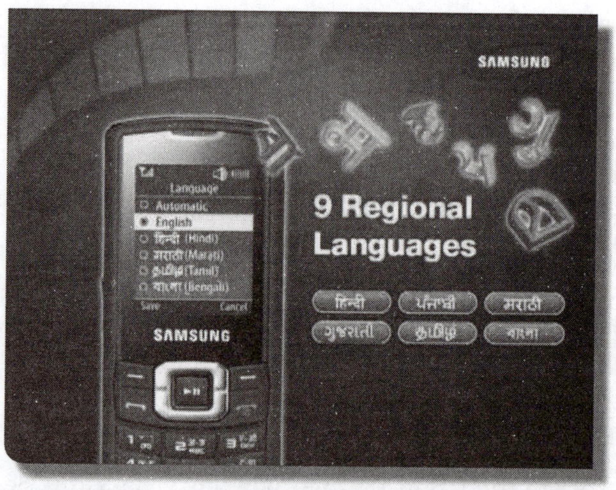

Samsung Mobile

3. **Language:** In almost every country, the language is different. Although English is widely spoken all across the world, yet the languages are different in many countries. In India also, an international company has to take care of so many languages besides Hindi to cater to the whole market.

4. **Legal:** Each country has its own legal system and a company needs to follow the system to market the products. In every country, the export-import procedures and documentations are also different. All of these need to be taken care of, while dealing with the international markets. Sometimes, a company can also benefit from the legal system. For example – In India Ford sells Ecosport in less than four meter size, while it sells the same compact SUV over four meter length in Chin, to take advantage of the excise duty structure for small cars.

5. **Trade Barriers**: Each country imposes certain trade barriers, to restrict the trade. These barriers can either be tariff or non-tariff barriers. A company is affected by the trade barriers in different countries. It needs to find out better ways to access the international markets.

6. **Mobility of Factors of Production:** Internally, in any country the factor of production are highly mobile. But internationally, there is limited mobility due to the difference in legal structure. Now, with the various advancements, the mobility of labour is increasing, while money or capital is also becoming more mobile. Overall, mobility of factors of production impacts internal marketing a lot.

All the above factors make international marketing a complex exercise. The only way to counter this is to implement the right kind of marketing mix, in this changed scenario.

Reasons for going International

Now the question arises, why does a company go international? Is it just the need of the hour or are there different reasons for going international. A company may go international for growth and diversification. It may also look out for minimising competitive risk, gaining economies of scale or may look forward to cushioning the economic cycle.[5] Following are the different reasons:

1. **Insufficiency of Domestic Demand**: Before getting into production, a company does lot of research to forecast the demand for the products. But sometimes, it does not match the actual demand. Based on the inputs of a thorough market research, Tata Motors decided to put up a plant for 20,000 Tata Nano per month. But the actual sale is hovering below 2000 units every month, which leads to a lot of unutilised capacity in the plant. In that scenario, a company like Tata Motors looks out abroad to sell Tata Nano in other countries. Now Nano is selling in Sri Lanka, Nepal and Indonesia. Tata Motors is even planning to launch in Europe and USA. Thus, in case of insufficient domestic demand, a company looks forward to international markets.

airtel

Airtel

2. **Growth and Diversification:** Every company faces competition in whichever market, it operates. The market may be hyper competitive with more than 8 to 15 competitors in the market and thus limiting the chances of a market player to grow the market share. It happens more with the market leader and the market challenger in the market. In this scenario, the only way to go forward is to look out for new markets. Airtel has been facing the same situation for the last few years in Indian market. It has been the leader for quite some time, but the growth is not very encouraging in the hyper competitive

telecom market. Now the only option left to Airtel is to get into new markets and that's what they have done. In 2010, Airtel acquired the African operations of the Kuwait based Zain Telecom, which gave access to the markets of 17 countries. Now, Airtel is the world's third largest mobile telecommunications company by subscriber base and operates across 20 countries with over 275 million subscribers.

3. **Minimising Business Risks**: Business risks can also be minimized by a company, if it has got international operations. The downward fluctuation in one country may be mitigated by the growth in the other country. It may be due to competitive and other forces in the economy. It happened with Tata Motors in 2013, when it was badly hit in the Indian market due to the competitive forces. But overall Tata Motors did well due to its international markets, which was contributed mostly by its Jaguar Land Rover (JLR) operations.

Tata Consultancy Services

4. **Cushioning the Economic Cycle:** A company can also minimize the risk from the fluctuations in the business cycle, if it operates in many countries. So, if there is slowdown in one country, it can be made up by another one. But if the market is concentrated just in one country or few countries, it will have to bear the impact. It happened with the leading IT companies in India like Infosys, TCS, Wipro etc., when these companies were badly hit by the recession in European and American markets. These companies were too much dependent on these markets, which lowered their growth pattern.

Renault Duster

5. **Economies of Scale**: A company needs to invest a lot of money in the research and development to develop a new product. Once the product is developed, a company can put up plant in all its markets, as it may not be viable. That's why a company looks forward to take the advantage of economies of scale, so that the production costs can be lowered. The same has also been by done by Renault Duster and Ford Ecosport, besides others. In India, Renault has put up a plant to produce Duster and it also exports the same to UK, Ireland and South Africa. Having production base in one country and exporting it to other countries provide economies of scale for the companies. Besides producing Duster in India, Renault caters to Brazil, Argentina and Chile market from its plant in Brazil, while it sells duster from Columbian plant to Mexico, Ecuador and Columbia.
6. **Obtaining Cheaper Inputs:** To manufacture a product, a company require lots of inputs. The inputs may not be available in all the countries. That's why a company expands internationally to take the advantage of obtaining cheaper raw materials and supplies, to produce the products. A Korean conglomerate POSCO, the world's fourth largest steel producer wants to put up a plant in India at Odisha to take the advantage of ease and cheper cost of raw materials for the steel industry.

All the above are the reasons for going international. Whatever may be the reason; this is the need of the hour to go international. Otherwise, a company may not maintain its growth trajectory. A company like Tata Motors would have been stranded in 2013-14, if there would not have been a company like JLR as a subsidiary with them.

Market Entry Strategies

There are different ways of getting into international marketing, depending upon the cost and the involvement concerned.[6] Following are the different ways:

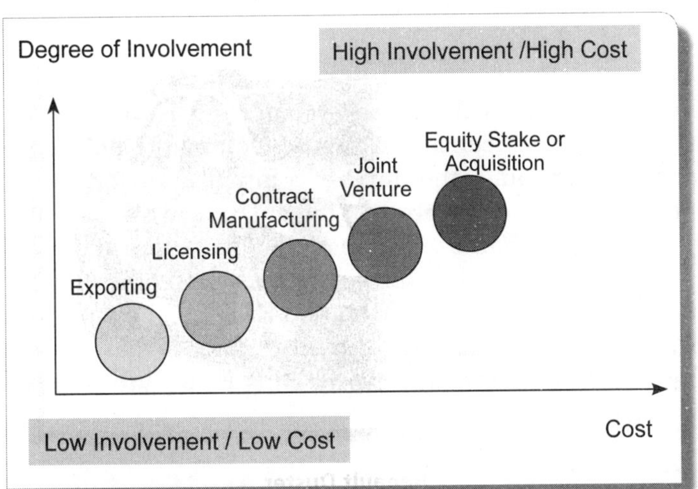

1. **Exporting**: Exporting is the easiest way to get an entry into international markets. Export simply means shipping the goods and services out of the country. The cost as well as the investment from the company is minimal. Export either can be done directly or indirectly. Generally a company gets into exports directly. In this case, the company bears the risk as well as earns good profits. But many small companies, who do not know the international markets or not interested in bearing the risk of selling into international markets, generally get into exports through a merchant exporter or Export House in India. These export houses buy the products from domestic manufacturers and sell them abroad. Here the risk is also borne by them. On a similar format, there are many visiting or resident buyers' representatives, who do the procurement on behalf of their foreign companies. Many big retail organizations like Walmart, Carrefour, Metro, Tesco etc. have their resident buyers' representative in many countries like India, China, Brazil and so on.

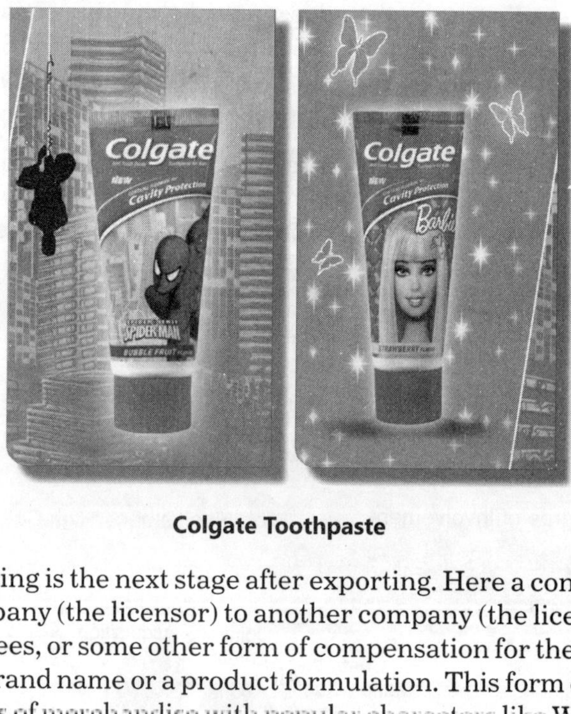

Colgate Toothpaste

2. **Licensing**: Licensing is the next stage after exporting. Here a contractual agreement is made by one company (the licensor) to another company (the licensee) in exchange for royalties, license fees, or some other form of compensation for the usage of a patent or a trade secret or a brand name or a product formulation. This form of licensing is popular in the areas of sales of merchandise with popular characters like Walt Disney's character – Micky Mouse, Donald Duck etc., Marvel Comics characters like Barbie, Spider-Man, the X-Men, the Fantastic Four, Iron Man, the Hulk etc. Few retail companies also get into licensing, which could not enter the international markets directly. Brands like Tommy Hilfiger, Wrangler, Arrow, Beverly Hills Polo Club (BHPC) are sold in India through licensing only.

Lilliput

3. **Contract Manufacturing:** Under contract manufacturing, a company provides technical specifications to a subcontractor or local manufacturer, which allows company to specialize in product design, while contractors accept responsibility for manufacturing facilities. Kidswear brand Lilliput has a contract manufacturing arrangement in China; which helps them source the products for the Indian market.

Air Asia

4. **Joint Venture:** Joint venture as well as equity stake or acquisition falls into the category of direct investment. This is also known as Foreign Direct Investment (FDI). Here the company acquires partial or full ownership of operations outside of home country. Both these formats are very popular all across the world. In the case of joint venture, a company gets into joint venture with local company in a country. It shares the investment as well as the business risk. Recently a joint venture named AirAsia India between Tata Sons and AirAsia has been announced with AirAsia holding 49% of the airline, while Tata Sons is holding 30% and the rest 21% is held by Amit Bhatia.

Munjal Showa is another example, which is a joint venture between Hero group's Munjal and Showa Corporation of Japan to manufacture shock absorbers and struts for leading two wheeler and four wheeler companies.

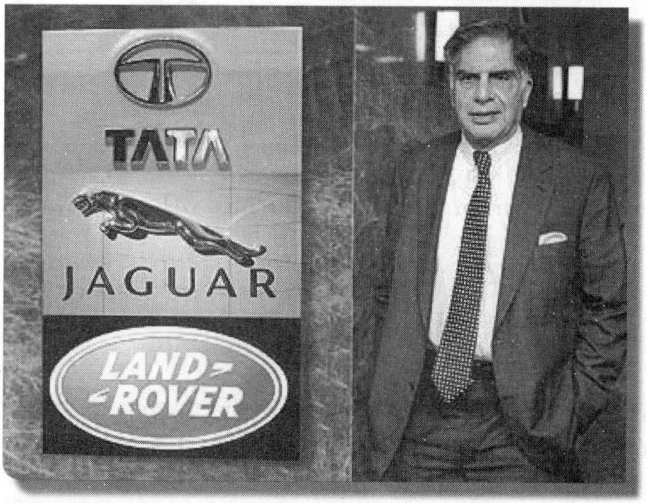

Tata JLR

5. **Equity Stake or Acquisition**: Through equity stake or acquisition, a company may enter into the foreign markets. It can start up a new operation or may merge with an existing enterprise or, can acquire an existing enterprise. Tata Motors acquired Jaguar Land Rover (JLR), while Airtel acquired Zain Telecom's Africa business. Here the cost as well as involvement is the highest. Following are the biggest mergers and acquisition by Indian companies.

India's Billion Dollar Deals			
Acquirer	**Acquired Company / Assets**	**Deal Size ($ billion)**	**Deal Date**
Tata Steel	Corus	13.6	Apr 02, 2007
Vodafone	Hutchison	10.9	Feb 11, 2007
Bharti	Zain (Africa)	10	Mar 30, 2010
Vedanta	Cairn India	9	Aug 16, 2010
Hindalco	Novelis	6	Feb 11, 2007
Vodafone	Essar	5	Mar 31, 2011
Daiichi	Ranbaxy	4.6	Jun 12, 2008

India's Billion Dollar Deals			
Acquirer	**Acquired Company / Assets**	**Deal Size ($ billion)**	**Deal Date**
Abbott	Piramal	3.7	May 21, 2010
ONGC	Imperial	2.6	Dec 30, 2008

Thus, a company may decide to go for one of these five routes to get into international markets. A business conglomerate like Tata group or Aditya Birla group may go for any one of these or a combination for these to enter into international markets, based upon their requirement. Tata has gone into joint venture with Air Asia to launch the airlines business, while it acquired JLR and Corus Steel for their respective companies Tata Motors and Tata Steel.

International Marketing Mix

In International marketing also, the marketing mix i.e. 4Ps of marketing – product, price, place and promotion remains as effective as in case of domestic marketing. But, it needs to be tweaked in terms of the changes in culture, language, currency etc. Let us check out the product first.

1. **Product**: If we talk about product, then in international marketing, a company needs to plan its strategy in accordance with its product or service portfolio. Certain products like Consumer Electronics items, Mobile Phones, MP3 players, LCD & LED TVs, Digital Cameras & Camcorders, Laptops, Desktops and so on, require no adaptation and can be sold directly in all the international markets. Like, currently Apple iPhone is selling in around 100 countries all across the world, while Dell is present in 180 countries across the globe. But few other products like food products, clothing, shoes, furniture etc require adaptation by a company.

McDonalds

To be successful in the International markets, a company needs to revalidate and rethink its marketing mix elements to suit that market, as Mc Donald's is doing in different countries all across the world. In India, you won't find a beef burger due to cultural considerations, sold by McDonalds, which has operations in 122 countries to be precise. While in US, you won't find a Mc Aloo Tikki Burger. In Germany, the burgers are served with a chilled beer - Pilsner, not with a Pepsi. In Japan, they serve shrimp burger called Ebi Filet-O and a green tea flavored milkshake. In Costa Rica, McDonald's serve rice. They call it Gallo Pinto, which means rice and beans in Spanish. In Hong Kong also, you will not find a bun, instead you will get rice burgers served between two rice patties. It means McDonalds needs to set up its menu in accordance with the local requirements of a country.

Apple iPhone

Samsung Galaxy

Marketing Insight 16.3

Competing to Go Native

Global fast food giant KFC launches a cheap potato burger exclusively for India just as rival McDonald's had done earlier.

Recent visitors at KFC outlets across the country have been getting a surprise - there is a new, 10-item, **low-price menu on offer**. Its highlight is the 'Potato Krisper', a vegetarian burger costing Rs 25, where the fried patty within consists almost entirely of potato. This was created exclusively for the Indian market, the first time the global fast food giant has done so. Indeed, it is also the first time KFC - known for its chicken items, marinated in a 'secret sauce' - has ever created a potato burger.

KFC

Other items on the new menu, called the 'Wow' menu, include 'Chicken Shotz - pieces of fried chicken - again available for Rs 25. 'Combos', where a fizzy drink or other accompaniments are offered along with the burger or the chicken fries, are available for just Rs 59. It is a steep price slash for KFC, where all other items cost a lot more - the popular 'Chicken Zinger', for instance, sells at Rs 99 a plate.

Not surprisingly, even more than the trendy music and decor at KFC outlets, the new bargain-basement menu has proved a great attraction for young people, especially students, whose disposable income is limited.

At the outlet in New Delhi's Connaught Place, for instance, a group of three - two girls and a boy - were relishing the Chicken Shotz. "We usually spend around Rs 100 per head when we come here with our friends," says Husna Syed, a student at Mata Sundri College for Women in the city. "Now we can eat a lot more for the same amount."

What prompted KFC to go native in India, 18 years after it entered the country? Industry watchers believe it is a belated effort to measure up to rival chain **McDonald's 'Happy Price Menu'** launched in 2004. That, in turn, was a cheap variant of McDonald›s ‹Dollar Menu› available in the United States.

The key feature of the Happy Price Menu too is a potato burger called McAloo Tikki, also priced currently at Rs 25. (It used to be Rs 20 when launched in 2004.) In comparison, McDonald's well known Chicken Maharaja Mac costs Rs 95. A part-bypart evaluation of the KFC and McDonald's potato burgers shows there is hardly any difference between them, though McAloo Tikki is a shade heavier. (See Counterpunch.)

Both McDonald's and KFC acknowledge that the low price strategy was adopted to expand their Indian presence. Indian taste buds were secondary this time - both already have vegetarian burgers on their menus. "India is a price sensitive market and the Happy Price Menu has helped us take our brand to the masses," says Vikram Bakshi, Joint Venture

Partner and Managing Director, McDonald's India, North and East. Sandeep Kataria, Brand General Manager and Chief Marketing Officer, Yum Restaurants International, which owns KFC, echoes him. "Value never goes out of fashion," he says. "The current economic situation has put more strain on consumers' purses. But we want them to have a memorable experience without worrying too much about the cost."

Is it viable, selling at such rockbottom prices? Both outlets claim it is. "We are certainly not losing money," says McDonald's Bakshi. "We serve millions every day. The volumes help us build and sustain profits." Tarun Lal, KFC's General Manager for India and surrounding countries, agrees. "We also source our ingredients locally, and that helps," he says.

Industry watcher Ankur Bisen, Vice President and Head of Retail at consultancy firm, Technopak Advisors, points to the small size and low weight of the cheap offerings. "The product size is small," he says. "They save on the amount of food."

KFC's Lal never once mentions the McDonald's precedent, and maintains it was KFC's own research which led it to the Wow menu. "Our research showed consumer needs are different at different times of the day," he says. "Between 11 and 1 pm, as well as between 3 pm and 6.30 pm, people want snacks. They don't want heavy meals at these times and we wanted to meet this need."

Potato Krisper was test-marketed in Bangalore from October last year, and following its success there, launched at all of KFC's 230 stores across Indian cities from February this year.

Many more KFC stores are also in the offing. "We've grown three times in five years and plan to expand to 500 stores by 2015," adds Lal.

2. **Price**: Price is a crucial factor in international marketing. A product may have a sound value proposition in one country, but it may not be the same in other. A country like India is too price sensitive for foreign marketers. In India, Apple has not been a great success in selling iPhones, as the pricing was conducive only for the upper class customers. But the strategy of selling iPhones on EMIs has done wonders for the company and the business has grown by an amazing 400%. On the other hand, Samsung has played their cards well in India through their Galaxy range in the middle and upper segments and guru series in the lower segments of customers. McDonalds sells its burgers at different prices in different countries, based on its cost structure and the customers' affordability. LG is very successful in India with its value pricing with respect to the domestic consumer durable companies in India. Suzuki is the leader in four wheeler category with the right kind of price strategy in the Indian markets. On the whole, the pricing of a product should justify the value in the respective country.

Marketing Insight 16.4

Marketing Insight 16.4

Apple's Amazing 400% India Growth Story Shows Success of EMI Scheme

iPhone 5s

Apple's EMI schemes for its iPhone series seem to have paid off and the sales figures are growing at 400 percent. A report in *Economic Times*, quotes Credit Suisse's research analyst Sunil Tirumalai's note to clients as saying, *"From our channel checks we believe that iPhone sales are nearing 400,000 units per month in India – that is nearly 3% share of handset sales for a single top-end product in a market that has long been dominated by low-end feature phones."*

If that is indeed the sales number, then it is clearly a big gain for Apple. It should be noted however that these numbers are by an *analyst* and Apple has never released sales or shipments numbers according to specific countries. The Swiss brokerage firm and research agency said its estimates were based on checks with mobile store retailers across the country and from distributors mandated to sell Apple products.

Apple's EMI scheme for India began this year in February when it began offering users the latest iPhone 5 (16GB version) for 16,990 down payment plus the option of 6 EMIs at Rs 4,752 per month with zero processing fee or the option of 12 EMIs at the rate of Rs 2,376 per month plus a one time processing fee. Apple also extended the offer to the iPhone 4S and iPhone 4 devices with a down payment option of Rs 9,990.

For students Apple has amped up the offer in May by assuring them Rs 7,777 off on the iPhone 4, and it has even extended its option of buyback to the popular online shopping portal infibeam.

We had previously noted on *Firstpost*, that Apple had risen to the number two spot in terms of revenue for smartphone vendors in India in Q4 of 2012.

Apple's steady growth is of course not just due to the EMI scheme or cashback offers but also due to its changed distribution pattern. Apple ditched the mode of supplying the smartphone via network providers such as Airtel and Aircel and instead signed up with national level distribution partners such as Redington and Ingram Micro thus ensuring nationwide presence both in small shops and the big retail brands.

Apple's EMI scheme of course faces tough competition in a price-sensitive market like India where there is no dearth of cheap quad-core devices starting at as low price as Rs 9,000. Of course rival Samsung is also offering an EMI scheme on all its top-line Android products. For Apple, despite the EMI scheme India remains a tough market primarily due to the existence of too many price-points.

3. **Place**: A company's distribution channel is also equally important for the success in the foreign markets. Every market is different and in accordance with the local requirements, a distribution channel needs to be set up. While coming to India, Apple adopted it's tried and tested strategy of supplying the iPhones with network providers, as it has done in the USA. But thes strategy of supplying the iPhones with network providers such as Airtel and Aircel has not worked in India. That's why Apple has to adopt the strategy of signing up with national level distribution partners such as Redington and Ingram Micro, to ensure nationwide presence, both in small shops and in the big retail brands. Initially in India, Fiat formed a distribution alliance with Tata. But the strategy did not work. Now Fiat is on their own and building their own dealer base in India. In fact, many foreign automobile giants like Ford, Nissan, Renault etc. are struggling to expand the dealer base, which, in turn, has been hampering their growth.

4. **Promotion**: Besides the above 3Ps, a company also needs the fourth P i.e. promotion to excel in the market. A company should have the right kind of communication strategy to be successful in the foreign markets. The same communication message may not work in all the countries. It needs to be adapted to the local environment, as there are cultural limitations also. Sometimes, the meaning of a word or colours may signify something else in different countries. Mitsubishi changed the name of its SUV Pajero to Montero in USA, as pajero in Spanish, is used as a slang term for sexual self gratification. Similarly colour purple is a mourning colour in Japan, while it is associated with death in most of Latin America. In European countries, purple is a colour of royalty. Media also needs to be chosen carefully, in accordance with the different countries' requirements. In some countries, newspapers may be very popular; while in some other TV may do a great job.

Thus, a company needs to 'Think Global and Act Local', which is also known as 'Glocal' as Japanese call it. This is also the philosophy for MNCs like Hindustan Unilever Limited (HUL), Tata, Birla, Dabur, Marico, Unilever, Sony, LG, Samsung, Maruti Suzuki etc., which has been highly successful in international marketing. HUL, a subsidiary of Unilever in India, calls itself multi-local multinational, with market presence in more than 100 countries for their food and beverages and home and personal care products.

Summary

- International marketing means marketing across borders. When a company expands its operations beyond the national boundaries, it is said to be doing International Marketing. Sometimes the term global marketing is also used to denote International Marketing.
- Multinational Corporation (MNC) is a term widely used in international marketing. MNC simply means a corporation or a company, which operates in more than one country.
- A company may go international for growth and diversification. It may also look out for minimising competitive risk, gaining economies of scale, finding cheaper inputs or it may look forward to cushioning the economic cycle.
- There are different ways of getting into international marketing, depending upon the cost and the involvement concerned. A company may enter the international markets through exporting, licensing, contract manufacturing, through joint venture and by taking equity stake or acquiring a company.
- Just like a domestic marketer, an international marketer can only be successful, if he comes out with the right kind of products or services with an attractive price tag. The product or service also needs to be widely available and the communication needs to be effective. But there are a lot of differences also like the differences in currency, culture, language and legal environment. There are also tariff and non tariff trade barriers and mobility of factors of production is also restricted.
- In International marketing also, the marketing mix i.e. 4Ps of marketing – product, price, place and promotion remains as effective as in case of domestic marketing. But, it needs to be tweaked in terms of the changes in culture, language, currency etc.
- Certain products like Consumer Electronics items, Mobile Phones, MP3 players, LCD & LED TVs, Digital Cameras & Camcorders, Laptops, Desktops and so on, require no adaptation and can be sold directly in all the international markets. But few other products like food products, clothing, shoes, furniture etc require adaptation by a company.
- The pricing of a product should justify the value in the respective country.
- Every market is different and in accordance with the local requirements, a distribution channel needs to be set up.

- A company should have the right kind of communication strategy to be successful in the foreign markets. The same communication message may not work in all the countries. It needs to be adapted to the local environment, as there are cultural limitations also.
- A company needs to 'Think Global and Act Local', which is also known as 'Glocal' as Japanese call it. This is also the philosophy for MNCs like Hindustan Unilever Limited (HUL), Tata, Birla, Dabur, Marico, Unilever, Sony, LG, Samsung, Maruti Suzuki etc., which has been highly successful in international marketing.

Discussion Questions

1. Define international marketing? How is international marketing different from domestic marketing?
2. What do you mean by Multi National Corporation (MNC)? Write a brief note Indian MNCs.
3. What do you mean by international marketing? Why does a company go international?
4. Discuss the difference between domestic marketing and international marketing. How can you minimize business risk by going international?
5. 'Think Global and Act Local', Discuss the statement with relevant examples from different MNCs operating in India.
6. Discuss the International marketing mix. How does promotion play an important role in international marketing?
7. An MNC needs to price their products differently in different markets. Do you agree with the statement? Support your answer with relevant examples.
8. A product needs to be adapted to suit the local requirements in any country. Do you agree with the statement? Support your answer with relevant examples.
9. The success of international marketing largely depends upon the right kind of distribution strategy in the different markets, they operate. Do you agree with the statement? Justify.
10. Short Notes:

    a. MNC

    b. Export

    c. Acquisition

    d. Licensing

    e. Think Global and Act Local

    f. Sachet Marketing

References

1. Keegan, W.J., (2002), Global Marketing Management, Prentice Hall, 7th Ed.
2. Prahalad, C. K., Hart Stuart L., (2000), Raising the Bottom of the Pyramid: Strategies for Sustainable Growth.
3. Doob, Christopher M. (2013). Social Inequality and Social Stratification in US Society. Upper Saddle River, NJ: Pearson Education Inc.
4. Varshney R. L., Bhattacharya B. (1995), International Marketing Management, Sultan Chand & Sons, 9th Ed.
5. Varshney R. L., Bhattacharya B. (1995), International Marketing Management, Sultan Chand & Sons, 9th Ed.
6. Keegan, W.J., (2002), Global Marketing Management, Prentice Hall, 7th Ed.

CHAPTER 17

Green Marketing

Chapter Structure

According to American Marketing Association (AMA), 'Green marketing is the marketing of products that are presumed to be environmentally safe.'

Green Marketing

Panasonic

Green is the new buzzword in the marketing. The world is going Green and so are the companies and the governments. Now going green has become the new success mantra in marketing to differentiate the products and services from their competition. It has also become a platform for innovation. Now, more and more organisations are trying to follow the green path either directly or indirectly. The harmony among the three P's – People, Planet and Profit is taking the centre stage for the companies as well as for the governments. Whether it is the case of Panasonic with the 'Eco-Ideas' implemented in their production facilities or the case of ICICI Bank with the 'E-statements' saving hundreds of trees every month; marketers all across the world are trying to relate their products and services to the 'Green' to be more marketing savvy and innovative.[1] Now, Interbrand not only ranks the Best Global Brands every year, it also ranks the best global green brands across the world.

Marketing Insight 17.1

Marketing Insight 17.1

Best Global Green Brands 2013

In the 2013 annual ranking of the 50 best global green brands, automotive and tech companies have been leading the list. The 2013 Best Green Global Brands is produced by Interbrand and is powered by Deloitte. The study measures the environmental perception of 100 global brands and compares it to those companies' actual environmental performance. Toyota, Ford, Honda, Panasonic and Nissan are the top five brands in the list.

Best Global Green Brands 2013

History of Green Marketing

Although green marketing came into prominence in the late 1980s and early 1990s, it was first discussed in the workshop titled "Ecological Marketing" in 1975, undertaken by American Marketing Association (AMA). The proceedings of this workshop resulted in one of the first books on green marketing entitled 'Ecological Marketing' by Henion and Kinnear in 1976. Since that time a number of books on this topic have been published by different authors like Charter in 1992, Coddington in 1993 and by Ottman in 1993.

In the last fifteen years, concern for the environment has been steadily increasing, due to increased media coverage, greater awareness of environmental problems, the impact of major industry disasters and the rise of activist groups on the environment (Kalafatis et al. 1999). Thus the first wave of Green Marketing occurred in the 1980s and 1990s, when the products were designed and developed by causing less damage to the environment; while in the late 1990s and early 2000, the focus was on sustainable green marketing. The same has been discussed by Peattie in 2001, where he has talked about the evolution of green marketing into three phases. These phases are as the following:

1. **Ecological'** green marketing : To help solve environment problems through remedies.
2. **'Environmental'** green marketing: With focus on clean technology that involved designing of innovative new products, which take care of pollution and waste issues.
3. **'Sustainable'** green marketing: To produce and market environment friendly products, as a number of customers started demanding eco-friendly products and technologies. It gained prominence in the late 1990s and early 2000.

Defining Green Marketing

Green marketing is also known as environmental marketing (Coddington, 1993), ecological marketing (Fisk, 1974; Henion and Kinnear, 1976), green marketing (Peattie, 1995; Ottman, 1992), sustainable marketing (Fuller, 1999) and greener marketing (Charter and Polonsky, 1999). A majority of people believe that green marketing refers solely to the promotion or advertising of products with environmental characteristics. Consumers often associate green marketing with terms like phosphate free, recyclable, refillable, ozone friendly, and environmentally friendly. While these terms are green marketing claims, in general green marketing is a much broader concept, which is applied to goods as well as services.

The AMA workshop in 1975 was the first attempt to bring together academics, practitioners, and public policy makers to examine marketing's impact on the natural environment. At that point of time, the term ecological marketing was used for green marketing. Based on the proceedings of the workshop,

Henion and Kinnear defined ecological marketing as: **'the study of the positive and negative aspects of marketing activities on pollution, energy depletion and non energy resource depletion.'**

According to American Marketing Association (AMA), **'Green marketing is the marketing of products that are presumed to be environmentally safe.'**

Although green marketing incorporates a broad range of activities; yet it puts a special emphasis on the 1st and the 4th P of the marketing mix i.e. product and promotions. Primarily it means changes in the production process, as in the case of Panasonic or it may just be product modification like Toyota Prius, the hybrid car. There might be changes in the packaging as well as in the advertising.

From time to time, green marketing has also been defined by several authors like Jain and Kaur, Pride and Ferrell, Grant and Kangis. On the whole they defined green marketing as an activity, which involves designing, promoting, pricing and distributing products and services according to the customers' want and need, with minimal detrimental impact on the natural environment. Thus green marketing incorporates a broad range of activities, including product design, product modification, changes to the production process, packaging changes, as well as modifying advertising and promotions.

Green Marketing in Marketing

Prior to Sept., 2007, Marketing by American Marketing Association (AMA) was defined as, 'Marketing is an organizational function and a set of processes for creating, communicating, and delivering value to customers and for managing customer relationships in ways that benefit the organization and its stakeholders.' Now with the ever changing business environment, the definition of Marketing also underwent a lot of change from Oct.,

2007. Now, AMA defines Marketing as, 'Marketing is the activity, set of institutions, and processes for creating, communicating, delivering, and exchanging offerings that have value for customers, clients, partners, and society at large.'

The major difference in the definition lies in the last three words that say 'Society at large'. Earlier marketing was only meant for benefitting the organisation and its stakeholders. Now it also means that the product and services should benefit the society on the whole. It is for that reason only that a company like Pepsi India has only one out of four major links to talk about its products, that too by saying 'Nourishing and Delighting India'. The other three links deals with 'Innovation to Transform Lives', 'Tomorrow Better than Today: Environment' and 'Empowering Growth with Fun at Work'. Here the environmental concerns are shown more than the junk nature of their aerated drinks and food products. Now, societal welfare is as important as the company's welfare.

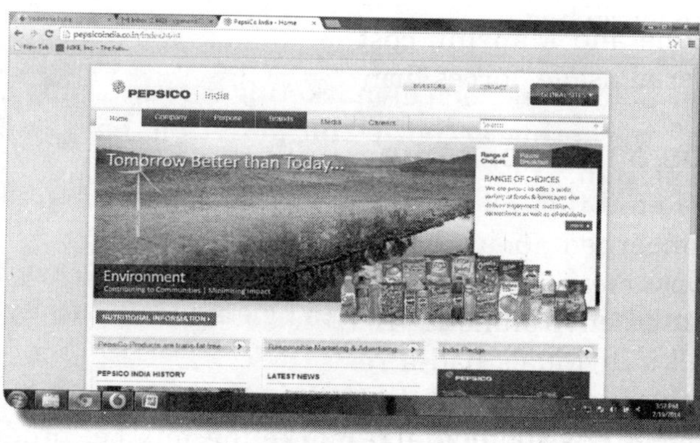

Pepsico India

The marketing concept is further strengthened with the term called Holistic Marketing Concept, which is based on integrated marketing, internal marketing, relationship marketing and social responsible marketing. It includes the development and implementation of marketing programs within the organisation as well as outside the organisation. Integrated marketing tries to build synergy among the product and services, channels of distribution and communications. Whereas internal marketing deals with the relationship and the coordination among the marketing department with the senior management and other departments like finance, accounts, human resources, information technology etc. Relationship marketing deals with effective implementation of CRM (Customer Relationship Management) and PRM (Partner Relationship Management); while socially responsible marketing calls for ethical, legal and environmental concerns for the organisation. And here the socially responsible marketing is making its presence felt 'Green Marketing'. Again, there is a new concept called Societal Marketing Concept, which talks about marketing beyond the objective of just making profits. It talks about fulfilling the need of a customer in such a way that will help to preserve the ecology and enhance the customers and society welfare. With the growing concern, the concept 'Green Marketing' is gaining popularity day by day.

Reasons for Going Green

There are various reasons as to why does a company 'go green'. These are as follows:

1. According to Keller and Shearer, organizations perceive environmental marketing to be an opportunity that can be used to achieve its objectives.
2. According to Davis, Freeman and Liedtka, Keller, McIntosh and Shearer; organizations also believe they have a moral obligation to be more socially responsible.
3. According to NAAG, Competitors' environmental activities pressurises firms to change their environmental marketing activities.
4. According to NAAG, Governmental bodies are also forcing firms to become more responsible and
5. According to Azzone and Manzini, cost factors associated with waste disposal, or reductions in material usage, forces firms to modify their behavior.

Green Marketing as an Opportunity

Generally it has been found that all types of consumers, both individual and industrial are becoming more concerned about the environment. In a 1992 study of 16 countries, more than 50% of consumers in each country, other than Singapore, indicated they were concerned about the environment.[2] A 1994 study in Australia found that 84.6% of the sample believed all individuals had a responsibility to care for the environment. A further 80% of this sample indicated that they had modified their behavior, including their purchasing behavior, due to environmental reasons [EPA-NSW 1994]. As demands change, many firms see these changes as an opportunity to be exploited. In turn, it means that the companies selling environment friendly products will have a competitive advantage over other companies. Few examples are:

Toyota Prius

a. Toyota is trying to push gas/electric hybrid technology into much of its product line. Toyota Prius with hybrid technology, has been a huge success all across the world. It is also making the single largest R&D investment in the hydrogen car and promoting itself as the first eco-friendly car company. That's why Toyota has also been ranked no. 1 Best Global Green Brand by Interbrand in 2013.

b. Xerox introduced a "high quality" recycled photocopier paper in an attempt to satisfy the demands of firms for less environmentally harmful products.

Nike Air Jordan Shoes

c. Nike is the first among the shoe companies to market itself as green. It is marketing its Air Jordan shoes as environment-friendly, as it has significantly reduced the usage of harmful glue adhesives. It has designed this variety of shoes to emphasize that it has reduced wastage and used environment-friendly materials.

d. Indian Tobacco Company (ITC) has introduced environmental-friendly papers and boards, which are free of elemental chlorine.

e. Donna Karen New York is introducing a line of sustainable clothes.

f. Tuna manufacturers modified their fishing techniques because of the increased concern over driftnet fishing, and the resulting death of dolphins [Advertising Age 1991].

g. Frito Lay's Sun Chips are made with the help of solar energy.

h. International business machines Corporation (IBM) has revealed a portfolio of green retail store technologies and services to help retailers improve energy efficiency in their IT operations. The center piece of this portfolio is the IBM SurePOS 700, a point-of-sale system that, according to IBM, reduces power consumption by 36% or more.

ITC Paperkraft

i. Philips Light's "Marathon - Philips Lighting's first shot at marketing a standalone compact fluorescent light (CFL) bulb was Earth Light, at $15 each versus 75 cents for incandescent bulbs. The product had difficulty climbing out of its deep green niche. The company re-launched the product as "Marathon, " underscoring its new "super long life" positioning and promise of saving $26 in energy costs over its five-year lifetime. Finally, with the U.S. Energy Star label to add credibility as well as new sensitivity to rising utility costs and electricity shortages, sales climbed 12 percent in an otherwise flat market.

   Although in some cases, it has been a genuine effort by the company. In most of the other cases, companies are merely looking for jumping to the green bandwagon for immediate gains. That's why sometimes these companies make false or misleading green marketing claims.

Green Marketing as Social Responsibility

Many companies are taking the initiative to become environment friendly. Sometimes it also acts like a marketing tool, while in some cases they are doing it without promoting this fact.

Panasonic Eco Ideas

a. Panasonic's 'Eco Ideas' to produce energy efficient products, to reduce CO_2 emissions across all their manufacturing sites and to spread awareness about the environmental activities through celebrity endorsers in India and all across the world.

Coca Cola

b. Coca Cola does not promote its environmental initiatives. Although they have invested large sums of money in various recycling activities and also modified their packaging to minimize the environmental impact. Coca-Cola pumped syrup directly from tank instead of plastic.

HP McDonalds

c. HP's 'Power to Change' campaign to save electricity is also one of the social responsibility measures.

d. McDonald's replaced its clam shell packaging with waxed paper, because of increased consumer concern relating to polystyrene production and Ozone depletion. McDonald's restaurant's napkins, bags are also getting made of recycled paper.

e. Wal-Mart and Target are both reducing the amount of toxic materials contained in some of its products and packaging.

British petroleum (BP) **Canon**

f. British petroleum (BP) displays gas station which its sunflower motif and boasts of putting money into solar power.

g. Canon is making "green friendly" printers through its Generation Green initiative.

Green Marketing due to Governmental Pressure

Many governments all across the globe are also trying to do their bit for the environmental concern.

Governmental regulations relating to environmental marketing are designed to protect consumers in several ways,

1 To reduce production of harmful goods or byproducts,

2 To modify consumer and industry's use and/or consumption of harmful goods, or

3 To ensure that all types of consumers have the ability to evaluate the environmental composition of goods.

Governments establish regulations designed to control the amount of hazardous wastes produced by firms. Many by-products of production are controlled through the issuing of various environmental licenses, thus modifying organizational behavior. In some cases, governments try to induce final consumers to become more responsible. For example, some governments have introduced voluntary curb-side recycling programs, making it easier for consumers to act responsibly. In other cases, governments tax individuals, who act in an irresponsible fashion.

Bureau of Energy Efficiency (BEE)

- Bureau of Energy Efficiency (BEE) Label in India has also been helping the customers to buy energy efficient electrical appliances with its five star labels.[3]
- In 2002, a Supreme Court directive made all the difference to curb pollution by issuing an order to completely adopt Compressed Natural Gas (CNG) in all public transport systems in Delhi. Now it is followed all across India to curb pollution.
- In Delhi, Bureau of Energy Efficiency (BEE) has also introduced a scheme called the Bachat Lamp Yojana (BLY) to promote the use of energy saving compact fluorescent lamps (CFLs) amongst households. It is expected that at the household level, every electricity consumption bill may be reduced up to 20%-30% if CFLs are used.
- In Australia, there is a higher gas tax associated with leaded petrol.

Marketing Insight 17.2

Bureau of Energy Efficiency (BEE) Star Labels

The Bureau of Energy Efficiency (BEE) is an agency of the Government of India, under the Ministry of Power created in March 2002 under the provisions of the nation's 2001 Energy Conservation Act. The agency's function is to develop programs which will increase the conservation and efficient use of energy in India. The mission of Bureau of Energy Efficiency is to "institutionalize" energy efficiency services, enable delivery mechanisms in the country and provide leadership to energy efficiency in all sectors of the country. The primary objective would be to reduce energy intensity in the economy.

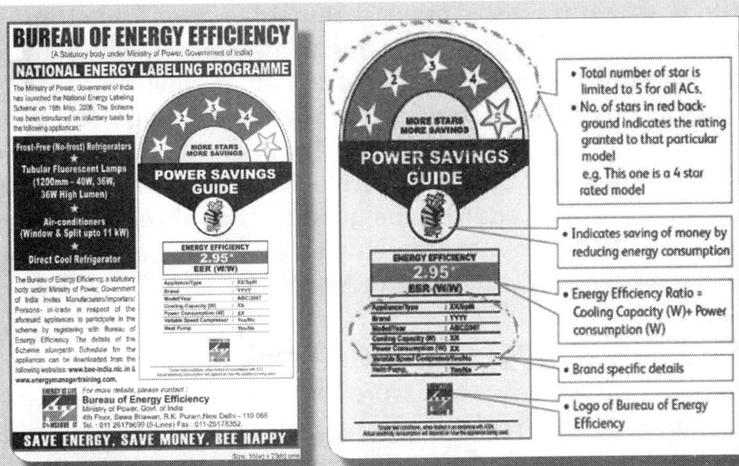

BEE introduced Star labels to help customers choose the more energy efficient appliances in the market. One to five stars are used to show varying energy efficiency levels of appliances, five stars denoting the most energy efficient. Under this scheme, initially an appliance is put in the voluntary list where manufacturers have the option to affix the label. After a fixed period of time, the appliances are included in the compulsory list where the labels become mandatory. Frost-free refrigerators, tubular fluorescent lamps, distribution transformers and air-conditioners were the first to get the compulsory rating. By 2013 end, star labels would be made optional for office equipment such as printers, scanners and photo copiers and also for a host of other equipment such as motors, fans, diesel generators, pump sets and voltage stabilisers.

Green Marketing due to Competitive Pressure

Xerox

Due to competitive pressure also, many companies are forced to look after the environmental concerns, as consumers are more aware and educated than before. In many cases firms observe competitors promoting their environmental behaviors and attempt to emulate this behavior. In some instances this competitive pressure has caused an entire industry to modify and thus reduce its detrimental environmental behavior. For example, it could be argued that Xerox's 'Revive 100% Recycled paper' was introduced a few years ago in an attempt to address the introduction of recycled photocopier paper by other manufacturers. In another example when one tuna manufacture stopped using driftnets the others followed suit [Advertising Age 1991].

Green Marketing due to Cost or Profit Issues

Companies also need to address the cost issues and profit issues, which heads them to go green. Companies can reduce harmful wastes, which may incur substantial cost savings. When attempting to minimize waste, firms are often forced to re-examine their production processes. In these cases, they often develop more effective production processes that not only reduce waste, but reduce the need for some raw materials. This serves as a double cost savings, since both waste and raw material are reduced. In other cases firms attempt to find end-of-pipe solutions, instead of minimizing waste. In these situations firms try to find markets or uses for their waste materials, where one firm's waste becomes another firm's input of production.

In the era of going green, many new businesses are also coming up to cater to the new needs of the industry like

1. A company may develop a technology for reducing waste and sells it to other firms, or
2. A waste recycling or removal industry can develop [Yurman 1994].

   For example, firms that clean the oil in large industrial condensers increase the life of those condensers, removing the need for replacing the oil, as well as the need to dispose of the waste oil. This reduces operating costs for those owning the condensers and generates revenue for those firms cleaning the oil.

   In India, many companies are working in the area of waste management and thus, saving the environment from devastation.[4] Few of these companies are :

VA Tech Wabag

Hanjer

- Arora Fibres recycles discarded plastic bottles into polyester used as packaging material.
- VA Tech Wabag is helping companies clean up their act by reusing waste water.
- Hanjer Biotech Energies is turning solid waste into fuel to run power plants.
- Microqual Techno uses power transmission towers as telecom towers.
- Cerebra Integrated Technologies extracts precious and other metals from mountains of e-waste.

Marketing Insight 17.3

India's Leading 'Green' Companies

It's easy to feel vulnerable and frustrated when one hears news stories and articles highlighting the hazards of global warming, environmental pollution and other ill-effects of environment abuse. But, increasingly companies are doing their bit to support the 'Go Green' campaign.

Although most companies fall under categories that have more to do with reducing emissions or saving power, there are brands that have nothing to do with power and energy, who are working towards developing a greener environment. These companies give us products like television sets, computers, clothing, cosmetics, and so on . . . products that we use on a daily basis. Here is a list of such companies who are doing their bit to save their environment:

LG

LG

South Korean consumer durables major LG Electronics recently introduced LG LED E60 and E90 series monitors in the Indian market. The LED E60 and E90 series monitors are packed with the eco-friendly features such as 40 per cent less energy consumption than the traditional LCD monitors. Also, the use of hazardous materials such as halogen or mercury is kept to minimal in this range.

LG Electronics' environmental policy is centered on its "Life's Good when it's green" program. Globally, LG launched a range of eco-friendly products 'Eco-Chic' such as the platinum coated two-door refrigerator and washing machine with steam technology.

HCL

Last year, HCL launched its range of eco-friendly notebooks, HCL ME 40. HCL claims that this was India's first PVC free and eco-friendly notebook.

This notebook is completely free from polyvinyl chloride (PVC) material and other harmful chemicals.

Further, Bureau of Energy Efficiency has given HCL eco-friendly products a five-star rating, and they also meet REACH (REACH is the European Community Regulation on chemicals and their safe use) standards and are 100 per cent recyclable and toxin free.

Haier

Haier Eco-life

Haier India launches the green initiative with its 'Eco-Life' series, as a part of its global rebranding exercise. This is aimed at designing smart products which not only meet customer needs, but also adhere to environmental norms. The company's eco-friendly offerings include refrigerators, semi and fully automatic washing machines, split and windows air conditioners, a wide range of LED & LCD TVs and the Spa range of water heaters.

Samsung Electronics

Samsung Electronics, a leading brand in display products, is continuing to evolve LED monitor technology by offering environmentally friendly monitors with its range of 50 and 30 series LED monitors. Samsung products have eco-friendly LED backlight,

Samsung Electronics

Samsung Electronics, a leading brand in display products, is continuing to evolve LED monitor technology by offering environmentally friendly monitors with its range of 50 and 30 series LED monitors. Samsung products have eco-friendly LED backlight, which contain few or no environmentally hazardous substances, such as mercury or lead. Additionally, it uses about 40 per cent less energy. Also, Samsung's Touch of Color (ToC) technology doesn't use paints, sprays or glues, ensuring they contain no Volatile Organic Compounds (VOCs), making recycling simpler and safer. Its other eco feature allows users to adjust a monitor's brightness based on different energy consumption levels with four preset energy-saving options to choose from.

Samsung has also launched its advanced range of Split ACs, which claim to save up to 60 per cent energy.

Voltas

Voltas AC

Air-conditioners, refrigerators and plasma or LCD TVs are going green with a vengeance. Next in the line is, Voltas from the Tata Group. In 2007, Voltas initiated the 'Green' range of air-conditioners, following which the government made it mandatory for home appliances to have energy star ratings. Energy Star is an international standard for energy efficient consumer products that originated in the US. Thus, devices carrying the star logo, such as computer products and peripherals, kitchen appliances and other products, use about 20-30 per cent less energy than the set standards.

Panasonic India

Panasonic has an Econavi range of air conditioners and LCD screens which is once again based on energy conservation. Econavi home appliances use sensor and control technologies to minimise energy consumption, based on a family's lifestyle. For instance, a door-opening sensor and lighting sensor allows the refrigerator to learn the time periods when the family typically doesn't use - when they're sleeping or away from home. The refrigerator goes into sleep mode accordingly.

Globally, Panasonic is aiming to become top green innovation company in the electronics industry by 2018 and is laying a lot of emphasis on eco-friendly products.

Nokia

Nokia Bicycle Charger Kit

Nokia has always takes steps to develop eco-friendly initiatives. It has also won the Greenpeace Award. The Finnish mobile company scored won this award mainly because of its back take-back program in India. It is also known for launching models free of PVC, brominated flame retardants and antimony trioxide.

Now, it has launched a Nokia Bicycle Charger Kit (DC-14) in India. The bicycle charger kit works at walking speed (6 km/h) and when the speed reaches 50 km/h it stops charging. The charger is compatible with Nokia phones that have a 2mm charging interface, which includes most mid-range Nokia phones. The Nokia bicycle charger has an ergonomic design to make installation easier to suit different types of bicycles. The phone holder also has a rubberised design to hold the phone securely and protect it from shocks and vibrations.

Wipro

The other company to launch wide range of eco-friendly desktops is Wipro. Introduced under the Wipro Green Ware initiative, these products aim to cut down e-waste in environment. Here, the systems launched are toxin free and operate under a total recycling policy. With the removal of the toxins, recycling of the electronic products would be safer, say company executives. Wipro has 17 e-waste collection centres in India where products are collected and recycled. Also, 12 Wipro campuses in the country have been certified as green buildings.

MRF Tyres

MRF ZSLK Tyres

Next in the line to join the eco-friendly product wagon is the Indian tyre manufacturer MRF with its ZSLK series. The premium eco-friendly tubeless tyres MRF ZSLK are made from unique silica-based rubber compounds and promises to offer fuel efficiency for vehicle owners.

The tyres had been tested extensively on Indian road conditions with emphasis on endurance, wet and dry braking, the company said in a statement. At present, the ZSLK series are available for models including Honda City/Civic, Ford Fiesta, Hyundai Santro, Maruti SX4, Wagon R, Skoda Octavia, Tata Indica, Nissan Micra.

ACC Ltd

India-based cement manufacturer ACC has recently launched its eco-friendly brand, 'Concrete+'. This brand uses fly ash (a hazardous industrial waste) to help conserve natural resources, thus making it an eco-friendly product. The new product has been designed exclusively to ensure high durability and resistance of structures under extreme climate.

Jayanta DattaGupta, chief commercial officer of ACC Ltd, said that the new product is a result of continuous feedback from customers, influencers and dealers.

Fevicol

Fevicol, a leading brand of adhesive in India, has introduced environment friendly synthetic resin adhesive. Claiming to be India's first eco-friendly adhesive, Fevicol AC Duct King Eco Fresh, boasts of being an all-in-one adhesive. The company says that this water-based adhesive has exceptional bonding strength and spreads smoothly at room temperature without emitting any toxic fumes. It is an ideal adhesive for AC Duct insulation for all residential and industrial projects.

Speaking on the launch, Vishal Malhan, chief - marketing, Fevicol Division at Pidilite Industries said, "We, at Fevicol, were always concerned and worked towards developing and offering adhesives that contributed immensely to the betterment of health, safety and environment. As market leaders, it becomes our responsibility to take lead in caring and conserving our planet by using strong and secure adhesives."

Fevicol

Grassroot Collection

Grassroot

Eco-friendly line of clothing is fast growing fashion trend. Though it had a slow take off, it now has many takers. Anita Dongre has now joined the line of eco-fashion with her brand, Grassroot. "My eco-friendly brand Grassroot is a 100 per cent environment-friendly brand. We use certified eco-friendly & organic fabrics; we have partnered with number of NGOs who are engaged into providing and promoting the work of local artisans," says Anita Dongre.

For the uninitiated, eco-fashion is a process of creating garments with environment friendly techniques and processes which are non-hazardous to the environment. Largely, eco-clothing uses organic cotton, bamboo jersey, viscose and linen, etc.

Vivanta by Taj Hotel Resorts & Palaces

Earth friendliness is the hallmark of the Vivanta line, just as it is at all Taj hotels. The parent company follows guidelines established at a United Nations Earth Summit and endorsed by nearly 200 countries. These green benchmarks are monitored by a leading worldwide certifier, Green Globe. Taj aims to bring the total of its Vivanta hotels to 30-plus in the next 2 years, totalling 5,000-plus guest rooms.

So, from LCDs to clothing, every brand is giving you an opportunity to ride the green wave. Go ahead, make a choice and join the green revolution.

Marketing Insight 17.4

TC's Hotel Royal Gardenia

TC's Hotel Royal Gardenia becomes the world's largest LEED Platinum rated Green Hotel -- first Hotel in India to achieve this recognition

ITC Hotel Royal Gardenia

ITC's new luxury hotel in Bengaluru, the ITC Hotel Royal Gardenia was conferred the highest rating for green buildings in the world – the LEED India Platinum Rating. This recognition makes it the world's largest platinum rated hotel and is yet another manifestation of ITC's leadership in Sustainability Practices. ITC is the only company in the world to be carbon positive, water positive and solid waste recycling positive.

The LEED Platinum Rating for the ITC Hotel is one more green milestone close on the heels of the ITC Green Centre in Gurgaon which was the world's first largest green building. This Centre was chosen by the US Secretary of State Hillary Clinton to announce her vision on Indo-US collaboration on Climate Change during her last visit to India. After a tour of the building she called it the "Monument to the Future".

ITC's exemplary commitment to green practices have also enabled it's hotel in Kolkata – the ITC Hotel Sonar to be the only hotel in the world to earn carbon credits. In keeping with the ITC Commitment to the "Triple Bottomline" philosophy, ITC Hotels has aspired to be an 'exemplar' in the service sector and truly provides leadership to positive environmental action in a sustainable manner.

The ITC Royal Gardenia is an inclusive blend of contemporary design and international green practices, a beacon in a bustling urban environment. Built on the ethos of "Responsible Luxury" the hotel has adopted contemporary 'Green Practices' that harness the element of nature in an inspired setting to deliver unique guest experiences.

According to Chief Executive, ITC Hotels Division, Nakul Anand, "The ITC Royal Gardenia exemplifies ITC's vision and is perhaps the perfect example of finding common rhythm between manmade and natural environment. The challenge was to see how luxury and responsibility could be in harmony together. Thus a series of sustainable measures and practices were embraced to ensure that elements of nature were effectively harnessed at every level inside the luxury hotel".

IThe hotel has utilised innovation, cutting edge technology and design integration to earn new benchmarks in energy efficiency, water efficiency and low carbon techniques, and is a model of environmental stewardship. The LEED-India Rating System encourages and facilitates the development of more sustainable buildings for innovation in design and environment practices.

Thus, the need of the hour today is to go green. By going green, a company can take advantage of the opportunities in the market, counter competition, meet governmental norms and can beat the competition through innovation.

Innovation and Green Marketing

In the era of technological developments, globalization and hyper competition, a company can only sustain and grow, when it can innovate consistently and continuously. "Because the purpose of business is to create a customer, the business enterprise has two-and only two-basic functions: marketing and innovation. Marketing and innovation produce results; all the rest are costs." It has been well told by Peter Drucker, the father of business consulting, in his famous book 'Innovation and Entrepreneurship', about the importance of innovation in business. Now companies can innovate on the front of Green Marketing, as seen from the above examples.

These innovations through green efforts lead to develop new and improved products and services with environment inputs in mind. It also gives access to new markets, thus increasing their profitability. On the whole, an organisation can enjoy a competitive advantage over the companies, which are not concerned for the environment.

In the last few years, two terms has been discussed widely in the area of green marketing i.e. green marketing myopia and greenwashing.

Green Marketing Myopia

Green marketing is still in its infancy at the consumer and producer level. The green marketers must understand the fact that they have to satisfy two objectives: improved environmental quality and customer satisfaction.[5] Misjudging either or overemphasizing the former at the expenses of the latter may cause a fatal result for companies. Research indicates that many green products have failed because of green marketing myopia; marketers' myopic focus on their product's greenness over the broader expectations of consumers.[6]

Greenwashing

The term greenwashing was first used by environmentalist Jay Westerveld. A hotelier used to ask his guests to reuse the towels, in order to save the environment. It was quite obvious that this measure was just taken to save the cost in washing the towel. In this context, the term greenwashing was first used. On the whole, it refers to all the industries, which adopt outwardly green acts with an underlying purpose to increase profits. The primary objective of greenwashing is to provide consumers with the feeling that the organization is taking the necessary steps to responsibly manage its ecological footprint. In reality, the company may be doing very little that is environmentally beneficial.[7]

Now more and more companies are willing to join the green bandwagon, as it provides an opportunity to market their eco friendly products. It also helps the companies to become socially responsible and it may happen due to governmental pressure or, due to competitive pressure or, due to cost or profit issues. On the whole, green marketing is going to benefit the consumers ultimately with better products and help the society on the whole, by building a green business ecosystem.[8]

Summary

- Green is the new buzzword in the marketing. Now going green has become the new success mantra in marketing to differentiate the products and services from their competition. It has also become a platform for innovation. Now, more and more organisations are trying to follow the green path either directly or indirectly. The harmony among the three P's – People, Planet and Profit is taking the centre stage for the companies as well as for the governments.

- According to American Marketing Association (AMA), 'Green marketing is the marketing of products that are presumed to be environmentally safe.'
- There are various reasons as to why does a company 'go green'. By going green, a company can take advantage of the opportunities in the market, counter competition, meet governmental norms and can beat the competition through innovation.
- In the era of technological developments, globalization and hyper competition, a company can only sustain and grow, when it can innovate consistently and continuously. Now a company can innovate on the front of Green Marketing and differentiate itself.
- The green marketers must understand the fact that they have to satisfy two objectives: improved environmental quality and customer satisfaction. Misjudging either or overemphasizing the former at the expenses of the latter may cause a fatal result for companies. Research indicates that many green products have failed because of green marketing myopia i.e. marketers' myopic focus on their product's greenness over the broader expectations of consumers.
- The primary objective of greenwashing is to provide consumers with the feeling that the organization is taking the necessary steps to responsibly manage its ecological footprint. In reality, the company may be doing very little that is environmentally beneficial.

Discussion Questions

1. Define green marketing? Discuss the role and importance of green marketing in the business today.
2. What do you mean by green marketing? How is it different from greenwashing?
3. Discuss the reasons for going green in detail, with relevant examples.
4. Discuss the importance of green marketing as an opportunity for marketers.
5. Write a note on the Best Global Green Brands.
6. Green marketing is nothing but greenwashing. Do you agree with the statement? Answer with relevant reasons to support your stand.
7. In India, Bureau of Energy Efficiency is doing a commendable job in the area of green marketing. Do you agree with the statement? Answer with relevant points.
8. How can a FMCG company like Hindustan Unilever Limited (HUL) exploit green marketing, as an opportunity for its products?

9. In the best global green brand 2013 listing, automobile and technology companies are leading the table. What may be the probable reasons for the same?

10. Short Notes:
    a. Greenwashing
    b. Green Marketing Myopia
    c. Bureau of Energy Efficiency
    d. Innovation and Green Marketing
    e. Best Global Green Brands
    f. BEE Labels

References

1. Anand, Vijay Prakash (2013). Go Green, The New Success Mantra in Marketing. *International Journal of Business Administration and Management, Vol. 3, Number 1 (2013),*
2. Ottman, J.A. (1993), Green Marketing: Challenges and opportunities, NTC Business Books, Chicago, IL.
3. http://www.beeindia.in/content.php?page=about_bee/about_bee.php?id=1
4. Nayak, Mahesh (2013). New age alchemists, Business Today, June 9, 2013
5. Levitt, T. (1960). Marketing Myopia. In Harvard Business Review. Accessed on 12/6/2011 http://www.casadogalo.com/marketingmyopia.pdf
6. Ottman, J., Stafford, E, Hartman, C. (2006). Avoiding Green Marketing Myopia. In Environment, 48(5), 22-36.
7. Naish, J. (2008). Lies...Damned lies...And green lies. Ecologist, 38(5), 36-39. Retrieved from Academic Search Complete database
8. Anand, Vijay Prakash (2013). Green Marketing and Its importance for Companies. International Journal Of Research In Commerce & Management Volume No. 4 (2013), Issue No. 08 (August)

REFERENCES

Marketing Insight References

1.1: Luharia, Jaimini, "What made Maruti Celerio a grand success in India", CarDekho.com, April 09, 2014

1.2: Narayanan, Chitra, "The monk who wants a billion-dollar company", Hindu Business Line, Dec. 07, 2015

1.3: Hunt, Shelby D., "Marketing Theory", Yes Dee Publishing, Indian Reprint, 2011, p. 61-64

1.4: Anand, Vijay Prakash, "Deodorant marketing getting hotter in India", https://marketingbyvijay.wordpress.com/2014/07/02/deodorant-market-getting-hotter-in-india/

1.5: Anand, Vijay Prakash, "Nirma Vs. Wheel", https://marketingbyvijay.wordpress.com/2014/07/07/nirma-vs-wheel/

2.1: Thakkar, Ketan, "Maruti Readies Plan for LCV Foray", Economic Times, Mumbai Edition, 20th Dec 2012

2.2: Somvanshi, Kiran Kabtta, "Asian Paints Enters the Kitchen with Sleek Deal", Economic Times, Mumbai Edition, 20th Mar 2013

2.3: http://www.ndtv.com/photos/business/wipro-from-a-vegetable-oil-maker-to-an-it-major-14100/slide/

2.4: Mukherjee, Writankar & Malviya, Sagar, "ITC Takes a Big Bite of FMCG Pie", Economic Times, Mumbai Edition, 19th Oct 2012

3.1 Malviya, Sagar, "Cadbury Steps Up the Game as Sales Slip", Economic Times, Mumbai Edition, 20th Feb 2014

4.1: "Honda goes all out to woo customers with Amaze", Business Standard, Mumbai Edition, 14th March 2013

4.2: Sachitanand, Rahul, "Marketing Mavens Making Data Work", Economic Times, Mumbai Edition, 23rd Oct 2012

4.3: Phadnis, Shilpa & John, Sujit, "India a global analytics hub as cos dig for data", The Times of India, Mumbai Edition, 8th Oct, 2012

4.3: Mukherjee, Writankar, "India Inc Suddenly Rises to Sleep Disorder", Economic Times, Mumbai Edition 5th Jan 2013

4.4: "From big databases to the big screen", The Times of India, Mumbai Edition, 26th May 2013

5.1: Malviya, Sagar, "A Perfect 10! HUL's 1,000cr Club Swells", Economic Times, Mumbai Edition, 5th June 2013

5.2: Sarkar, John, "PepsiCo bats for IPL, Coke votes for polls", The Times of India, Mumbai Edition, 13th March 2014

5.3: Ganguly, Dibyendu, "Natural Selection", Economic Times, Mumbai Edition, 14th June 2013

5.4: Jain, Dipti, "Growth Formula", The Times of India, Delhi Edition, 18th April 2013

6.1: Manu Aiyappa, TNN | Apr 23, 2014, 08.43PM IST

Aiyappa, Manu, "New JSW steel plant may make cars cheaper", Economic Times, Mumbai Edition, 23rd April 2014

6.2: Mahalingam TV & Kandavel Sangeetha, "All the Way Up", Economic Times, Mumbai Edition, 18th No. 2012

7.1: Vijayraghavan, Kala, "Colgate Brushes Aside Foes With an Array of Offerings", Economic Times, Mumbai Edition, 5th Oct 2012)

7.2: "Culture Customisation: Wrangler, McDonald's, And Starbucks", Business World, 25th Oct 2012

7.3: Rathore, Vijaya, "For Luxury Watch Makers, Festive Season's Right Time to Drive Sales", Economic Times, Mumbai Edition, 23rd Oct 2012

7.4: Malviya, Sagar, "TIGI Products will be sold through Salons", Economic Times, Mumbai Edition, 13th June 2013

8.1: Malviya, Sagar & Bhushan, Ratna, "Happy with Surprise Toy, Kinder Joy for Ferrero", Economic Times, Mumbai Edition, 23rd April 2013

8.2: Bhushan, Ratna, "Kurkure, Lays slipping", Economic Times, Mumbai Edition, 23rd Nov 2012

8.3: Chamikutty, Preethi, "No Instant Karma Here", Economic Times, Mumbai Edition, 28th Nov 2012

8.4: Malviya, Sagar, "Combined share of local brands slips to 2%", Economic Times, Mumbai Edition, 13th Feb 2014

8.5: PTI Apr 11, 2014

8.6: Philip, Joji Thomas, "Airtel, Vodafone and Idea dominate Indian telecom sector ", Mint, Mumbai Edition, 5th Sept. 2014

8.7: Anand, Vijay Prakash, "The Great Indian Mobile Phone War", https://marketingbyvijay.wordpress.com/2014/08/29/the-great-indian-mobile-phone-war/

9.1: Chamikutty, Preethi, "How Fevicol went on to enjoy equity that billion dollar cola and soap labels do", Economic Times, Mumbai Edition, 26th Sept. 2012

9.2: Upadhyay, Anindya, "Cool Branding Lands IndiGo in Biz Class", Economic Times, Mumbai Edition, 20th March 2013

9.3: Anand, Vijay Prakash, "Welcome to Rs. 1000 Cr. FMCG Club", https://marketingbyvijay.wordpress.com/2014/11/12/welcome-to-rs-1000-crore-fmcg-club/

9.4: Gangal, Ashwini, "Airtel: 'Second insight' on friendship", Afaqs, Mumbai, 8th August 2012

10.1: sagar.malviya@timesgroup.com

11.1: Sharmistha Mukherjee, "TripAdvisor survey: IndiGo is preferred airline third year in a row", Business Standard, New Delhi, 2nd Dec. 2013

11.2: Tata Consultancy Services Press Release dated 26th June, 2008

11.3: Parmar, Beena, "Now, banking on tablets to win customers", Business Line, Mumbai Edition, 3rd March 2014

11.4: "Starbucks' India operations fastest growing in its history", PTI, 20th May, 2014; http://articles.economictimes.indiatimes.com/2014-03-20/news/48402127_1_tata-starbucks-tata starbucks-avani-davda

12.1: Thakkar, Ketan "Ford's EcoSport to Kick up Dust-er with Pricing", Economic Times, Mumbai Edition, 29th Mar 2013

12.2: Subramaniam, Nikhil, "With Moto E priced at Rs. 6,999, Motorola aims to disrupt Micromax and Co's low cost strategy", Tech.firstpost.com, 15th May 2014

12.3: Bhushan, Ratna & Pande, Bhanu, "Rs 5 price point becomes a magic word for marketers across products", Economic Times, Mumbai Edition, 24th Dec 2010

12.4: Mukherjee, Writankar & Bhushan, Ratna "Food Firms Give up Popular Price Points on Rising Costs", Economic Times, Mumbai Edition, 5th Apr 2013

12.5: Law, Abhishek, "Hidesign changes pricing strategy; affordable products soon in multi-brand stores", Business Line, Mumbai Edition, 21st Apr 2014

13.1: Acharya, Bhavana, "Dabur India, Hindustan Unilever's tech route to rural markets", Business Line, Mumbai Edition, 14th July 2013

13.2: Malviya Sagar & Bhushan, Ratna, "Chemists Turn Key Sales Partners for FMCG Cos", Economic Times, Mumbai Edition, 21st Nov 2012

13.3: Mukherjee, Writankar, "Tata Group's Croma store hits 101 mark as retail battle heats up ", Economic Times, Mumbai Edition, 14th May 2014

13.4: Malviya Sagar & Bhushan, Ratna, "Chemists Turn Key Sales Partners for FMCG Cos", Economic Times, Mumbai Edition, 21st Nov 2012

13.5: Anand, Nupur, "Mom & pop stores upgrade staff", DNA, Mumbai Edition, 28th March 2013

14.1: Manral, Kiran, "Difference between 'Above the Line' and 'Below the Line" www.thadvertisingclub.net, 22nd August 2011

14.2: Bhushan, Ratna, "Krrish 3 May Net $3 m from Off-screen Action", Economic Times, Mumbai Edition, 23rd May 2013

14.3: Dasgupta, Pritha Mitra, "Amazon Raises Stakes with High-Decibel Ad Pitch", Economic Times, Mumbai Edition, 8th May 2014

14.4: Shran, Anita, "Celebrity Ad Fever", Hindustan Times, Mumbai Edition, 25th Nov 2012

14.5: Team ET, "Ad Wars Rage Again", Economic Times, Mumbai Edition, 21st March 2013

14.6: Singh, Namrata & Mukherjee, Shubham, "Companies offer freebies to beat slowdown blues", Economic Times, Mumbai Edition, 17th April 2013

14.7: Bhushan, Ratna & Mukherjee, Writankar, "White Goods Cos in Shop-Floor Push for Sales", Economic Times, Mumbai Edition, 27th May 2013

14.8: Shashidhar, Ajita, "Digital advertising spend to grow the most in 2014", Business Today, 11th Feb 2014

15.1: Sen, Nandini, "Gearing up for Rural Ride", Economic Times, Mumbai Edition, 30th Mar., 2013

15.2: The Hindu, November 29, 2012; http://www.thehindu.com/business/companies rural-india-market-of-the-future/article4147251.ece

15.3 Sengupta, Debjoy, "Expanding Footprint - Sun Shines on Coke's New Rural Push", Economic Times, Mumbai Edition, 9th Nov 2012

15.4: Hindustan Unilever Ltd.

16.1: Source: Sagar Malviya Mumbai, Economic Times, 20 Oct, 2013 Issue

16.2: Business World, 25 Oct, 2012 Issue

16.3: Dearton Thomas Hector, Business Today, May 12, 2013

16.4: 31 May 2013, http://tech.firstpost.com/news-analysis/apples-amazing-400-percent india-growth-story-shows-success-of-emi-scheme-214020.html

17.1: http://www.interbrand.com/en/best-global-brands/Best-Global-Green-Brands/2013 Best-Global-Green-Brands-2013.aspx

17.2: Wikipedia and Rajwi, Tiki, 2013, BEE All Set to Revise Star Rating System for Appliances, The New Indian Express, 28th November 2013

17.3: http://www.rediff.com/business/slide-show/slide-show-1-world-environment-day-some-of-indias-leading-green-companies/20110603.htm#1

17.4: Press Release, 24 Dec 2009, http://www.itcportal.com/media-centre/press-releases-content.aspx?id=14&type=C&news=ITC%E2%80%99s%20Hotel

INDEX

A

B

E

F

G

H

I

Q

R

S

T

U

V

W

Y